The Good
Cook's Encyclopedia

The Good Cook's Encyclopedia

General Editor Richard Olney

Contributing Editor Lewis Esson

Quadrille Publishing

Both metric and imperial quantities are given.
Use either all metric or all imperial, as the two are
not necessarily interchangeable.

Compiled by Lewis Esson
Editor & Project Manager: Lewis Esson
Publishing Director: Anne Furniss
Art Director: Mary Evans
Design: Paul Welti
Production: Candida Jackson
Typesetting: Pete Howard

First published in 1997 by
Quadrille Publishing Ltd
Alhambra House
27-31 Charing Cross Road
London WC2H 0LS

This paperback edition first published in 1998
Reprinted in 1999

The Good Cook's Encyclopedia
© 1997 Time-Life Books B.V.
First published jointly by Time-Life Books B.V. and
Quadrille Publishing Limited. Material in this book was first
published as part of the series The Good Cook
© 1979 Time-Life Books B.V.
Additional material, design & layout © 1997 Quadrille Publishing Ltd

Cataloguing in Publication Data: a catalogue record
for this book is available from the British Library

ISBN 1 899988 53 X
Printed in Hong Kong

Contents

Foreword 7

Section One
Buying Food 8

Meat 10
A Guide to Beef Cuts 10 A Guide to Veal Cuts 12
A Guide to Lamb Cuts 14 A Guide to Pork Cuts 16

Poultry & Game 18
A Guide to Poultry 18 A Guide to Game Birds 20 Game Animals 22

Fish & Shellfish 24
Fish 24 Shellfish, etc. 32

Vegetables, Fungi & Pulses 34
A Guide to Vegetables 34 A Guide to Fungi 47 Pulses 48

Fruit & Nuts 50
Types of Fruit 50 A Guide to Nuts 61

Grains & Pasta 62
Types of Grains 62 Types of Pasta 64

Eggs & Cheese 66
Types of Eggs 66 A Guide to Soft & Blue Cheeses 68
A Guide to Hard Cheeses 70 A Lexicon of European Cheeses 72

Herbs & Spices 74
A Guide to Herbs 74 A Guide to Spices 76

Section Two
Preparing Food 78

Beef & Veal 80
Barding Beef & Veal Cuts 80
Larding 82 Stuffing a Breast of Veal 84
Dressing & Flavouring Steaks 85 Mincing Beef by Hand 86
The Basic Hamburger & Variations 87
Steak Tartare 88 Beef Carpaccio 89

Lamb 90
Boning Lamb 90 Trimming a Leg plus Trimming & Stuffing a Shoulder 92
Preparing Racks of Lamb & Guard of Honour 94
Stuffing a Leg Under the Fat 96 Stuffing a Rolled Breast 97
Trimming Chops 98 Trimming Cutlets & Slicing Lamb Fillet 99

Pork 100
Boning Loin of Pork 100
Boning a Neck of Pork & Preparing a Leg of Pork 101
Stuffing a Rolled Pork Loin & Scoring Crackling for Roast Pork 102

Poultry 104
Jointing Poultry 104 Boning Whole Birds 106 Trussing Poultry 108
Spatchcocking Poultry & Stuffing a Spatchcocked Bird Under the Skin 110
Boning Chicken Suprêmes 112 Stuffing Boned Chicken Breasts 113

Game 114
Plucking & Drawing Game Birds 114 Trussing Game Birds 116
Jointing Rabbit & Hare 118 Larding & Barding Game 119
Preparing a Haunch of Venison 120 Preparing Saddle of Venison 121

Offal 122
Preparing Various Types of Offal 122

Fish & Seafood 126
Cleaning & Trimming Fish 126 Filleting Fish 128
Boning Round Fish via the Belly 130 Cutting up Uncooked Lobster 132
Dressing Squid 133 Preparing Molluscs 134

Vegetables, Pulses & Fungi 136
Vegetable Preparation Techniques 136 Preparing Pulses 143

Rice, Grains & Pasta 144
Preparing Couscous 144 Preparing Polenta 145
Making Fresh Pasta 146 Using a Pasta Machine 148 Shaping Fresh Pasta 150
Colouring & Flavouring Pasta 152 Stuffed Pasta 154

Fruit & Nuts 158
Preparing Fruit & Nuts 158 Simple Steps to Smooth Purées 163

Marinades & Stuffings 164
Marinades 164 Stuffings for Poultry 166 Gravlax 168

Section Three

Cooking Food 170

Boiling 172
Boiling Eggs 172   Boiling Vegetables 174
Cooking Rice & Grains 176   Boiling Pasta 177

Steaming 178
Steaming Potatoes & Rice 178   Steaming Shellfish 179
Steak & Kidney Pudding 180   Steamed Winter Pudding 182

Poaching 184
Poaching Eggs 184   Poaching Whole Fish 185
Poule au Pot 186   Poaching Fruit 188

Stewing 190
Lamb with Haricots 190   Coq au Vin 191
Mediterranean Fish Stew 194   Ratatouille 196

Braising 198
Osso Buco 198   Beef Olives 199   Boeuf à la Mode 200
Braised Vegetables 202   Glazing Vegetables 204

Grilling 206
Grilling Steaks 206   Grilling Fish 208   Grilling Vegetables 210

Roasting 212
Roasting Meat 212   Roast Rib of Beef with Yorkshire Pudding 214
Roasting Poultry 216   Roasting Game Birds 217

Baking 218
Baked Eggs 218   Pâté de Campagne 220   Baked Potatoes, Onions etc. 222
Vegetable Gratins 224   Cheese Soufflé 226

Frying & Sautèing 228
Frying Eggs 228   Omelette Fines Herbes 230
Poulet Sauté à la Crème 232   Lyonnaise Potato Cake 234

Deep-frying 236
Deep-fried Marinated Chicken 236   Chips & variations 238
Pineapple & Frangipane Fritters 240

Stocks & Sauces 242
Making Veal & Chicken Stock 242   Making Court-bouillon & Fumet for Fish 244
Basic White Sauce 246   Basic Brown Sauce 248
Sabayon & Beurre Blanc 250   Vinaigrette & Sauce Bâtarde 251
Hollandaise & Mousseline 252   Aïoli, Pesto & Salsa Verde 253
Butterscotch & Caramel Sauce 254   Chocolate Sauce 255
Custard & Bavarian Cream 256   Pastry Cream 257

Soups 258
Consommé 258   French Onion Soup 260
Borscht 262   Crayfish Bisque 264

Bread-making 266
Basic Bread-making 266   Making Croissants 269
Making Long Loaves 272   Pizza, etc. 274

Pastry-making 276
Shortcrust Pastry 276   Double-crust Apple Pie 278
Pear Upside-down Tart 280   Puff Pastry 282
Layered Fruit Bande 284   Making Choux Pastry 286   Eclairs, etc 288

Cake-making 290
Making Meringue 290   Making Whisked Sponge Cakes 294
Rich Fruit Cake 296

Section Four

Serving Food 298

Carving Meat & Poultry 298
Carving Leg & Saddle of Lamb 300   Carving Leg of Pork 302
Carving a Ham 303   Carving a Turkey & Other Poultry 304

Serving Fish & Shellfish 306
Serving Whole Poached Fish 306   Serving Flat Fish off the Bone 307
Dressing Crab 308   Dressing Lobster 310

Garnishing & Presentation 312
Assorted Garnishes 312   Piping Decoration 314
Decorating a Cake 318

Index 319

Foreword

When cooking is easy, the kitchen is a place of fun and excitement. When a cook's gestures and grasp of fundamentals become assured and automatic, the act of cooking is, at the same time, a tonic relaxation and an exhilarating creative experience. One cannot learn to draw by marking lines between strategically positioned dots around the contours of a bunny or a cat; neither can one learn to cook by slavishly following the steps of a printed recipe with no understanding of the underlying principles that impose those steps.

The preparation of a good meal begins in the marketplace and the garden. That is where *The Good Cook's Encyclopedia* begins. It is not a recipe book, it is an *exposé* of eternal culinary verities, which know no geographical or historical boundaries. It is about *how to cook*, how to recognize perfect produce, how to master simple, mechanical procedures, such as chopping, slicing, boning, filleting, stuffing, trussing, larding, barding, moulding and unmoulding, carving and serving. And it is about understanding the principles of basic cooking methods — roasting, baking, grilling, frying, deep-frying, sautéing, braising, boiling, poaching and steaming — the magical transformation of foods under the influence of different intensities and qualities of moist or dry heat or of cold.

The illustrated preparations on these pages demonstrate basic culinary techniques, each of which can lend itself to a kaleidoscope of interpretations. For example, the chicken, split down the back and stuffed beneath the skin on pages 110-111 is a recipe only in the sense that a specific stuffing is suggested. Guinea fowl, pigeon squab or farm-raised quail can be treated in the same way (hunted birds often have damaged skin, the skin of duck and goose is too fatty and turkey is too large). Stuffings based on spinach or chard, with or without an addition of sorrel, mirepoix, duxelles of wild or cultivated mushrooms (chopped truffle is a welcome addition), parboiled and chopped broccoli, diced and sautéed aubergine, chopped chicken livers, and so forth, are all equally successful. Fresh breadcrumbs lend lightness and body, an egg binds but is often not necessary (liver binds as well), spices and herbs are a matter of personal experience and taste — they do not affect the physical performance. The birds may be baked in the oven or grilled — smaller birds are better grilled. The inspiration of the moment is often the best and, in any case, is never a disaster.

Cooking is a question of passion, of experience, mechanics, intuition, imagination and, least of all, of recipes. The *raison d'être* of *The Good Cook's Encyclopedia* is to rupture the binds of frustration, to give wings to the reader. It addresses both amateur and professional alike — nothing goes unexplained and nothing is falsely simplified: good cooking is easy.

RICHARD OLNEY, France 1996

Buying Food

The real key to good cooking is buying the best and freshest of ingredients. This does not necessarily mean buying the most expensive items on display – a good cook can make wonderful meals from the cheapest of meat cuts or fish – but simply being able to judge the quality of what is available in any given price range.

Shopping for food should be one of life's greatest pleasures. Instead it often seems to become a mere chore and part of the weekly round of household duties. Obviously if you are still getting your ingredients from a series of specialist suppliers, butchers, fishmongers, greengrocers and the like, there is more of the stimulus that goes with being able to handle and judge the raw material, ask advice from an expert, etc. It is also usually possible to get them to do a great deal of the more fiddly preparation, like boning and filleting. On the other hand, shopping in a supermarket, however speedy and economical, frequently involves taking a calculated risk with food that it already pre-packaged and can't be examined, felt or smelled – let alone tasted. The answer there is to be ready to return anything that does not live up to expectations.

The quality of the food you buy can also be seriously impaired by poor handling and storage, so get it back home as soon as you can and unpack it immediately. Take the time to unwrap or re-wrap items as appropriate and put it straight into the refrigerator, freezer or vegetable basket.

Buying and Storing Meat

All meat is, of course, muscle; groups of fibres composed mostly of protein and bound together in bundles by gelatinous connective tissue. The well-exercised muscles of a mature beef animal, for example, have a coarse grain and stronger walls of connective tissue than the undeveloped muscles of a veal calf and are therefore potentially tougher.

The ability to judge tenderness and flavour of meat requires years of experience and a knowledge of the technicalities of the modern industry. Many visual clues, such as the whether lean beef is bright or dull red and whether the grain of the meat is coarse or fine, may prove inconclusive. For the home cook, however knowledgeable, there is no substitute for a trustworthy butcher who will select good carcasses and prepare them skilfully.

In general, however, always buy meat that looks and smells appealing, with a clean colour bearing no hint of grey, and firm waxy fat with no hint of yellow. Avoid any meat that looks or feels moist or clammy and it is obviously wiser to buy joints that have already been well trimmed.

To develop its full flavour and tenderness – apart from pork, which is eaten fresh – even the best meat is customarily allowed to hang, or age, in conditions of strictly controlled temperature and humidity, before being cut up for sale. During this time enzymes in the meat break down the fibres, with a resulting improvement in both flavour and tenderness.

Most meat will keep for a few days in the coldest part of the refrigerator and during that time the flavour will continue to improve a little. Since the cut surfaces of closely wrapped meat will remain wet, bacteria can thrive and the meat spoil. So remove all close wrappings and put meat on a small rack over a plate so that air can circulate around it. To prevent any exchange of flavours with other foods, cover it with an inverted bowl. Beef and lamb keep well for 3-5 days; veal and pork for 2-4 days, while any offal or minced meat should be used within 24 hours.

CUBED NECK

1 **Neck or sticking piece**. The neck is a very muscular cut with a high proportion of connective tissue. It needs very long, moist cooking to achieve tenderness, but it is well-flavoured and cheap. It is usually sold cubed or minced.

MINCED CLOD

2 **Clod**. The primal cut contains the long heavy 'arm' bone or humerus, which is removed and sold as a marrow bone. The relatively high proportion of fat is trimmed out by the butcher. Meat from the clod is similar in quality to neck meat (1) and is usually prepared in the same way by cubing or mincing.

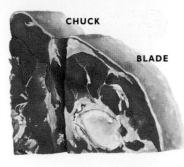

CHUCK

BLADE

3 **Chuck**. A large and fairly lean cut of high-quality braising meat, this complex area of shoulder muscle is boned and cut into slices to be sold as chuck steak. The meat may also be cubed for stewing. It needs long cooking by the moist heat method to tenderize the connective tissue.

4 **Blade**. The shoulder blade contained in the primal cut is removed by the butcher and the muscles are divided in different ways to yield steaks or larger pieces for braising. The flavour is good and the meat fairly lean. Some pieces contain a thick seam of gelatinous tissue that attaches the muscles to the blade bone. This is left on the meat because it melts down and becomes tender when cooked by moist heat.

BLADE STEAK

CHUCK STEAK

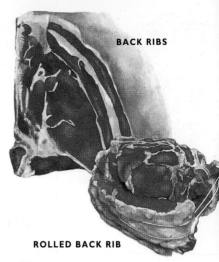

BACK RIBS

ROLLED BACK RIB

5 **Back rib**. The primal cut contains 4 or 5 ribs, with relatively tender and fine-grained meat. To make a good slow roast, the rib bones are sawn off short and the meat is usually tied; or it can be boned out completely, rolled and tied. The meat may also be pot-roasted or braised in a piece.

THICK RIB

LEG-OF-MUTTON CUT

16 **Thick rib**. This structure is often considered part of the shoulder, with its large associated muscles; the ribs and their muscle formation lie beneath. The division of this section varies with local practice, but thick rib is often butchered to produce a good cut of well-flavoured boneless meat (sometimes known as leg-of-mutton) that is excellent for slow roasting (page 213). The meat may also be cut into steaks for braising.

A Guide to Beef Cuts

The diagram of a side of beef in the centre of these pages indicates the basic divisions, known as primal cuts, into which the butcher traditionally separates the carcass before subdividing the meat for his customers. The primal cuts on the carcass are keyed by number to detailed drawings showing some of the ways in which the meat is usually sold over the counter. The names of the different cuts and the details of the cutting

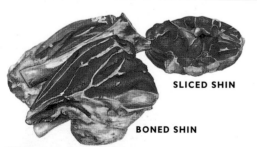

SLICED SHIN

BONED SHIN

15 **Shin**. The well-muscled foreleg, or shin, contains a marrow bone and several narrow well-defined muscles with thick connective tissue and strong sinews. The bone is removed and the meat usually cut across the grain in rounds, or cubed for braising or stewing. With moist cooking, the gelatinous tissues melt down to give rich juices. Shin is especially suitable for braising (page 198).

14 **Brisket**. The breastbone and ribs are removed to leave the brisket, a long, flat piece of meat that is usually rolled and tied. The roll may then be divided for sale in sections of any length. The layered structure of these muscles is interspersed with fat, and the flavour is good. Brisket needs moist cooking. It may be braised, but is usually poached, either fresh or salted – brisket is one of the cuts for salting.

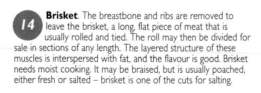

BRISKET

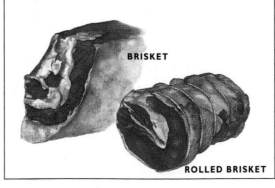

ROLLED BRISKET

13 **Thin rib**. This cut, overlying the rib bones, is composed of muscle interlayered with some fat. It is very well suited to poaching, since the flavour of the meat is good and the interlarding of fat keeps it moist. The meat may also be braised on or off the bone, sliced or cubed. The meat is also often minced.

THIN RIB

CUBED THIN RIB

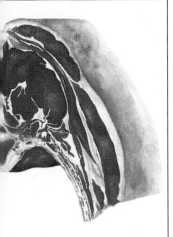

6 **Forerib**. The primal cut contains 4 or 5 ribs, from which 2-rib and 3-rib roasts are usually prepared. The classic prime rib roast, forerib is very tender. To retain its flavour and juices, forerib should be roasted on the bone at high heat, after chining (page 94). Rib steaks and single ribs on the bone are excellent grilled. When boned out a rib roast becomes *entrecôte*.

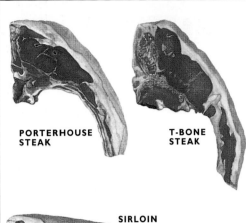

PORTERHOUSE STEAK

T-BONE STEAK

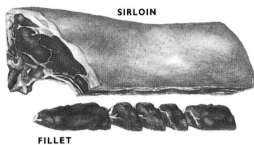

SIRLOIN

SIRLOIN STEAK

FILLET

7 **Sirloin**. This large section of very tender, prime meat includes the last 3 ribs (wing ribs). Sirloin may be roasted on or off the bone or the meat may be divided into various combinations of steaks for grilling or frying. Sirloin steaks are boneless; Porterhouse steaks are cut on the bone from the rib end of the sirloin; T-bone steaks, cut from the hind section, include a section of the tender fillet that lies beneath the backbone. If the fillet is removed separately, it may sometimes be roasted whole, but it is more often cut up across the grain for steaks.

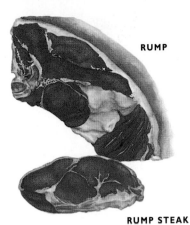

RUMP

RUMP STEAK

8 **Rump**. The primal cut contains the lowest vertebrae of the back and the pelvic bone. These are removed and the meat is usually sliced across the grain to give tender steaks of good flavour suitable for grilling or frying. Pieces over 1.5 kg (3 lb) are excellent for roasting by the high-heat method (page 212).

methods used may differ from region to region, but the cooking information summarized here applies to any cut from a given part of the carcass.

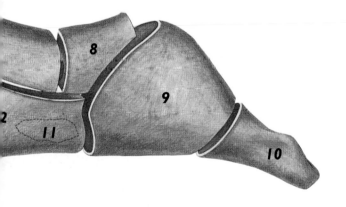

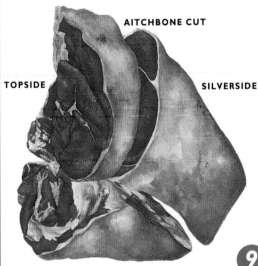

AITCHBONE CUT

TOPSIDE

SILVERSIDE

TOP RUMP

ROLLED SILVERSIDE

ROLLED TOPSIDE

ROLLED TOP RUMP

9 **Topside, silverside, aitchbone cut, top rump**. These four major cuts compose the upper hind leg. Topside, a lean, fine-grained cut from the inside leg, may be slow-roasted or braised. Silverside, with a coarser grain and good flavour, may be slow-roasted, braised or salted and poached. The aitchbone cut, a well-flavoured piece cut from around the pelvic bone, makes a good slow roast. Top rump (also known as thick flank) may be slow-roasted or braised, but it is also sliced into steaks to be braised, or sometimes fried.

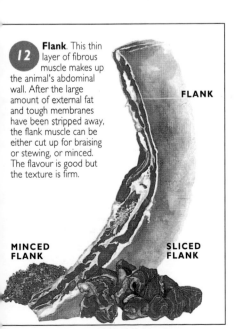

12 **Flank**. This thin layer of fibrous muscle makes up the animal's abdominal wall. After the large amount of external fat and tough membranes have been stripped away, the flank muscle can be either cut up for braising or stewing, or minced. The flavour is good but the texture is firm.

FLANK

MINCED FLANK

SLICED FLANK

GOOSE SKIRT

11 **Skirt**. Skirt is a name for various small internal muscles of which the most important are the goose skirt, from inside the flank (sometimes called 'flank steak'), and rump skirt, from inside the rump. Coarse-grained but of excellent flavour and very lean, skirt steaks may be grilled or fried if kept rare. If they are to be cooked well done, they should be braised and given a long cooking. A third type of skirt steak is called the 'hanging tender', 'butcher's piece' or 'bloody skirt'. Though only occasionally available from retail butchers (it is a central internal muscle, so there is only one from each beef carcass), its tenderness and flavour make it one of the best cuts for grilling; buy it when you can. It is a favourite cut in France, where it is known as *onglet*.

10 **Leg**. The well-sinewed and fleshy hind leg, like the shin, contains a marrow bone and a high proportion of tissue. It is boned out and usually cut into thick slices, or cubed. Its fine flavour and gelatinous quality make it an excellent stewing meat.

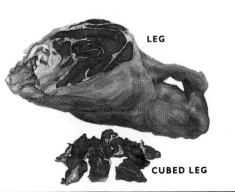

LEG

CUBED LEG

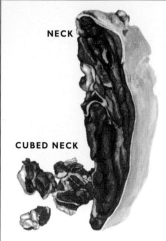

NECK

CUBED NECK

1 **Neck**. The neck contains bones and sinews that are removed by the butcher. The meat may be sold in a large piece for braising, or cut up for poaching in a blanquette. It may also be cubed or diced for stewing. Pieces of neck on the bone are useful for veal stock (page 242).

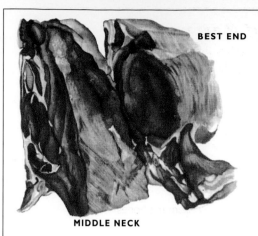

BEST END

MIDDLE NECK

2 **Middle neck**. This cut includes the first 4 or 5 ribs of the back. Removal of the shoulder (11) leaves these rib bones exposed; meat from the middle neck is then usually boned completely and sold either in one piece for roasting or sliced into cutlets for braising.

3 **Best end of neck**. The prime meat of the central ribs is usually sliced into cutlets on or off the bone for grilling or frying. The meat may also be prepared in large pieces on or off the bone for roasting.

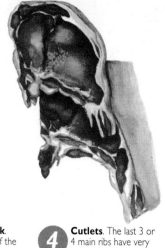

4 **Cutlets**. The last 3 or 4 main ribs have very tender meat and are usually sold as cutlets for grilling or frying. They may be prepared by chining (removing the tip of the vertebra) and trimming off the ends of the rib bones; or they may be boned. The ribs may also be divided into thick chops as for loin (5).

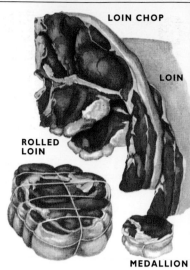

LOIN CHOP

LOIN

ROLLED LOIN

MEDALLION

5 **Loin**. A tender cut of very lean meat, the loin may be divided into chops for grilling or frying. It may also be boned and rolled for roasting, with or without the fillet that lies beneath the backbone. When the fillet is removed, it may be sliced into rounds, called medallions, for frying.

A G*uide to* V*eal* C*uts*

The numbered diagram of a side of veal on the right is divided to show the position of the major, or primal, cuts. The enlarged drawings in the corresponding numbered boxes show how the cuts are prepared for sale. The cutting pattern used here is based on French butchery practice.

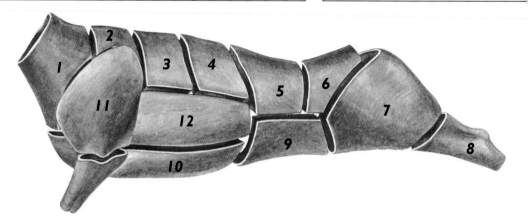

11 **Shoulder**. The muscles of the shoulder are divided into cuts of varying degrees of tenderness depending on their positions. The meat is used according to its qualities – usually for roasting off the bone, or for braising. Some butchers trim one or more of the shoulder muscles carefully for slicing into escalopes, but these will not be of top quality.

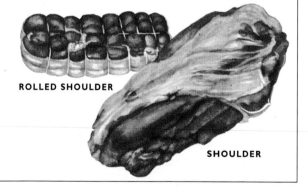

ROLLED SHOULDER

SHOULDER

12 **Ribs**. The central section of the ribcage is usually boned and sliced for braising or poaching, since moist cooking is needed to soften the high proportion of connective tissue. The layered structure of the flesh is similar to that of the breast (10) – and many British butchers cut the breast to include some of this rib area. The flavour is good, and the interlarding of integral fat helps to keep the meat moist while it cooks.

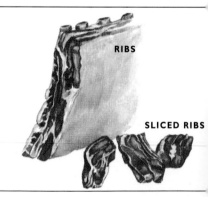

RIBS

SLICED RIBS

10 **Breast**. In this bony cut, layers of muscle are interlarded with fat and membrane. The fore part contains the breastbone and ribs; the hind part (*tendrons de veau*) contains cartilaginous rib tips and is the classic cut for *blanquette de veau*. A whole or half breast may be boned, stuffed and rolled for poaching; or the meat sliced for braising or poaching.

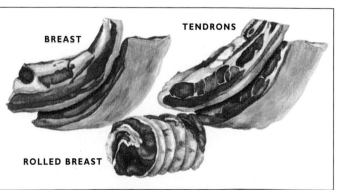

BREAST

TENDRONS

ROLLED BREAST

9 **Flank**. The calf's abdominal wall is a thin cut, composed of layers of meat with plenty of connective tissue that requires moist heat to tenderize it. The flank may be rolled and poached – sometimes with a stuffing – or cut up into slices or cubes for stewing. Flank is also suitable for minced veal.

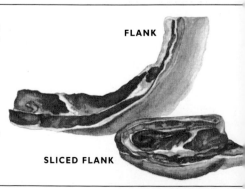

FLANK

SLICED FLANK

6 **Rump**. The rump is a prime cut that may be roasted, grilled as steaks or fried as escalopes. French practice separates the smaller *culotte* section from the larger *quasi* for roasting, but British butchers often treat the rump and leg (7) together as one piece, and slice all the meat into escalopes. The rump end of the fillet may be sliced into medallions.

QUASI

CULOTTE

STEAK

MEDALLION

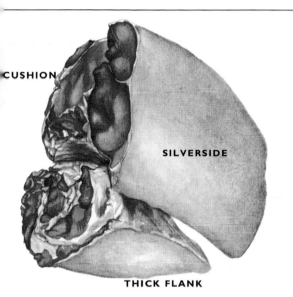

CUSHION

SILVERSIDE

THICK FLANK

7 **Leg**. The leg is divided by seaming out the 3 main muscles, any of which may be roasted or braised successfully in a large piece, or thinly sliced into escalopes for frying. The cushion, or topside, is a very tender fine-grained muscle from the inside leg, yielding large escalopes of excellent quality. The thick flank, also very tender, provides fine, but smaller escalopes. The silverside, or undercushion, with a coarser grain, is less tender and an internal muscle seam that makes the escalopes cut from it less satisfactory. Silverside is a good roasting or braising cut when barded (page 80-1) or larded (page 82-3).

ESCALOPES

OSSO BUCO

8 **Knuckle and shin**. Both the knuckle (hind leg) and the shin (foreleg) are sinewy well-flavoured gelatinous cuts that need moist cooking. Meat from the shin and knuckle may be braised or poached on or off the bone. For braising in slices as *osso buco* (page 198), the heavier knuckle has more meat around the bone and the bone contains more marrow. The less meaty shin is often used for diced veal. Both shin and knuckle are excellent cuts to use for making veal stock.

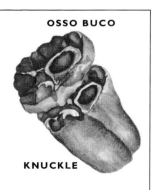

KNUCKLE

The Beef Marrow Bonus

Beef bones, especially the heavy leg bones, are large enough to yield a usable quantity of marrow. This light, fatty substance is highly nutritious, and its smooth texture and slight meaty flavour make marrow a welcome addition to many beef and veal dishes. Marrow may be taken from the bones with or without preliminary cooking. For easy extraction ask the butcher to saw the bones into 10 cm (4 inch) sections.

Raw marrow removed from the bones (below, left) can be chopped up for use in dumplings, hamburgers (page 86-7), or stuffings (pages 165-7). Poached marrow may be employed as an ingredient in sauces, used as a garnish for steaks or served on toast. To extract the marrow, simmer the beef bones in water until the marrow will slip out easily (below, right). Cut a section of marrow into slices; then, just before serving, poach the slices in salted water for a minute or less until the pieces are heated through and translucent.

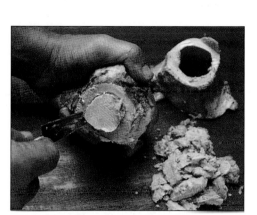

Cutting out raw marrow. Loosen the marrow from the bone with a small sharp knife and prise it out little by little until the bone is empty. Raw marrow can be refrigerated in a tightly covered container for 2 to 3 days or frozen for up to 2 months.

Extracting poached marrow. Put the marrow bones in a pan with enough water to cover. Bring the water to the boil, reduce the heat and simmer for a few minutes until heated through. Drain, then shake each bone gently over a plate to slip the marrow out in one piece.

Calf's Foot: A Rich Source of Gelatine

Calves' feet are among the richest sources of natural gelatine. A single calf's foot will yield enough gelatine to give body to a poaching broth or make 1/2 litre (18 fl oz) of simmered braising liquid set to a firm jelly as it cools.

To prepare a calf's foot for cooking, remove the bone at the joint if it is still attached (right, top) – the bone would take longer than the rest of the foot to give up its gelatine and it would occupy valuable space in the cooking pot. (But you should keep the bone to use when you are next making stock.) Split the foot in half lengthwise (right, bottom); it will fit into the cooking pot more easily and will yield its gelatine more quickly if it is divided.

Calves' feet are not always available at the butcher's, but you can usually obtain them if you order them in advance. If you cannot get them use pigs' trotters instead; two will do instead of one calf's foot.

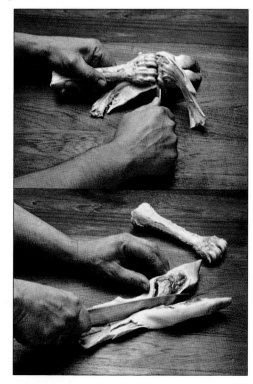

NECK RINGS

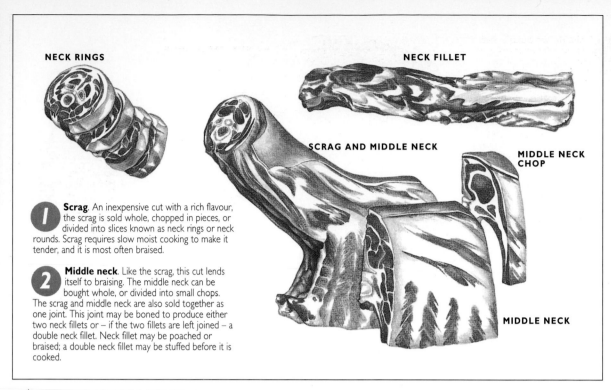

NECK FILLET

SCRAG AND MIDDLE NECK

MIDDLE NECK CHOP

MIDDLE NECK

1 **Scrag**. An inexpensive cut with a rich flavour, the scrag is sold whole, chopped in pieces, or divided into slices known as neck rings or neck rounds. Scrag requires slow moist cooking to make it tender, and it is most often braised.

2 **Middle neck**. Like the scrag, this cut lends itself to braising. The middle neck can be bought whole, or divided into small chops. The scrag and middle neck are also sold together as one joint. This joint may be boned to produce either two neck fillets or – if the two fillets are left joined – a double neck fillet. Neck fillet may be poached or braised; a double neck fillet may be stuffed before it is cooked.

3 **Best end of neck**. This tender rib cut is sold whole or divided into cutlets. The cutlets may be fried, grilled or baked. A single rack of best end of neck provides an elegant small roast. For a special occasion, a pair of racks can be interlaced to make a guard of honour, or joined in a circle to make a crown roast (pages 94-5).

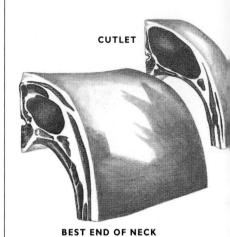

CUTLET

BEST END OF NECK

A Guide to Lamb Cuts

The central diagram on the right shows the major or primal cuts obtained from a lamb carcass. The primal cuts on the carcass are keyed by number to detailed drawings showing some of the ways in which the meat is usually sold over the counter. The names of the different cuts and the details of the cutting methods used may differ from region to region, but the cooking information summarized here applies to any cut from a given part of the carcass.

The lean meat of grass-fed lamb – between about three and 12 months old – is a clear rose colour. As the animal ages, the colour progressively deepens, and in mature mutton, over two years old, the meat is a purplish red. A muddy tinge in the colour of the meat of either lamb or mutton is a sign of poor quality. The bones of a young lamb have a pinkish-blue tinge and are slightly porous; mutton has hard white bones. The fat of both should be white, firm and dry to the touch.

A milk lamb is an unweaned lamb, usually under eight weeks old. The flesh of milk lambs is very pale pink in colour. Milk lamb is sold whole, with its pluck – the lungs, liver, spleen and heart – or cut into quarters. It is usually available only in late winter or spring.

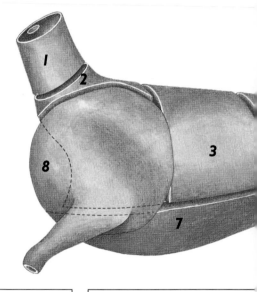

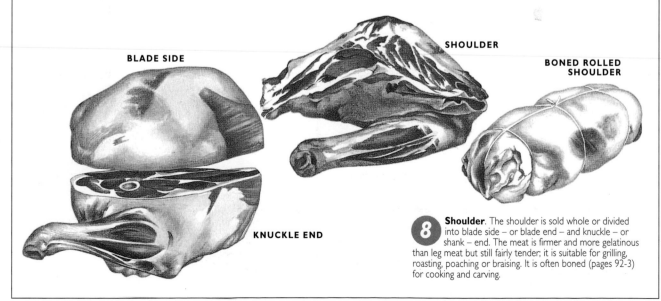

BLADE SIDE

SHOULDER

BONED ROLLED SHOULDER

KNUCKLE END

8 **Shoulder**. The shoulder is sold whole or divided into blade side – or blade end – and knuckle – or shank – end. The meat is firmer and more gelatinous than leg meat but still fairly tender; it is suitable for grilling, roasting, poaching or braising. It is often boned (pages 92-3) for cooking and carving.

7 **Breast**. This is a fatty but economical cut with a good flavour. A whole breast may be roasted or braised on the bone, but it is often first boned (page 90) and stuffed (page 97). The breast – with or without bone – may be divided into strips for braising.

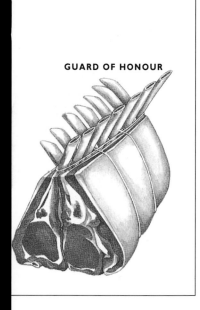

GUARD OF HONOUR

4 **Loin**. The loin is usually divided into chops for either grilling or frying. Left whole, it makes a good small roast. The loin includes the fillet, the most delicate meat of the lamb, and the eye of the loin, a tender, completely lean section. A pair of loins left joined by the backbone may be sliced to produce double loin or butterfly chops. A whole pair of loins provides the handsome joint known as a saddle. A 'long' saddle includes a pair of chumps as well as a pair of loins.

5 **Chump**. Like the loin, the chump is often divided into chops for grilling or frying. A whole chump makes a compact small roast or can be gently braised.

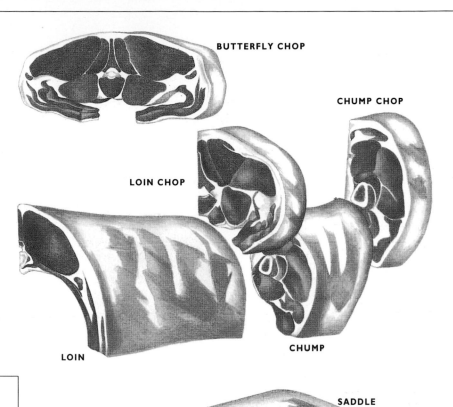

BUTTERFLY CHOP

CHUMP CHOP

LOIN CHOP

LOIN

CHUMP

SADDLE

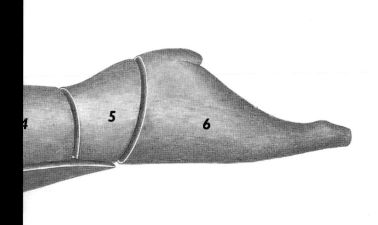

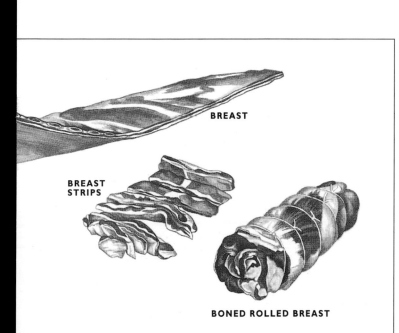

BREAST

BREAST STRIPS

BONED ROLLED BREAST

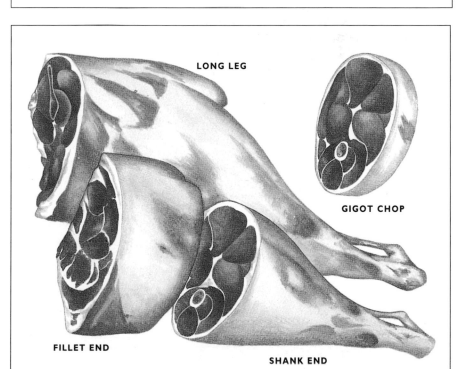

LONG LEG

GIGOT CHOP

FILLET END

SHANK END

6 **Leg**. The most popular lamb joint for roasting, the leg provides a high proportion of lean tender meat to a very small proportion of bone. A leg is sometimes divided into the fillet end and the shank – or knuckle – end; the fillet end may be cut into several slices to provide gigot chops for grilling or frying. A 'long' leg or haunch includes a section of chump as well as the leg.

1 **Head**. This may be sold whole, or split in half. Much of the meat that it contains, such as the tongue and brains, is normally retailed as offal. If you are cooking a whole suckling pig, be sure not to waste any of this meat; it will be ready to eat when the pig is cooked and should be cut away from the bone and served with rest of the roast. Pigs' ears are a delicacy in their own right; they are prepared by lengthy poaching and can then be coated with mustard and breadcrumbs and grilled.

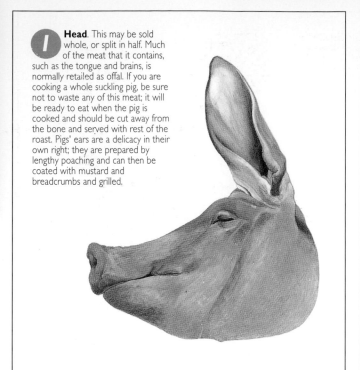

2 **Neck end**. This large cut is often sold in two sections; the spare rib – not to be confused with the spare ribs (9, opposite page) from the thick end of the belly – and the blade, which includes the shoulder bone. Both are tender meaty cuts interlarded with fatty tissue, that make good economical choices for roasting or braising. The spare rib can also be cut into chops for frying or grilling; front chops contain a section of the vertebral column, while back chops are cut on the rib. The whole cut can be boned and rolled for roasting or braising. Bacon-cured meat from this cut is sold as collar; it may be sliced into rashers for frying or grilling, or sold whole for poaching and braising.

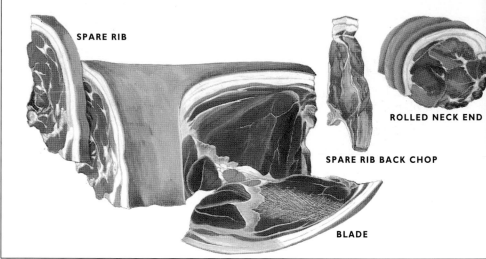

SPARE RIB

ROLLED NECK END

SPARE RIB BACK CHOP

BLADE

A Guide to Pork Cuts

The diagram of a side of pork in the centre of these pages shows the major cuts derived from a pig's carcass. The primal cuts on the carcass are keyed by number to detailed drawings showing some of the ways in which the meat is usually sold over the counter. The names of the different cuts and the details of the cutting methods used may differ from region to region, but the cooking information summarized here applies to any cut from a given part of the carcass.

Most cuts of pork are sold with the outer skin, or rind, attached. Many butchers score the rind to prevent it both from deforming the cut as it shrinks during cooking, and to enable excess fat to escape. If you want the rind unscored, warn the butcher in advance.

Cured pork is offered for sale either as ham or as bacon. To make ham, legs of pork are removed from fresh pork carcasses and cured separately; some processed hams – known as shoulder hams – are now also made with meat from the neck end and hand and spring. Bacon is cured in entire sides from which the head, tail, trotters and fillet have been removed. All bacon is salted and some is smoked as well; unsmoked cuts are known as 'green' bacon.

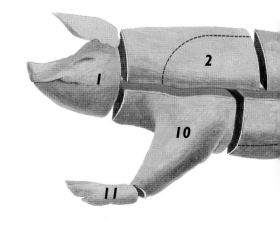

11 **Trotters**. Trotters are cooked by lengthy poaching; they can then be coated with breadcrumbs and grilled or served with a piquant sauce. The gelatine that they contain makes them useful for enriching stews and jellied stock.

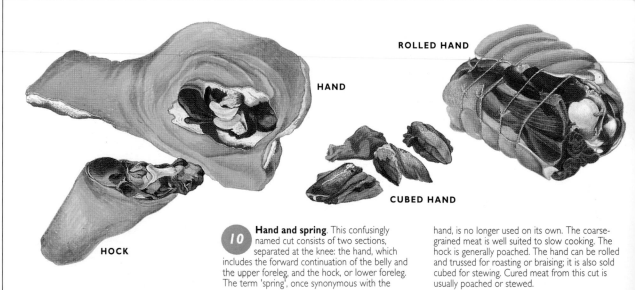

ROLLED HAND

HAND

HOCK

CUBED HAND

10 **Hand and spring**. This confusingly named cut consists of two sections, separated at the knee: the hand, which includes the forward continuation of the belly and the upper foreleg, and the hock, or lower foreleg. The term 'spring', once synonymous with the hand, is no longer used on its own. The coarse-grained meat is well suited to slow cooking. The hock is generally poached. The hand can be rolled and trussed for roasting or braising; it is also sold cubed for stewing. Cured meat from this cut is usually poached or stewed.

3 **Foreloin**. This prime cut of tender meat is often divided between the ribs into chops. Whole, it is an excellent choice for roasting. A crown of loin, made by curving two rib sections into semi-circles and stitching them together, is taken from the fore-and middle loin; stuffed and roasted, it makes an arresting main course for a formal dinner. The cured meat of the loin cuts and chump end is sold as back bacon – a prime cut for frying or grilling.

4 **Middle loin**. This prime cut can be roasted on the bone, or boned and rolled. It is also divided into chops; some contain a slice of kidney. The 'eye' is sometimes removed and sliced for sautéing . Beneath the middle loin and the chump end lies the fillet, or tenderloin, a choice lean cut which can be cooked with the loin or braised, roasted whole, or sliced for frying.

5 **Chump end**. This tender cut is roasted whole or divided into chops. Chops from the back of the cut have a distinctive wrap-around shape, and contain more meat than chops from other cuts.

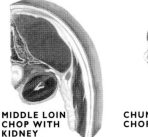

MIDDLE LOIN CHOP WITH KIDNEY

CHUMP CHOP

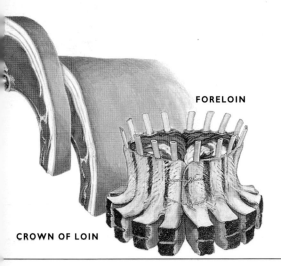

FORELOIN

CROWN OF LOIN

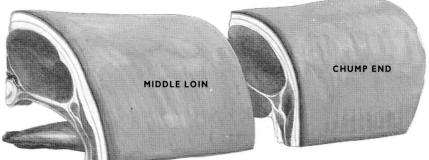

MIDDLE LOIN

CHUMP END

SLICES FROM THE EYE OF LOIN

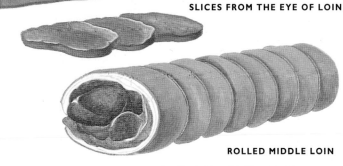

ROLLED MIDDLE LOIN

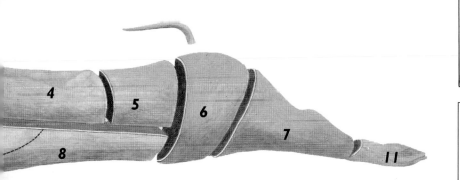

FILLET END

KNUCKLE END

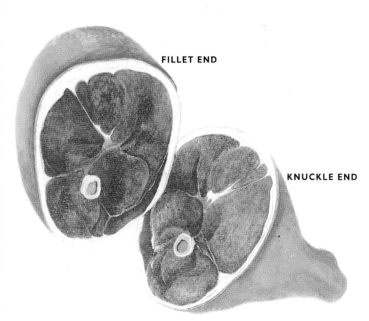

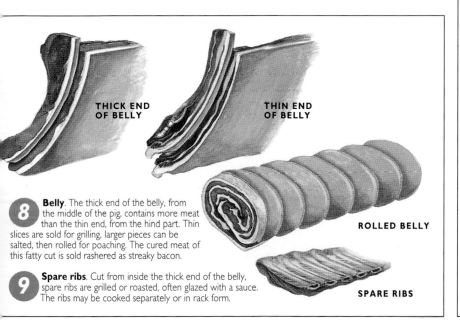

THICK END OF BELLY

THIN END OF BELLY

ROLLED BELLY

SPARE RIBS

8 **Belly**. The thick end of the belly, from the middle of the pig, contains more meat than the thin end, from the hind part. Thin slices are sold for grilling, larger pieces can be salted, then rolled for poaching. The cured meat of this fatty cut is sold rashered as streaky bacon.

9 **Spare ribs**. Cut from inside the thick end of the belly, spare ribs are grilled or roasted, often glazed with a sauce. The ribs may be cooked separately or in rack form.

6 **7** **Leg**. Legs of pork can be roasted or braised whole. A whole leg is too large for the needs of most households, however, and the cut is often divided across the thigh into two parts which are retailed separately. The upper section, or fillet end (above, left) provides excellent lean meat for roasting on the bone; it can also be sliced into steaks for grilling and frying. The lower section, called the knuckle end (above, right) has a much higher proportion of bone, but is still a good roasting cut; it can also be salted down for poaching. When cured, the leg is sold as ham – unless it is bacon-cured, in which case it is called gammon.

A Guide to Poultry

As a rule, young birds are tender and subtly flavoured; they are ideal for roasting, grilling or sautéing – rapid cooking methods that seal in flavour and preserve succulence. The breast meat of the lean birds – chicken, turkey and guinea fowl – is particularly delicate and cooks in a shorter time than the darker meat of the legs.

As a bird matures, it becomes increasingly tough – especially its active leg muscles. However, the flesh develops a depth of flavour that is rarely found in young birds. In addition, it acquires a gelatinous quality that enables it to tolerate the long cooking required to tenderize the fibres. If an old bird is gently braised or poached with vegetables it will retain its flavour and the liquid will itself become suffused with enough of the bird's essence to stand on its own as a soup, stock or sauce.

The age of freshly killed poultry can be gauged without difficulty. The beak and the tip of the breastbone are flexible to the touch in a young bird, rigid in old ones. However, when you buy pre-packaged birds, whether fresh or frozen, you will have to rely on labels and what you can see through the wrappings. The skin of a young bird should look smooth with no visible hairs. The colour of the skin differs from breed to breed and according to diet; it is therefore not a reliable guide to age or quality. When buying frozen poultry, avoid packages that are limp or contain pinkish ice, a sign that the bird was accidentally defrosted and then refrozen.

Fresh poultry keeps for up to 3 days in the coldest part of the refrigerator. Unwrap as soon as you get it home, place in a shallow container and cover loosely to let air circulate without flavours being transferred. Always defrost frozen poultry thoroughly in the refrigerator before cooking (up to 48 hours for a large goose or turkey) and use as soon as possible after defrosting.

The display of poultry shown right reflects the relative proportions of eight different birds and lists the range of weights at which they are customarily sold. When buying undressed poultry, allow about 350 g (12 oz) for each serving of pigeon squab, guinea-fowl or chicken; a little less for turkey and capon; but up to 750 g (1¹/₂ lb) for goose and duck. This is because a goose or duck will lose as much as 50 per cent of its weight when it is dressed and still more in the cooking process, which melts out the copious quantities of fat that lie under the skin. In contrast, lean birds – such as turkey and chicken – lose only perhaps 25 per cent of their weight when they are dressed.

GOOSE
4.5 TO 8 KG (10 TO 18 LB)

TURKEY
4 TO 14 KG (9 TO 30 LB)

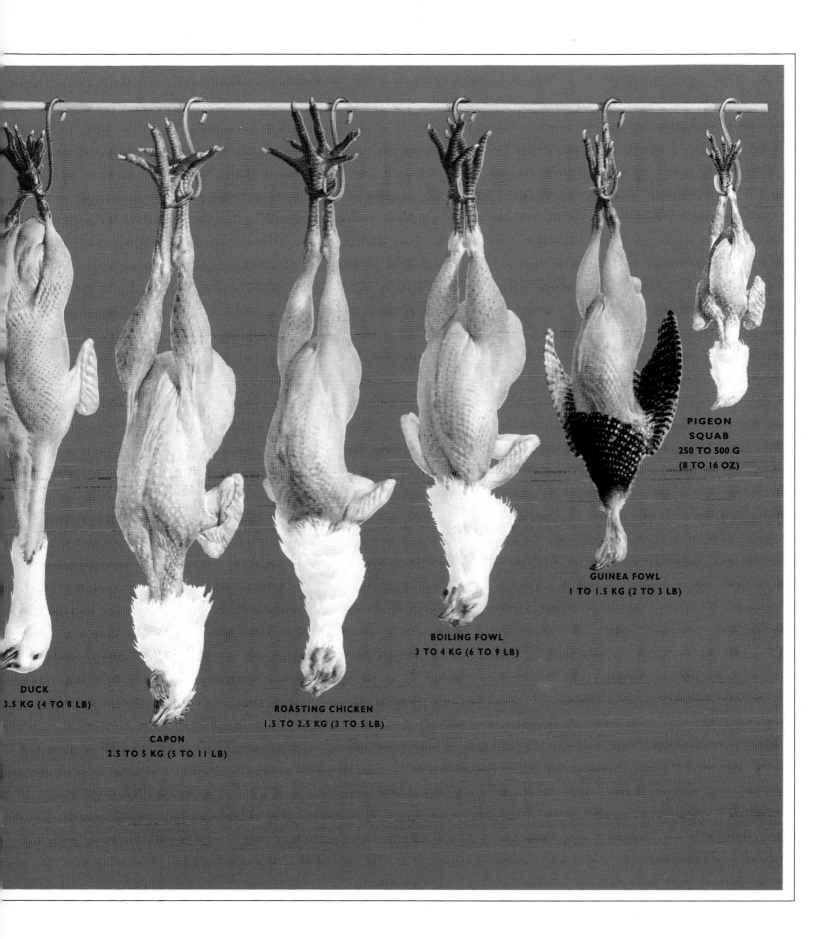

DUCK
3.5 KG (4 TO 8 LB)

CAPON
2.5 TO 5 KG (5 TO 11 LB)

ROASTING CHICKEN
1.5 TO 2.5 KG (3 TO 5 LB)

BOILING FOWL
3 TO 4 KG (6 TO 9 LB)

GUINEA FOWL
1 TO 1.5 KG (2 TO 3 LB)

PIGEON
SQUAB
250 TO 500 G
(8 TO 16 OZ)

A Guide to Game Birds

The guide on these pages shows the main British game bird species. Where the male and female of a species differ markedly in appearance, both are shown. The guide gives the average length and weight of the birds, when they can be hunted – known as the 'open season' – and the best time for eating. After being dressed – plucked and drawn – a bird's weight is reduced by about 25 per cent.

The most commonly eaten waterfowl are wild ducks – especially mallard, teal and widgeon – which are found on the coast and in marshy areas. The mallard eats a variety of plants, the teal feeds on seeds and small invertebrates, while the widgeon is grass eating.

Pheasants inhabit woodlands and hedgerows, although some are reared on farms and then released into the wild. Whether wild or farm

bred, their flesh always has the flavour of game. The hen pheasant provides meat that is more moist and more delicately flavoured than that of the cock. Partridges and quail belong to the same family as pheasants. Both grey and red-legged partridges prefer dry open country. It is illegal to hunt wild quail in Britain, but farm-bred birds of a sub-species close to the wild variety are available from shops.

WIDGEON
Anas penelope
Length: 45 cm (18 inches)
Weight: 750 g (1^1/2 lb)
Open season: *inland* 1 Sept-31 Jan;
foreshore 1 Sept-20 Feb
Best time for eating: Oct-Nov

TEAL
Anas crecca
Length: 35 cm (14 inches)
Weight: 400 g (14 oz)
Open season: *inland* 1 Sept-31 Jan;
foreshore 1 Sept-20 Feb
Best time for eating: Oct-Nov

GREY PARTRIDGE
Perdix perdix
Length: 30 cm (12 inches)
Weight: 400 g (14 oz)
Open season: 1 Sept-1 Feb
Best time for eating: Oct-Nov

RED-LEGGED PARTRIDGE
Alectoris rufa
Length: 34 cm (13^1/2 inches)
Weight: 450 g (15 oz)
Open season: 1 Sept-1 Feb
Best time for eating: Oct-Nov

MALLARD
Anas platyrhynchos
Length: 57.5 cm (23 inches)
Weight: 1.25 kg (2^1/2 lb)
Open season: *inland* 1 Sept-31 Jan;
foreshore 1 Sept-20 Feb
Best time for eating: Nov-Dec

PHEASANT
Phasianus colchicus
Length: 70 cm (28 inches)
Weight: 1.5 kg (3 lb)
Open season: 1 Oct-1 Feb
Best time for eating: Oct-Jan

QUAIL
Coturnix coturnix japonica
Length: 17.5 cm (7 inches)
Weight: 150 g (5 oz)
Availability: all year round
Best time for eating: all year round

The largest member of the grouse family is the capercaillie. It is found in mountainous forests and its flesh is sometimes perfumed by the pine needles that it eats. Black grouse prefer rocky hillsides, while the smaller red grouse inhabit the heather moors which give their meat its distinctive flavour. Other species of grouse are hunted and eaten but they are less common.

Snipe and woodcocks inhabit marshy inland areas, though woodcocks – as the name implies – also like a woodland environment. Snipe meat is strongly flavoured, while the flesh of

woodcock is prized for its fine, delicate flavour.

The ubiquitous wood-pigeon inhabits woods, fields and gardens. The birds are most succulent in the summer months when they feed on new grain shoots.

When buying birds, choose plump, firm specimens, with supple skin and smooth, firmly attached feathers. Avoid birds that have been badly damaged by shot. Game birds have a characteristic 'wild' odour, but they should never smell of decay. Young birds are generally regarded as the best choice.

Certain characteristics distinguish a young specimen from an old one. On young partridges and grouse the two outermost large flight feathers have pointed tips; younger partridges and grouse also have supple breastbones and flexible beaks. The spurs on young pheasants are softly rounded at the ends, while old birds have long sharp spurs. In some species, the colour of the birds' legs alters with age. Young grey partridges have yellowish legs that turn slate-grey with age; pigeons' legs deepen from a soft, rosy pink to red.

WOODCOCK
Scolopax rusticola
Length: 34 cm (13¹/2 inches)
Weight: 325 g (11 oz)
Open season: 1 Oct-31 Jan;
Scotland 1 Sept-31 Jan
Best time for eating: Nov-Dec

SNIPE
Gallinago gallinago
Length: 26 cm (10¹/2 inches)
Weight: 125 g (4 oz)
Open season: 12 Aug-31 Jan
Best time for eating: Dec-Jan

WOOD-PIGEON
Columbo palumbus
Length: 40 cm (16 inches)
Weight: 600 g (1¹/4 lb)
Open season: all year round
Best time for eating: April-Oct

RED GROUSE
Lagopus lagopus
Length: 38 cm (15 inches)
Weight: 750 g (1¹/2 lb)
Open season: 12 Aug-10 Dec
Best time for eating: Aug-Oct

CAPERCAILLIE
Tetrao urogallus
Length: 86 cm (34 inches)
Weight: 4 kg (9 lb)
Open season: 1 Oct-31 Jan
Best time for eating: Oct-Nov

BLACK GROUSE
Lyrurus tetrix
Length: 53 cm (21 inches)
Weight: 1.5 kg (3 lb)
Open season: 20 Aug-10 Dec;
Devon, Somerset, New Forest
1 Sept-10 Dec
Best time for eating: Aug-Sept

Common Species of Deer

All deer meat is known as venison. The three most common species of deer in the British Isles are the red deer, roe deer and fallow deer. The illustrations show the male and female of each species; the captions give average height (from the shoulder) and live weight, the hunting season and the best time to eat venison.

Red deer are the largest of the three species.

They inhabit forests and moorlands. Roe deer, the smallest, like woodlands, as do fallow deer, though the latter may also be found captive on parkland. Deer feed on grass, foliage and, occasionally, farm crops. Their meat is at its best in the autumn when they have fattened on abundant food supplies.

Good deer meat should be dark-red with a

fine grain and firm white fat. The same cooking techniques can be applied to venison from any type of deer, but cuts from roe and fallow deer will be smaller than corresponding joints of red deer.

The diagram of a side of venison (far right) shows the main cuts derived from a deer carcass and the ways in which the joints are usually cooked.

ROE DEER *Capreolus capreolus*
Height: 60 cm (24 inches)
Weight: 25 kg (4 stone)
Open season: *bucks* I April-30 Oct;
does I Nov-28/29 Feb.
Scotland: bucks I May-20 Oct;
does 21 Oct-28/29 Feb.
Best time for eating: *bucks* Oct;
does Dec-Feb

FALLOW DEER *Dama dama*
Height: 85 cm (34 inches)
Weight: 76 kg (12 stone)
Open season: *bucks* I Aug-20 April;; *does* I Nov-28/29 Feb.
Scotland: bucks I Aug-30 April; *does* 21 Oct-15 Feb. Best time for
eating: *bucks* Oct-Nov; *does* Dec-Feb

Rabbits and Hares

Wild rabbit has darker flesh and a gamy taste, while the pale flesh of hutch rabbit is reminiscent of poultry in its delicate flavour.

Hares belong to the same family as rabbits, but are a larger long-legged species. A young hare, up to the age of six months, is known as a leveret. Hare meat is dark, with a robust flavour.

To identify young rabbits and hares, look for soft ears that tear easily, white teeth and smooth fur. Their meat is usually roasted or sautéed while that from older animals is best braised.

HUTCH RABBIT
Oryctolagus cuniculus
Length: 50 cm (20 inches)
Weight: around 2 kg (4 lb)
Availability: all year round
Best time for eating: Sept-Nov

WILD RABBIT
Oryctolagus cuniculus
Length: 30 cm (12 inches)
Weight: around 1.5 kg (3 lb)
Open season: all year round
Best time for eating: Sept-Nov

RED DEER
Cervus elaphus
Height: 1.2 m (48 inches)
Weight: 127 kg (20 stone)
Open season: *stags* 1 Aug-30 April;
hinds 1 Nov-28/29 Feb.
Scotland: stags 1 July-20 Oct;
hinds 21 Oct-15 Feb.
Best time for eating: *stags* July-Aug; *hinds*
Dec-Feb

BROWN HARE
Lepus europaeus
Length: 60 cm (24 inches)
Weight: around 4 kg (8.5 lb)
Open season: all year, except Sundays or
Christmas day; must not be sold March-July
Best time for
eating: Oct-Jan

LEVERET OF BROWN HARE
Lepus europaeus
Length: 40 cm (16 inches)
Weight: 2 kg (4 lb)
Open season: all year, except Sundays or Christmas
Day; must not be sold March-July

HAUNCH OR LEG. A prime cut for
roasting; may be cut short or long.

FLANK. May be poached, braised, or
minced for sausages.

SADDLE. A prime cut for roasting;
includes the fillets. The ribs may be divided
into chops for sautéing and grilling.

SHOULDER. Braised in one piece or
cut into cubes for stewing.

NECK. Cut up for stewing or minced for
sausages.

A Guide to Fish and Shellfish

Of the hundreds of fish and shellfish species sold in Europe as a whole, most shoppers have access to several dozen but can identify only a fraction of those available. Even if you are familiar with all the species that are customarily sold in your locality, the changing patterns of commercial fishing and marketing mean that you are likely to encounter new types of seafood from time to time.

The guide on the following pages shows 121 of the important food fish and shellfish caught in Mediterranean and North-east Atlantic waters. By familiarizing yourself with the appearance of the seafood, you will be able to identify fish that are displayed without a label – and perhaps detect misleading labels. Many fishmongers endow commonplace fish with euphemistic names: dogfish, for example, is traditionally sold as 'rock salmon', although its appearance and flavour have nothing in common with those of true salmon. Also, for the cook who moves home from one part of the country to another, visual clues may at first be the only means of identifying a fish since the names of many species differ from region to region.

The guide will also help you to choose a substitute if the fish that you ask for is not available or is too expensive. Most of the recipes for fish later in the book provide one or more suitable substitutes for the fish specified; recipes that do not call for a particular fish include a list of options. All the fish given as options are included here. Finally, the guide should encourage you to try some of the delicious, but strange-looking, species you come across.

Size is an important consideration when choosing fish; for this reason, all the fish and shellfish in the guide are drawn to scale – necessarily a sliding scale, since the range of sizes is great (see below). For ease of reference and for comparison, the entries are divided into nine groups: freshwater fish; white fish (herring and cod families); flat fish; mackerel, bonito, tuna and swordfish; sharks, skates and rays; other sea fish; crustaceans; squid, cuttlefish and octopus; shellfish.

All but two groups are arranged in accordance with the scientific system of classification. Not surprisingly, fish belonging to the same family, or to closely related families, tend to have culinary features in common and can be prepared in the same ways. All the cod family, for example, have lean white flesh; and the recipes for species in this group are interchangeable. The general cooking characteristics of each group – together with salient information about individual species – are given in the text that accompanies the illustrations.

The two groups that do not conform to this system are the freshwater fish (opposite) and the species arranged under the heading 'Other Sea Fish' (page 30). Both groupings list species from many different families and with varying flavours, textures and cooking requirements. The so-called freshwater fish include some species, such as bream and carp, that are found only in fresh water, and others, such as salmon and eel, that spend part of their lives in the sea but are caught in rivers and lakes. In the sea fish grouping, Mediterranean species are well represented. Unlike the colder waters of the North Atlantic, which contain relatively few species mostly occurring in huge numbers, the Mediterranean contains numerous species, mostly in relatively small numbers. Local cuisines reflect this difference, since they feature many dishes of mixed fish and shellfish – including the sea fish stews for which the Mediterranean region is famous.

Since seafood is more perishable than meat or poultry you should take care to ensure that it is absolutely fresh when purchased. Both the appearance and odour of fish provide clues to its condition. When buying whole fish, look for shining skin, pink gills and full bright eyes with black pupils and transparent corneas. If you can, press the fish with your fingers; it should be soft and springy. Genuinely fresh fish has a clean pleasant odour; reject any that have even the suggestion of a 'fishy' smell. When buying pieces of fish, look for translucent rather than milky flesh. Fillets that are dried up around the edges and show traces of discoloration will be stale. Shellfish deteriorate even more rapidly than fish and should, where possible, be bought still live or pre-cooked. As a general rule, however, fresh shellfish can be recognized by their lack of smell.

Fish and shellfish keep in the refrigerator for no more than a day, loosely wrapped in film or foil to prevent their flavour permeating the fridge. Neither fish nor shellfish freeze well at home.

A Key to the Fish Drawings

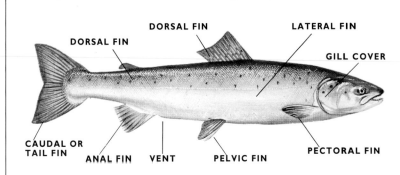

DORSAL FIN

DORSAL FIN

LATERAL FIN

GILL COVER

CAUDAL OR TAIL FIN

ANAL FIN

VENT

PELVIC FIN

PECTORAL FIN

The fish illustrated in the guide range in size from the porbeagle shark, which may attain a length of 4 metres (13 feet), to the sardine. In order to show species of greatly differing sizes on the some page, gradations in the fish's length are represented on a diminishing scale (below). Thus the Atlantic salmon (left) appears only twice as large as the brown trout on the opposite page, but is actually four times as long. The drawing of the salmon also gives the terms for the main external features of fish: the terms are those used throughout the book. Each fish is identified by its common and scientific names.

Freshwater Fish

Among fish caught in fresh water, members of the salmon and trout family are universally esteemed, but there are many less familiar species that make fine eating – notably grayling, powan, perch, pike-perch and eel.

Both grayling, which has a scent of thyme when freshly caught, and powan are related to trout. Perch has an especially good flavour but is very bony; its relative, the pike-perch, has flesh that has been likened to that of sole. Eel has firm, moist flesh that is enhanced by highly flavoured sauces; its young, called elvers, are delicious sautéed, deep-fried, or stewed with garlic. Sturgeon can be braised like tuna.

The other fish shown include gudgeon, which is good pan-fried or deep-fried; carp, admired for its firm sweet flesh; barbel and bream, two less distinguished cousins of carp that need well-seasoned sauces; pike, a flavourful fish that is a good choice for mousselines but is rarely served in its natural form because of the many tiny bones in its flesh; and burbot, a relative of cod.

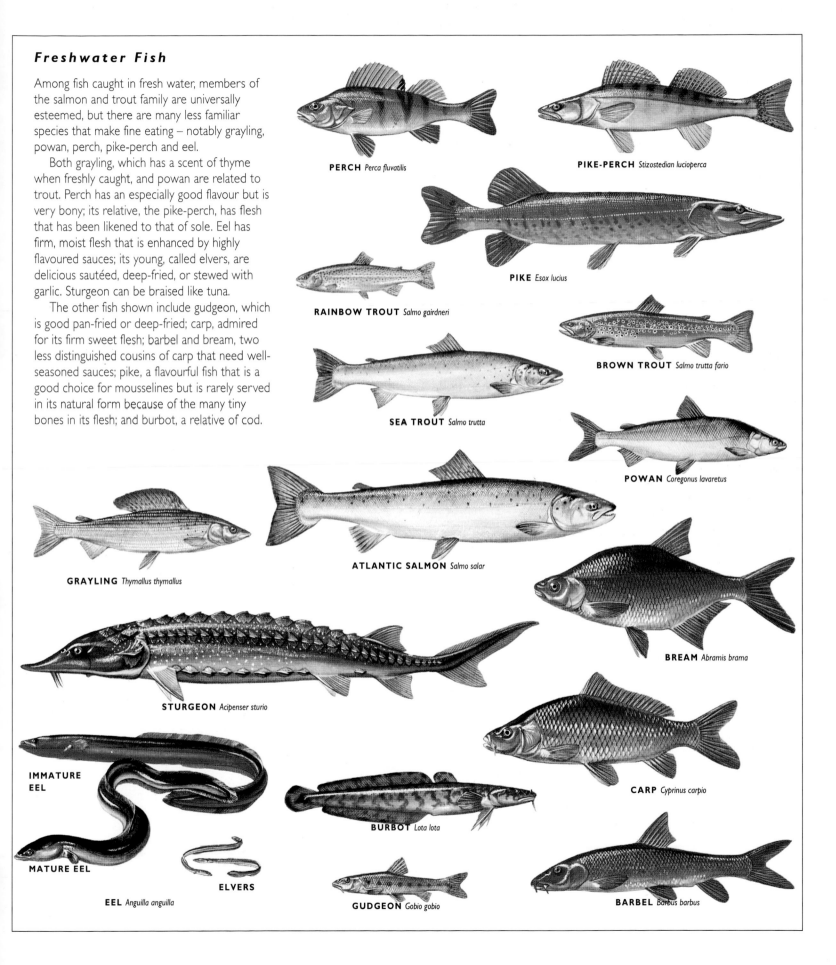

PERCH *Perca fluvatilis*

PIKE-PERCH *Stizostedian lucioperca*

PIKE *Esox lucius*

RAINBOW TROUT *Salmo gairdneri*

BROWN TROUT *Salmo trutta fario*

SEA TROUT *Salmo trutta*

POWAN *Coregonus lavaretus*

GRAYLING *Thymallus thymallus*

ATLANTIC SALMON *Salmo salar*

BREAM *Abramis brama*

STURGEON *Acipenser sturio*

CARP *Cyprinus carpio*

IMMATURE EEL

MATURE EEL

ELVERS

EEL *Anguilla anguilla*

BURBOT *Lota lota*

GUDGEON *Gobio gobio*

BARBEL *Barbus barbus*

The Herring and Cod Families

Richly flavoured, with somewhat fatty flesh, fish of the herring family – herring itself, sprat, anchovy, shad, pilchard and its immature form, sardine – are usually grilled or fried. The smelt is a delicately flavoured relative that is delicious grilled, fried, poached in a wine court-bouillon or braised.

Herrings, sprats and anchovies are sold in a variety of cured forms. Salted anchovies make a valuable flavouring agent in many sauces and stuffings.

The members of the cod family are lean white fish. The North Atlantic cod, its Baltic cousin and haddock have firm sweet flesh. Whiting has an especially delicate flavour and fine texture. Hake resembles cod, but has closer-grained flesh. The other members of the cod family – pollack, coley, blue whiting and ling – tend towards blandness, but they are inexpensive choices for any recipe that simply calls for white fish.

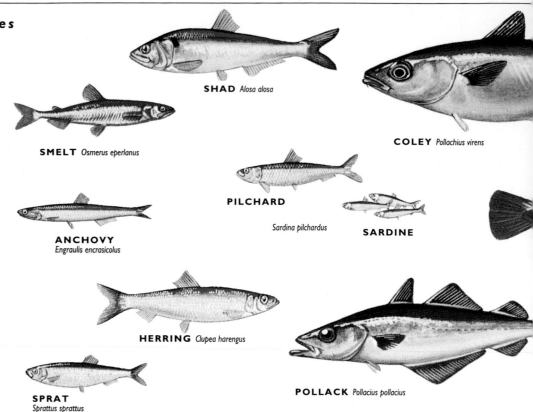

SHAD Alosa alosa

SMELT Osmerus eperlanus

COLEY Pollachius virens

PILCHARD

Sardina pilchardus

SARDINE

ANCHOVY
Engraulis encrasicolus

HERRING Clupea harengus

POLLACK Pollacius pollacius

SPRAT
Sprattus sprattus

Flat Fish

Two of the most exquisitely flavoured sea fish – sole and turbot – belong to this group. Both have firm, yet tender and succulent flesh. Sole, in particular, has fired the imaginations of chefs, and features in a wide range of dishes.

Like the other smaller flat fish – lemon sole, French sole, plaice, the dabs, witch, flounder, brill and megrim – sole can be cooked whole or filleted. The shallow bodies of all these species make them suitable for grilling and sautéing. Turbot is often so large that it requires a special lozenge-shaped vessel, the *turbotière*, for poaching it whole; however, it is generally cooked as steaks or fillets. The turbot's bones are rich in gelatine, which makes the flesh succulent and gives body to sauces made from a liquid in which the bones have been poached.

The largest flat fish is the halibut, which is always sold as fillets or steaks. It has a pleasing flavour, but a tendency to dryness: take special care to keep it moistened during cooking.

DAB Limanda limanda limanda

PLAICE Fleuronectes platessa

LONG ROUGH DAB
Hippoglossoides platessoides

HALIBUT Hippoglossus hippoglossus

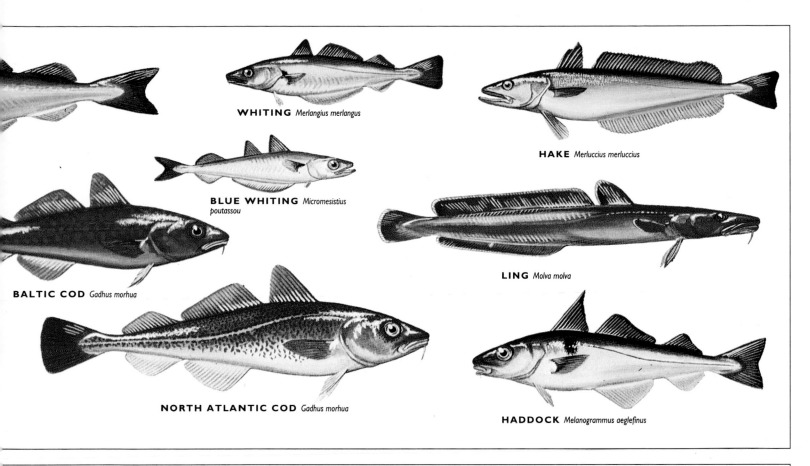

WHITING *Merlangius merlangus*

HAKE *Merluccius merluccius*

BLUE WHITING *Micromesistius poutassou*

BALTIC COD *Gadhus morhua*

LING *Molva molva*

NORTH ATLANTIC COD *Gadhus morhua*

HADDOCK *Melanogrammus aeglefinus*

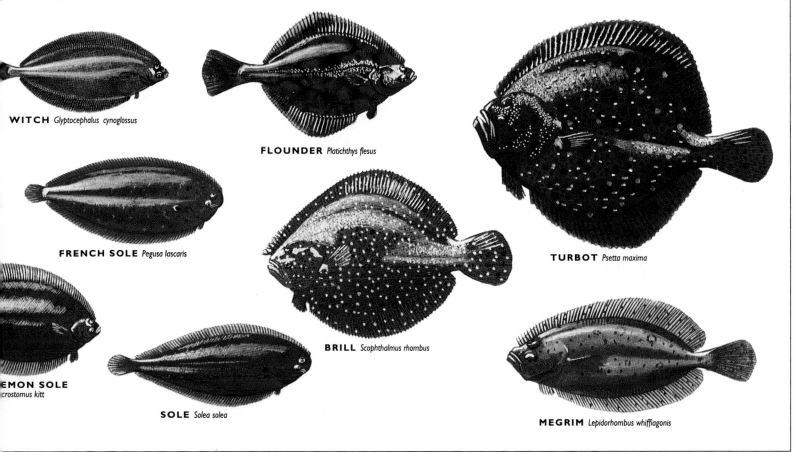

WITCH *Glyptocephalus cynoglossus*

FLOUNDER *Platichthys flesus*

TURBOT *Psetta maxima*

FRENCH SOLE *Pegusa lascaris*

EMON SOLE *crostomus kitt*

SOLE *Solea solea*

BRILL *Scophthalmus rhombus*

MEGRIM *Lepidorhombus whiffiagonis*

Mackerel, Bonito, Tuna and Swordfish

Powerful swimmers with compact muscular flesh, these surface fish can be divided for practical cooking purposes into two groups – mackerel and the rest.

Mackerel is distinguished by its comparatively soft texture and by its oiliness. During summer and autumn, its fat content may rise to 20 per cent – a very high proportion for fish. Traditional ways of countering mackerel's fattiness include poaching it in white wine and serving it with sharp sauces based on gooseberries, sorrel or mustard.

Swordfish, bonito, tuna, skipjack and the misleadingly named frigate mackerel (actually a member of the tuna family) have firm, close-grained flesh. These fish lend themselves to grilling and lengthy oven braising with vegetables.

The colours of their flesh range from the near-white of the swordfish to the deep red of the bonito and frigate mackerel; lighter-coloured flesh indicates a more delicate flavour. The larger fish are usually sold as steaks.

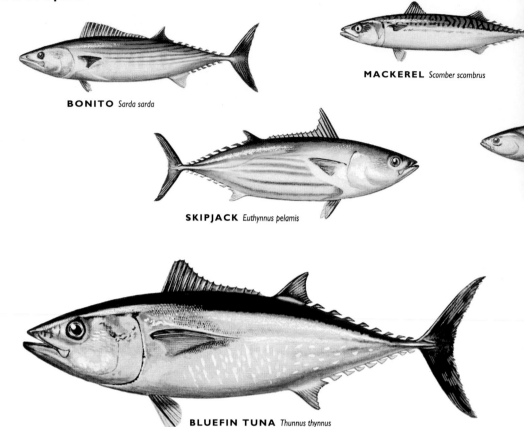

BONITO *Sarda sarda*

MACKEREL *Scomber scombrus*

SKIPJACK *Euthynnus pelamis*

BLUEFIN TUNA *Thunnus thynnus*

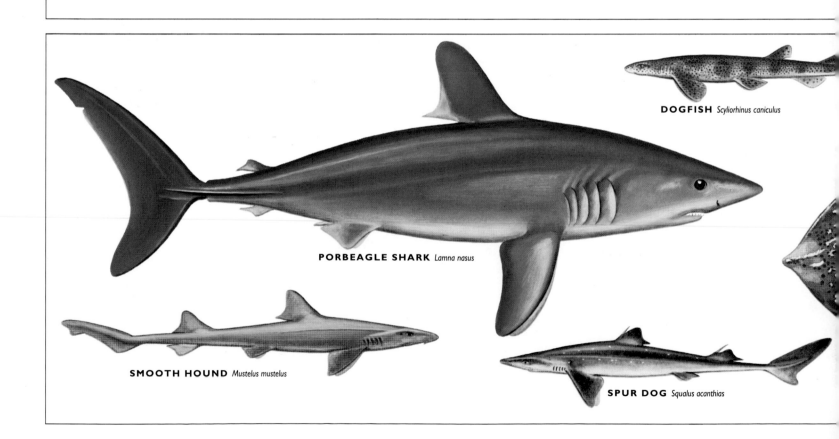

DOGFISH *Scyliorhinus caniculus*

PORBEAGLE SHARK *Lamna nasus*

SMOOTH HOUND *Mustelus mustelus*

SPUR DOG *Squalus acanthias*

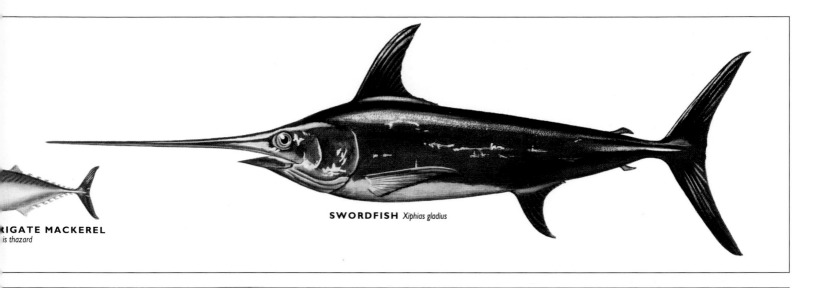

RIGATE MACKEREL
is thazard

SWORDFISH *Xiphias gladius*

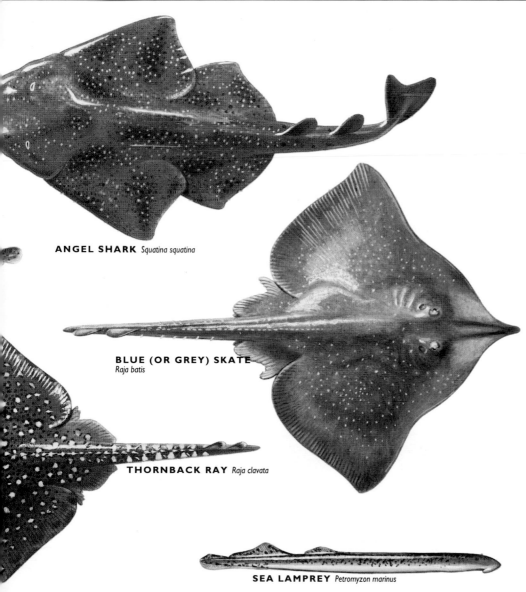

ANGEL SHARK *Squatina squatina*

BLUE (OR GREY) SKATE
Raja batis

THORNBACK RAY *Raja clavata*

SEA LAMPREY *Petromyzon marinus*

Sharks, Skates and Rays

One characteristic of these fish that should endear them to the diner is their lack of true bones. Their skeletons are composed of a cartilaginous material that separates easily from the flesh after cooking. The skeletons yield gelatine during cooking: a fumet (page 244-5) made from a shark or skate carcass will have enough body to set after cooling. These fish can have a slightly ammoniac smell when freshly caught, which disappears on cooking. However, do not buy any which still smell of amonia by the time they reach the shop, it will not vanish.

Of the sharks and dogfish, the porbeagle enjoys the most favourable culinary reputation. It has several features in common with veal: close-textured pink flesh with a delicate flavour and a tendency to dryness, which can be countered by larding the flesh with strips of pork fat. Porbeagle is good for grilling or braising. Angel shark, spur dog, smooth hound and dogfish have less refined flavours, but they lend themselves well to highly seasoned dishes. Their flesh can be cut into cubes and steeped in an aromatic marinade to make excellent brochettes.

Only the 'wings' of blue skate and thornback ray are used in cooking. Delicately flavoured but delicious when fried or poached, they are traditionally sauced with *beurre noisette*, butter heated until nut-brown, and then sharpened with a dash of vinegar and a sprinkling of capers.

The sea lamprey can be prepared and cooked like an eel; braised in red wine, it is a great Bordelais speciality (*lamprois à la Bordelaise*).

Other Sea Fish

Unlike the cold waters of the Atlantic, the Mediterranean contains many different species, most of which occur in relatively small numbers. Shown here are some of the most important Mediterranean species, with preference given to those that range around the Iberian peninsula into the Bay of Biscay and as far north as the English Channel. In addition, some of the less familiar North Atlantic species are exhibited. All of these fish make good eating.

Among the finest flavoured is red mullet, the liver of which is a delicacy; grouper, with its firm and relatively bone-free flesh; the sea bass; John Dory; and the family of sea breams – notably, sea bream itself, red sea bream, pandora, gilt-head bream and dentex – all with firm lean flesh.

The wrasse, gurnards, weever and grey mullet are often included in the fish stews for which the Mediterranean region is famous. Grey mullet – no relation of red mullet – has rather soft flesh, and is prized chiefly for its roe.

An unappetising appearance has prevented some of the species shown here from winning the favour they deserve. The angler-fish, for example, has a hideous head; but the flesh from its tail is firm and sweet. The wolf-fish has an array of fearsome teeth that enables it to feed on mussels and whelks – a diet that gives its firm flesh a delicious flavour. The garfish's green bones do not affect its delicate flavour, but do keep down its price. Conger eel is another inexpensive fish, with firm and delicate flesh usually relegated to fish soups because of its abundance of tiny bones.

Of the remaining species illustrated, small bluefish and the robustly flavoured dolphin fish are especially worth seeking out. Sar commun and bogue can be substituted for the sea breams. Ombrine can be treated like sea bass. Scad is similar, but inferior, to mackerel. Redfish is undistinguished, but economical.

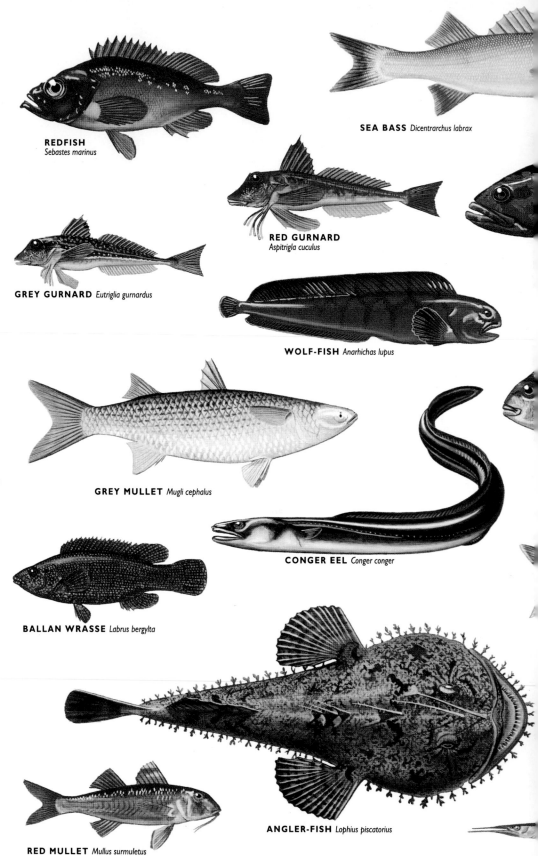

REDFISH *Sebastes marinus*

SEA BASS *Dicentrarchus labrax*

RED GURNARD *Aspitrigla cuculus*

GREY GURNARD *Eutriglia gurnardus*

WOLF-FISH *Anarhichas lupus*

GREY MULLET *Mugli cephalus*

CONGER EEL *Conger conger*

BALLAN WRASSE *Labrus bergylta*

ANGLER-FISH *Lophius piscatorius*

RED MULLET *Mullus surmuletus*

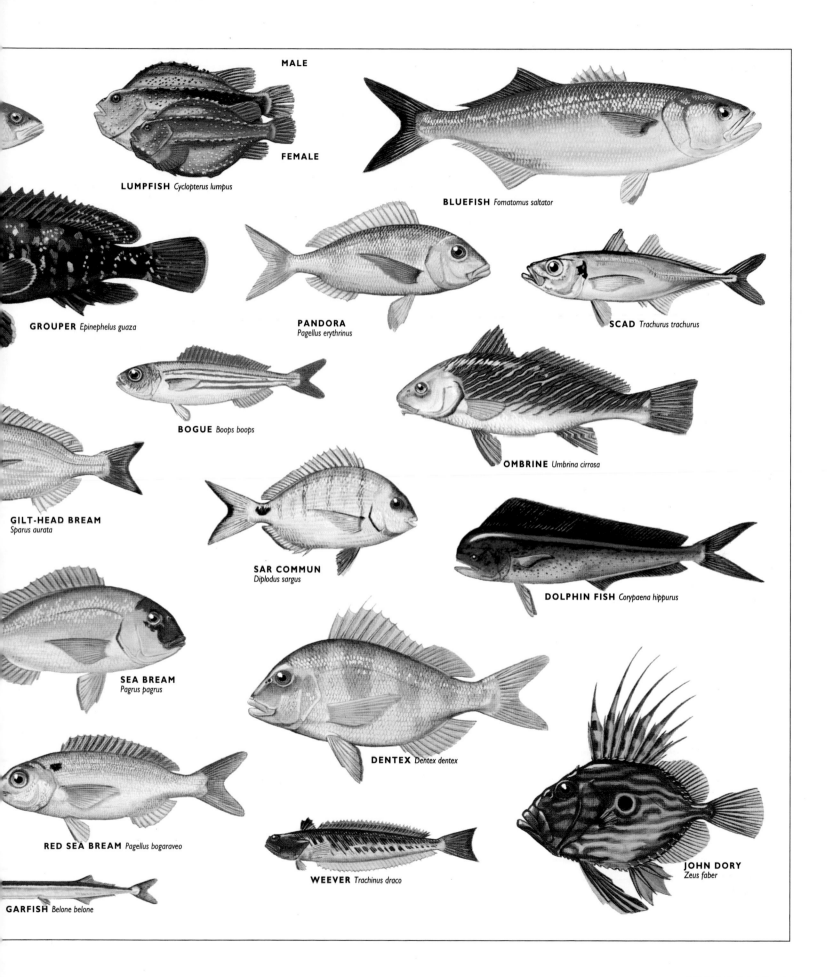

MALE

FEMALE

LUMPFISH *Cyclopterus lumpus*

BLUEFISH *Fomatomus saltator*

GROUPER *Epinephelus guaza*

PANDORA *Pagellus erythrinus*

SCAD *Trachurus trachurus*

BOGUE *Boops boops*

OMBRINE *Umbrina cirrosa*

GILT-HEAD BREAM *Sparus aurata*

SAR COMMUN *Diplodus sargus*

DOLPHIN FISH *Corypaena hippurus*

SEA BREAM *Pagrus pagrus*

DENTEX *Dentex dentex*

RED SEA BREAM *Pagellus bogaraveo*

WEEVER *Trachinus draco*

JOHN DORY *Zeus faber*

GARFISH *Belone belone*

Crustaceans

All of the crustaceans have firm sweet flesh and hard jointed shells that are shed periodically as the creatures grow. The European lobster, the spiny lobster and the flat lobster are of comparable quality and lend themselves to the same dishes. All three species are prepared for cooking in basically the same way (page 132).

Shrimps, prawns and deep-sea prawns are often poached and used as garnishes; but like the larger Dublin Bay prawns and mantis shrimps, they can be prepared as dishes in their own right – coated in batter and deep-fried, for example, or skewered with vegetables and grilled. Crayfish are especially esteemed for their delicate flavour. These freshwater crustaceans can be rapidly boiled in a court-bouillon and eaten, or they can be braised in a sauce enriched with their pounded heads and tail shells.

The edible and spider crabs are usually cooked in a court-bouillon and served in their shells. The small swimming and shore crabs yield little meat and are used mainly for flavouring soups and stews. However, if they are collected at the moment of moulting, they can be cooked, usually dipped in batter and deep-fried, and eaten whole.

DEEP-SEA PRAWN *Pandalus borealis*

SPINY LOBSTER *Palinurus elephas*

FLAT LOBSTER *Scyllarides latus*

SPIDER CRAB *Maja squinado*

SHORE CRAB *Carcinus maenus*

MANTIS SHRIMP *Squilla mantis*

FRESHWATER CRAYFISH *Austropotamobius pallipe*

EDIBLE CRAB *Cancer pagurus*

SWIMMING CRAB *Macropipus corrugatus*

EUROPEAN LOBSTER *Homarus gamman*

Squid, Cuttlefish and Octopus

Members of the cephalopod family, squid, cuttlefish and octopus are unusually rich in flesh for their weight, since their bag-like bodies and tentacles do not contain true skeletons. Yet until recently, their firm, rather spicy flesh has been widely appreciated only in the Mediterranean region and the Far East.

The squid of European coasts, its relative, the flying squid, and the cuttlefish can be cut up and fried or stewed – or their bodies can be stuffed and braised. Small octopus can be fried, but octopus more than 30 cm (12 inches) long have rubbery flesh that should be beaten and then tenderized by long cooking in a liquid. Little cuttlefish are usually cleaned and fried whole.

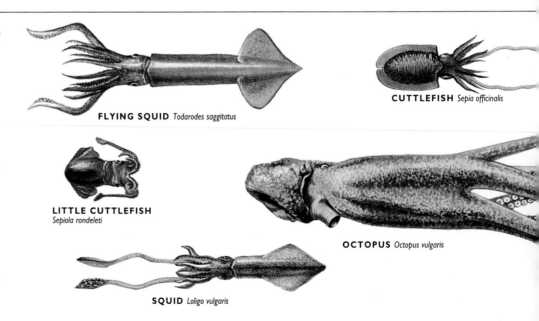

FLYING SQUID *Todarodes saggitatus*

CUTTLEFISH *Sepia officinalis*

LITTLE CUTTLEFISH *Sepiola rondeleti*

OCTOPUS *Octopus vulgaris*

SQUID *Loligo vulgaris*

Shellfish

Despite their abundance and the variety of ways in which they can be served, molluscs are neglected by most cooks. Eaten raw, many of them make a delicious *hors d'oeuvre*; they can be used in soups or stews; or they can serve as garnishes and stuffings for other seafood dishes. Advice on choosing and opening molluscs appears on pages 134-5.

Oysters are most often eaten raw, with their juices, from the half shell. Most of the other bivalves – cockles, razor-shells, tellins, clovisses, carpet-shells and the different kinds of Venus shells – can also be eaten raw. They also make delicious soups and stews.

Mussels and clams are often steamed in their own juices, which are served as a broth or transformed into a sauce. Scallops can be poached, sautéed, baked or grilled, with or without a sauce, but should be cooked only until just firm.

Winkles and whelks, boiled in their shells and served with lemon juice or vinegar, make good appetisers. The white muscle of the ormer is tough; it should first be tenderized by beating and then braised or fried.

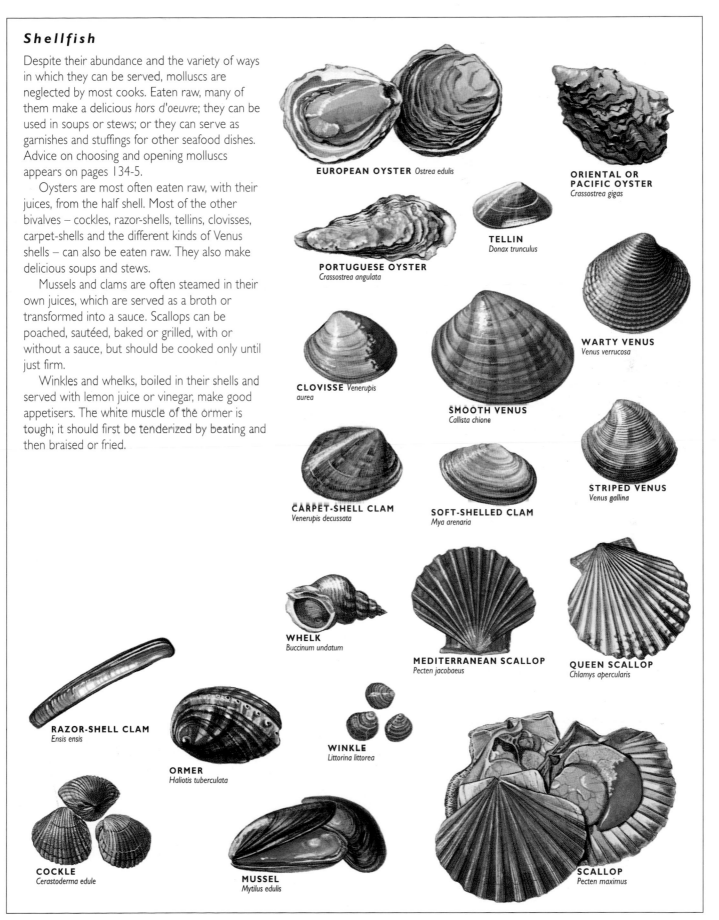

EUROPEAN OYSTER *Ostrea edulis*

ORIENTAL OR PACIFIC OYSTER *Crassostrea gigas*

PORTUGUESE OYSTER *Crassostrea angulata*

TELLIN *Donax trunculus*

WARTY VENUS *Venus verrucosa*

CLOVISSE *Venerupis aurea*

SMOOTH VENUS *Callista chione*

CARPET-SHELL CLAM *Venerupis decussata*

SOFT-SHELLED CLAM *Mya arenaria*

STRIPED VENUS *Venus gallina*

WHELK *Buccinum undatum*

MEDITERRANEAN SCALLOP *Pecten jacobaeus*

QUEEN SCALLOP *Chlamys apercularis*

RAZOR-SHELL CLAM *Ensis ensis*

ORMER *Haliotis tuberculata*

WINKLE *Littorina littorea*

COCKLE *Cerastoderma edule*

MUSSEL *Mytilus edulis*

SCALLOP *Pecten maximus*

DUBLIN BAY PRAWN
Nephrops norvegicus

SHRIMP
Crangon crangon

PRAWN
Palaemon serratus

A Guide to Vegetables

CAULIFLOWER

WHITE CABBAGE

RED CABBAGE

BRUSSELS SPROUT

KOHLRABI

PURPLE BROCCOLI

The Cabbage Family

The members of the large and diverse cabbage family – the brassicas – range in size from massive winter cabbages to tiny Brussels sprouts and in appearance from the nubbly whiteness of the cauliflower to the smooth, sometimes purple-tinged, cream-coloured, bulb-like stem of the kohlrabi. Yet all these disparate plants share a common descent from the wild cabbage that still grows in some coastal areas of Britain and France.

The closest cultivated link to the cabbage family's wild progenitor is kale, a hardy vegetable whose strong-flavoured, curly leaves are often sold as 'winter-greens', since they can be picked after the heavy frosts that kill other plants. Kale is supplanted later in the year by 'spring greens' – a leafy thick-ribbed variety of cabbage without a compact head.

Firm-headed cabbages – red, white or green – are most widely available in winter and are at their best when tightly formed and with firm unblemished outer leaves. If cored (see page 138) and shredded, green and white cabbages are good boiled briskly and served semi crisp; either buttered or with olive oil and vinegar; the shredded leaves may also be braised or pan-fried, or the whole cabbage can be stuffed and simmered slowly. Cabbage is best cooked either rapidly or for a long time. Red cabbage, too, is cored and shredded. Boiled in plain water, red cabbage will turn an unappetizing blue; it is usually braised with red wine or vinegar, whose acidity balances its flavour and helps preserve its colour.

Chinese cabbage owes its recent popularity in the West to the crisp delicate flavour of its pale

CHINESE CABBAGE

LEAFY CABBAGE

GREEN CABBAGE

BROCCOLI

CURLY KALE

crinkly leaves. Shredded, it may be cooked in the same way as other cabbages. It is also very good when rapidly sautéed, or may be stir-fried in the Oriental fashion, using a wok, on its own or in combination with other vegetables.

Brussels sprouts are miniature cabbages that grow clustered on stalks; as their name suggests, they were first cultivated in Belgium. They are best when bright green, small and tight-leaved; soft, loose heads and wilted or yellow leaves are signs that betray age. Trim the bases and remove the outer layer of leaves; the pale green

spheres that remain can be boiled in a very few minutes.

The cauliflower has been steadily improved by selective cultivation over the past 200 years; earlier cultivated strains had heads that were no bigger than golf balls. The plant's florets (or curds) must be firm and white with no spots, speckles or other discolorations. Cauliflower can be boiled or steamed whole; however, if it is first separated into individual florets, it will cook both faster and more evenly.

Broccoli – purple-budded, or green in the

form known as calabrese – also benefits from careful preparation. The stems should be stiff, the buds compact; wilted stems or leaves and open or yellowing buds indicate poor quality.

Perhaps the most unusual of all brassicas is kohlrabi – a swollen, edible stem that is at its best when it reaches a size of about 8 cm (3 inches) in diameter. Kohlrabi is sometimes sold with its leaves still attached: if they are crisp and fresh, prepare them like kale; the stem is cooked in the same way as turnip – but its flavour is mild and distinctly cabbage-like.

Leaf Vegetables

Leaf vegetables range in flavour from the near sweetness of some varieties of lettuce to the refreshing bitterness of endive and the pronounced tartness of sorrel. Many – especially lettuce, endive and chicory – are associated with the salad bowl; but they are just as good, and totally different, when cooked. Some, such as spinach, can be found in almost every market; others, such as sorrel and chard, may be less widely available, but well worth searching out. All are rich in vitamins A and C, as well as in iron and other minerals essential to health.

All leaves should be cooked as soon as possible after they are picked: both flavour and food value suffer if leaves are stored too long. Chicory is sold only in the winter months, but most other leaf vegetables are available all the year round; the development of air-freight and greenhouse cultivation have blurred most of the former seasonal distinctions. Leaves are always best when they are young and tender, but small size is not always an index of age; each vegetable is available in many varieties, and young leaves of one variety may be larger than the fully grown leaves of another. There are, however, a few basic tips: young leaves are glossy, so avoid vegetables that have developed the dull surface of maturity; and, of course, reject specimens that are discoloured or limp. When you buy chicory, look for thick, cigar-shaped, firm buds with no brown discoloration.

If you must store leaves for a few days, keep them cool and moist. Sealed, airtight wrappings will prevent the still-living leaves from breathing and cause them to rot; always make sure that air can circulate around the leaves. Before storing, rinse the leaves in cold water and shake off the excess. Place the leaves inside a loose-fitting open bag, or wrap them in a damp cloth, and keep them in the salad drawer of a refrigerator: the moist atmosphere slows down the rate at which their cells lose water and they will retain their crispness longer.

Spinach and chard are most commonly simply served boiled; they might equally well be baked in a gratin, or chopped and used in stuffings for meat, poultry or for other vegetables; chard leaves are also strong enough to enclose stuffings.

Sorrel has a comparatively delicate leaf structure that breaks down to a purée on contact with heat. Young sorrel leaves may be stewed with butter for a few minutes; older leaves should first be parboiled – for a few seconds only. The clean sharp taste of sorrel makes it an excellent accompaniment to fish, veal and chicken; sorrel's tartness also suits fatty and full-flavoured meats such as goose and duck. In small quantities, it is a flavouring element in sauces and stews. However you cook sorrel, do not use iron or aluminium pans; it reacts chemically with these metals and becomes acrid.

When prepared as a cooked vegetable, lettuce is most often braised whole by itself or filled with a meat and vegetable stuffing. The greener outer leaves contain much of the flavour and almost all of the vitamins, do not discard them unless they are badly bruised. When shredded, lettuce leaves become a *chiffonnade* – a scattering of green that can be sprinkled over stews and baked dishes to sweat flavour and moisture into the other ingredients as the dish cooks.

Endive and Batavian endive may look like curly-leaved lettuce, but their pleasantly bitter flavour is quite different. Both types of endive can be prepared in ways similar to those used for lettuce.

The tight, white shoots of chicory may be stewed in butter, braised or baked. The rather bitter flavour of chicory may be lessened by removing the plant's core (see page 138).

Grape-vine leaves have acquired a specialized role, particularly in the cooking of Greece and the Middle East. Strong and – if parboiled – supple, they serve as wrappers for a wide range of fillings. Vine leaves are often preserved by pickling in brine: such leaves, which must be soaked in water to remove the salt, are only good to eat when stuffed and cooked slowly. When very small, vine leaves or vine tendrils are also good chopped and used as flavourings for stews and gratins.

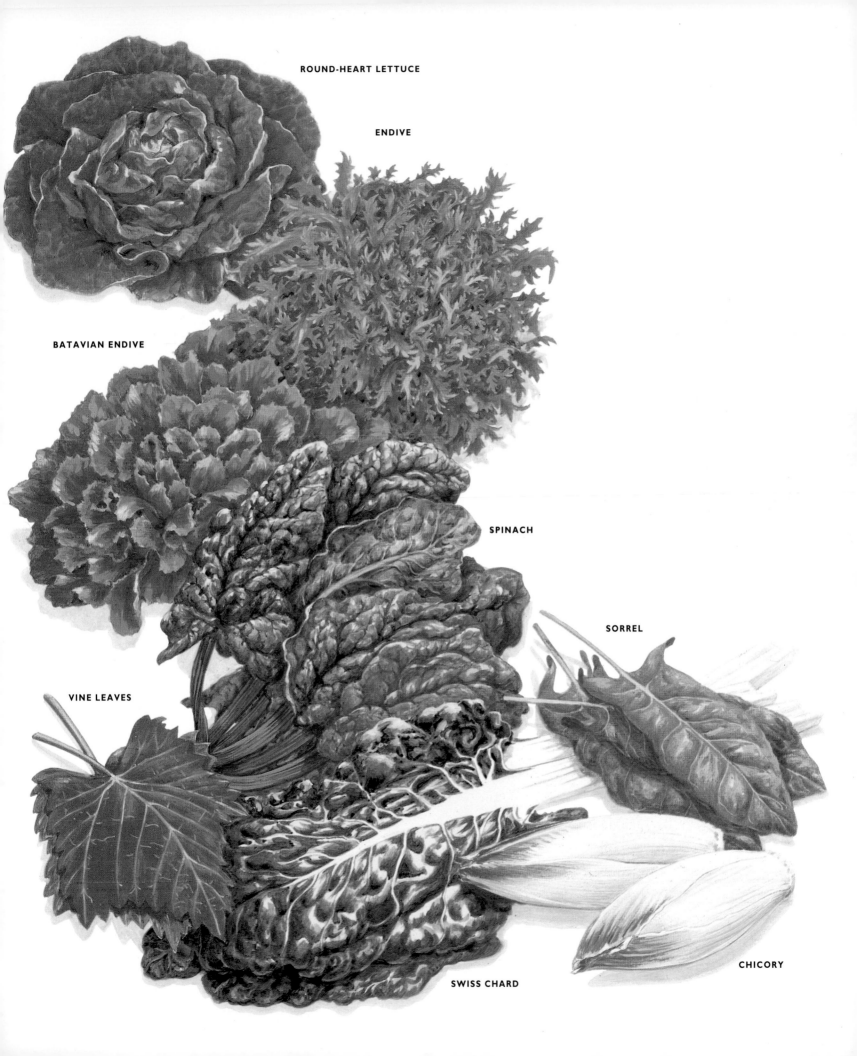

ROUND-HEART LETTUCE

ENDIVE

BATAVIAN ENDIVE

SPINACH

SORREL

VINE LEAVES

SWISS CHARD

CHICORY

Salad Leaves

Whole or torn, leaves add colour and flavour to salads; shredded, or shaped into cups for individual portions, they also play an important supporting role in the presentation of cold dishes made with other vegetables, meat, poultry or fish.

Lettuces fall into three main categories: cabbage-type, long-leafed (or cos) and loose-headed. Cabbage-type lettuces include the supple-leafed round-heart variety shown here, which has a mildly sweet flavour; the delicate little garden lettuces; and the crisp Iceberg varieties. Cos lettuces have sturdy leaves with a stronger flavour than round-hearts. Even more pronounced in flavour are loose-headed lettuces such as oak leaf lettuce. All lettuces are at their best in summer.

Other leaves are at their peak during winter. These include chicory, endive and lamb's lettuce – which are available for most of the year, but are most valued for winter salads. There are several varieties of chicory; shown here are white Belgian chicory, which has brittle leaves and is pleasantly bitter, and red chicory or radicchio, which is well worth seeking out for its glorious colour. Curly endive has a chewy texture while Batavian endive is very crisp; both have a strong flavour. Lamb's lettuce grows wild but is worth cultivating for its velvety leaves and refreshing flavour.

Many other leaves add contrasts of flavour to salads. Watercress, for example, has a peppery freshness. Young spinach leaves are agreeably acrid, while sorrel is sharply acidic. Watercress and spinach are available most of the year, except in high summer; sorrel grows from March until the first winter frosts. Rocket, with its fiery taste, is easy to grow if you cannot find it at the greengrocers; pick it in spring and autumn. Dandelion leaves have an astringent bitterness, while purslane – a garden weed rarely found in the shops – has a delicate cool taste; pick them both when young, dandelion in the spring and purslane during summer.

Whichever salad leaves you are buying, choose foliage that looks fresh, resilient and bright. Use the leaves as soon as possible; they can be kept for up to 3 days in a refrigerator if dried, wrapped in a damp cloth and enclosed in a plastic bag.

LAMB'S LETTUCE

ROCKET

BATAVIAN ENDIVE

CHICORY

COS LETTUCE

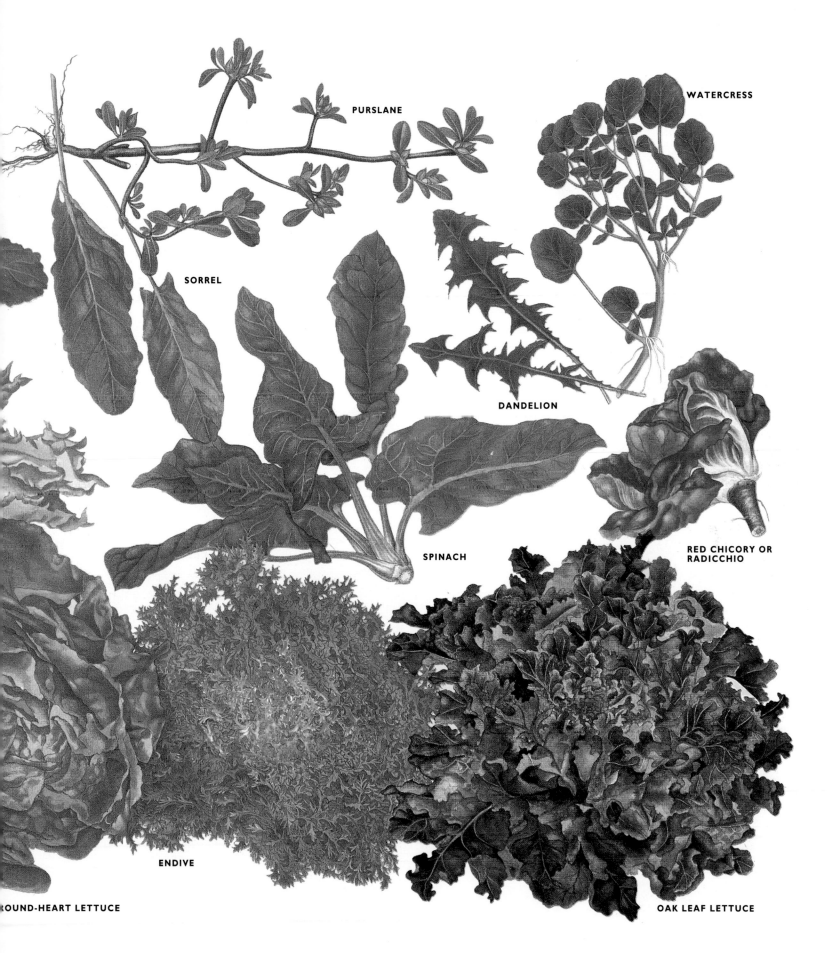

PURSLANE

WATERCRESS

SORREL

DANDELION

SPINACH

RED CHICORY OR
RADICCHIO

ENDIVE

ROUND-HEART LETTUCE

OAK LEAF LETTUCE

Roots and Tubers

Vegetables that grow underground are either the enlarged roots of leafy plants or the tubers from which both plant stems and roots develop. Carrots, for example, are roots; potatoes are tubers. Together, roots and tubers comprise an extensive group, ranging from staples to less common plants – such as salsify or Jerusalem artichokes – that deserve greater recognition than is usually given them.

Virtually all roots and tubers can be stored for long periods under controlled conditions and familiar varieties are widely available during winter months, when other vegetables may be scarce. But the difference between stored and newly harvested roots and tubers is profound. Baby carrots only 5 to 8 cm (2 to 3 inches) long are delicious when served simply: briefly boiled and topped with butter. As they age, carrots toughen and develop woody cores that should be removed before cooking (see page 139). Even cored, they must be boiled for 30 minutes or more to tenderize them.

Parsnips have a strong fruity smell and ivory-coloured, starchy flesh. Like carrots, they develop tough cores as they age; even after removing these, older parsnips need longer cooking.

Turnips and swedes are related roots. Swedes usually grow larger than turnips; their flesh is dense and usually yellow, whereas that of the turnip is white and crisp. Both vegetables require relatively long cooking at any season; they are best boiled and puréed or stewed in butter.

The long, slender roots of salsify and scorzonera (black-skinned salsify) have a milky-white flesh the flavour of which is more delicate and less sweet than that of parsnips and other tubers. Even in late autumn when freshly harvested, both roots can be tough; they are best parboiled and then sautéed in butter or gratinéed.

Celeriac's piquant flavour contradicts its drab colour and gnarled appearance. Peel this root thickly, then cut it into chunks or shred it before boiling. Serve celeriac with butter or a cream sauce. It can also be included in mixed vegetable purées or cooked in stews.

Beetroot, with its sweet red flesh, is usually baked or boiled in its skin and served without embellishment; young and tender, peeled and cooked until glazed with a bit of water, a pinch of sugar and some lemon juice, it is exquisite.

The tiny 'new' potatoes of spring and early summer are also cooked, and eaten, in their skins – boiled, steamed or stewed in butter or oil. Later crops of mature potatoes come in two distinct types – waxy and mealy. Unfortunately, the outward appearance of the fully grown tuber gives no clue as to whether the potato has a waxy texture – which is best for frying or baking in a gratin – or a more starchy, mealy quality, suited to baking whole or boiling and puréeing. Only by trying a variety of the potatoes available locally can you select the sort best suited to the requirements of a particular recipe.

Sweet potatoes, although unrelated to their common namesake, will lend themselves to many of the same preparations as the mealy or floury type of ordinary potatoes. The red-skinned variety can be either round or elongated and both types are available throughout the winter.

The Jerusalem artichoke is neither an artichoke

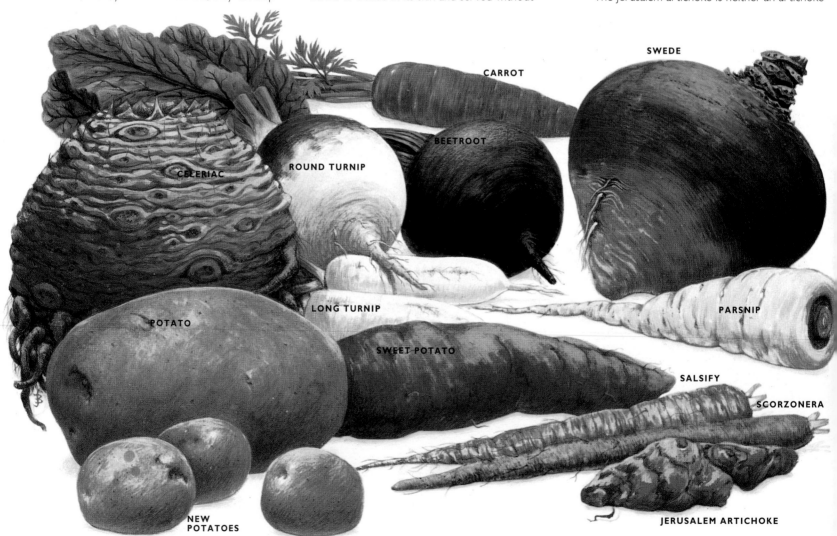

CELERIAC

ROUND TURNIP

CARROT

BEETROOT

SWEDE

POTATO

LONG TURNIP

SWEET POTATO

PARSNIP

SALSIFY

SCORZONERA

NEW POTATOES

JERUSALEM ARTICHOKE

nor from Jerusalem (it came from North America). The faint resemblance between the flavour of its cream-coloured flesh and that of the globe artichoke earned it one part of its name; the other part comes from the Italian girasole – a sunflower, to which the plant is related. Available during the winter and early spring, Jerusalem artichokes can be boiled and puréed, sliced and pan-fried, parboiled and deep-fried, baked or stewed.

When buying roots or tubers, select firm, unwrinkled specimens. Any leafy tops should be crisp and fresh. The greens of turnips, swedes, beetroot, salsify and scorzonera can be cooked and eaten like other leafy vegetables. Store roots and tubers in a cool, dark, dry place.

The Onion Family

Onions, leeks and garlic – all members of the allium family – have been indispensable to the art of cookery since the beginnings of civilization, both as flavourings for other foods and as main elements in many dishes. The ancients considered them sacred, and more recent peoples have been hardly less appreciative: when Paris was besieged by the Prussian Army in 1870, its citizens reckoned the shortage of onions as the worst of their many wartime deprivations.

Over the centuries, countless onion types have been developed, varying in water content and in sweetness: the less water and sugar an onion has, the stronger its flavour. As a general rule, purple, violet-tinged or white onions are the mildest, and yellow varieties are the most pungent. But there are many exceptions, and the only way to be sure is to taste for yourself. In any event, the long baking or braising typical of most onion dishes will mellow the most powerful flavour.

Peeling strong onions can be made less tearful by holding the onion under running water. Peeling very small onions – often glazed whole and used as a garnish – can be especially tedious, for their skins cling stubbornly. A preliminary dip in boiling water simplifies the task.

Spring onions – which are that only in name, since they can be purchased all year round – are young onions that have been picked before the bulb is fully grown, or varieties that attain their full growth without a bulb forming. Both the white

RED ONION

GARLIC

YELLOW ONION

SPANISH ONION

WELSH ONIONS

LEEK

SHALLOTS

SMALL ONIONS

SPRING ONIONS

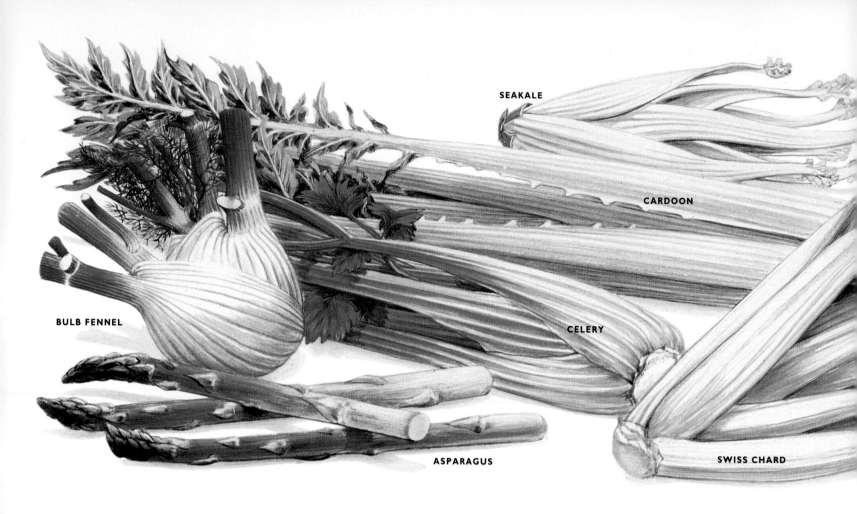

SEAKALE

CARDOON

BULB FENNEL

CELERY

ASPARAGUS

SWISS CHARD

bottom and the green top are best known as lively additions to salads, but they also have potential in cooked dishes: the white portion and greens can be mashed together with boiled potatoes, or coated with batter and deep-fried.

Welsh onions – *ciboules* – are a distinct species and especially common as a seasoning agent in French and Eastern dishes. Despite their name, they originally came from Siberia or China. Only the brown husk on the bulb need be discarded: the rest of the onion can be eaten – perhaps baked in the oven, or as part of a mixed vegetable stew.

Leeks combine delicacy and wide availability, long ago earning themselves their French sobriquet 'asparagus of the poor'. They lack a clearly defined bulb and shoot: instead, the leek's leaves form a tight-packed scroll. However, grit can penetrate between the layers, and the leaves always need careful washing. The dark-green fibrous tops, the roots and outer leaves must be removed, but the rest of the plant is edible. Cooked leeks have a mild but pleasantly sweet flavour; in addition to their frequent use as a

garnish to meats and poultry, they can make superb dishes on their own – baked with a gratin topping, cooked in a pie or perhaps braised in wine.

Shallots, similar in appearance to small onions, grow in clusters around a single root base. Although strongly flavoured, they are the most refined of the alliums, and seasoning is their role. Finely chopped, shallots are used in sauces such as béarnaise or in savoury butters that dress grilled meat.

Garlic, when raw, is the most pungent of the whole family, although cooking subdues it. It ranked as a vital component of Mediterranean cooking even before the Romans made it a regular part of their soldiers' diet. Yet in England only 40 years ago, one cookery writer doubted 'on account of its appalling odour' whether garlic would ever be popular 'among northern races'. Nowadays cooks almost everywhere regularly rely on the garlic's ability to lend an exciting spark to the foods it seasons. And after it has been tamed and transformed by long slow cooking, it can be used not just as a flavouring, but also as a vegetable in its own right – baked whole, as a stuffing for onions, or even puréed and spread on toast.

Stalks and Shoots

Vegetable stalks and shoots have been prized since ancient times. Celery is mentioned in Homer's *Odyssey*; cardoon and asparagus were enjoyed by the Romans. Such lengthy cultivation has drastically altered the original wild plants, most of which can still be found today. Wild asparagus, for example, is delicious but bootlace-thin; wild celery is a dark green, bitter weed. Selective propagation has produced today's plump juicy asparagus, and the pale colour of celery and most other stalks is due to the technique of blanching – banking up earth round the growing plants. When thus deprived of light, the stalks are white and succulent, with only a hint of bitterness.

Asparagus is the undoubted aristocrat of stalk vegetables. Available fresh and unforced for only a few weeks in spring and early summer, asparagus is highly prized for its exquisite flavour. Look for evenly shaped plump stalks with firm tightly budded tips. According to variety and growing methods, asparagus may range in colour

The Globe Artichoke

The artichoke is a thistle: stiff, sharp-pointed leaves, each with a fleshy base, surround an inedible choke – a mass of hairs that, in unharvested plants, eventually forms the artichoke's purple flower. The choke itself nestles in a tender, cup-shaped base – the artichoke bottom. Artichokes are available in European markets all the year round except in the early winter and late summer. Freshness is indicated by a tight-packed green globe, with no brown leaves.

The age of the plant – and its suitability for various sorts of cooking – can be judged by comparing the size of the globe with the thickness of the stem. Since the growth of the stem is completed first, the smaller the globe in relation to the stem, the younger the plant.

Young artichoke globes need only be trimmed of their outer leaves to furnish the artichoke 'hearts' – composed of the delicate inner leaves clasped around still-unformed chokes – which may be deep-fried, stewed or baked. Mature artichokes can be boiled whole; the tough parts

GLOBE ARTICHOKE

of the leaves are discarded when the globe itself is eaten, a leaf at a time. But the tender bottom of a mature plant may be the only part required – perhaps for stuffing. In that case, the artichoke must be 'turned' (see page 141).

---

from green to white, often with violet tinges. All are good, and all are prepared and cooked in the same ways.

The whole asparagus stalk is edible; but the tough skin must be peeled from the lower part of the stem (see page 142). Usually, the asparagus is served boiled, accompanied by melted butter or a sauce. Asparagus can also be parboiled, cut into finger-length sections, dipped in batter and deep-fried; or the stalks can be sliced thinly, parboiled for a few seconds and rapidly pan-fried.

Unlike asparagus, celery is available all the year round; it is at its best in winter. An important flavouring element in many dishes, celery is also a delicious vegetable in its own right – braised, for example, or baked in a gratin. Choose plants that are crisp and unblemished, with white or pale green stalks clustered in a tight head. The darker its colour, the coarser the texture of the celery. Even young celery plants have stringy fibres running along the outside of each stalk; these should be removed before cooking (see page 142). The outer stalks have a

stronger taste; chopped, they are often included, together with the plant's leafy top, as flavourings in vegetable stews. Celery hearts – the closely packed inner stalks – do not need stringing; they are the best parts for a braise. To prepare them, snap off the coarser, outer stalks and then trim away the discoloured surface of the root base. Cook the hearts whole or halved lengthwise, depending on size. To speed cooking time and attenuate celery's penetrating flavour, the hearts are often parboiled first.

Bulb fennel – sometimes called Florence fennel – resembles a bulbous head of celery, but its mellow, aniseed flavour is unmistakably its own. It is available during autumn, winter and spring. Look for crisp fully formed round bulbs. Like celery, even young fennel needs stringing and trimming (see page 142). Halved or quartered, fennel bulbs can be cooked in the same ways as celery hearts; braised fennel is a good accompaniment to fish or roast meats.

Swiss chard, also known as seakale spinach or beetroot spinach, appears in markets throughout

the year. The stalks – or ribs – of the plant should be firm and white, the leaves unwilted and dark green. Chard leaves are prepared like other leaf vegetables (see page 138); the ribs are appreciated for their sweet, nutty flavour. Chard ribs are less stringy than celery or fennel stalks, but they are covered by a thin fibrous membrane that should be removed before cooking. Cut into finger lengths, chard ribs are usually parboiled before being braised, or they can be coated with a sauce and gratinéed.

In flavour, the long white stalks of seakale – available during spring and summer – are similar to chard ribs and they are prepared in the same way; the leaves are also good, raw, in salads.

The cardoon, harvested in late autumn, is part of the thistle family, and its flavour has a faint resemblance to that of the related globe artichoke (above). Popular in Italy and France, cardoons are still unusual delicacies in other parts of Europe and in the USA. Only the stalks are eaten – trimmed in the same way as celery and parboiled before being baked or braised.

Vegetable Fruits

Most vegetable fruits were comparatively late arrivals to European kitchens. Both okra and aubergines were brought to Europe from the tropics of Africa and Asia during the Middle Ages; sweet peppers and tomatoes came from Central and South America in the 16th century.

The Mediterranean countries quickly incorporated these tropical newcomers into their cookery, but people in northern Europe and, later, in the USA, were often deeply suspicious of vegetable fruits. Well into the 19th century, myths persisted that one or another of them was a dangerous aphrodisiac, a deadly poison or led to incurable insanity.

Tomatoes often had the worst reputation of all; but once accepted as a food, they changed the cooking and eating habits of the world. All the vegetable fruits combine well with other foods – and with each other – but none matches the tomato's versatility. Cooked or raw, whole or sliced, or skinned and seeded (see page 140) for use in soups, stews or sauces, the tomato figures in a multitude of dishes in almost every cuisine.

Enthusiastic cultivation has furnished a wide range of tomato varieties, including low-acid yellow types. Red tomatoes are the most common: some varieties are smooth and round, while other, 'Mediterranean-type' or 'beef' tomatoes are flattened and ridged. Plum tomatoes, despite their name, are pear-shaped; their relatively small seed clusters make them particularly suitable for sauces and stews.

Tomatoes should be firm-fleshed, with unwrinkled skins. The best fruits are those that have ripened in the sun on the plant; tomatoes ripened artificially have much less flavour. A sign of a naturally ripened tomato is a faint flush of green at the stem end. Such tomatoes are, unfortunately, only available in high summer. However, canned tomatoes retain flavour if not a firm texture, so they serve well for most cooking purposes when the best quality fresh fruits are not available.

Sweet peppers can be obtained fresh all the year round. Compared to a ripe tomato, a pepper is surprisingly light for its size; it consists of a firm case of flesh surrounding only a cluster of flat seeds and a few ribs of whitish pith. Seeds and pith should be discarded (see page 140); the remaining shell makes an attractive container for stuffing, or it may be sliced or chopped and included in stews, or other dishes. As peppers ripen, their colour changes from green to yellow or red; the riper the fruit, the sweeter it is.

Aubergines are glossy and colourful; most run the spectrum of purples from mauve to near-black, but white and green varieties also exist. Some types are round, some elongated. All have the same mildly sweet flavour; the best are young and firm, with unblemished skins. The fruit is available all the year round. Aubergines play their part in the mixed vegetable stews of Mediterranean cooking, but are good alone, grilled or baked. Brush unpeeled halves or slices with olive oil first.

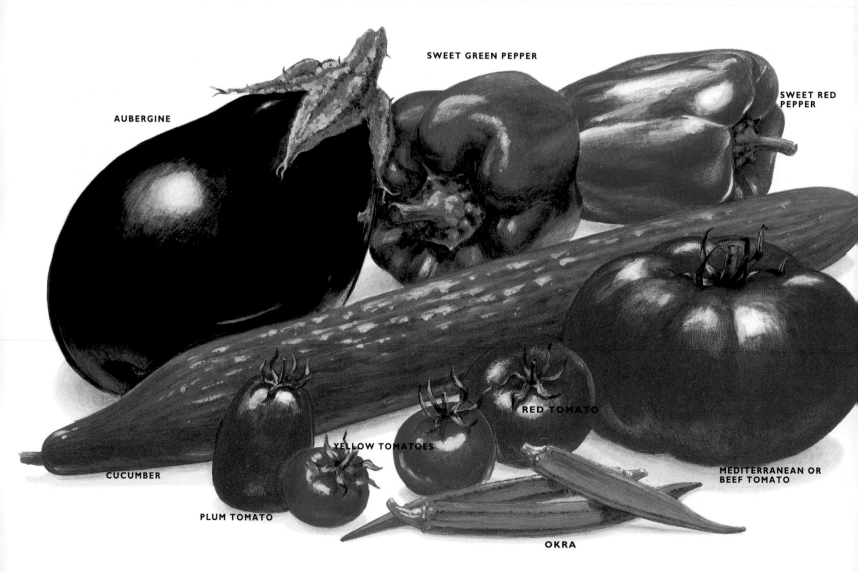

AUBERGINE

SWEET GREEN PEPPER

SWEET RED PEPPER

CUCUMBER

PLUM TOMATO

YELLOW TOMATOES

RED TOMATO

OKRA

MEDITERRANEAN OR BEEF TOMATO

PUMPKIN

MARROW

HUBBARD SQUASH

CUSTARD MARROW

CROOKNECK SQUASH

CHAYOTE

BUTTERNUT SQUASH

COURGETTE

Cucumbers are mild and refreshing whether raw, cooked or preserved. Japanese cooks use cucumber rounds to garnish steamed fish; Eastern Europeans pickle cucumbers with dill. The French stew them in butter, and almost everyone eats them raw. Cucumbers are closely akin to squashes and may be boiled, sautéed, baked and braised in many of the same ways. For most dishes that include cooked cucumber, the fruit must be peeled and seeded; to do this, split the cucumber in half lengthwise and scoop out the soft core of seeds with a teaspoon or fingertip. Like many vegetable fruits, cucumbers are available all year round, but are most abundant in summer. Size does not affect their quality, but texture does; the best are very firm.

Okra is widely eaten throughout Africa and the Middle East. It is an essential element in the Creole cookery of the southern USA and the Caribbean. In Creole stews the cut pods release a glutinous liquid that serves as a thickening agent. If okra is to be eaten whole, the pods must be trimmed carefully so that their liquid is retained (see page 140); otherwise they will lose their shape during cooking. In any case, okra should be eaten young – pods more than 5 cm (2 inches) long develop a tough stubble on the outside. You will find okra in vegetable markets during the spring and in autumn; select only those pods that are a clean, unblemished green.

The Squashes

Marrows, pumpkins and their relatives – all members of the family cucurbitaceae – are popularly called squashes, a term derived from the American Indian word *askutasquash* which means 'eaten raw'. Ranging in size from finger-length courgettes to huge pumpkins, squashes have a sweetish, rather elusive flavour and a high water content.

Many of the squashes are available most of the year, but they are categorized as 'summer' varieties and 'winter' varieties. Summer squashes are picked when they are immature; the whole vegetable – skin and seed included – is edible. Winter squashes are picked when they are full-grown; most types have a tough, inedible skin and hard seeds.

Courgettes, vegetable marrow, and the crookneck, straightneck and patty-pan squashes are all summer varieties. They are at their best when very small, bright in colour, smooth-skinned and firm. They should be washed and trimmed at both ends, but require no peeling. Summer squash recipes sometimes call for excess moisture to be removed before cooking: sprinkle the vegetable lightly with salt and leave it to stand for at least half an hour. The salt draws off liquid from the vegetable, which can be drained away, taking most of the salt with it.

None of the summer squashes needs lengthy cooking. Courgettes up to about 10 cm (4 inches) long can be parboiled whole for two minutes and then sautéed in oil or butter – or they may be eaten raw. Courgettes of all sizes can be sliced and sautéed, or baked in the oven, or they can be coated with batter and deep-fried.

Vegetable marrows less than 15 cm (6 inches) long, taste very like courgettes and can be cooked similarly. The larger specimens can be halved, seeded, filled with a stuffing and baked; but marrows over 20 cm (8 inches) long have watery, rather bitter flesh and are best avoided.

The familiar globe-shaped pumpkin, with its orange skin and the butternut and hubbard squashes are well-known winter varieties. Look for uniformly hard skins that show no cracks or bruises.

The more fibrous winter squashes need longer cooking than the summer varieties; they can be baked, or steamed and puréed. Large specimens should be cut up, seeded and peeled before cooking. With smaller winter squashes, you can cut off a lid section, remove the seeds and fill the seed cavity with butter, cream, or a stuffing; the lid is then replaced and the squash baked.

The pear-shaped chayote has a thick, often prickly, skin surrounding crisp, but succulent, flesh and a single, long seed. After it has been peeled, and the seed taken out, chayote can be cooked in the same way as summer squashes.

In addition to their fruits, the golden flowers of all squash plants are good to eat. They can be sautéed briefly in oil, or braised and can also be dipped in batter and deep-fried.

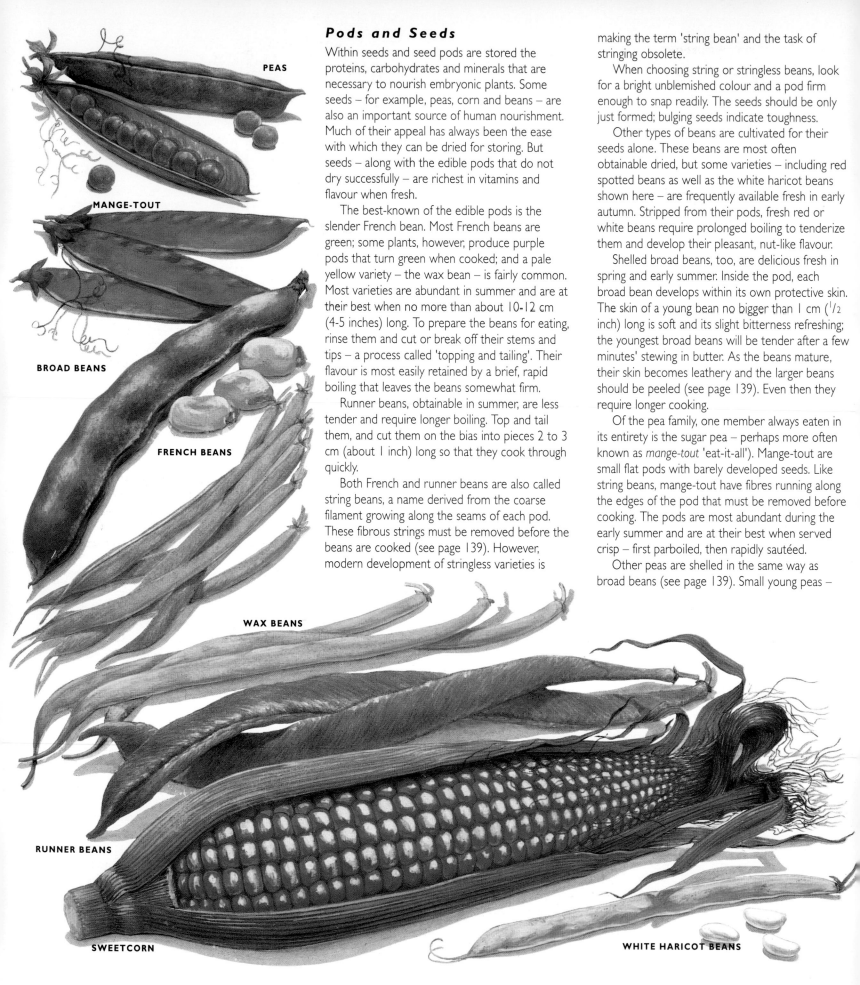

Pods and Seeds

Within seeds and seed pods are stored the proteins, carbohydrates and minerals that are necessary to nourish embryonic plants. Some seeds – for example, peas, corn and beans – are also an important source of human nourishment. Much of their appeal has always been the ease with which they can be dried for storing. But seeds – along with the edible pods that do not dry successfully – are richest in vitamins and flavour when fresh.

The best-known of the edible pods is the slender French bean. Most French beans are green; some plants, however, produce purple pods that turn green when cooked; and a pale yellow variety – the wax bean – is fairly common. Most varieties are abundant in summer and are at their best when no more than about 10-12 cm (4-5 inches) long. To prepare the beans for eating, rinse them and cut or break off their stems and tips – a process called 'topping and tailing'. Their flavour is most easily retained by a brief, rapid boiling that leaves the beans somewhat firm.

Runner beans, obtainable in summer, are less tender and require longer boiling. Top and tail them, and cut them on the bias into pieces 2 to 3 cm (about 1 inch) long so that they cook through quickly.

Both French and runner beans are also called string beans, a name derived from the coarse filament growing along the seams of each pod. These fibrous strings must be removed before the beans are cooked (see page 139). However, modern development of stringless varieties is making the term 'string bean' and the task of stringing obsolete.

When choosing string or stringless beans, look for a bright unblemished colour and a pod firm enough to snap readily. The seeds should be only just formed; bulging seeds indicate toughness.

Other types of beans are cultivated for their seeds alone. These beans are most often obtainable dried, but some varieties – including red spotted beans as well as the white haricot beans shown here – are frequently available fresh in early autumn. Stripped from their pods, fresh red or white beans require prolonged boiling to tenderize them and develop their pleasant, nut-like flavour.

Shelled broad beans, too, are delicious fresh in spring and early summer. Inside the pod, each broad bean develops within its own protective skin. The skin of a young bean no bigger than 1 cm ($^1/_2$ inch) long is soft and its slight bitterness refreshing; the youngest broad beans will be tender after a few minutes' stewing in butter. As the beans mature, their skin becomes leathery and the larger beans should be peeled (see page 139). Even then they require longer cooking.

Of the pea family, one member always eaten in its entirety is the sugar pea – perhaps more often known as *mange-tout* 'eat-it-all'). Mange-tout are small flat pods with barely developed seeds. Like string beans, mange-tout have fibres running along the edges of the pod that must be removed before cooking. The pods are most abundant during the early summer and are at their best when served crisp – first parboiled, then rapidly sautéed.

Other peas are shelled in the same way as broad beans (see page 139). Small young peas –

PEAS

MANGE-TOUT

BROAD BEANS

FRENCH BEANS

WAX BEANS

RUNNER BEANS

SWEETCORN

WHITE HARICOT BEANS

FLAT MUSHROOMS

CUP MUSHROOM

CEP

MOREL

BUTTON MUSHROOMS

CHANTERELLES

BLACK TRUFFLE

the *petits pois* of French cooking – are the most tender and sweet; they appear in markets in early summer and require only the briefest of boiling. As the summer advances and the peas grow larger, their natural sugar gradually turns to starch and their texture becomes increasingly pasty; medium-size peas need longer boiling and large peas are best reserved for purées or soups.

Like peas and beans, the seeds of the sweetcorn – the kernels – are enclosed. But the wrapping on an ear of corn is a sheath of silky threads covered by a husk of green outer leaves. Corn kernels can be scraped from the cob (see page 140) and boiled, added to stews or made into puddings. Whole, the ear of corn can be boiled or grilled. Served with butter, salt and pepper, the tender, juicy kernels are eaten directly from the cob.

Corn is sweetest when prepared as soon as possible after being removed from the stalk. Once picked, its sugar content rapidly turns into starch. Late summer is the best time to look for corn with moist green husks that completely enclose the ears. Open up the husks slightly to expose a few kernels. Those at the tip of the cob should still be unformed, but the rest should be plump and smooth. When you pierce a fresh kernel with your thumbnail, it will spurt milky juice.

Mushrooms and Truffles

Mushrooms, once a seasonal delicacy for those with the skill to find them, are now accessible to all. *Agaricus bisporus*, the common mushroom, was cultivated in a haphazard fashion for 300 years before 19th-century scientists perfected the means to grow it all the year round.

The youngest of these fungi, button mushrooms, have the mildest flavour. Their neat shape and size suit them for garnishes. As they mature, their caps partially open and they are known as cup mushrooms, adaptable to most cooking purposes. Fully mature, the mushrooms become flatter and a useful size for stuffing; they are also good in stews.

To prepare cultivated mushrooms for cooking, cut off the earthy base of the stalk and wipe the caps with a damp cloth . If they are dirty, wash them quickly – and dry them thoroughly – just before cooking. Use the whole mushroom.

No other variety of mushroom has been cultivated on a large scale in Europe and America – which is a pity since some of the wild relatives of *Agaricus bisporus* surpass it in flavour. Hunting for wild mushrooms is so risky that it should be left to experts; however, the wild varieties are occasionally available in markets. Among the best

are morels – which appear in late spring – and chanterelles and ceps, both available in summer and autumn. Chanterelles are smooth-textured and fragrant; morels are perhaps the most delicate; and ceps have an earthy flavour and an almost meaty firmness.

When buying ceps, choose those with firm light-coloured tubes on the undersides of their caps. Wipe them clean with a damp cloth and peel the base of the stem. Ceps are popular with insects as well as cooks, so remove any damaged parts before cooking. Morels are hollow shells that trap sand; they should be split and washed under running water. Chanterelles have irregular surfaces that also trap dirt and they, too, need careful washing.

Dried wild mushrooms are worth buying if you cannot obtain fresh ones. Before cooking, soak them in water so that they swell to their natural size and regain their tenderness.

Truffles, rarest of the edible fungi, grow underground; any clinging earth must be cleaned off with water and a brush. Tinned or fresh, they are always expensive, but only fresh truffles have the wonderful fragrance that justifies their cost. Even a few slices will permeate an entire dish, and if the truffles are peeled the peelings can be used as a flavouring.

Types of Pulses

Lentils, peas and beans, collectively known as pulses, are the seeds of leguminous plants – a group whose common feature is that the seeds are borne in pods. Strictly speaking, the word pulse covers both fresh and dried peas, beans and lentils, however, pulses are invariably the dried vegetables.

Hundreds of types of pulses are sold dried, many of them available in several different colours. To add to the complexity, many pulses have several names. The pulses illustrated below are a good cross-section of those available in Europe and America – but you should not be deterred from trying other pulses that you can buy just because of an unfamiliar appearance or name.

All pulses consist of two sections encased in a strong skin. Some pulses are sold in split form – with the skin removed so that the two halves fall apart. Without its skin, a pulse may look quite different: split mung beans, for example, are yellow, although the whole beans are green. Split pulses cook more quickly than their whole counterparts, but will not usually retain their shape as well.

Dried pulses can be safely kept almost indefinitely. However, you should avoid using any that are more than a year old: pulses become harder with age and require longer cooking; eventually they dry out so much they fall to pieces in the water without becoming properly tender. Since it is impossible to tell a pulse's age from its appearance, the best safeguard is to buy small quantities at a time from a reputable shop which has a quick turnover, like a large multiple or an ethnic grocer.

The Latin name for lentil is *lens* – a word since borrowed to describe glass ground to a lentil's flattened form. The most widely available lentils are the split red variety; sometimes known as Egyptian lentils, and the larger beige lentils. Red lentils are bland-tasting; the beige ones have

RED LENTILS   **GREEN SPLIT PEAS**   **SOYA BEANS**   **CHICK PEAS**

PUY LENTILS   **YELLOW SPLIT PEAS**   **FIELD BEANS**   PI

BEIGE LENTILS   **GREEN WHOLE PEAS**   **BROAD BEANS**   **BLACK-EYED PEAS**

a more pronounced flavour. Puy lentils, a small mottled green or slate-coloured variety, are more rare but prized for their subtle flavour and ability to hold their shape when cooked.

Although all lentils belong to the same botanical grouping, the names pea and bean are both umbrella terms that cover a number of species. Round pulses are generally called peas, oval or kidney-shaped pulses are called beans. However, black-eyed peas are sometimes referred to as black-eyed beans.

Yellow and green peas are different types of common pea. Both are sweet but green peas

have somewhat more flavour. Both are available whole and split.

The yellow soya beans illustrated here have a mild taste: a black variety of soya bean, however, is renowned for its sweet, full flavour. Chick peas have an almost nut-like taste and a crunchy texture. Mealy textured broad beans and field beans – also known as *foul* (or *ful*) *medames* – are enveloped in a leathery skin which you should remove after soaking or cooking. Pigeon peas and black-eyed peas are both succulent and have an earthy flavour.

The other pulses illustrated belong to the

huge kidney bean family. Mung beans and aduki or adjuki beans have a sweetish taste; butter beans are mild-flavoured and smooth. The remaining beans – black or turtle beans, Dutch brown, haricot, pinto, borlotti, flageolet, cannellini and red kidney beans – are all variants of the common kidney bean. They share a mealy texture, but their flavours range from robust to delicate. Red beans have the most full and meaty taste; pinto and borlotti beans a nut-like flavour. A relative of the pinto bean much used in Mexican cooking is the pink bean. Flageolets are the jewel of the kidney bean family, with a subtle fresh and delicate flavour.

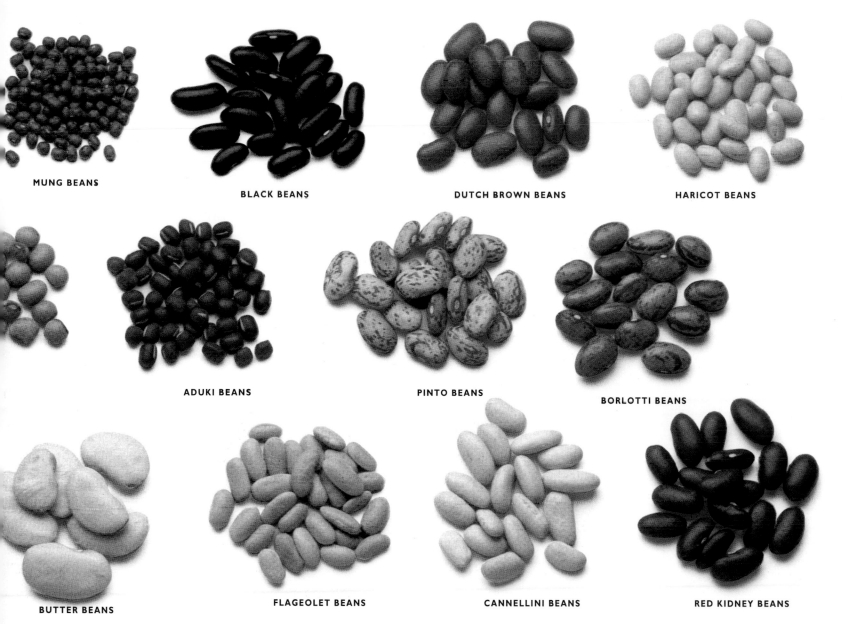

MUNG BEANS

BLACK BEANS

DUTCH BROWN BEANS

HARICOT BEANS

ADUKI BEANS

PINTO BEANS

BORLOTTI BEANS

BUTTER BEANS

FLAGEOLET BEANS

CANNELLINI BEANS

RED KIDNEY BEANS

Types of Fruit

Orchard Fruit

The apple is without doubt the most popular member of the firm-fleshed family. The ancestor of many modern apples was probably a tiny, inedible crab apple. But so splendidly has the apple responded to cultivation over the centuries, that today there are over 3,000 named varieties.

Apples vary greatly in colour, taste and texture. Their skin may be green and waxy like the Granny Smith, streaked with red like the Starking Delicious, mottled like a Cox's Orange Pippin, or brown and rough-skinned like a russet.

Their flesh may be crisp or mealy, tart or sweet. Most apples are also suitable for cooking, in either sweet or savoury dishes. Firmer varieties – such as russets or Cox's – keep their texture after cooking. Whatever the variety, choose fruit with a healthy skin that is free from bruises. The firmer-textured apples store for several weeks if wrapped individually and placed in single layers in a cool airy place.

Unlike its popular cousin, the apple, the medlar is not widely available commercially; however, the tree grows wild throughout

Europe. In size and shape, the medlar resembles a small apple with yellow-brown skin and an open end crowned with calyces. It is unusual in that it can only be eaten when the white or green flesh turns brown and begins to soften, two to three weeks after the fruit is picked. The soft, buttery flesh may then be eaten spooned from the skin, added to fruit fools, made into preserves or served as a sauce with meat or game.

Loquats, or Japanese medlars, are grown widely around the Mediterranean. The yellow,

GRANNY SMITH APPLE

STARKING DELICIOUS APPLE

RUSSET APPLE

COX'S ORANGE PIPPINS

MEDLARS

orange or red-brown fruit has a juicy, slightly tart flesh. When buying, choose firm, well-coloured fruit with a faint bloom. Loquats are delicious raw; cooked, they enliven any fruit compote. They are best used soon after purchase, but keep for several days in a cool place.

Crab apples and quinces, very different from one another in appearance, have similar uses in the kitchen. While both fruits are too acrid for eating raw, their high pectin content makes them suitable or jams, jellies and preserves. Choose crab apples that have a brightly-coloured, unwrinkled skin. The aromatic quince – at its best when the skin is tough, downy and golden – may also be stewed or baked. Its strong, slightly tart-flavoured flesh turns from yellow to pink when cooked. Quince is often used in small quantities to bring out the flavour of other cooked fruits – a few slices in an apple and pear pie will greatly enhance the dish. Crab apples and quinces can be stored in the same way as firm apples.

The pear is a close rival to the apple in popularity but a more temperamental fruit. Its season is shorter and, although the skin is sometimes tough, the flesh bruises easily. Pears are at their best for only a short time, and should be bought and used when they are just ripe. A pear is ready to eat when the flesh at the stem yields to the touch and the fruit gives out its distinctive aroma. Ripe pears will keep for about a week in a cool room.

Like apples, pears have been extensively cultivated to produce thousands of named varieties, although few are grown commercially. The best pears have been developed in relatively recent times: the superlative Doyenné du Comice, for example, first appeared in 1849. The fruit varies considerably in appearance, from the long Conference pear, which has a dark green skin heavily spotted with russet and creamy-pink flesh, to the Comice, large, oval and pale yellow, with yellow flesh. The William's, similar in colour to the Comice, has a waisted shape; the Beurre Hardy is a round pear with rough bronze skin and pink flesh. Pears may be substituted in many recipes that call for apples. For cooking, the fruit should be slightly underripe.

COMICE PEAR

WILLIAM'S PEAR

BEURRE HARDY PEAR

CONFERENCE PEAR

QUINCES

CRAB APPLES

LOQUATS

Stone Fruits

With the exception of the mango, a tropical fruit, and the date, grown mainly in the Middle East, stone fruits – those with one central, woody seed – flourish throughout the temperate regions of the world. Different varieties and hybrids of stone fruits abound, but all of them have in common a pulpy flesh and a thin skin. Because of their tenderness, ripe stone fruits must be handled carefully, and are best used the same day they are bought. They can be kept for about a week, however, in a cool place.

Peaches and nectarines are closely related; but while peach skins have a fuzzy bloom, nectarines are smooth-skinned – like plums – and are usually sweeter than peaches. Both fruits have juicy flesh that may be white, yellow-orange or red. Depending on whether the flesh adheres to the central stone, they are described as cling-stone or free-stone. White-fleshed peaches and nectarines – either cling- or free-stone – are often believed to have the best flavour for eating raw. All varieties, however, may be eaten raw, poached, stewed or baked in pastry.

Like its larger cousin, the peach, the apricot has white to orange flesh and may be cling-stone or free-stone. When ripe, apricots have a deep golden-orange skin. The warm, rich flavour of the fruit lends itself equally well to either sweet or savoury dishes, and it particularly complements the flavours of lamb and pork. All cherries fall into one of three types: sweet, sour, or semi-sweet. Semi-sweet cherries are hybrids, and are known as Duke or Royale cherries. They may be red or black-skinned. Sweet dessert cherries may be red, black or pale-skinned, and either firm-fleshed – the Bigarreau, or Heart varieties – or plump and tender – the Geans. Of the sour cherries, the most popular is the dark acid morello. While sour cherries are suitable only for cooking – in sweet and savoury dishes, as well as conserves – the other two types may be eaten raw or cooked. Whatever the variety, choose

WHITE PEACH

YELLOW PEACH

NECTARINE

APRICOT

DATES

MANGO

cherries that are firm and dry.

The plum is another stone fruit with many distinctive varieties. The damson – a small, blue-black plum with a tough skin – is too tart to be eaten raw, but it is excellent in jams and preserves. The Victoria – an oval, yellow or red-skinned fruit with sweet juicy flesh – is one of the best-known plums; other popular varieties are the large red Santa Rosa, and the Kirke's Blue – a succulent plum with a purple-black skin that has a dusty bloom. Gages, one of the oldest types of plum, are smaller and more tender and highly scented than the other varieties. Greengages have a yellow-green skin and flesh; golden gages, such as the small soft

fragrant Mirabelle, are golden-yellow. Delicious raw, plums may also be baked in pies, stewed, or cooked in meat dishes. The firmer-fleshed plums – early Victorias, and most blue-black varieties, for example – are excellent for bottling. When buying plums, select those that have unblemished skins, a good colour and a healthy bloom.

Date varieties are either soft, semi-dry or dry. By far the most delicious are fresh soft dates, plump and golden or reddish brown, with smooth, shiny skins. Their buttery flesh is highly nutritious, and combines well with nuts and other fruits. Dates are delicious stuffed with cream cheese, or cooked in savoury meat

dishes. Soft dates are also available pressed into blocks for cooking. Semi-dry dates, often packed into long boxes, can be used in the same way; dry dates are seldom available in Europe.

The mango is the largest and heaviest of the stone fruits, weighing from 150 g to 1 kg (5 oz to 2^{1}/$_{2}$ lbs). Mangoes are either oval with a beak-like protuberance at the top, or kidney-shaped. When ripe, their smooth skins may be green, yellow, orange, red or a combination of these colours. At its best, the mango's pale orange flesh is sweet and aromatic. Ripe mango is delicious in fruit salads, mousses and ice-cream; the unripe green fruit is used for chutneys and relishes.

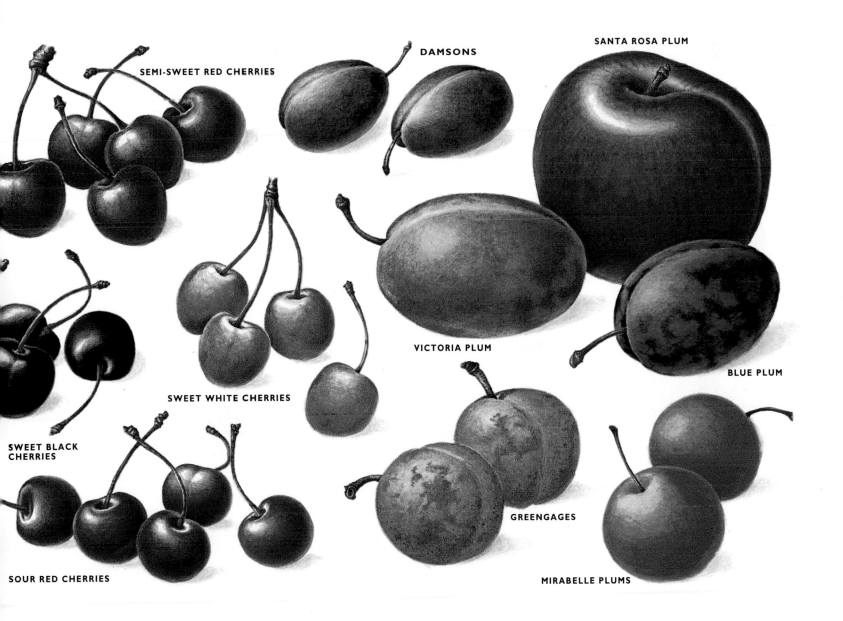

SEMI-SWEET RED CHERRIES

DAMSONS

SANTA ROSA PLUM

VICTORIA PLUM

BLUE PLUM

SWEET WHITE CHERRIES

SWEET BLACK CHERRIES

GREENGAGES

SOUR RED CHERRIES

MIRABELLE PLUMS

Berries and Grapes

The family of small soft fruits includes currants, grapes and a wide range of different berries. Fresh soft fruits – with the exception of grapes, cranberries and cape gooseberries – should be used within one to two days of purchase. Keep the fruits spread out on trays, so that they do not touch, in a cool airy place. Most berries are associated with summer; and none more so than the strawberry. However, the large bright-scarlet cultivated berry, with its sweet juicy flesh and distinctive fragrance, has been with us only since 1821: the result of a chance cross between two American wild varieties. Wild strawberries, such as the European alpine, are softer, smaller and more scented than the cultivated berries.

Raspberries, blackberries and loganberries are closely related. Of the three, the velvety raspberry is the most fragrant and sweet. Usually eaten raw, its clear, deep-pink juice can also lend colour and flavour to many desserts. Blackberries grow wild all over northern Europe; the cultivated varieties, larger and sweeter, are better dessert berries. Blackberries may be eaten raw; or cooked with other fruits in tarts and compotes. The loganberry – believed to be a hybrid between the raspberry and blackberry – has the advantages of both. Sharper-tasting than a raspberry, this oblong fruit is delicious raw, and a substitute for blackberries in any cooked dish.

Succulent and very soft, with a purple juice that leaves a persistent stain, the mulberry is not often found in shops. Its tart yet sweet flavour makes it equally good raw, or cooked like blackberries.

The savoury use of cranberries, in a sauce for poultry and game, is widely known. Too bitter to eat raw – except crushed, as a relish – cranberries are also delicious cooked in pies and

CRANBERRIES

CAPE GOOSEBERRIES

BLACKBERRIES

BLUEBERRIES

GREEN GOOSEBERRIES

PINK GOOSEBERRIES

MULBERRIES

STRAWBERRIES

RASPBERRIES

WILD STRAWBERRIES

LOGANBERRIES

tarts. To avoid toughening the skins, cook the berries before you sweeten them. Because of their waxy skins, cranberries keep fresh longer than most soft fruits – about a week if refrigerated. The cranberry's sweeter cousin, the blueberry, can be cooked in the same way or eaten raw.

Red and white currants are delicately flavoured, with gleaming, translucent skins. They are often frosted – dipped in egg white and sugar – or used to garnish creams and jellies. The blackcurrant has a pungent aroma that, to some palates, makes it unpleasant raw. But cooked for jams and sauces, sweet or savoury dishes, its

rich colour and flavour are invaluable.

Gooseberries – members of the currant family – vary considerably in size and appearance. Their skins are smooth, downy or hairy, and any colour from pale-green to dark-red. Unripe gooseberries, with their sharper flavour, are the best choice for cooking: in pies, or puréed to make a sharp sauce that balances rich oily fish. Cape gooseberries, physalis fruit or Chinese Lantern fruits, are not gooseberries at all – they belong to the tomato family. These shiny, golden-orange fruits encased in a papery inedible husk have a sweet-sharp taste that goes well with other fruits, raw or cooked.

Inside their husks, the berries will keep in a cool place for several weeks.

Table grapes are divided into black or white varieties. Black grapes range in colour from red to blue-black with a dusty bloom; white grapes include those with green, golden or amber skins. Among the most popular dessert grapes are the white Italia, the seedless Almeria, the Black Hamburgh, a sweet hothouse variety, and the Golden Chasselas, a grape with a rich flavour and musky scent. Fresh grapes, unlike other soft fruits, store very well: kept dry, they can be refrigerated for up to two months.

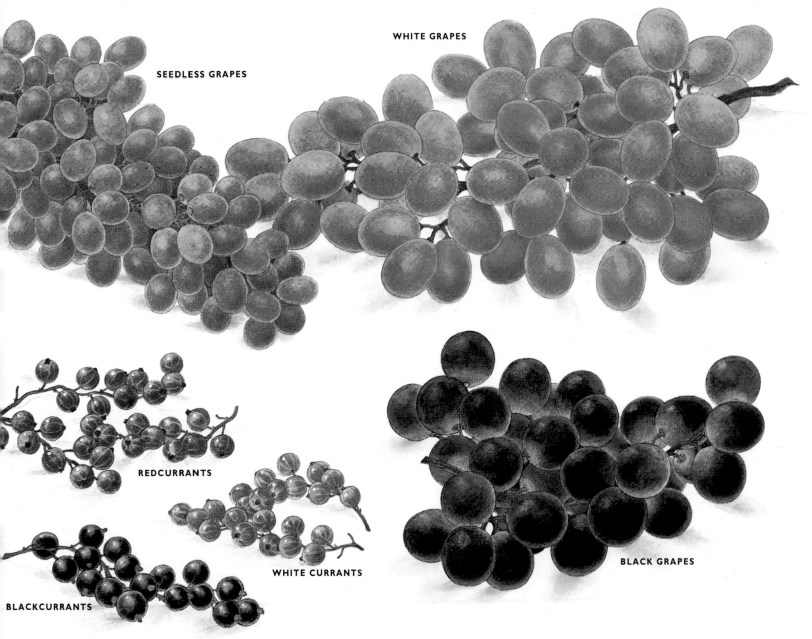

SEEDLESS GRAPES

WHITE GRAPES

REDCURRANTS

WHITE CURRANTS

BLACKCURRANTS

BLACK GRAPES

The Citrus Family

Citrus fruits span a spectrum of flavour from sharp to sweet. There are only a few basic types of citrus fruit, but centuries of cultivation and cross-breeding have produced numerous varieties and hybrids; those illustrated below are necessarily only a selection of the fruits available.

Oranges, tangerines and kumquats all originated in China. The earliest orange varieties known in Europe were bitter – such as the modern Seville, which, as well as being used to make marmalade, lends piquancy to meat and game dishes. Sweet oranges first became popular in Europe in the 16th and 17th centuries. They are now grown widely around the Mediterranean, in Israel, Africa and the USA. Among the most popular sweet varieties are oval oranges, such as the Jaffa Shamouti, the tight-skinned juicy varieties like the Valencia, and the navel, which has well-defined segments and is distinguished by the embryonic orange embedded at one end of the fruit. Blood oranges have red or red-streaked skin and flesh, and a bittersweet flavour.

Choose oranges that are firm and have a soft shine and, as for any citrus fruit, avoid any which are discoloured, bruised or have soft or dry patches. The high sugar and acid content of oranges makes them a most refreshing fruit to eat raw; but their flesh, rind and juice are also used extensively in cooking.

Orange rind is almost as useful as the fruit it encloses. It can be finely grated to flavour many dishes, cut into julienne for a garnish, or dried in wide strips to be used in bouquets garnis.

The satsuma and the clementine are both varieties of tangerine: a loose-skinned fruit that is similar in flavour and appearance to a small sweet orange. Clementines have bright orange-red skin and juicy flesh; satsumas have paler skin and flesh, and are less rich in flavour.

GRAPEFRUIT

UGLI FRUIT

PINK GRAPEFRUIT

KUMQUATS

Kumquats are like little golden oranges with a thin tender skin. They are unique among citrus fruits in that they are eaten whole; the sweetness of the skin balances the flesh's tartness. Kumquats are often cooked in sweet-and-sour dishes.

Citrus-fruit juice contains differing proportions of sugar and acids, and sugar predominates in most of the fruits. Lemons and limes, however, contain a higher proportion of acids – mainly citric acid – which makes them unpalatable raw. But the very sourness of these fruits renders them invaluable in the kitchen. While lemons and limes are interchangeable in their culinary uses – both, for instance, enhance the flavour of other fruits – the lime has a very much stronger flavour and should be used sparingly.

Lemons, because they are milder and widely available, are the more useful of the two fruits. Their juice lends a sharp note to many different sauces, and their scented rind is both a flavouring and a garnish. The acid in lemon juice helps to prevent fruits such as apples and pears from discolouring after being peeled.

There are many varieties of lemon, but the main difference between them lies in the texture of their skin. Smooth-skinned lemons that feel heavy for their size are usually juicier than those varieties with a knobbly rind.

The grapefruit is one of the younger members of the citrus family, first sold commercially in the 1880s. Its flesh and thick skin may be either yellow or flushed with pink – pink grapefruits are sweeter but not as strongly flavoured as yellow ones. Grapefruit halves, sprinkled with sugar or liqueur, are often eaten as appetisers, but the halves are also excellent baked, with a sugared gratin surface. The craggy-skinned ugli fruit – a hybrid of the grapefruit and the tangerine – can be substituted in any grapefruit dish.

NAVEL ORANGE

VALENCIA ORANGE

LIME

LEMON

JAFFA ORANGE

CLEMENTINE

SEVILLE ORANGE

BLOOD ORANGES

SATSUMAS

Soft Fruit

Soft-fleshed, heavily seeded fruits – ranging from the creamy banana to the luscious persimmon – lend their abundant pulp to mousses, ice-creams and jellies. In some of these fruits, such as the papaya, the seeds are massed in the centre; in others – the guava, for example – they are distributed throughout the flesh. Early varieties of the banana were pitted with bitter dark seeds; but by the time the fruit appeared commercially in the West, towards the end of the 19th century, selective propagating had virtually eliminated the seeds.

For eating raw, all the fruits shown here are best bought ripe and used as soon as possible; but they will keep for about a week in a cool humid place.

The largest of the soft-fleshed seedy fruits, the papaya or pawpaw, resembles an elongated melon. The pink or orange flesh of the ripe fruit is similar in flavour to melon, and can be treated in the same ways – halved, seeded and served with ham, for instance. Green, unripe papayas can be stuffed and baked as a savoury dish, or the flesh can be used in soups and curries. Papaya juice makes an excellent marinade; like the leaves, it contains an enzyme that tenderizes meat.

The kiwi fruit – which was named after the national bird of New Zealand, its main centre of cultivation – is also known as a Chinese gooseberry, because of its place of origin and its hairy skin. The bright-green pulp and tiny black edible seeds are often eaten spooned from the skin; the attractive pattern of the seeds when the flesh is sliced also makes the kiwi fruit a useful garnish for desserts.

The Sharon fruit from Israel is one of the many varieties of persimmon and has seeds arranged in a star pattern. It is the only persimmon that can be eaten when it is firm. All other varieties must be left until the orange-red skin turns translucent and the flesh becomes almost like jam. When they are ready to eat, persimmons can be spooned from their skins

PAPAYA

PRICKLY PEARS

KIWI FRUITS

CHERIMOYA

PERSIMMONS

and served with cream; they are also excellent stewed, baked in tarts, or puréed for sauces.

The cherimoya is a member of a large family of fruits that are often known collectively as custard apples, because of their creamy, soft flesh. Heart-shaped, with smooth, bumpy or scaly skin, the cherimoya has a flavour reminiscent of pineapple. In spite of its leathery appearance, the skin is fragile; the cherimoya should be handled carefully. The sweet white flesh can be eaten from the skin or sieved for a natural custard.

Just as the Chinese gooseberry is no gooseberry, so the Indian fig is not a fig. Better known as the prickly pear because of the ribs of hair-like spines on its skin, it is actually the edible berry of a cactus. A prickly pear should be handled cautiously until its spiny skin has been removed. Peeled and sliced, the sweet juicy flesh is delicious raw, with a dash of lime or lemon juice; or it can be stewed or puréed.

The true fig is one of the earliest of the cultivated fruits. There are about 700 known varieties. Figs are most commonly white or purple-black; but they may also be green-, gold-, red- or brown-skinned. The flesh, too, varies considerably in colour and flavour. Best eaten raw and sun-warmed, figs may also be crystallized or chopped and used in cakes and puddings.

The guava is a highly aromatic fruit with a soft, grainy flesh and a smooth or ridged skin that may be white, yellow, green, red or purple. The flesh can be eaten raw, stewed or puréed. Guavas can also be halved and stuffed with a sweet or savoury filling.

Bananas develop their full flavour when the yellow skin becomes speckled with brown. For cooking, however, use the fruit slightly underripe, before the skin changes colour. Banana is often added to cooked savoury dishes – to offset the spiciness of a curry, for example – but the fruit is perhaps at its best as a dessert, flamed in rum or kirsch and served with brown sugar and cream.

BLACK FIGS

BANANAS

GUAVAS

Melons: Cool and Refreshing

On a hot day, a slice of chilled melon is just as refreshing as a long cool drink – not surprisingly, since a melon's flesh is almost 95 per cent water. Cultivated for thousands of years in Egypt, this thirst-quenching fruit reached northern Europe only in the 15th century, to be greeted as a rare delicacy. Today, thanks to increased imports, melons are widely available.

The heavy watermelon, with its crisp scarlet flesh and dark seeds, is quite different from other melons. The latter fall broadly into three types – the musk or netted melons; cantaloupes; and winter melons, which ripen later in the season.

Musk melons, such as the Gallia, are distinguished by a raised net pattern on the skin. Cantaloupes may be grooved and knobbly in appearance or smooth-skinned. Two popular varieties of the cantaloupe melon are the Charentais and the Ogen – both often small enough for a half to be served as an individual portion. Both cantaloupes and musk melons have scented green or orange flesh. Winter melons, such as the honeydew, have a pale flesh with less flavour than the scented melons; but as they ripen slowly, they can be stored for much longer and are thus usually cheaper to buy.

To choose a prime melon, weigh several in the hand and pick the heaviest for its size. Cantaloupe and musk melons should also be fragrant and very slightly soft round the base.

A Mixed Crop

While most fruits can be grouped together according to shared characteristics, a few defy simple classification. Lychees have a central seed, like stoned fruits, but the flesh is enclosed in a papery shell. Passion fruits and pomegranates are filled with seeds, but unlike other seedy fruits each seed is enclosed in a sac of juicy pulp. The pineapple is not one fruit but many, formed by the fusion of about 100 separate flowers; and rhubarb is not a fruit at all, but a leaf stem.

Pineapple's sweet flesh grows heavily scented as the fruit ripens. When you buy a pineapple, tap its base – a dull, solid sound indicates ripeness. The ripe fruit may be stored in the refrigerator for two to three days. The sweet-sour flavour of pineapple makes it a good companion to rich foods such as glazed ham. But raw pineapple contains an enzyme that attacks gelatine; if you use pineapple in a recipe that includes gelatine, cook the fruit beforehand to destroy the enzyme.

Passion fruit, when ripe, has a dimpled purple-brown skin. Its fragrance enhances drinks and cold desserts. Lychees reach their prime when the skins are deep-red and look slightly crumpled. Add them raw to salads, or poach them in syrup and serve cold. Pomegranates are at their best when the skin is brightly coloured and firm. The fruit's translucent-pink seeds garnish sweet or savoury dishes; the juice lends a delicate flavour to soups and jellies. All these fruits will store for a month or longer in a cold, humid place.

Fine pink rhubarb stems are delicious stewed or in pies. Rhubarb keeps for up to two weeks in a cold place.

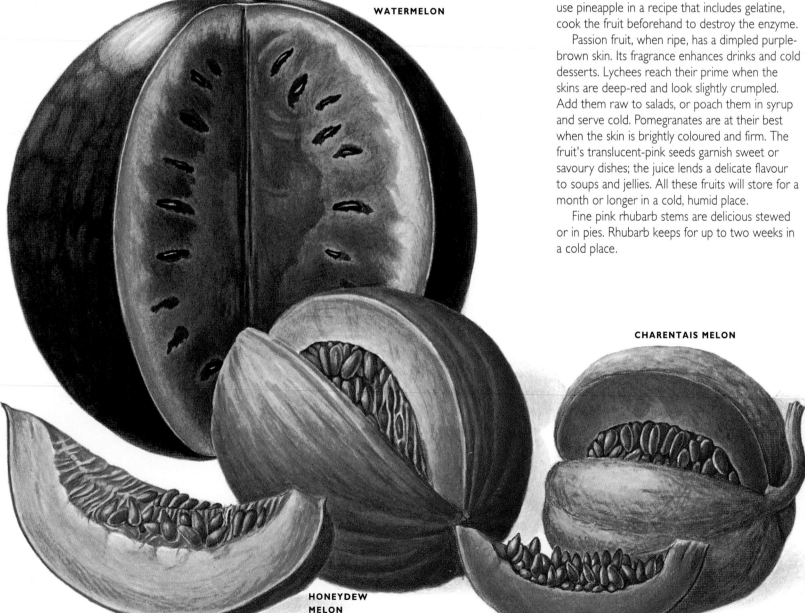

WATERMELON

CHARENTAIS MELON

HONEYDEW MELON

A Guide to Nuts

True nuts are one-seeded fruits with hard shells. The extended family of nuts, however, includes any seed or fruit with an edible kernel inside a hard or brittle husk. Most nuts, shelled or unshelled, keep for several months in an airtight container in a cool larder. The ripe kernels of most nuts are rich in oils which dry out with age; when choosing nuts, avoid any that feel light for their size or rattle.

The coconut is protected by a fibrous husk. When buying a coconut, make sure the shell is not cracked, and shake the nut to ensure it contains liquid. The coconut's sweet flesh, flaked or grated, is valued as a flavouring and garnish, while its milk may be added to drinks.

Walnuts, at their best, have a faintly damp sheen to their shells. With their pronounced flavour, walnuts are equally good raw in salads, or cooked in sauces and stuffings. The rich oily Brazil nut and the sweet hazelnut are useful in baking and confectionery. So is the almond, often ground for pastes and fillings. Bitter almonds are usually distilled into an essence for flavouring cakes and sauces. The pecan nut, a relative of the walnut with a smoother and elongated shell, may be baked in pies and pastries.

The chestnut has many culinary uses, both sweet and savoury. Its dry flesh may be cooked and puréed for desserts and stuffings; it can be boiled or roasted, like a vegetable, or preserved in sugar syrup. Chestnuts will keep for up to two weeks in an airtight container in a cool place.

The smaller nuts – pine nuts, pistachio nuts, cashews and peanuts – may be pounded as a base for sauces, toasted and served as a snack, or used as garnishes.

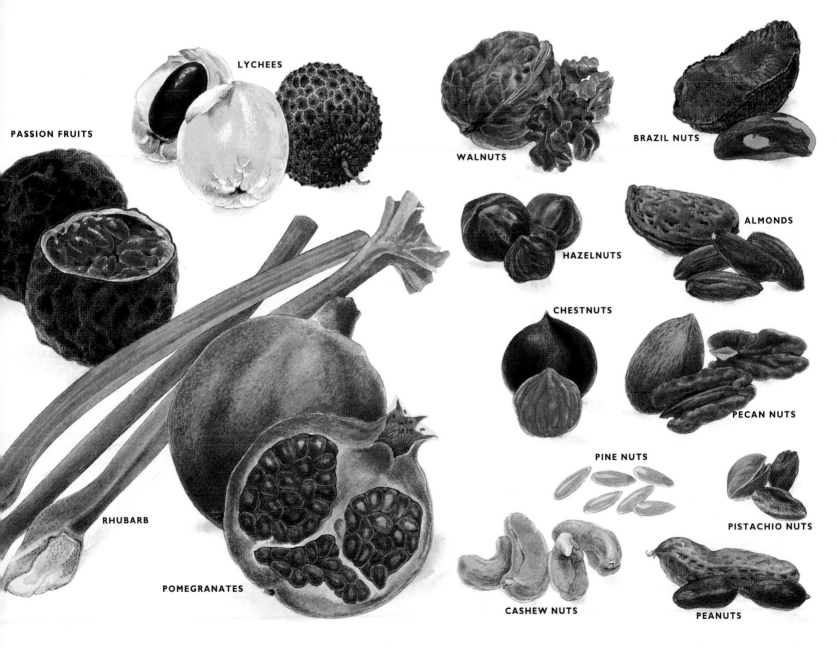

PASSION FRUITS

LYCHEES

WALNUTS

BRAZIL NUTS

HAZELNUTS

ALMONDS

CHESTNUTS

PECAN NUTS

RHUBARB

POMEGRANATES

PINE NUTS

PISTACHIO NUTS

CASHEW NUTS

PEANUTS

Types of Grains

All grains are capsules of starch with a protein-rich embryo or germ, outer layers of bran and more protein, and an inedible husk enclosing the whole. Cultivated grains, the fruits of no more than a dozen grasses, supply the staple diet of most of the world. Dried grains, displayed below, can be obtained as groats – that is, complete except for the husks – or in a range of processed forms.

Some grains – notably rice and barley – are available 'pearled', with the outer layers and the germ removed by friction. Treated thus, the grains have a smoother texture than whole grains and cook more quickly. Alternatively, whole grains may be cracked into pieces – which may in turn be ground coarsely to produce grits, or more finely to produce meals and various flours. When cracked grains are heated and pressed flat, the result is sold as flaked or rolled grain.

Wheat is available whole, cracked, flaked and ground – and, of course, as flour. The whole grains keep their shape well when cooked, and have an attractively robust flavour. Many wheat products have their own names. Burghul is a kind of cracked wheat made by boiling and baking whole grains before they are cracked. Semolina is the meal ground from a hard wheat known as durum wheat. Couscous is a processed semolina; at home, it is made by rubbing coarse and fine semolina into small balls, which are passed through coarse sieves to form pellets and a fine sieve to remove loose semolina. Couscous is

WHOLE WHEAT

RYE GROATS

BROWN RICE

CRACKED WHEAT

BURGHUL

LONG-GRAIN WHITE (PEARLED) RICE

COUSCOUS

SEMOLINA

WHEAT FLAKES

made commercially by machine-extruding semolina.

Darker in colour and stronger in flavour than wheat – although similar in texture – rye is available in whole and processed forms. It can be used in recipes where wheat is called for.

Rice is grown in a continuum of shapes and sizes, each with a slightly different internal chemistry that affects its cooking qualities. Long-grain rice remains separate when cooked correctly; rice with shorter, rounded grains tends towards stickiness. Both long and round-grain rice are sold in whole (brown) and pearled (white) forms. Glutinous rice, a less common and

quite separate variety, is available from Oriental delicatessens; it looks similar to ordinary round-grain rice, but when cooked it will form a sticky mass.

Wild rice, in spite of its name, is not related to rice. It is a rare grain harvested from a grass that grows wild in marshes in parts of North America. Much prized for its strong nutty flavour, wild rice is always sold as a whole unpolished grain.

By contrast, white and yellow maize – also known as corn – are more often sold as a meal. Sometimes, however, dried maize kernels are soaked in lye, a powerful alkali that removes the

tough outer layers. Maize treated in this way, then boiled to wash off the lye, is termed hominy. Dried hominy can be whole, cracked or coarsely ground into grits.

Barley is available both as a whole grain – pot barley – and in pearled form. It may also be cracked or ground to a meal. Buckwheat is not a true grain, but the fruit of a plant related to rhubarb and sorrel; it is, however, cooked like grains. Whole or coarsely ground, buckwheat is often roasted to deepen its flavour. Millet is a mild-flavoured fragile grain which, even in whole form, quickly cooks to a porridge. Oats are another soft grain with a distinctive sweet flavour.

ILD RICE

POT BARLEY

BUCKWHEAT GROATS

OAT GROATS

JND-GRAIN WHITE RICE

PEARL BARLEY

ROASTED BUCKWHEAT GROATS

OATMEAL

RACKED HOMINY

CORNMEAL

WHOLE MILLET

ROLLED OATS

Types of Pasta

Pasta is prepared from flour or semolina, first moistened to make a dough, then formed into any one of a vast range of shapes. These pages illustrate a representative selection of what you may find in shops and markets. Although all the pasta shown is sold commercially, many of the shapes can be made at home (see page 150). Homemade pasta is most often used immediately; commercial dried pasta can usually be kept for up to three years; check the package for shelf-life.

The semolina used in Western commercial pasta is milled from a particularly hard variety of wheat, called durum wheat, which yields an elastic, easily shaped dough. In Oriental food shops, however, you will find pasta made of other materials. The distinctively flavoured soba is prepared from buckwheat flour; rice noodles are soft and delicate in flavour and texture; cellophane noodles, made from soya or mung bean flour, are springy and slippery when cooked.

Spaghetti and macaroni are perhaps the most widely available pasta shapes, but there are hundreds of others, including numerous flat sheets, noodles and small shapes, that may resemble anything from wheels to butterflies. Most shapes can be obtained in a variety of sizes and many are sold with both smooth and ribbed surfaces.

The names for the various shapes can be confusing. Italy originated much of the Western world's pasta and most shapes are sold under their Italian names – but different regions of Italy use different names for the same or similar shapes. When buying pasta, look for the shape you want rather than concerning yourself too much with the name.

Common sense will tell you that some shapes are suited to particular purposes. To make a dish in which pasta is layered with a sauce, large flat shapes such as lasagne are an obvious choice. Long strands of macaroni can be coiled to make a casing that could not be imitated with any other pasta. Otherwise, there are few constraints; even when recipes associate particular shapes with certain sauces, it is still up to you whether or not you follow the convention.

TAGLIATELLE VERDI (GREEN NOODLES)

RUOTE ("WHEEL

CAPELLI D'ANGELI ("ANGELS' HAIR")

TAGLIERINI (FINE NOODLES)

TAGLIATELLE (NOODLES)

ZITI (BROAD MACARONI)

RICE NOODLES

SOBA (BUCKWHEAT NOODLES)

CELLOPHANE NOODLES

LASAGNE VERDI (GREEN LASAGNE)

CHINESE EGG NOODLES

FUSILI ("SPINDLES")

GNOCCHI SARDI
("SARDINIAN DUMPLINGS")

FARFALLE
("BUTTERFLIES")

PENNE
("QUILLS")

CONCHIGLIE
("SHELLS")

SPAGHETTI

WHOLE WHEAT SPAGHETTI

LINGUETTINE
("LITTLE TONGUES")

ELBOW MACARONI

NETTE
PLED NOODLES)

NARROW TRENETTE

CANNELLONI
(LARGE TUBES)

MILLE RIGHE
("A THOUSAND RIDGES")

RIGATONI
(LARGE RIDGED TUBES)

LASAGNE RICCIE UN LATA (LASAGNE WITH ONE SIDE RIPPLED)

LASAGNE

Types of Egg

Eggs vary widely in freshness, size and quality. Gauging these factors and understanding their effects is one of the keys to successful egg cookery.

Of the three variables, freshness is the hardest one to assess. EU regulations – which apply to all packaged eggs – require a date on every box to indicate the week when the eggs were packed (usually a numeric code: week I is the first week in January). But eggs may have been laid as much as a week before packing. One way of roughly gauging the age of an egg is to shake it gently close to your ear; there will be no audible movement in a really fresh egg, but you will hear the contents of an older egg shifting inside the shell. Other methods of judging freshness are the flotation test for whole eggs shown below or the dispersion test for broken eggs (opposite).

The flotation test depends on the fact that an egg's buoyancy increases with age. A newly laid egg fills the entire shell, except for a tiny pocket of air at the broader end. As the egg ages, however, water evaporates through the porous shell and the air pocket expands. After two to three weeks, the egg will be buoyant enough to stand upright in

Buoyancy: a Test for Freshness

A newly laid egg. To test the age of an egg, place it in water. A newly laid egg has only a tiny air pocket, it sinks and lies flat on the bottom.

A week-old egg. The air pocket, which forms in the broad rounded end, expands and gives the egg buoyancy. The egg tilts in the water, round end up.

A two-to-three-week-old egg. As the egg ages, the air pocket continues to expand until the egg becomes buoyant enough to stand upright.

SIZE 1: 70 G OR OVER　　　**SIZE 2: 65-70 G**　　　**SIZE 3: 60-65 G**

Grading sizes: Eggs are graded by weight on a scale ranging from size 1, the heaviest – 70 g (2^1/$_2$ oz) or more – to size 7 – less than 45 g (1^1/$_2$ oz)

water. After five to six weeks it will float to the surface; it should then be discarded.

At the same time, chemical changes make both the white and the yolk more fluid. These changes in consistency affect the suitability of eggs for cooking. The firm, well-centred yolks and cohesive whites of fresh eggs are particularly advantageous for poaching or frying. But it is best to use slightly older eggs when boiling for shelling; the contents of new-laid eggs cling so closely to the shell membrane that the eggs are difficult to peel. Eggs that are two to three weeks old, while no less nutritious than fresher eggs, are best used where appearance is not a factor – for baking or in sauces.

Eggs, however fresh, must be stored correctly, in a cool place at a constant temperature – ideally between 7° and 13°C (45° and 55°F) – or in the least cold part of the refrigerator. The pores in their shells make eggs vulnerable to invasion by airborne bacteria and odours; keep them away from strong-smelling foods.

Egg size is regulated by an EU grading system based on weight (see below); sizes 3 and 4 make up the bulk of those sold.

The Effects of Ageing

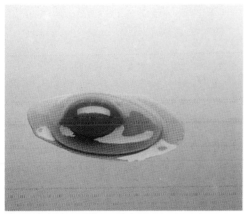

A newly laid egg. The yolk is compact and rounded, held near the centre by a thick layer of white surrounded by a small thin outer layer.

A week-old egg. The thick layer of white becomes progressively more fluid, merging into the thinner white. The yolk moves away from the centre.

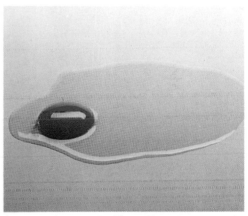

A two-to-three-week-old egg. The yolk spreads out and flattens. The egg's white thins to a uniform watery consistency.

SIZE 4: 55-60 G

SIZE 5: 50-55 G

SIZE 6: 45-50 G

SIZE 7: UNDER 45 G

A Guide to Soft and Blue Cheeses

The hundreds of varieties of soft cheese range from mild Port-Salut to aromatic Gaperon, and from creamy Brie to moist crumbly goats' cheeses. A selection of soft and blue cheeses is shown below; the cheeses are described individually on pages 72-3.

Cows', goats' and sheep's milk are all used to make soft cheeses. Both sheep's and goats' cheeses have a distinctive tang, although their flavour may vary from mild to very strong. Cows' milk cheeses are produced throughout the year, but goats' and sheep's cheeses are seasonal; and since the milking period falls between the months of March and December, these fast-ripening cheeses are not at their best in winter.

Soft cheeses owe their textures to their high moisture content – the consequence of draining the whey only partially from the curds. To achieve this result, soft cheese manufacture takes place at moderate temperatures, and little or no pressure is used to expel the whey. Unlike simple curd cheeses, all of the cheeses illustrated here have been left to ripen; they derive their individual character from moulds or bacteria

GORGONZOLA

SAINTE-NECTAI

STILTON

GAPERON

BLEU D'AUVERGNE

EDELPILZ

CROTTIN DE CHAVIGNOL

POULIGNY-SAINT-PIERRE

SAINT-MARCELLIN

TOMME AU MARC DE RAISIN

SANCERRE

VALENÇAY

LANGRES

SELLES-SUR-CHER

CHABICHOU

SAINTE-MAURE

BANON

LIMBERGER

that spread during the ripening process.

Soft cheeses can be grouped according to the particular type of micro-organisms they harbour. The so-called 'bloomy-rind' cheeses – Brie, Camembert and many goats' cheeses – develop a thick white fuzz of penicillin mould on their surfaces. The 'washed-rind' type, among them Pont-l'Évêque and Livarot, have been regularly wiped with a cloth soaked in brine or some other liquid such as cider or wine to keep the cheese moist and supple and to encourage the growth of surface micro-organisms. In 'blue' cheeses such as Stilton and Roquefort, a blue-green penicillin mould – often artificially added – branches out from the centre through the tiny fissures that remain in a lightly pressed cheese; holes punched in the curd help the mould to spread evenly.

When choosing soft cheeses, bear in mind that those with surface organisms ripen from the outside inwards, while the blue cheeses ripen from the inside – where the mould develops – outwards. An immature Brie has a hard chalky centre; an immature Stilton has no blue veins near the rind. Cheeses with an ammoniac smell, brown discoloration beneath the rind or a very liquid interior are past their best or have been incorrectly ripened.

MÜNSTER

FOURME D'AMBERT

MUROL

TOMME DE SAVOIE

DAUPHIN

LIVAROT

PORT-SALUT

CAMEMBERT

PONT-L'ÉVÊQUE

BRIE

REBLOCHON

BANON

HARZERKÄSE

A Guide to Hard Cheese

In the realm of cheese, the term 'hard' is applied to such diverse textures as those of well-aged Parmesan that is almost too firm to cut with a knife, of crumbly Caerphilly and of resilient Gruyère. A selection of hard cheeses is illustrated below and described in the glossary overleaf.

Hard cheeses are distinguished from soft ones (previous pages) by their low moisture content – less than 50 per cent. The dryness is the result of close cutting of the curd, relatively high temperatures during manufacture, and lengthy pressing, all of which help expel whey from the curd. Ageing further increases a cheese's dryness

and therefore its hardness; for example, a three-month-old Gouda might be classified as semi-soft, but a year-old Gouda is indisputably hard.

An important group of hard cheeses, Emmenthal and Gruyère among them, are heated during manufacture to relatively high temperatures – about 55°C (130°F) – and are

SAGE DERBY

BOERENKAAS

CHESHIRE

DOUBLE GLOUCESTER

COMTÉ

GOUDA

EDAM

FRIESE NAGELKAAS

CHEDDAR

BURRINO

TALEGGIO

TILSIT

therefore called 'cooked cheeses'. Heating and subsequent heavy pressure give them a very close, but somewhat flexible texture. A class of bacteria which is traditionally added to some of these cooked cheeses, such as Emmenthal, produces chemical changes that release carbon dioxide gas trapped in the ripening cheese. These bubbles of gas give the cheese its characteristic holes.

Most other hard cheeses are heated to around 40°C (105°F) during manufacture; they are known as 'scalded cheeses'. After scalding, some cheeses, such as Cheddar, are pressed firmly; others, such as Caerphilly, more lightly.

To make Provolone and Burrino, the curd is not pressed; instead, it is immersed in warm whey and kneaded until its texture is elastic and malleable enough to be moulded into a variety of shapes. The technical term for such a product is 'plastic-curd' cheese.

Gjetost, unlike all the other cheeses illustrated, is made from whey, not curds, boiled down to a thick paste. Gjetost's sweet flavour and brown colour come from the natural milk sugar – lactose – which caramelizes during boiling.

When you buy hard cheese, enquire about its age; choose younger cheeses for mild flavour and flexible nature, well-aged cheeses for a stronger flavour and a texture suitable for grating.

A Lexicon of European Cheeses

The brief descriptions of more than 70 cheeses on these pages are intended to help you explore the extraordinary variety of cheeses available. Technical terms such as 'starter' or 'bloomy-rind' are explained in the preceding pages. The cheeses are made from cows' milk unless otherwise specified.

The fat content of a cheese determines how smooth and rich it is but has less influence than moisture content on the cheese's degree of hardness or softness. Unless the entry specifies otherwise, the cheeses have a fat content of 45 per cent.

Cheeses described here as small are generally sold whole; medium and large cheeses are sold by weight, though you may occasionally want to buy a whole medium-sized cheese. The shapes given are the most typical, but many cheeses are made in several different forms.

Because it is impossible to describe subtle differences of flavour accurately, the only sure way to get to know each cheese is to taste it.

Appenzell. A hard, cooked, pressed Swiss cheese in the form of a medium-sized wheel. It has a fat content of up to 50 per cent and is steeped in white wine or cider and treated with herbs and spices during ripening.

Banon. A French goats'-milk cheese. Traditionally, it is made as a small cylinder that may be wrapped in chestnut leaves, but is sometimes formed into a stick and topped with savory. See Goats' Cheese.

Beaufort. A hard, cooked, pressed French cheese in the form of a large wheel, similar to Gruyère but richer than either, with a 50 percent fat content. It has narrow fissures rather than holes.

Bel Paese. A soft washed-rind Italian cheese with a 45 to 50 per cent fat content. It is sold as a medium-sized disc packaged in trademarked foil. The cheese has a close creamy consistency and a very mild taste.

Bleu d'Auvergne. A sharp-tasting French blue cheese in the form of a medium-sized short cylinder. Its thin rind is protected by foil.

Bleu de Bresse. A French blue cheese with a 50 per cent fat content, made as cylinders of various sizes. It is creamy in texture and fairly bland for a blue cheese.

Boerenkaas. A hard, lightly pressed Dutch cheese, formed in the shape of a large wheel. It is made exclusively on farms, with raw, unpasteurized milk. A glossy orange-brown rind encloses the nutty-flavoured cheese.

Brie. A soft unpressed French cheese with a fat content of at least 45 per cent, formed into a medium-sized disc. The bloomy rind is downy white, spotted with reddish pigments, and the inside uniformly creamy when perfectly ripe. The flavour is extremely subtle.

Brousse. A soft unripened French sheep's-milk cheese with a fat content of 45 per cent, called *brocciu* or *broccio* in Corsica. The curd is drained in a basket, which gives it its shape. It is sometimes salted and dried. See Ricotta.

Burrino. A hard plastic-curd Italian cheese. It has the form of a small gourd, surrounding a lump of whey butter – made from the small amount of fat that remains in whey. Cacetto is similar but with no butter in the centre.

Caerphilly. A medium-sized cylindrical hard, lightly pressed cheese originating in Wales but now made mainly in England. It has a flaky texture and a light salty flavour.

Camembert. A soft unpressed French cheese with a 45 to 50 per cent fat content. It is a small disc with a bloomy rind and a creamy texture.

Cantal. A hard, pressed French cheese in the form of a large cylinder, with a greyish rind and a supple light-yellow interior.

Chabichou. A French goats'-milk cheese formed into a small cylinder or flat-topped cone. See Goats' Cheese.

Chaource. A medium-sized cylindrical soft French cheese with a fat content of 45 to 50 per cent. It is a mild cheese with a soft white bloomy rind and a supple interior.

Cheddar. A hard, pressed English cheese, now made world-wide. It is a large cylindrical cheese; when young, it is mild-flavoured and pale, but flavour and colour deepen with age.

Cheshire. A hard, pressed English cheese. Shaped in tall cylinders, it comes in three versions: white, red (stained with a vegetable dye) and blue. The white and red Cheshires are mild-flavoured, salty, and somewhat crumbly. Blue Cheshire is richer in flavour, with blue veins developed in long maturing.

Comté. A hard, cooked, pressed French cheese; it is similar to Gruyère in form, taste and texture.

Cottage cheese. Traditionally, cottage cheese is a fresh, renneted curd cheese. Commercial cottage cheese is made from the curds of skimmed milk, heated to make them firm and dense and finished with a little cream. The fat content is very low – usually about 4 per cent.

Coulommiers. A soft bloomy-rind French cheese with a 45 to 50 per cent fat content. It is similar to Brie but smaller.

Cream cheese. Any fresh soft cheese made from cream or cream and milk. The fat content of cream cheese must be at least 45 per cent; if it contains 65 per cent fat it is called 'double cream cheese'. Cream cheese is generally prepared with rennet as well as a starter; for double cream cheese the cream is usually simply soured with starter and drained.

Crottin de Chavignol. A small cylindrical French goats' cheese traditionally kept for eating in winter: several months of ageing give it a dry texture and strong taste. See Goats' Cheese.

Curd cheese. Any soft fresh cheese made by coagulating milk and draining some of the whey from the resulting curds. The fat content varies between 4 and 18 per cent.

Danish Blue. A blue Danish cheese with a fat content of up to 60 per cent. A medium-sized cheese, it is made in cylinders, rectangles and square blocks. It has blue-green veining, with a creamy consistency and a sharp taste.

Dauphin. A soft unpressed French cheese with a 50 per cent fat content and a washed brown rind; most commonly it takes a rectangular loaf shape. The cheese is a relative of Maroilles (see opposite) flavoured with tarragon and pepper.

Derby. A large cylindrical hard, pressed English cheese with a close texture and a mild flavour. Sage Derby is flavoured with finely chopped sage leaves and is mottled green.

Double Gloucester. A medium to large cylindrical hard, pressed English cheese, coloured with a vegetable dye. Its texture is smooth and firm and its flavour well-rounded.

Edam. A hard, pressed Dutch cheese with a fat content of up to 40 per cent. Edam is a medium-sized spherical cheese that is encased in wax for export. It has a rather elastic texture and a bland flavour which sharpens with age.

Edelpilz. A medium-sized cylindrical blue German cheese with a piquant flavour.

Emmenthal. A hard, cooked, pressed Swiss cheese. It is produced in enormous wheels weighing around 80 kg (180 lb). It has the characteristic holes or 'eyes' often as large as a cherry, and a distinctive mild sweet taste.

Feta. A soft unpressed Greek cheese with a fat content around 40 per cent. It may be made from sheep's, goats' or cows' milk, or a mixture of these. It is a white rindless cheese, made in rectangular blocks usually kept in brine until sold. The taste is slightly sharp and quite salty.

Fontina. A hard, cooked, pressed Italian cheese with a fat content of between 45 and 50 per cent. In shape it is a medium-sized wheel whose rind is covered by a thin layer of wax. The interior has tiny holes, a sweetish, nutty flavour and a smooth texture.

Fourme d'Ambert. A medium-sized cylindrical blue French cheese. The grey rind is often spotted with red and yellow moulds. The flavour is full, with a pungent edge.

Friese Nagelkaas. A hard, pressed Dutch cheese with a fat content of 20 to 40 per cent. It is a medium-sized wheel, spiced with cloves either alone or combined with cumin.

Gaperon. A soft, pressed French cheese with a 30 per cent fat content. It is a small, dome-shaped cheese made from buttermilk or skimmed milk, flavoured with garlic.

Gjetost. A hard Norwegian cheese made of whey boiled down to form a thick, fudge-like mass. Its brown colour and sweetish flavour come from the milk sugar which caramelizes as it is boiled. It contains cream and 10 per cent or more goats' milk, and has a 38 per cent fat content. It is sold in rectangular blocks.

Goats' cheese. Any cheese made from goat's milk. Most goats' cheeses use a fresh curd cheese as the starting point. The cheese may be lightly pressed or not pressed at all before it is packed into small moulds. The character of the cheeses depends chiefly on their age. Initially they are soft; as they mature they become harder, acquire various surface moulds and taste stronger. They may be sold at any stage in their maturation. Some goats' cheeses are rolled in powdered charcoal, which forms a matt blue-black coating.

Gorgonzola. A medium-sized cylindrical blue Italian cheese with a 50 per cent fat content and a soft creamy texture.

Gouda. A hard, pressed Dutch cheese with a fat content of 48 per cent, made in the form of a medium-sized wheel. The texture is compact. The flavour is bland when the cheese is young, but becomes more distinctive with age.

Gruyère. A large wheel-shaped hard, cooked, pressed Swiss cheese with a nutty flavour, a smooth dense texture, and small widely dispersed holes.

Harzerkäse. A small soft German cheese with a 10 per cent fat content. The gelatinous, slightly sour-tasting cheese is made as a stick or disc. It is often sprinkled with caraway seeds.

Kefalotyri. A hard, cooked, pressed Greek cheese made from sheep's or goats' milk. It takes the form of a medium-sized cylinder, and has a fat content of 40 to 45 per cent.

Langres. A soft unpressed French cheese. It is made as a small flat-topped cone with a smooth washed orange-red rind. The smell is penetrating, the flavour quite strong.

Leyden. A hard, pressed Dutch cheese with a 20 to 40 per cent fat content. The rind is stamped with a design of two crossed keys and waxed. The cheese is spiced with caraway and cumin seeds.

Limberger. A soft unpressed cheese originating in Belgium but now made in Germany, with a fat content of 30 to 40 per cent. It is a medium-sized cheese, made in a roughly rectangular shape with a yellow-brown rind. The smell is extremely pungent – almost rotten – and the taste is strong.

Livarot. A soft unpressed French cheese with a fat content of between 40 and 50 per cent. In shape it is a small cylinder, with a glossy, washed, orange-brown rind, sometimes banded with rows of marsh grass. It has a strong smell and a strong spicy flavour.

Maroilles. A soft unpressed French cheese with a fat content of 45 to 50 per cent. It is a medium-sized square cheese with a glossy orange-brown rind and a potent flavour.

Mozzarella. A soft kneaded Italian cheese with a fat content of 40 to 50 per cent. It is usually made of cows' milk, but the original buffalo milk version has a more interesting taste. It is made in a small ball shape and kept moist in a water bath. It has a delicate, spongy texture when fresh, but soon becomes rubbery.

Münster. A small cylindrical soft unpressed cheese made in Alsace, with a fat content of 45 to 50 per cent. The flat discs, which are sold boxed, have a washed orange-red rind and a very pungent smell.

Murol. A soft pressed French cheese. It is made as a small disc with a 5 cm (2 inch) hole in the centre. The washed rind is pinkish, the flavour mild.

Mysost. Any Norwegian whey cheese; Gjetost (see opposite) is one example.

Parmesan. A hard, cooked, pressed Italian cheese, made in large cylinders with a 32 per cent fat content. It is aged for 2 to 3 years or longer. It has a distinctive flavour, which becomes sharp with age. The oldest hardest cheeses are the best for grating. Younger Parmesan is an excellent table cheese.

Pecorino. A group of hard, cooked, pressed Italian sheep's-milk cheeses with a fat content of about 38 per cent, made as large cylinders. The texture is granular and the taste is sharp; the cheese is generally grated for cooking. Pecorino Romano, Pecorino Sardo and Pecorino Siciliano are made around Rome, in Sardinia and in Sicily respectively. Similar cheeses are made from goats' and cows' milk, and are generally called simply 'Romano'.

Pont-l'Évêque. A soft pressed French cheese with a 50 per cent fat content, made in small squares and usually sold boxed. The washed rind is golden. The cheese is supple with a strong smell and a subtle flavour.

Port-Salut. A soft, pressed French cheese with a fat content of 45 to 50 per cent. Shaped as a medium-sized wheel, it has a thin washed orange rind and a creamy yellow interior. The texture is resilient, the taste mild and buttery.

Pouligny-Saint-Pierre. A French goats' cheese in the form of a flat-topped pyramid. See Goats' Cheese.

Provolone. A hard, plastic-curd Italian cheese with a 44 to 47 per cent fat content. It comes in a variety of shapes and sizes. Its golden-yellow rind is marked by the cords used to hang it. The cheese is smooth and creamy white. *Dolce provolone* is not aged and has a fairly mild flavour; *piccante provolone* is aged for a more pronounced flavour.

Reblochon. A soft, lightly pressed French cheese with a 50 per cent fat content. It is a small disc, and is usually sold boxed. The washed rind is pinkish white, the interior pale with a full creamy flavour.

Ricotta. A soft Italian cheese made from cow or sheep whey nowadays mixed with whole milk. The fat content varies from 20 to 30 per cent depending on how much whole milk has been mixed in. It is usually an unripened soft cheese with a mild flavour,

sold in the form of the basket in which it drained, or it is made into balls and dried for grating.

Romano. See Pecorino.

Roquefort. A blue French cheese made from sheep's milk. It is produced in medium-sized cylinders with a natural rind; the cylinders are matured in limestone caves. The cheese is usually wrapped in foil. The taste is strong and sharp, the texture creamy.

Sage Derby. See Derby.

Saint-Marcellin. A soft French cheese with a 50 per cent fat content, made from cows' or goats' milk: it takes the form of a small disc whose rind develops a bluish-grey mould. It is sometimes known as Tomme de Saint-Marcellin.

Sainte-Maure. A log-shaped French goats' cheese. See Goats' Cheese.

Saint-Nectaire. A soft, pressed French cheese that is shaped into a medium-sized wheel with a natural greyish rind, often scattered with yellow and red moulds. It has a subtle taste.

Samsoe. A hard, cooked, pressed Danish cheese. It is a medium-sized, wheel-shaped or square cheese with small to medium holes and a bland flavour.

Sancerre. A French goats'-milk cheese made in a flat-topped cone shape. See Goats' Cheese.

Selles-sur-Cher. A French goats'-milk cheese shaped as a flat-topped cone and covered with powdered charcoal. See Goats' Cheese.

Stilton. A blue English cheese with a 55 per cent fat content. It is a medium-sized cylinder evenly veined with blue. The texture is firm but slightly creamy.

Stracchino. Both the generic name for a group of soft Italian cheeses and the name of one rich soft white cheese with a 50 per cent fat content, which is eaten very fresh.

Taleggio. A hard, pressed Italian cheese with a 48 per cent fat content. It is a medium-sized square with a rough greyish-pink rind and a cream-coloured interior. It has a full flavour.

Tilsit. A hard, pressed cheese produced in Germany, Switzerland and Scandinavia. It is a supple-textured cheese, shaped as a medium-sized wheel or loaf, sometimes with small irregular holes. The taste is piquant and mildly sour. Caraway seeds are sometimes added for extra flavour.

Tomme de Savoie. A soft, pressed French cheese with a 20 to 40 per cent fat content, made as a medium-sized wheel. It has a rough grey rind dotted with bright red and yellow pigments. The interior is yellow, with a supple texture and a nutty taste. Tomme au Marc de Raisin is a version of the cheese coated in marc.

Valençay. A French goats'-milk cheese made as a flat-topped pyramid and dusted with powdered charcoal. See Goats' Cheese.

Wensleydale. A hard, pressed English cheese in the form of a medium-sized cylinder which comes in white and blue versions. The white version is crumbly, with a fresh clean flavour; blue Wensleydale is rich and creamy.

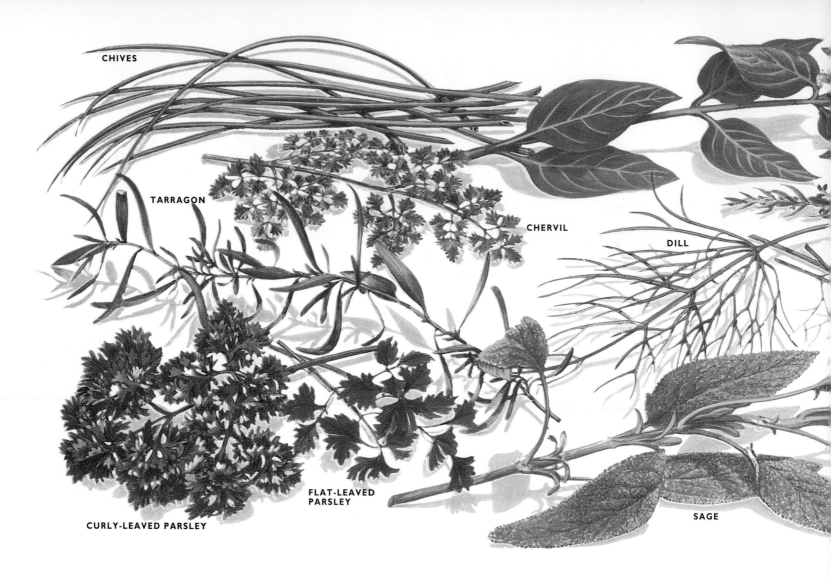

CHIVES

TARRAGON

CHERVIL

DILL

FLAT-LEAVED
PARSLEY

CURLY-LEAVED PARSLEY

SAGE

A Guide to Herbs

Herbs have been gathered or cultivated since ancient times – and not only for the kitchen. Four thousand years ago, Egyptian and Sumerian doctors were concocting curative herbal potions; less benignly, secret combinations of herbs have been used in many eras for casting magic spells. But the medical and magical functions have receded, leaving herbs their main role of improving the taste of food.

Vegetables, because of their great variety, offer the widest scope for cooking with herbs. Some combinations – such as mint with peas or dill with cucumber – have become traditional. But there are no cast-iron rules dictating that only certain herbs can be used with particular vegetables. The best guides are, as always, common sense, based on familiarity with each herb and its special characteristics – and the cook's own imagination.

A herb's flavour derives largely from its volatile oils, which are generally more intense when the herb is picked fresh. Fortunately, many herbs – particularly those illustrated on this page – retain much of their fragrance and flavour when dried. In the case of oregano and its stronger relative, dittany of Crete, drying actually increases potency.

Both oregano and dittany add zest to cooked tomato dishes. Sweet marjoram, also called 'knotted marjoram', marries well with almost any vegetable; so does pot marjoram, which has a flavour between that of the mild sweet marjoram and the more powerful oregano.

Rosemary also dries well, but it should be used with discretion; the herb is strongly scented and it can easily dominate other flavours. Its most important use in vegetable cookery is in outdoor grilling: the smoke from a few sprigs of rosemary

that have been tossed on the coals will subtly perfume the food.

The most widely used of the dried herbs are bay leaf and common thyme. Both can improve a broad range of dishes; together – dried or fresh – they form an important part of a bouquet garni. Used to add flavour to vegetable stews, the bouquet garni is a bundle of herbs bound with string that usually includes bay leaf, thyme and fresh parsley; the herbs are often enclosed in an aromatic outer wrapping of leek greens and celery stalk. Winter or summer savory may also be included in a bouquet garni.

The bouquet garni is only one way of exploiting herbs in combination. Equally useful are mixtures of dried herbs in which each element contributes its own nuances to a dish. Experience will help you to decide on a selection that best suits your taste. You

BASIL

LEMON THYME

LEAF THYME

HYSSOP

LOVAGE

CORIANDER

FENNEL LEAVES

SPEARMINT

can begin your experimenting with a well-balanced blend made of 3 parts of thyme, 2 parts each of oregano and sweet marjoram and 1 part of winter savory. The dried herbs should be blended together to form a homogeneous mix, and then stored in an airtight container in a cool dark place.

Other herbs, especially basil, sage, hyssop, mint, dill, leaf thyme, lemon thyme, lovage and the *fines herbes* – parsley, chives, chervil and tarragon – are best used fresh. Each of the *fines herbes* can also be employed on its own. Freshly picked flat-leaved parsley has a finer flavour than the curly variety. It is exhilarating when combined with raw garlic, both finely chopped separately and then together, in a *persillade* to be added at the last minute to a rapid sauté of mushrooms, vegetables, fish or white meats, alone or in combination. Chives, delicately onion-flavoured, and chervil, with its hint of anise,

are equally versatile. Tarragon is often used in chicken preparations; it is also the dominant flavour in Béarnaise Sauce, a traditional accompaniment to grilled fish and meats.

Other fresh herbs have their own distinctive flavours. Chopped fresh winter savory or, if that is unavailable, summer savory, whose flavour is neither so strong nor so clear, will complement broad beans. Hyssop, basil, lovage and leaf thyme (as distinct from common thyme) share a mild pleasant bitterness that improves many stews and baked vegetable dishes; lovage is particularly useful for its strong scent of celery, and for this reason it is often included in bouquets garnis. Sage is a pungent herb that is best used on its own and in small quantities; it is well suited to onion-based stuffings and whole fresh leaves may be pressed to the oiled surfaces of pork chops or slices of calves'

liver before grilling. Dried sage has a musty flavour.

Fresh dill and wild fennel leaves are sweet herbs that combine well with many vegetables – chopped and sprinkled over boiled new potatoes, for example – and are traditionally used in many fish preparations. The dried stalks and seeded flower heads of wild fennel flavour fish stews the year round. Mint – especially spearmint – is another refreshing addition to boiled young vegetables. Coriander leaves have a musky, penetrating flavour; also called cilantro or Chinese parsley, this herb is a common seasoning in Latin American, Oriental and Middle Eastern cookery. Lemon thyme has a startling aroma of citrus and is delicious scattered over salads or grilled vegetables; and it is a herb which is well worth cultivating for its scent alone.

A Guide to

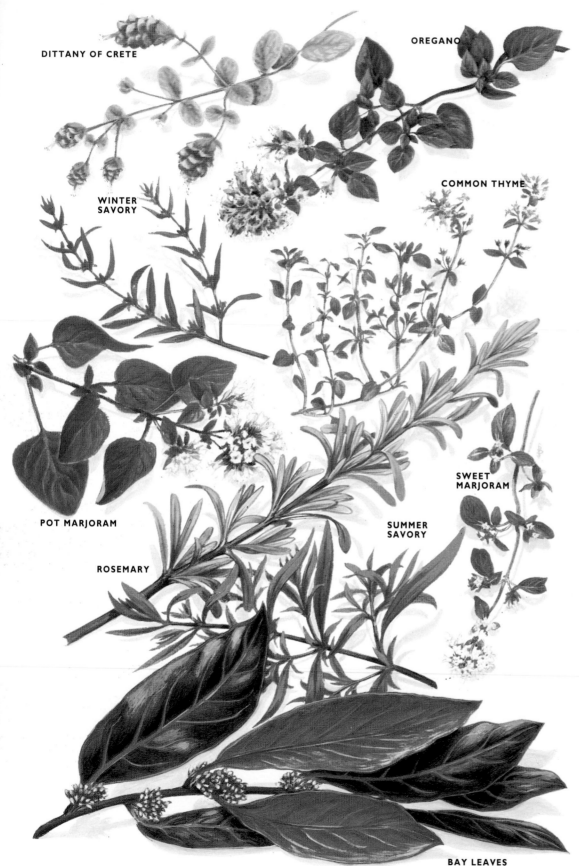

DITTANY OF CRETE

OREGANO

WINTER SAVORY

COMMON THYME

POT MARJORAM

ROSEMARY

SUMMER SAVORY

SWEET MARJORAM

BAY LEAVES

The term spices when used in cooking was originally applied to those aromatics imported from the Orient. Today that definition has broadened to include dried seeds and berries. Whatever their origin and whether they are hot, sharp or bitter, spices are generally strong in flavour. As they are usually dried, spices are often sold ready-ground, but such powders lose their flavouring powers very rapidly. Buy spices in small quantities as you need them, and keep them in a cool dark place.

Cinnamon's warm flavour has been popular in baking since the Middle Ages, especially in conjunction with dried fruit and apples. It is made from the dried bark of a tree, which is planed thinly so that it curls into the familiar 'quills' or sticks.

Nutmeg is the highly aromatic seed of a tropical tree. The lacy outer covering of the seed is striped off and used as mace. The kernel is usually sold whole for grating as required. Nutmeg has many savoury and sweet uses, from flavouring custards and soufflés to béchamel sauce and vegetables like spinach. Mace is sold as flakes or in powder form and has a flavour more akin to cinnamon than the inner nut. It is used mainly in pork dishes and with some seafood, like potted shrimp.

Cardamom seeds come from a plant which is related to ginger. In India, they are used to flavour rice and sweetmeats, while the Arabs drop whole pods into cups of coffee. The flavour of cardamom is quite delicate and is lost from ground varieties very rapidly, so it is a spice much better bought still encased in the pale pods.

Paprika is a mild sweet or hot spice made by drying a variety of red pepper and then grinding it to a powder. It is most associated with the cooking of Hungary and of Spain, where it is known as *pimenton*. It is used to flavour and colour some cheese and, indeed, its bright crimson colour makes it one of the most popular of garnishes.

Spices

Cayenne pepper is made by drying and grinding a particularly hot variety of chilli pepper, including the fiery seeds. It was the favoured means for 'devilling' dishes such as kidneys.

Black and white peppercorns are the berries from the Oriental pepper vine used as our most common flavouring after salt. The black are picked when just ripe and allowed to dry in the sun; the white are allowed to become very ripe before harvesting and the outer shell allowed to ferment before being stripped off, to give a purer flavour. Green peppercorns are picked when unripe and then usually pickled in brine or vinegar. Their sour fruity flavour is good with fish and duck, and in cream sauces and terrines.

Juniper berries have a pungent resinous flavour often used in marinades and stocks, especially with pork and game. They are also used to flavour many alcoholic drinks, like gin.

Coriander seeds have a much stronger flavour than the fresh leaf, with warm citrusy overtones. Their preservative powers have led them to being much used in pickles, chutneys and marinades.

Cumin seeds are possibly the most essential element in the flavouring of curries and are common in Middle-eastern and Indian cooking. In Europe, cumin has long been used in the baking of bread and to flavour cheeses like Gouda.

Saffron is possibly the most expensive and valued of the spices, as it is dried stigmas of a variety of crocus and it takes several hundred to make just 1 gram of the spice. Fortunately only a tiny pinch is required to impart its characteristic golden colour and subtle flavour. It is used most notably in rice dishes like *pilaffs* and *paellas*, and in Mediterranean seafood soups and stews. It is a good idea first to soak the strands briefly in stock or water before use.

Cloves are the dried buds of an Oriental tree, and probably best know to us as the warm background flavour in mulled wine and baked hams. The flavour of many a stew is deepened by the spiking of an onion with one or two cloves.

Allspice is the unripe berry of a Central American tree, with a flavour like a mixture of nutmeg, cinnamon and cloves – hence its name. It is popular in baking, especially with dried fruit and apples and pears, and features in marinades and cures for salt beef, as well as in pickles.

MACE   CARDAMOM   CORIANDER SEEDS   CINNAMON

PAPRIKA   CAYENNE PEPPER   BLACK PEPPER   WHITE PEPPER

CUMIN   SAFFRON THREADS   CLOVES   ALLSPICE

Preparing Food

There is really no point in buying the best of ingredients if you don't then prepare them for cooking with some degree of skill and sensitivity. This applies as much to simple essential everyday tasks like peeling fruit and vegetables correctly as it does to more ambitious endeavours such as boning a bird or gutting a fish.

A significant element in easy and successful food preparation lies in equipping yourself with the right utensils, from a set of good sturdy chef's knives – which you keep well sharpened – to a good pair of scissors, a ball of kitchen twine or a capacious mortar and pestle. Many such tools are obviously expensive items, particularly when you are setting up home, but the better the quality of your knives, for example, the longer they will last and the better service you will get from them. It is also surprising how many otherwise sensible people will gladly invest in a plethora of quite unnecessary and over-elaborate gadgets for slicing eggs and making chips, etc. – which are destined to fall apart in months – yet resent paying the price of a good basic chef's knife, which if well maintained and used will accomplish the same tasks just as speedily.

Becoming skilled in food preparation techniques also has other advantages in areas as diverse as economy, flavour, nutrition and presentation. For instance, you get much more value for money buying, say, whole chickens and cutting them into pieces yourself than buying ready-trimmed chicken portions – two breast fillets can be the price of a whole bird. As a bonus you also get all the benefit of the trimmings for making stocks and sauces. Whole fish filleted at home usually retains much more of its flavour and nutrients than pre-prepared fillets or steaks. Moreover preparing joints of meat at home can allow you to make carving easier or incorporate a stuffing.

This section of the book can also help you to widen your experience and culinary repertoire. After all many quite confident cooks are loathe to experiment with things like artichokes or squid – or even some less familiar types of dried beans – at home because they are uncertain about how to prepare them. You will soon see that they are probably no more difficult to with deal with than more familiar items like poultry.

Apart from all these obvious practical considerations, there is also the immense satisfaction to be found in, say, mastering the art of boning a chicken or creating a guard of honour from two racks of lamb, or even making your own fresh pasta, allowing you to bring to the table wonderful examples of culinary craft that really are all you own work.

Barding Beef & Veal Cuts

Cuts of beef that would remain tough if cooked more briefly at high heat – such as the thick ribs, top or back ribs, or topside – respond well to steady cooking at a moderate heat. Although not quite so tender as the back cuts, these have an excellent flavour and, with such leisurely roasting, yield juicy slices. Such cuts, however, have little natural fat, so ways have to be found to nourish and protect the meat as its cooks. The simplest method is the addition of a bard or sheet of beef or pork fat (see below) which is tied in place on top of, or around, the joint and which then bastes the meat as it cooks.

Barding can make it difficult to achieve a nice crisp brown finish to the meat. You can, of course, remove the bards towards the end of the cooking time and increase the heat, to produce a more traditional finish. Alternatively, you can create a lattice of barding fat, as shown opposite, which will perform the basting function efficiently while still allowing the surface of the meat to brown nicely. The presence of solid bards can also make it more difficult to judge the meat's degree of doneness by pinching (see page 214) as it cooks, so it is best to calculate the cooking time using the slow-roasting section of the chart on page 212.

A whole beef fillet, being so very lean, really benefits from a protective covering of barding fat when roasted.

Barding Lean Beef & Veal Cuts

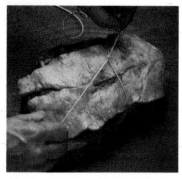 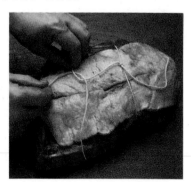 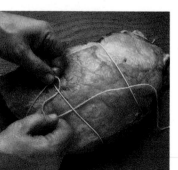 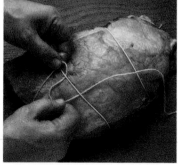

If you are roasting a lean cut of beef with little external fat of its own, barding by covering it with a sheet of extra fat will help protect it from the drying heat of the oven. Use beef fat, sliced thinly by the butcher, for its contribution to the flavour as well as the protection it can give. Trim the bard to the shape of your beef, place it over the meat and tie the meat and fat securely into a trim shape. Use strong thin string, looping it firmly and neatly around the length and width of the beef (above). Finish with a double knot, and trim off the string ends.

How to **K**eep **V**eal from **D**rying **O**ut

Roasting veal presents a special challenge. The best veal comes from a milk-fed animal a few months old. Since meat from such a young animal is difficult to digest unless cooked through, it must not be served underdone. At the same time, veal is one of the most delicate of meats – and high heat will leave it dry and tough, especially if the roast is small. For a veal roast that is fully cooked but still juicy, choose a cut that weighs at least 1.5 kg (3 lb), and roast it in a moderate oven for a relatively long time. The chart on page 00 will guide you – but the shape of the cut may affect the timing, so check that the veal is ready by one of the methods described for roast beef on page 214. Veal is done when its internal temperature reaches 75°C (165°F).

Lean veal cuts suitable for roasting – such as rump, loin, or the silverside shown here – need extra fat to keep them moist. Smear your veal with butter before roasting; or, better still, bard it (right) with fat that will partly melt and baste the meat as it roasts. Fresh pork fat, mild and smooth-textured, is the best material; a young calf has not developed enough fat of its own to provide extra barding pieces, and beef fat has too strong a flavour for barding veal. Cut the fat in 1 cm (¹/₂ inch) strips and lay it over the veal in an open pattern; if the meat is completely enclosed in a cocoon of fat, the surface of the meat will not brown. Barding in a pattern also creates an attractive dish: during roasting, the arrangement of barding strips forms a crisp, golden lattice around the meat.

1 Barding the veal. Lay strips of veal or pork fat in an open pattern over the veal. Here lengths of pork fat create a lattice design. Enclose the sides of the veal with broader slices of fat.

2 Tying the veal. Tie the fat around the meat to make a compact parcel. Place the veal in a flat pan large enough to hold it easily and cook it in a moderate oven until the roasting is three-quarters complete. The juices will run pink when the meat is pierced with a thin skewer.

Larding Lean Beef and Veal Cuts

Lean beef and veal cuts tend to be better endowed with flavour than with the internal fat that is so important in keeping meat from drying out during the cooking. One way to guarantee the meat's succulence is to introduce fat. This can be done quite easily through larding – a process that enables you to take advantage of less expensive, lean cuts such as shin (opposite).

In larding, strips of fresh pork fat – known as *lardons* – are inserted through the raw meat with the aid of a knife or one of the special larding tools demonstrated here. As cooking proceeds, the strips melt, thus basting the meat from within. And since the melted fat rises to the surface of the liquid in the pan or pot, it can be skimmed off. The remnants of the lardons will also chequer the meat

attractively when it is carved into slices for serving.

For the best lardons, choose firm white fat from the back and cut it into uniform strips about 5 mm (4 inch) wide and thick (right). Allow about 100 grams of fat to 1 kilogram meat (1½ ounces to 1 pound).

If you coat the lardons with seasonings, they will carry flavour right into the heart of the meat. You can first marinate them in an aromatic mixture of herbs and wine, or dip them in fresh or dried chopped herbs. Take care to insert the strips with the grain of the meat, not across it.

When you are larding a large piece of meat, arrange the lardons in a symmetrical pattern; this will give an extra distinction to the final appearance, as well as distributing the fat evenly throughout the meat.

Cutting the lardons. Trim off any rind from your pork fat, then slice it into lardons 5 mm (¹/₄ inch) wide and thick. The fat will be easier to handle while you are cutting the strips if you first chill it well in the refrigerator to firm it up.

Larding a Large Cut

Larding the interior. Use a *lardoire*: a tool with a U-shaped groove along the top. Thrust the point through the meat following the grain. Let the tip protrude well beyond the opposite side of the meat – here silverside. Lay a lardon, shown on the left, into the groove. Draw back the *lardoire* until the lardon fills the channel made by the point. Ease out the *lardoire*, leaving the lardon lying through the meat. Repeat at regular intervals. Trim the ends within 2.5 cm (1 inch) of the meat.

Larding at the Surface

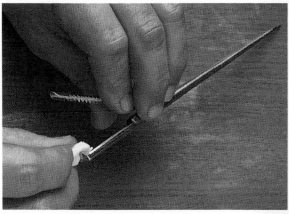

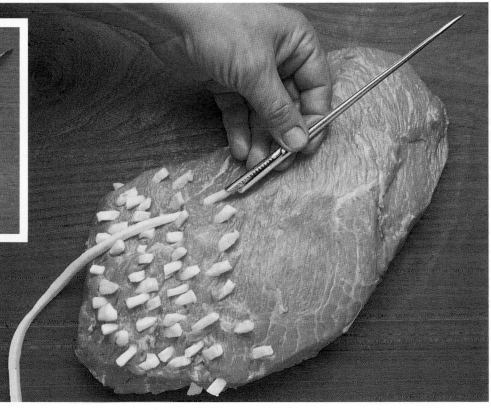

Stitching with lardons. Using a hinged larding needle, close the toothed clip at the handle to grasp the end of the lardon securely (above). Push the point of the needle under the surface of the meat – here veal silverside. Draw the lardon through the meat just far enough to make a single stitch (right). Release the clip and snip off the surplus fat, leaving the short length in place. Rethread the needle and repeat, one stitch at a time, in neat rows.

Larding a Small Cut

Inserting flavoured lardons. With the tip of a small, sharp knife (right) pierce the centre of each piece – in this case beef shin. With your fingers push a short lardon into the hole (far right). Here the lardons are seasoned first rolling them in a *persillade* (see page 164) consisting of chopped fresh parsley and garlic. After larding, each chunk of beef will contain a nugget of fat and flavour.

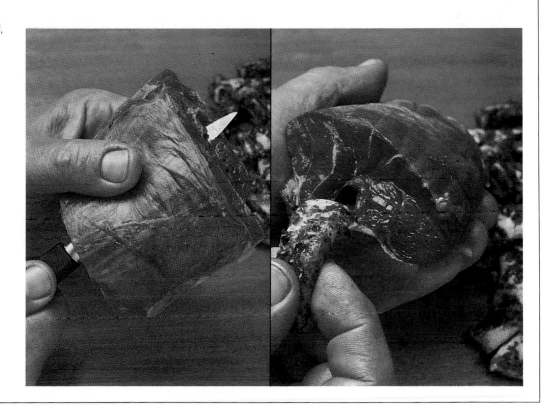

Stuffing a Breast of Veal

Breast of veal is a cut of excellent flavour, well suited to poaching. It is a flat, irregularly shaped piece with a series of rib bones on the inner side, but when boned, stuffed and rolled, as demonstrated here, it becomes a highly decorative as well as delicious dish.

Start with either a whole breast of veal or, as here, a half breast. Although your butcher can bone the breast for you, you can easily do this yourself; no elaborate skills are required. Place the meat rib side down and insert a knife just above the bones. Slice the meat away from the ribs in a single integral piece. (Reserve the bones for your stock-pot.)

Then, by making a pocket in the meat, you can create a space for stuffing (Steps 1 and 2). Forming the pocket is short work if you follow the structural layers of the meat. The natural division between the two main layers will separate easily; just widen and extend it using your fingers and a stout sharp knife.

For the stuffing, you can choose whatever ingredients will contrast with, yet not dominate, the veal; chard, breadcrumbs and herbs, ham or bacon and chopped eggs are possibilities (see page 165). Here the colour, contrast and flavour are contributed by a stuffing made with about 1 kg (2 lb) spinach – parboiled, squeezed dry and chopped – 100 g (3 to 4 oz) raw beef marrow, two beaten eggs and enough breadcrumbs to bind all the ingredients together.

When the breast is stuffed, simply fold the two longest sides over the pocket and stitch them together (Step 3) to give the meat a neat presentable form. Since the veal is flavoured from within by the stuffing, you can poach it in water with aromatic vegetables and seasonings: the resultant broth will be light and pure. If you like a more assertive tone, add some white wine to the water, or substitute stock.

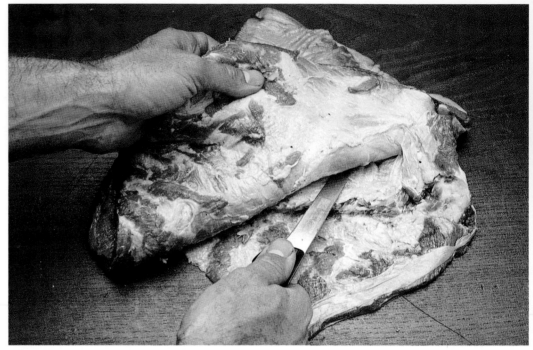

1 Forming a pocket. Start by working your knife blade between the two main layers of muscle to open up a pouch in the boned breast of veal. Make the pocket as deep and capacious as possible, while taking care not to detach the upper from the lower layers completely. Season the inside of the pocket.

2 Stuffing the breast. Lay the breast skin side down and fill the pocket loosely with whatever stuffing you are using. To seal the pocket, tuck the top flap of flesh gently but firmly around and under the stuffing, to form a neat cylindrical shape.

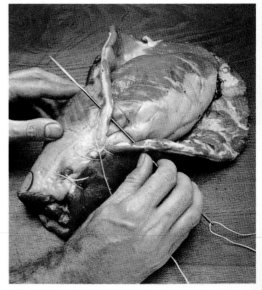

3 Rolling and stitching. Draw the two long edges of the breast together over the stuffed pocket. If they overlap you can, if you prefer, trim them off until they just meet. With a trussing needle and string, stitch the edges together at about 3.5 cm (1¹/₂ inch) intervals. Knot the ends of the string securely.

Dressing and Flavouring Steaks

Grilling time for a steak is measured in minutes; but best results require that you make a generous advance investment of time in properly preparing the meat.

First, allow the steak to come to room temperature: if the meat is chilled, the rate of cooking will be slowed down, and in a thick steak the outside will be overcooked while the inside is still raw. Dress and season the meat before placing it on the grill. And, since you should not be distracted from minding the steak every moment while it is grilling, be sure to prepare any accompanying sauces in advance.

1 Starting preparation. Remove the steak from the refrigerator about an hour before you intend to grill it. Trim off excess fat but, if you like, leave a 1 cm (½ inch) wide margin along the outer edge of large cuts such as this rump steak, since the cooking time will be long enough to make the fat appetisingly crisp.

2 Dressing the steak. Between the fat and the lean meat is a very thin membrane that shrinks when exposed to the heat. To prevent the steak from buckling, slit the membrane by cutting right through the fat to the lean at 3 cm (1¼ inch) intervals.

A Peppery Crust

Peppering the steaks. First crush the coating mixture – here, a combination of black and white peppercorns with a few allspice berries – and spread the spices on a work surface. Place the steak – rump, in this case – on the mixture and press down hard (above) to encrust the surface; repeat on the other side.

3 Seasoning the steak. To promote even searing and enhance the flavour, rub both sides of the steak with olive oil before cooking; use a brush or your hands to distribute the oil evenly.

Season the steak with salt and pepper. The salt will not have time to draw the juices before the surface is sealed by searing.

Mincing Beef by Hand

When a dish is not supported by sauces, strong seasonings or long cooking, it is particularly important that the basic ingredients should be perfect. If the key ingredient is minced beef or veal, the cook who chops it by hand can make doubly sure that the meat is immaculately fresh and free of unwanted fat or gristle.

The best equipment for chopping meat is a pair of heavy cook's knives that are the same length and of equal weight. With matched knives, you can easily achieve a chopping rhythm that will permit the heft of the cutlery to do most of the work. If you lack two such knives, don't try to improvise; a single knife will do the job better than two that are out of balance. Whether you use two knives or one, be sure the blade has a keen edge; a dull edge will mash the meat into an unpalatable pulp instead of cutting it cleanly.

1 Trimming the meat. Using a very sharp knife, cut the meat away from the bone, if any. Then divide it along the muscle seams into lean sections, paring away all sinewy connective tissue. The cut being trimmed here is chuck – a good choice for hamburgers or steak tartare, since its flavour is excellent and the mincing makes it certain to be perfectly tender.

2 Cubing. Trim off every trace of fat and membrane from the meat, and cut the trimmed sections of lean meat coarsely into fairly small cubes. The mincing will proceed more swiftly if you start with the meat in pieces of roughly uniform size.

3 Mincing. Spread the cubed meat in a single layer and chop it with a matched pair of heavy sharp knives, moving them alternately and rhythmically, as if beating a drum. Work with a loose-wristed action, holding the knives more or less parallel to each other in a relaxed grip and letting their weight do most of the work for you. As the chopping progresses the meat pieces will begin to spread out; stop from time to time and use one of the knife blades to flip the edges of the chopped mass back into the centre, turning the mass over each time. This helps to achieve a consistent texture. Continue chopping until the meat is minced as coarsely or as finely as required.

The Basic Hamburger and Variations

A lean cut of beef, such as rump, makes ideal mince for hamburgers. Less expensive cuts – topside or chuck, for example – are also excellent; they have a good flavour and, when minced, cannot be tough. Many people like the flavour and moistness imparted by the inclusion of a certain proportion of fat with the meat. But undercooked beef fat is not easily digested, so if you like rare hamburgers, use lean meat and mix it with a little butter. Season the meat mixture before cooking, but use a light hand: your aim is to bring out the flavour of the meat, not to conceal it. When you shape the patties, handle the mixture gently; a loosely formed hamburger cooks more evenly and has a more appetising texture, but it must be firm enough to hold together while it cooks.

Adding a Surprise Stuffing

One way to vary the nature of hamburgers is by mixing the raw chopped steak with special seasonings. But another way to lend variety is to conceal a stuffing of contrasting character and flavour inside it.

A nugget of soft cheese is a good basis for a hamburger stuffing. The Roquefort cheese shown here has a sharp enough flavour of its own, but you might prefer a mild cottage cheese, accented with capers or chopped anchovies or olives. The possibilities for improvisation are almost limitless. Try a pocket of chopped cooked vegetables, such as mushrooms or carrots, in the hamburger.

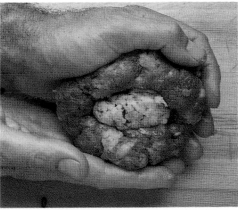

Filling the patties. To stuff a hamburger, simply press a cavity in the middle of it with your thumb, add the filling and close the meat around it. Shape the patty carefully and cook it in the usual way.

1 Seasoning the beef. Using your fingers, lightly toss the minced meat together with whatever seasonings you are using. Chopped fresh dill is shown above, but you can substitute any other fresh or dried herb that you like, or grated cheese, fried onion or minced capers.

2 Shaping the patties. Divide the mixture into portions and form each one into a ball. Flatten the ball on the top and bottom to give a good surface for searing but do not squash the patty. For a rare hamburger, make the patty as thick as 4 cm (2 inches); for well-cooked hamburgers, scale down the thickness to 2 cm (1 inch) so that the outside does not dry up before the middle is done.

Raw Beef Preparations

Almost invariably, the first forkful of raw beef is a happy surprise for people who are not usually blessed with an adventurous appetite. The two dishes shown here are found more often in restaurants than in home kitchens – but there is nothing difficult about their preparation. The indispensable first step is to be sure the beef is of perfect quality.

The name of steak tartare reflects its presumptive beginnings among the nomads of Mongolia. At daybreak – so the story goes – the provident Tartars would slip bits of raw beef under their saddles. By nightfall, dinner was tenderized from a hard day's riding and ready to be eaten. Nowadays, however, preparation of steak tartare is less time-consuming. The accompaniments may be prepared in advance; but the beef should be chopped – preferably by hand – at the last possible moment. Many cooks use fillet or sirloin steak – very tender but expensive cuts; rump steak is a slightly less expensive and better flavoured alternative. Whatever cut you use, every bit of fat and connective tissue must be pared away, for part of the merit of steak tartare rests in the perfect leanness of the beef.

Thin slices of raw beef with a piquant garnish became a celebrated dish at Harry's Bar in Venice, where they were first served to a favoured customer whose doctor advised him to eat only raw meat. The dish, named Carpaccio in honour of the great 15th-century Venetian painter, was prepared by slicing chilled beef paper-thin on a machine. Instead of using a machine, the method shown here relies on pounding small slices of beef gently until they spread into sheets so thin that they are almost translucent.

As with steak tartare, you can use beef fillet, or a cheaper cut thoroughly trimmed. Steak cut from the topside is used here; pounding takes care of toughness. It is economical: you can cut a dozen servings from 500 g (1 lb) of beef.

Steak Tartare

1 The presentation. Arrange patties of minced beef on a dish and surround them with chopped garnishes – parsley, capers, gherkins, onions and shallots are used here. Have coarse salt, pepper and olive oil at hand. To complete the presentation, make a small well in each patty; crack one very fresh egg for each serving, drain off the white, then slip the yolk into the well.

2 Final mixing. Give the diners two forks each so that they may garnish the dish to their taste; when they have chosen the blend of ingredients that suits their palates, they can use the forks to mix the seasonings gently through the meat, until they have a lightly blended mixture of contrasting flavours.

Beef Carpaccio

1 Slicing the meat. Trim a piece of raw steak of every trace of fat and connective tissue. Cutting across the grain of the meat, divide the steak into small pieces about 5 mm (1 inch) thick.

2 Pounding. Smear two sheets of clear plastic film with olive oil and place a slice of beef between them. Using a meat mallet, pound gently and evenly. The meat will spread very little at first, but once it becomes soft, it will spread rapidly.

3 Peeling off the plastic. To test the meat for thinness, hold the plastic sheets with the meat between them up to the light; if you can see through the meat, it has been pounded sufficiently. When it is thin enough, remove the top plastic film and invert the meat on to a plate. Gently peel away the other layer of film.

4 Garnishing. Fill the plate with slices of pounded beef arranged side by side. Decorate the beef with a criss-cross pattern of anchovy fillets and green peppers studded with capers and red peppers, and sprinkle with chopped chives; serve it at once. Lemon wedges, Parmesan shavings, French mustard, watercress, thinly sliced rye bread and mayonnaise could also be used.

B *oning* **L** *amb*

If the bones are removed from an unwieldy cut of lamb, such as breast, neck or shoulder, the cut at once becomes much more versatile. The meat can be formed into a regular shape that will fit neatly into a cooking pan and will cook evenly. Boned meat lends itself to stuffing. A boned joint is easy to carve. And, as a bonus, the bones themselves can be reserved for stock.

Before you begin to bone a joint, work out the positions of the bones. For boning, use your fingertips and a small sharp knife. A good deal of separation of flesh from bone can be done with the fingers alone. Where you need to use a knife, keep its sharp edge firmly against the bone so that you follow the contours without cutting into the flesh.

A breast of lamb (right) is easy to bone: the breast bone and the row of ribs can be detached in one piece.

Boning a neck (opposite) is a little more exacting. Each rib from the middle neck section must be twisted free and then the chain of vertebrae carefully cut out.

To remove the bones from a shoulder, you have a choice of boning methods: you can cut out the three bones to obtain a flat sheet of meat (overleaf, box, centre). Or you can bone the shoulder without slitting the flesh covering the humerus – the middle bone (overleaf, box, right). This method leaves a pocket for stuffing.

Leg of lamb is usually cooked on the bone. However, two partial boning operations make carving easier (overleaf). If you saw off the shank bone just above the knuckle, you will then be able to screw a carving handle – a *manche à gigot* – on to the straight shaft of bone which is left. And if you remove the pelvic bone, you will be able to slice the meat more neatly. The amount of pelvic bone in a leg varies. The leg as it is most often cut contains only a portion of it.

Boning a Breast of Lamb

1 Opening up a pocket. Position the breast rib bones uppermost, with the tips of the ribs closest to you. Lift up the flap of flesh at the thin end of the joint. Slip a knife inside the flap and cut under the flesh to separate it from the ridge of cartilage which lies beneath (above). With your fingertips, push the flesh away from the cartilage to open up a pocket.

2 Freeing the breast bone. With the breast bone nearest to you, insert a knife between the bone and the flesh under it. Work the knife blade along the entire length of the bone.

3 Detaching the ribs. Turn the joint round so that the thick end is closest to you. Grasp the breast bone and cut the bone and the ribs attached to it away from the flesh. With your knife, scrape along the ribs to free them from the flesh.

4 Cutting away the last ribs. As you work, the bones will fall to one side of the knife blade and the meat to the other. Cut away any tiny rib tips that still remain attached to the meat.

Boning a Neck of Lamb

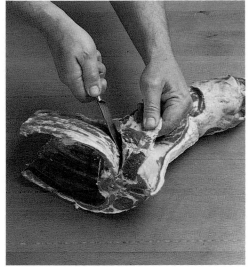

1 Exposing the rib bones. Place a scrag and middle neck joint on a wooden board. With a sharp knife held at a slant, scrape the flesh from the outside of the rib bones, so that the entire length of the bones is exposed.

2 Cutting between the ribs. Slit through the flesh that separates the end rib from the next one. Grip the end rib firmly; with your other hand, steady the neck. Twist the end rib free. If it does not come away easily, use the knife tip to sever the nervous tissue. Slit the flesh between the next rib and its neighbour. Grasp the rib and twist it free.

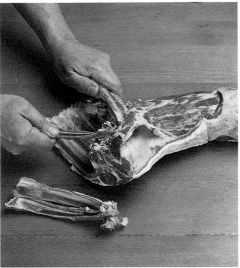

3 Freeing the remaining ribs. Continue to slit down the flesh between the ribs and twist the ribs free. When you have removed all of the ribs on one side, turn the joint over and remove the ribs from the other side in the same way.

4 Slitting the neck. Place the neck with the surface from which the ribs were removed uppermost and the scrag end pointing away from you. Feel along the neck to locate the vertebrae. With a sharp knife, slit down the centre of the flesh covering the chain of vertebrae.

5 Removing the vertebrae. Starting at the scrag end, and keeping the knife blade close to the bone, cut round one side of the vertebrae to free them from the meat. The flesh is very thin in places, so work carefully. Scrape down the length of the longer vertebrae at the middle neck end.

6 Cutting the vertebrae free. When one side of the chain of vertebrae is detached from the flesh, carefully cut away the flesh from the other side in the same way. When all of the vertebrae are freed except for their attachments to the back of the neck, cut the attachments free.

Trimming a Leg of Lamb

1 Sawing the shank bone of a leg. Cut through the tendon attached to the heel. To expose the shank bone loosen the flesh from the bone with a knife. Saw off the shank bone just above the knuckle.

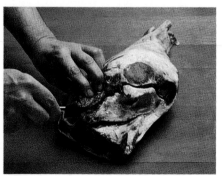

2 Loosening the pelvic bone. Turn the joint round. Cut round the exposed surface of the pelvic bone. Then cut deeper into the flesh, following the contours of the bone.

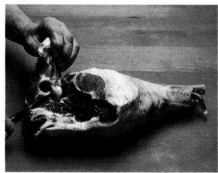

3 Removing the pelvic bone. When you expose the ball and socket joint that connects the pelvic bone to the thigh bone, sever the tendons joining the bones. Scrape flesh from the pelvic bone until it is entirely free.

Boning a Shoulder of Lamb

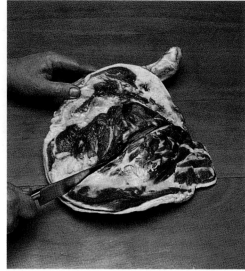

1 Slitting a shoulder. Set the shoulder skin side down. Bend the shoulder joints back and forth to familiarize yourself with the positioning of the bones. Make a straight incision in the flesh covering the blade bone, cutting from the point at which the blade bone joins the middle bone to the mid-point of its outer edge.

2 Exposing the blade bone. Cut away the flesh from the surface of the bone on either side of the incision. Fold back the flesh to the right and left, so that the blade bone is exposed.

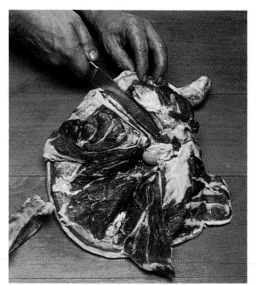

5 Freeing the middle bone. First bend the shoulder at the joint between the middle bone and the knuckle bone, so that you know where the middle bone ends, then slit along the length of the middle bone (above). Cut the bone away from the surrounding flesh.

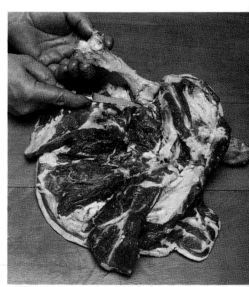

6 Removing the middle bone. When you reach the socket where the middle bone joins the knuckle bone, cut the tendons between the two bones and lift out the middle bone.

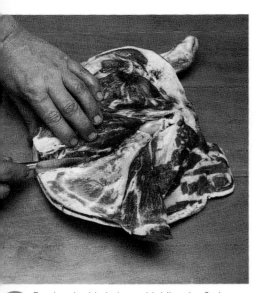

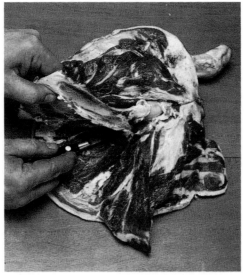

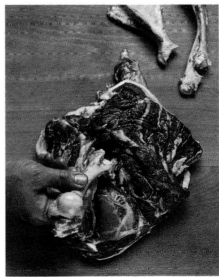

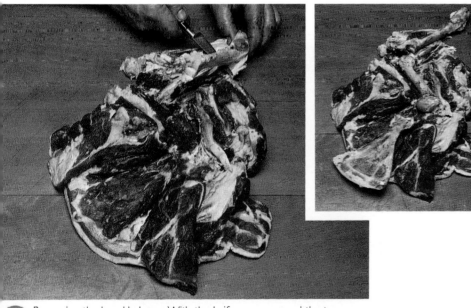

3 Freeing the blade bone. Holding the flesh back with one hand and keeping the blade of the knife firmly pressed against the bone, cut round the top and sides of the blade bone.

4 Removing the blade bone. Cut the flesh away from under the blade bone. Sever the tendons that join the blade bone to the middle bone (above). Bend the shoulder to loosen the ball and socket joint. Grasp the blade bone in one hand at the joint, steady the middle bone with the other hand and prise the blade bone away.

7 Removing the knuckle bone. With the knife, scrape round the top, sides and bottom of the knuckle bone to free it from the surrounding flesh (above). There is a thin extension which must also be freed of flesh. Cut out the bone. You will be left with a flat sheet of meat from which all the bones have been removed (inset).

A Pocket for Stuffing

1 Exposing the middle bone. Remove the blade bone (Steps 1 to 4, left). Leave the middle bone in place. Starting at the end of the knuckle bone, scrape away the flesh and remove the knuckle bone (Step 7, left). Scrape the flesh away from the knuckle end of the middle bone.

2 Removing the middle bone. Cut through the tendons at the blade end of the middle bone. Use your fingers to free the blade end of the bone from the flesh. Prise the length of the bone free of the flesh, then pull it away, leaving a tunnel.

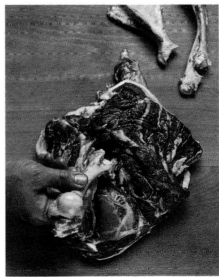

Depending on the way it is trimmed and arranged, best end of neck of lamb – the upper rib cut – will provide a simple or a spectacular presentation. A single rack of best end of neck forms a neat, easily manageable small joint. For a festive meal, you can serve a pair of racks, transformed either into a guard of honour (right) or a crown roast (see below).

For the simplest best end roast, ask the butcher to saw through the chine bone – the backbone – but not to remove it. Trim the rack and strip the rib ends as in Steps 1 to 3. Position the rack in the ovenproof dish rounded side up and resting on the severed chine bone. The bone will protect the meat as it cooks and can easily be removed before you carve the joint.

To make a guard of honour, ask your butcher for two matching racks, from the same animal – mismatched racks would mar the final symmetry of the dish. Have the chine bone removed by the butcher; you can trim the racks and strip the rib ends at home. Shape the rib tips neatly (Steps 4 and 5). Then, to turn the racks into a guard of honour – so called because of its supposed resemblance to an arch of swords – stand the racks up, press them together and interlace the bone ends.

If you want to make a crown roast, prepare two chined racks as you would for a guard of honour (Steps 1 to 5), then gently curve them into two semi-circles, stand them on end and join them in a circle. The central cavity logically demands to be filled. But an enclosed stuffing takes longer to cook than lamb does to roast medium-rare, so only cook a crown roast with a stuffing if you like the meat well done. If you prefer pink meat, garnish the roasted crown with a filling that has been cooked separately – sautéed mushrooms, for example, or a purée of peas.

1 Preparing racks. Position each chined rack, concave side up, on a wooden board. With the point of a knife, free the yellow strip of elastic connective tissue that runs underneath the backbone end of the ribs. Grasp the tissue and pull it out. Turn the rack over, slit open the shoulder end and slide out any remnant of the shoulder blade.

2 Exposing the rib ends. Score a straight line across the rack, about 10 cm (4 inches) from the tips of the ribs. Pull and cut off the layer of fat and meat between the line and the rib tips, to expose the ends of the bones.

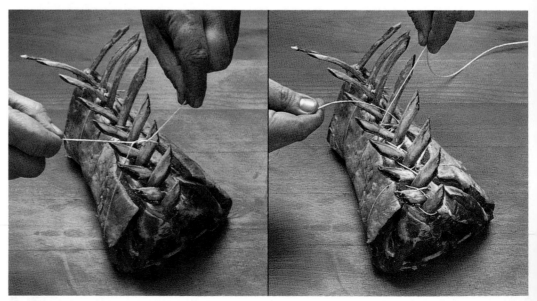

6 Joining the prepared racks. Stand the two racks up, concave sides facing each other, and press them together. Interlace the bone ends. Cut three lengths of string – each about 45 cm (18 inches) long – and tie each length vertically round the racks (above, left). Knot each string. Cut another length of string – about 75 cm (30 inches) – and weave it in and out of the crossed ribs (above, right) from one end to the other. Bring the ends of the string back along the outside of the crossed ribs and tie them in a knot.

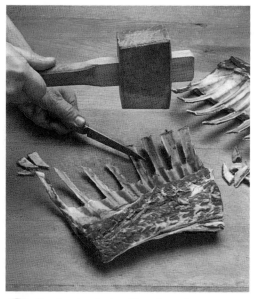

3 Slitting between the ribs. With a knife, cut out the meat and fat from between the bared rib ends (above). Save these strips of meat to use in stuffings or stews. Remove the bark – the outer membrane – and trim any excess fat from the meat remaining on the rack.

4 Shaping the rib tips. Turn the racks concave side up. Hold a sharp knife diagonally over each tip – making sure that the rib is flat against the board – then tap the knife sharply with a wooden mallet. If you like, graduate the length of the ribs so that when the racks are joined together the ribs decrease in height towards one end.

5 Scraping the ribs clean. Holding each rack firmly, scrape the exposed bones with the knife to remove any remaining bits of meat and fat. Be careful not to split the fragile bones.

Serve roast guard of honour in the classic French way with flageolets and French beans.

Stuffing a Leg of Lamb

An aromatic stuffing, which flavours a roast as it cooks, is a valuable addition to a joint. To create a space for a stuffing in a leg of lamb, some cooks remove the bone; but the meat will always be more succulent if the bone is left in. A better solution is to stuff the leg under the bark – the outer membrane.

The bark is pulled back, so that a stuffing can be smeared over the meat. Choose a light stuffing that can be spread in a thin layer. The stuffing used in this demonstration includes green bacon, mushrooms, herbs and butter. The butter helps the stuffing to adhere to the surface of the meat. Once the meat is covered with a layer of stuffing, the bark is moulded back into place.

The joint can be roasted in exactly the same way as an unstuffed leg. But if you want to give a crisp surface to the layer of stuffing, sprinkle the leg with breadcrumbs for the last 10 minutes of roasting.

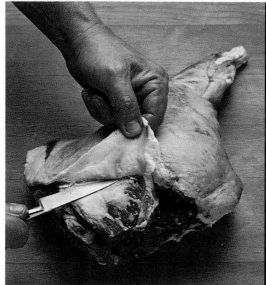 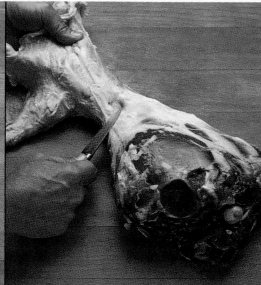

1 Peeling the bark from a leg of lamb. Remove the section of pelvic bone from the leg and prepare the shank bone according to your carving method (see page 90). Starting at the fillet end, carefully peel the bark and the underlying layer of fat away from the meat

(above, left). Gently force the bark free with your fingertips, using the point of a knife to loosen the bark where necessary. Try not to pierce the bark – but a hole or slight tear is not a disaster. Leave the bark attached at the shank end of the leg (above, right).

 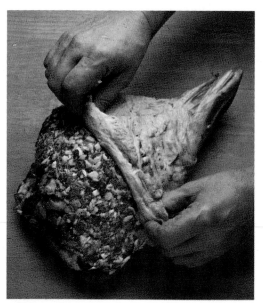 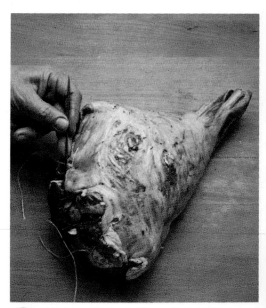

2 Stuffing the leg. Smear a 5 mm (¹/4 inch) layer of stuffing – here, a mixture of lamb trimmings, chopped green bacon, spring onions, mushrooms and herbs, spices and butter – over the exposed surface of the leg. Pat the stuffing down firmly so that it sticks to the meat in an even layer.

3 Putting the bark back in place. Ease the bark back over the stuffing, moulding it into place with your hands. Take care not to stretch and break the bark as you pull it back towards the fillet end.

4 Stitching the bark. Thread a trussing needle with kitchen string. To keep the stuffing in place, stitch the cut edges of the bark – at the fillet end – to one another. Put the leg, rounded side up, in a fireproof dish or roasting pan. Pat a little olive oil over the surface.

Stuffing a Rolled Breast of Lamb

Breast of lamb is a flat cut that must be boned and folded to make a compact roast. It is easy to incorporate a stuffing before the meat is tied up. And because the firm, gelatinous meat requires lengthy cooking, there will be plenty of time for an enclosed stuffing to cook through.

Here the pocket that is opened up when the breast is boned (page 90) is filled with stuffing, and stuffing is spread over part of the flat surface of the meat; the flap of meat left unstuffed is then folded over and the breast is sewn up in a pouch shape. During roasting, the meat will shrink and the stuffing swell, so that, by the end of cooking, the flat package becomes a plump cushion. Any substantial stuffing is suitable: here, a mixture of ricotta, ham and spinach is used.

Before the joint is stuffed, superficial fat should be cut from its boned surface. The fat and membrane on the outer surface should be left, to strengthen the stuffed breast and keep it intact during cooking.

1 Stuffing a breast of lamb. Bone a breast of lamb. Cut the fat from the boned surface. Spoon stuffing into the pocket opened up at one corner when the breast was boned. Spread a thick layer of stuffing over the exposed surface of the meat, to cover about two-thirds of the breast; leave the rest of the meat, and all the edges, free of stuffing.

2 Enclosing the stuffing. Fold the unstuffed flap of meat over the stuffed surface and the pocket. If you have difficulty in enclosing the stuffing, remove some of it; an overstuffed joint may burst in the oven while it is cooking.

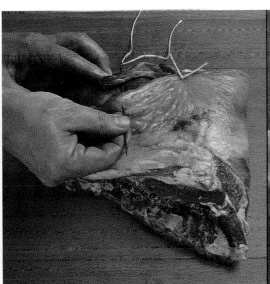

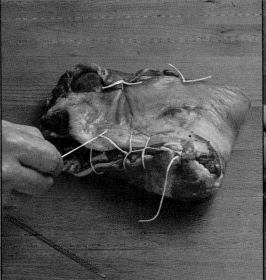

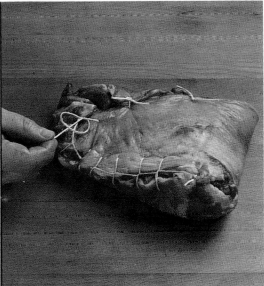

3 Sewing up the joint. Thread a trussing needle with string. Make two separate stitches, about 4 cm (1½ inches) apart, to attach the edge of the flap to the far edge of the pocket (above, left). Make a line of looped stitches to close the opposite, open, side of the parcel (above, centre). Finish off by stitching the short side of the flap to the pocket (above, right). Take care not to pull the stitches too tight.

Trimming Lamb Chops for Grilling

Exposed to the intense dry heat of a grill, small cuts of lamb quickly brown on the outside, while the inside stays pink and succulent. In the two techniques demonstrated here, thick loin chops are prepared for cooking on a traditional charcoal grill and chump chops are readied for cooking in a ridged grill pan.

Loin chops pose a particular challenge in grilling because they consist of three different types of meat with different cooking needs. On opposite sides of the bone are the tender eye and the smaller, still more delicate fillet; both of these need only brief cooking. However, the attached length of flank or 'apron' is best when well done, even slightly crisped. To cater to the different cooking requirements, wind the apron round the triangle of meat comprising eye and fillet, and secure it with a twig of rosemary or a wooden skewer (Step 3). The chop's five faces – the two sides of the eye and the three sides of the apron – can then be subjected in turn to the heat. For most of the cooking, the apron will protect tender meat from the direct heat of the grill.

For extra flavour, you can marinate lamb before grilling it (page 164). Here, the loin chops are marinated in olive oil with dried herbs. If the meat has not been marinated in oil, rub oil on the surface before you grill it, to nourish the meat and to keep it from sticking to the rack.

1 Trimming off fat. Ask the butcher to cut loin chops about 7.5 cm (3 inches) thick, and to leave the aprons long. If you refrigerate the meat, remove it from the refrigerator at least 1 hour before you place it on the grill: chilled meat tends to burn on the outside before the inside is cooked. Cut off the fat in the angle between the apron and the eye of the chop (above, left). Turn the chop over and trim the fat from the back. With your knife, loosen the fat from the thick end of the chop (above, right); pull it away from the flesh with your fingers.

2 Stripping fat from the apron. Loosen and pull away the fat from the apron end. To remove the whole layer of fat, cut through the fat at the point where it is still attached to the chop. To remove the fat embedded between layers of lean meat in the apron, cut into the apron and pull apart the lean layers. Strip away the exposed layers of fat with your fingers.

3 Skewering the chops. Trim most of the leaves from rosemary twigs, leaving a flourish of leaves at one end. Cut the other end of each twig to a point. Rub olive oil and dried herbs – here, thyme, savory, marjoram and oregano – into the chops. Roll the apron round each chop and secure it with a rosemary twig. Let the chops marinate, covered, for 2 to 3 hours before cooking.

Trimming Lamb Cutlets

Lamb cutlets are chops cut from the chined best end of neck. Suitable for grilling or frying, they are also often served cold as part of a buffet meal. The French style of butchery usually trims the rib bone of fat for about 5 cm (2 in). This gives a much more elegant presentation, allowing the addition of a paper frill, if so desired, and also providing a neat handle for buffet-style consumption.

You can, of course, now quite easily buy lamb cutlets ready-trimmed in the French style, but preparing them yourself does provide you with useful trimmings with which to enhance stocks, stuffings, etc.

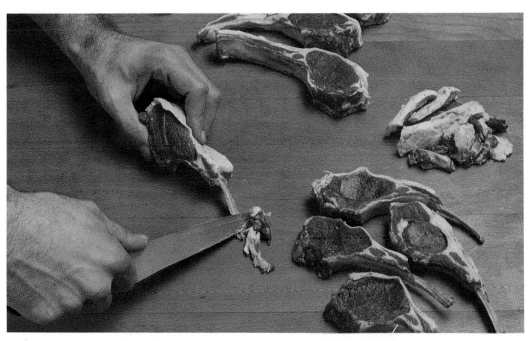

Stripping rib ends. Ask the butcher for best end of neck cutlets with the chine bone – the backbone – removed. With a sharp knife, trim any excess fat from each cutlet and pare all fat and meat from the last 5 cm (2 inches) of the rib bone. Scrape away any remaining tissue or flesh on the bone to leave it completely clean. Clean the meat from all trimmings for use in stuffings and stews.

Slicing Lamb Fillet for Sautéing

Both boneless slices of meat and cuts on the bone can be sautéed: loin and chump chops, best end of neck cutlets, slices from the leg, as well as the slices from the loin shown in this demonstration. In each case, the meat is pared of connective tissue and excess fat, dusted with flour and then seared in hot olive oil or butter.

Slicing lamb fillet. Trim any connective tissue and excess fat from the lamb – here, eye of the loin and fillet. Cut the fillet into three or four pieces. Slice the eye of the loin into médaillons – small, rounded slices – about 2 cm ($^3/_4$ inch) thick.

Preparing Chump Chops for Grilling

Trim excess fat from chump chops. Rub a garlic clove against the bone of each chop, then smear garlic purée over the meat (above). Rub olive oil into the chops, cover them and leave them to marinate for 2 to 3 hours before cooking.

Boning a Loin of Pork

All loin cuts of pork, including the chump end, contain a section of the spine; the foreloin and the middle loin also include some ribs. Removing the bones makes it easier to carve the cuts after cooking; and boning is an essential first step if you intend to roll the meat around a stuffing. Most butchers will bone the meat for you on request; but you will need nothing more complicated than a small sharp knife if you prefer to do the job yourself.

Although all loin cuts are boned similarly, details vary with the particular piece. Some middle loin cuts, as here,

are sold with the kidney. If you like, the kidney can be left in place rolled inside the loin for roasting. Or you can remove it (right) and cook it separately. The fillet, which runs beneath the middle loin and chump end, is also often prepared separately; left in place, it provides an additional layer of tender meat.

Before the spinal column itself can be loosened, the ribs must be cut free of the surrounding flesh and snapped away. The vertebrae that make up the spine are themselves embedded in flesh. Once they have been cut loose, the whole bone will come away easily.

1 Removing the kidney. Set the loin with the ribs uppermost. Lift the kidney away from the flesh, and use a small knife to sever the fatty membrane connecting it to the loin. Trim away any loose fat or meat to give the cut a neat shape.

2 Cutting around the ribs. Holding the loin steady, cut along both sides of one rib at a time. Press lightly on the knife to avoid cutting the flesh any deeper than the thickness of the rib.

3 Cutting under the ribs. With your fingers, prise the rib upwards and insert the knife blade crosswise under the rib's tip. Slide the blade towards the spine to cut the rib away from the flesh beneath.

4 Twisting the ribs free. Grip the rib firmly between your thumb and forefinger; with your other hand, hold the spine to steady the loin. Twist the rib to break it away from the spine. Remove the remaining ribs in the same way.

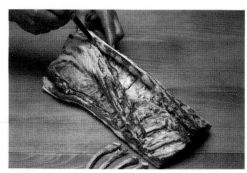

5 Loosening the fillet. The fillet is attached to the spine by a band of connective tissue. Cut through the connective tissue along its length; the fillet will fall away, exposing the spine (above). Keep the blade close to the bone so as not to slice into the meat.

6 Loosening the spine. Extensions of the vertebrae protrude at regular intervals from the point where the ribs end. Feel their position with your fingertips, then cut around and under them with the tip of the knife in order to free them from the surrounding flesh.

7 Cutting away the spine. To free the spine, work the knife blade along its length, lifting the bone away from the flesh as you cut. Save the spine and ribs to add to a pork stock.

Boning a Neck End of Pork

Neck end of pork includes the shoulder blade as well as a section of the spine; both of them should be removed if the meat is to be stuffed (overleaf).

In this cut, the spine supports a set of extensions, known as chine bones or spare ribs, as well as the stumps of the ribs proper. These must be cut loose (Steps 1 and 2) before the spinal column can be freed. The blade bone is sandwiched between two layers of flesh. The top of the bone is flat; but beneath, a protrusion called the keel bone extends into the flesh. To free it you must follow its contours carefully with the knife.

1 Loosening the chine bones. Set the neck end fat side down. Using a small sharp knife, cut under the chine bones that protrude from one end of the spine. Prise them in one piece away from the flesh beneath.

2 Removing the spine. Cut along the opposite side of the spine to the chine bones to free the vertebrae and the short rib sections attached to them. Lift the spine free as it comes away from the surrounding flesh.

3 Uncovering the blade bone. A layer of flesh covers the top of blade bone. Insert knife between the flesh and bone, and cut along the smooth surface of the bone to separate it from the meat. Lift away the meat as it comes free.

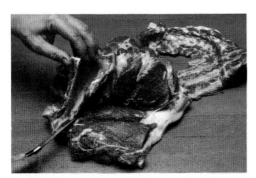

4 Removing the blade bone. The underside of the blade is irregularly shaped. Insert the knife under the bone. Keeping the cutting edge against the bone, cut around the curves of the protruding keel bone. Lift the bone away from the flesh as it comes free.

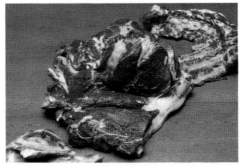

5 The boned neck end. Once the blade bone (foreground) and the spine with its attached bones (background) have both been removed, you will be left with a boneless cut, ready to be wrapped around a stuffing.

Preparing a Leg of Pork

Legs of fresh pork or whole hams, which are rarely stuffed, are always juicier when they are cooked on the bone. But you can usefully remove the pelvic bone at the top of the leg, to make it simpler to carve the cooked meat.

The pelvic bone is generally sawn in two when the carcass is divided, leaving only the small, easily removed section shown in this demonstration. If, however, you buy a leg containing a larger section of bone, you will have to cut more deeply into the flesh to free it.

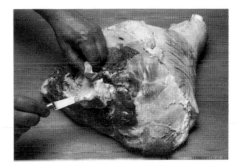

1 Loosening the pelvic bone. Set the leg or ham with its fillet end facing towards you. With a small sharp knife, carefully cut around the edge of the pelvic bone, to separate it from surrounding flesh.

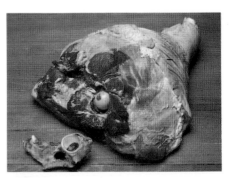

2 Removing the bone. Grasp the pelvic bone with one hand and pull it firmly to expose the cartilage connecting it to the thigh bone. Cut through the cartilage to separate the bones, leaving the tip of the thigh bone exposed.

Stuffing Pork Joints

Stuffings of fresh herbs or dried fruit are less substantial than the mixed stuffings described on page 165, but what they lack in body they make up for in delicacy of flavour.

Of the suitable herbs, sage and rosemary make the most strongly scented stuffings. For a more subtle flavour, use fennel leaves. Fruits that have an affinity with pork include prunes, apples and the apricots used opposite.

Herb-Filled Tunnels

1 Stuffing with herbs. Chop the herbs – here, fennel leaves – coarsely. Place a boned pork loin on a chopping board, pierce each end of the meat in several places with a paring knife, pressing in the blade to make an opening for the stuffing. With a finger, force some of the herbs into each opening.

2 Marinating the meat. Lay the meat in a bowl. Sprinkle over it any remaining herbs and pour in enough white wine almost to cover it. If you like, add a splash of pastis to reinforce the anise flavour. Leave the meat in the bowl to marinate at room temperature for 4 to 5 hours, turning it two or three times.

3 Drying and seasoning. Lift the meat out of the marinade, place a colander over the bowl, and set the meat in it to drain for a few minutes. Reserve the marinade for basting during roasting. Place the meat on a cloth and pat it dry. Season with salt and pepper.

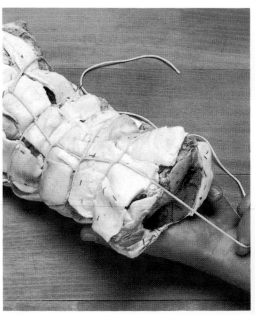

4 Barding and tying. Roll the loin into a cylinder shape. Cover exposed lean meat with pork fat – here, trimmings from rib chops. Truss the loin with string, looping it at 4 cm (1 1/2 inch) intervals along its length. Pass the string around the end of the loin (above) and secure through the loops on the other side.

Scoring Crackling

One of the delights of roast pork is the golden-brown crust of crackling that forms when the meat is cooked with the rind in place. Roasting makes the rind so brittle that it can simply be split down the middle, lifted away from the meat, and served in thin, crisp strips.

Before cooking, the rind must be scored all over and smeared with salt and oil. Scoring prevents the rind from deforming the shape of the roast as it shrinks during cooking; the salt and oil add flavour and help to crisp the crackling.

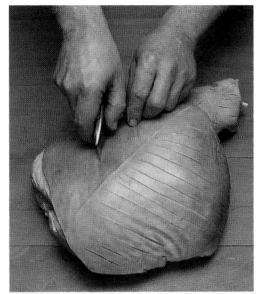

1 Scoring the rind. Remove the pelvic bone from a leg of pork (page 101). Trim loose fat from the fleshy fillet end. With a razor-sharp knife, or the craft knife shown here, score the rind lengthwise along the leg. Then make a herringbone pattern of incisions, each one only about 3 mm (1/8 inch) deep so as not to penetrate the flesh.

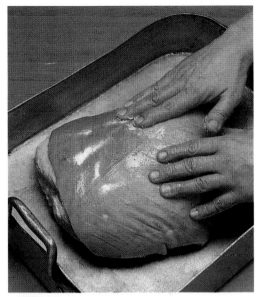

2 Smearing with oil. Place the leg in a large roasting pan. If you like, set it on a rack to raise it above the level of the fat and juices which it will exude as it cooks. Smear olive oil thickly all over the leg. Sprinkle salt over the leg, and rub it into the incisions (above).

Stuffing Pork Loin with Fruit

Loin is a good cut to stuff with herbs or fruits. It is simple to cut pockets for the herbs in the lean meat, and the fillet running along its centre provides a convenient prop to hold fruit stuffings in place. Before cooking, bone the loin (page 100) for easy carving, and bard exposed flesh with pork fat to prevent it from drying. The loin rind is excellent for this purpose; ask your butcher to reserve it for you.

1 Stuffing. Soak dried fruit – here, stoned apricots – in white wine for about 3 hours. Place the boned loin fleshy side up. Lay the softened apricots on it in two rows – one on each side of the fillet that runs down the centre of the loin.

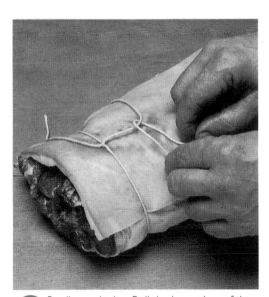

2 Barding and tying. Roll the long edges of the loin around the apricots and bard the exposed flesh with a thin layer of fat or rind. Tie the rolled meat and rind with string, as shown in Step 4, opposite. Place the trussed loin, barded side down, in an ungreased roasting pan.

Jointing Poultry for Economy

Poultry pieces purchased from a shop or supermarket are sometimes of poor quality and, weight for weight, are more expensive than a whole bird. By learning how to cut up poultry at home, you can save money and also provide neater-looking, more appetising portions. And there is a bonus, too, in the giblets if you are lucky enough these days to be supplied with them.

The process is simpler than it appears and, approached with confidence, can be accomplished in a few minutes. All you need are a chopping board and a heavy cook's knife with a sharp edge and pointed blade. However, the key to cutting up poultry into tidy pieces lies in your own hands. Learn to locate the joints by feel so that, when you bear down on the knife, you avoid the bones and cut through the less resistant tendons and cartilage.

On these pages, a chicken is used to demonstrate the technique, but since all birds have the same basic anatomy, you can adapt the steps to cut up duck, turkey, guinea-fowl and other poultry.

The lettered diagram above summarizes the simplest way to divide up a whole chicken. The most convenient place to begin is at the legs, which yield drumsticks (A) and thigh pieces (B). After the wings (C) are removed, the ribcage is cut through (Step 4) to separate the back and breast. The back is divided into two pieces (D and E) by cutting across the spine. The final step is cutting the breast into two portions (F) by splitting it lengthwise.

1 Removing the legs. Place the chicken, breast side up, on a board. Pull one leg gently away from the body and cut through the skin between the body and the thigh. Now bend the whole leg firmly outwards until the ball of the thigh bone pops from its socket. Cut down between ball and socket, and the leg will come cleanly away. Repeat this procedure with the other leg.

2 Dividing the legs. Place each whole chicken leg in turn on the board, skin side down, and cut firmly down through the joint to separate drumsticks from thighs. If the bird is a very small one, this step may be omitted.

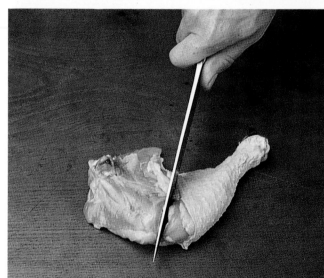

3 Removing the wings. Press one wing against the body of the bird, both ports of the shoulder joint will now be visible beneath the skin. Make an incision between the ball and socket of the joint, then pull the wing outwards and cut down through the skin at the base of the wing. Remove the other wing by the same method.

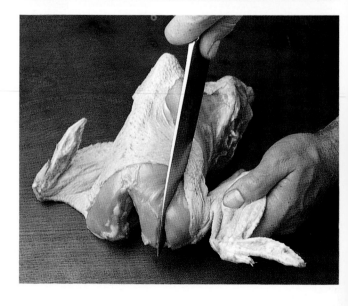

4 Splitting the carcass. Place the knife blade inside the cavity of the bird and pierce one side between the shoulder joint and the ribcage. Cutting towards yourself, parallel to the backbone, carefully slit the ribcage. Repeat the same steps on the bird's other side.

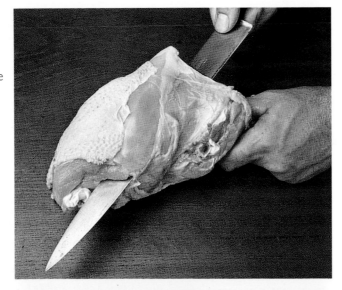

5 Separating the breast. Pull the breast away from the back to expose the shoulder bones. Cut down between these bones to detach the breast section (right). Next, divide the back into two pieces by cutting across the spine at the point where the ribcage ends.

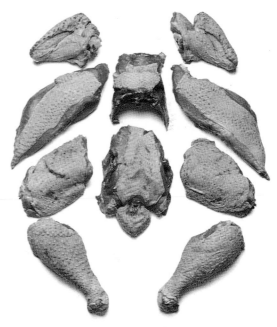

The method described on these pages yields 10 pieces. No part of the carcass is wasted, but the sizes of the pieces differ widely.

6 Halving the breast. Place the breast skin side up on the chopping board. Using a strong steady pressure on the knife, cut down through the breastbone on one or the other side of its keel. Larger birds, such as turkey or goose, can be cut again across to yield between four and six breast portions.

Boning Whole Birds

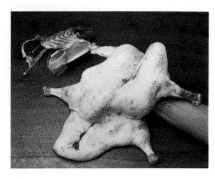

Stuffed, boned poultry is an impressive demonstration of the cook's art. With bones removed, a stuffed bird can be served in slices – a simple method of carving that wastes no meat. The extracted bones furnish rich stock for cooking the bird. Best of all, the method will provide six portions from a duck, instead of the usual two or three.

The apparently intricate boning technique can easily be mastered by any cook who has learned to cut up a chicken (see previous pages); it is identical for all types of poultry. All you need are a small very sharp knife and patience. The first try may take up to an hour; the second time it will go more quickly.

The boning process, demonstrated here on a duck, keeps the skin intact, with no slits except the openings where the butcher cleaned the bird. First, the structure comprising the wishbone, collar-bones and shoulder-blades is removed. The flesh can then be carefully peeled back from the carcass. At this stage the boned bird resembles a limp meaty sack (above). The main wing and leg bones are left in place, so that the bird – after it has been stuffed, trussed and cooked – will have a natural, untouched appearance.

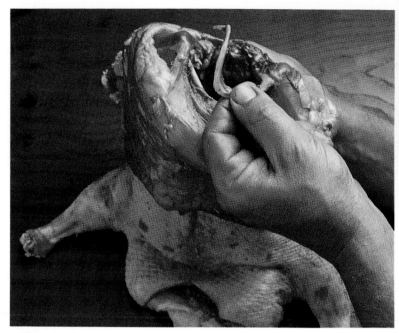

1 Removing the wishbone. Pull the flap of skin from the duck's neck down around the shoulders, turning it inside out until you can locate the wishbone with your fingers. Slit just deep enough into the surrounding flesh to expose the wishbone fully. Snap the wishbone from its attachment at the shoulder joints, where it meets the collar-bones, shoulder-blades and wing bones.

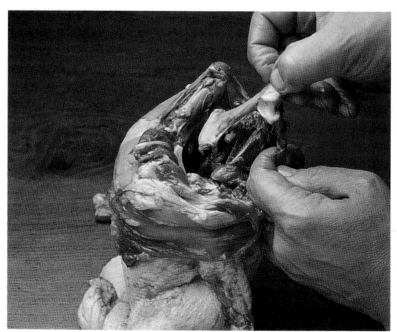

4 Removing the collar-bones and shoulder-blades. Each collar-bone is now attached only by a connecting joint to a shoulder blade – a thin strut whose other end is embedded in the flesh. Pare back the flesh around one joint to expose it fully. Then remove both bones by pulling steadily on the joint (above). If the bone breaks, cut out any remaining pieces with the knife. Repeat the procedure with the other collar-bone and shoulder-blade.

5 Exposing the skeleton. Pull back the flesh around the shoulders to reveal the top of the skeletal structure comprising ribcage, breastbone and backbone. Working towards the legs, scrape the flesh from the skeleton, using fingers and knife (above). To avoid damaging the skin, always cut towards the carcass. Where the backbone is attached by the cartilaginous tips of the vertebrae, slice through these tips, but leave them in the flesh.

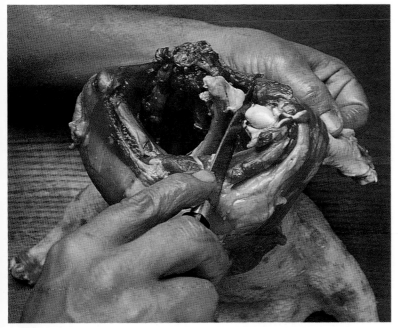

2 Freeing the wings. Pull back one wing as shown above, until you have exposed the tough bands of sinew that hold the wing bone to the collar-bone and the shoulder-blade. Cut through these sinews to separate the wing, but do not pull out the wing bone. Repeat the procedure with the other wing.

3 Snapping the collar-bones from the breastbone. One end of each collar-bone is attached to the corresponding shoulder-blade, the other end is joined to the breastbone by a weak and easily broken seam of cartilage. First, clear the surrounding flesh from the collar-bones with your fingers, scraping with the knife where necessary; then, snap them free from the breastbone.

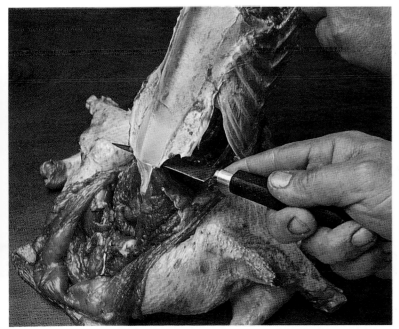

6 Separating the breastbone. When the knife reaches the legs, pop the bones from the ball-and-socket joints where they join the spine and cut through the connecting cartilage. Leave the leg bones in place. Continue peeling back the flesh until you reach the end of the breastbone: a thin strip of cartilage connects it to the body. Cut through this strip (above) to free the breastbone.

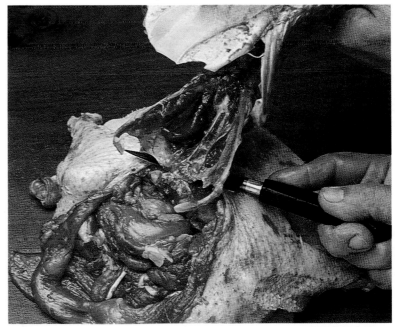

7 Removing the skeleton. The flesh will now be almost completely peeled away from the skeleton. Lift up the skeleton and cut through the backbone at the tail (above), leaving behind the last three or four vertebrae – the tail's bone structure. If the lower ribs, which are not firmly attached to the rest of the skeleton, remain in the flesh, cut them out. The boned duck is now ready to be filled with a stuffing (page 166), trussed and cooked.

Trussing Poultry

Oven-roasting is perhaps the simplest of all cooking methods: put the bird in the oven (see page 216 for temperatures and times), baste it, turn it periodically so that it browns evenly and take it out ready to eat. But a few preliminaries will greatly improve the dish.

Removing the wishbone from the uncooked bird (right) will enable you to carve the breast easily and more neatly, after roasting. If the bird – here a turkey – has a high-arched breast that might colour too quickly, thump the ridge of the breast with your fist to flatten it a little.

Stuffing, of course, adds variety of flavour and of texture, and it helps prevent the bird from drying out in the oven (see pages 166-7).

The next step – trussing the bird – provides a tidy look for any kind of poultry. More importantly, by holding the legs and wings close to the bulk of the body, trussing gives a compact shape that will cook at the same rate throughout.

The skin of a lean bird should be generously smeared with fat or barded – covered with strips of fat bacon – as a protection against the intense dry heat.

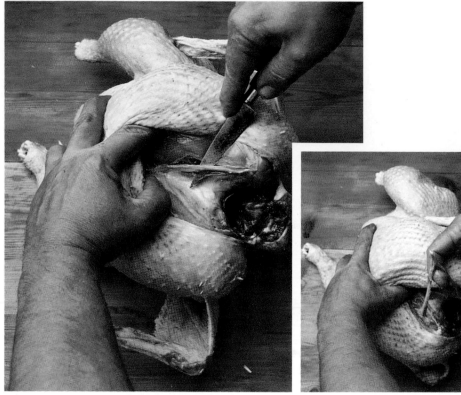

1 Removing the wishbone. Turn the bird breast-up and pull back the neck skin until you are able to locate the wishbone with your fingers. With the tip of a small knife, cut through the flesh under the contour of the bone on both sides just deeply enough to free it (above, left). When the bone is attached only at the ends, hook your finger under it (inset) and pull it out.

3 Closing the tail vent. Thread a trussing needle with butcher's twine or thin string. Starting at one end of the vent and leaving a tail of string about 10 cm (4 inches) long, sew up the vent by stitching through both edges of the flesh. Cut off the string, leaving a 10 cm (4 inch) length hanging. Omit this step if the tail vent is small and neat.

4 Securing the neck flap and wings. After threading the trussing needle again with twine or string – at least 60 cm (2 feet) is a convenient length for any bird – fold the wing tips as shown and fold the flap of neck skin on to the back. Pass the needle through one wing, the shoulder and the neck flap, and out through the other wing.

5 Securing the drumsticks. Turn the bird breast uppermost. Using the same string as in Step 4, pass the needle through the upper part of one drumstick and the body, and out through the same point in the opposite drumstick.

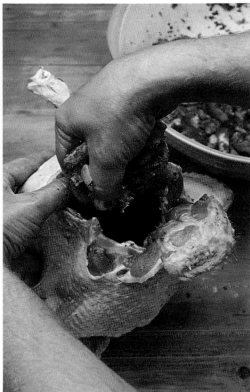

2 Stuffing the bird. Fill the cavity partly through its tail vent (above) and partly through its neck. Do not pack the stuffing tightly; stuffing expands slightly as it cooks and the skin of an overstuffed bird may split.

Tying with a Single Length of String

Although a long trussing needle is essential for dealing with bulky birds like turkey, smaller birds can be trussed effectively using just one long piece of string. You will need at least twice as much string as would be necessary to encircle the bird lengthwise; a generous length is easier to pull tight, and the excess can be cut off on completion.

Before you begin to truss the bird, pull down the flap of neck skin and fold it over to close the neck opening. If the bird has been stuffed, handle it carefully so that the stuffing does not spill out.

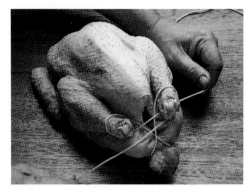

1 Securing the drumsticks. Place the bird on its back with the string underneath its tail. Cross the string ends and loop each end over and around the opposite drumstick. Pull both ends away from the bird to draw the drumsticks and tail tightly together over the vent.

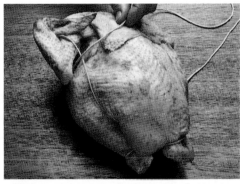

2 Completing trussing. Turn bird on its breast. Leaving one string end loose, bring the other end across the thigh, loop it around the upper wing, and pull it firmly across the neck flap. Still working with the same end, loop the string around the other wing, tie it securely with the loose end of string and cut off the excess.

6 Tying the first knot. Remove the needle from the string. Turn the bird on its side, with the loose ends of string from leg and wing on top. Pull the string tight, tie a secure knot close to the wing (above) and cut off the excess string.

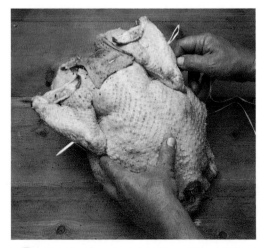

7 Securing the wing joints. Thread the needle with another length of twine or string 60 cm (2 feet) long. Turn the bird breast-down. Insert the needle through the wing near the middle joint, push it through the body and out through the other wing (above). Leave a length of string and do not unthread the needle.

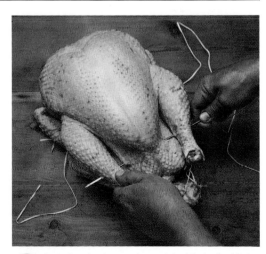

8 Securing the lower drumsticks. Turn the bird breast-up. Draw the string through the lower part of one drumstick, through the body and out through the opposite drumstick (above). Remove the needle. To finish, turn the bird on its side, with the two string ends nearest to you. Pull them tight, tie a knot at the wing, and cut off the excess lengths.

Spatchcocking Poultry

Spatchcocking is the name for the technique of flattening a bird to enable it to be more quickly and uniformly cooked, especially by grilling. Stuffing, traditionally confined to the body cavity of the bird, can turn plain roast or grilled spatchcocked poultry into elegant party fare if it is inserted between the skin and flesh instead. This unorthodox method is shown here with a chicken and a moist courgette and ricotta cheese stuffing, but the technique can be used with a large variety of stuffings and applied to guinea-fowl and capon, as well.

Supple and strong, poultry skin is firmly attached to the body in four places:

the backbone, the end of each drumstick and the crest of the breastbone. Elsewhere, only thin membranes join skin to flesh, and these membranes can be detached easily by working your fingers under the skin. If the bird's skeletal structure is first collapsed by splitting it along the backbone then flattening it with a sharp blow (below), the pockets between the skin and the flesh will accommodate a layer of filling up to 5 cm (2 inches) thick.

If the skin has been torn – either by the butcher or while being loosened and stuffed – use a large sewing needle and thread to make good the damage. Even a

small tear may enlarge drastically during the stuffing process.

The technique has several very practical advantages. Because the bird is flattened, it cooks quickly and evenly. The tender breast meat is protected from drying out by a thick coat of stuffing that keeps it moist while the whole bird cooks through. And the skin, capacious and flexible, can conceal an unusually generous amount of stuffing.

1 Cutting through the backbone. Place the chicken on its breast. Using poultry shears, cut along the entire length of the backbone, as near as possible to the centre of the bone so that the skin remains firmly attached to each side of the back. If you work without shears, lay the bird on its back, insert the blade of a long, heavy knife through the body cavity, and press down hard with a rocking motion to cut through the backbone.

2 Flattening the bird. Open the bird out as much as possible and place it on a flat surface with the breast uppermost and the legs turned inwards. Using the heel of your hand or the flat side of a wooden mallet, strike the bird firmly on the breast. Do not be gentle; the object is to break the breastbone, the collar-bones the ribcage and the wishbone. There will be more room inside the skin if the underlying bone structure is not rigid.

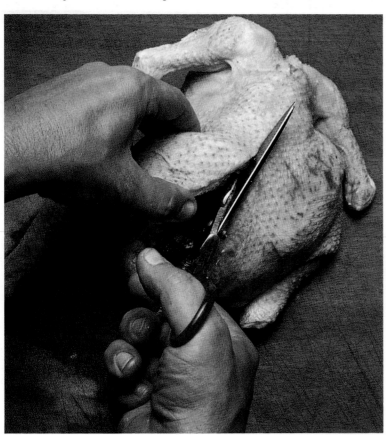

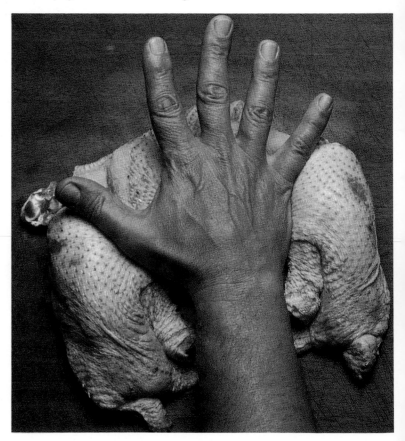

Stuffing **U**nder the **S**kin

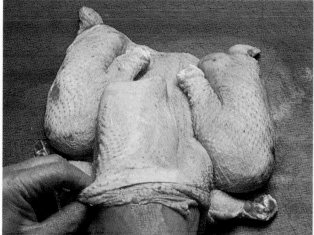

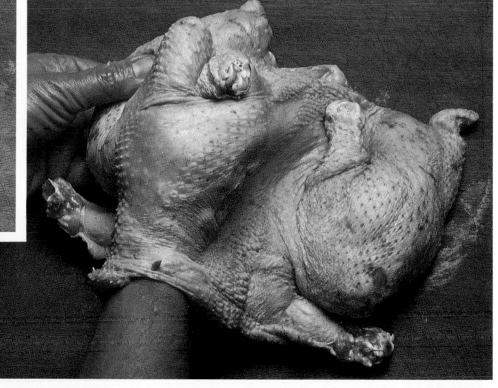

3 Loosening the skin. Starting at the neck, slip your fingers between the skin and flesh and work them towards the tail to loosen the skin over one side of the breast (above). With your entire hand underneath, free the skin by degrees from the leg, leaving the skin attached only at the tip of the drumstick (right). Do the same to the other side of the breast.

4 Stuffing the bird. From the neck, push the filling under the skin with one hand, using the other hand to settle the stuffing into place from the outside (right). After stuffing the thighs and drumsticks, push a thick coating over the breast. Finally, pull the neck flap over the opening and tuck it under the bird. If there is no neck flap, put less stuffing towards the neck.

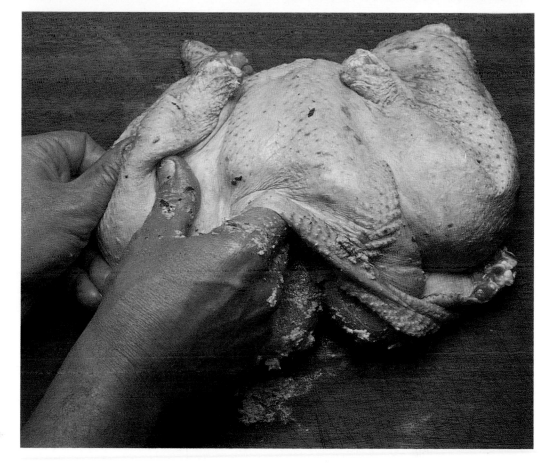

Boning Chicken Suprêmes

Chicken breasts that have been skinned, boned and halved are known in culinary parlance as suprêmes. Rapidly sautéed and coated with sauce as in the recipe on page 232, suprêmes are perfect for a luncheon or light supper. Each suprême makes an elegant single serving.

To prepare the chicken, start with a whole skinned breast prepared by the method shown on page 105. The bones and cartilage all have well-defined forms: using your fingers and a small, sharp knife, it is short work to remove them.

1 Freeing the breastbone. The breastbone is attached to the collar-bones. Place the breast skin side down and slit along the membrane covering the breastbone. Grasp the collar-bones and twist back the breastbone to snap them apart.

2 Removing the breastbone. Snap the breastbone from the piece of white cartilage attached to the narrow end of the breast. Gently prise the breastbone out of the breast. The ribs (foreground) may come away with it, as here.

3 Removing the ribs. Any ribs left attached to the breast can be pulled away with your fingers: if they resist, cut them away with the knife. Trim the tips of the ribs from the sides of the breast.

4 4 Removing the cartilage. Push your thumbs underneath the thin, flat piece of cartilage attached to the narrow end of the breast and pry the cartilage free.

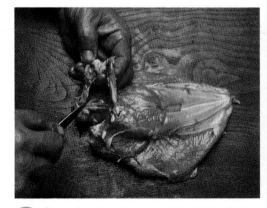

5 Removing the collar-bone. With the knife tip, cut through the thin layer of flesh that covers the collar-bone, carefully following the contours of the bone. When the bone is attached only at its two ends, pull it loose or cut it free.

6 Removing the wishbone. Feel the shape of the wishbone beneath the flesh, and carefully cut away the surrounding flesh with the knife tip. When it is uncovered, firmly grasp its prongs and pull it out.

7 Trimming the breast. Halve the breast along the cleft that held the breastbone. Trim off any fat or nervous tissue to shape each piece into a fillet.

Stuffing Boned Chicken Breasts

Presented in different guises, boned and stuffed chicken breasts are a delectable feature of many cuisines. Perhaps the most celebrated example is the Russian dish known as chicken Kiev, which calls for a flattened chicken breast that is rolled around a finger of garlic butter, dipped in beaten egg and flour, coated with breadcrumbs and then deep-fried. Italian versions of the dish substitute slices of prosciutto or cheese for the butter. Try creating your own simple stuffing mixtures, too – such as a combination of fresh herbs, butter, breadcrumbs and egg. The dish demonstrated here resembles a traditional chicken Kiev, except that instead of being rolled around the filling, the breast is slit to make a roomy 'purse' in which the butter stuffing – or any other suitable filling – is lodged securely.

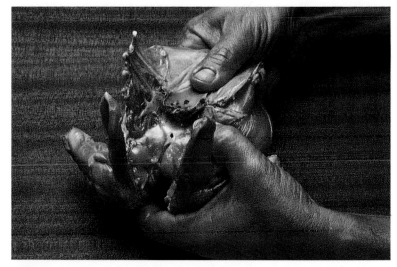

1 Boning the breast with wing attached. If you start with whole chickens, cut them up as shown on pages 104-5, but do not remove the wings as they will give the halved breast portion a neat cutlet shape. Skin the breast, turn it skinned side down and cut off the outer joint of each wing. Slit the membrane that covers the breastbone and the attached cartilage. Grasp the breast by its wide end and bend the breastbone back (above) to snap it from the collar-bones. Remove the breastbone, cartilage, any ribs remaining attached to the breast, collar-bones and wishbone as shown in Steps 2-6 opposite. Turn the breast over again and halve it along the cleft that held the breastbone. Each portion will now resemble a cutlet.

2 Cutting a pocket for the stuffing. With the knife tip, make a deep slit along the thick edge of each 'cutlet'. Be careful not to penetrate as far as the opposite side of the cutlet.

3 Stuffing the cutlets. Cut two pieces of plain or seasoned butter into finger shapes that can be slipped neatly into the pockets. It will be easier to shape the butter if it has been refrigerated for an hour or so beforehand.

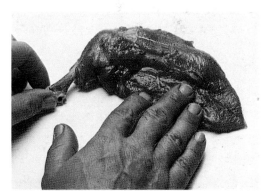

4 Sealing the stuffed cutlets. With your fingertips, press the edges of the pockets together. You will find that the two surfaces of raw flesh cling together; no skewers are needed. Refrigerate after applying any coating for cooking.

Plucking and Drawing Game Birds

Plucking game birds and drawing out their innards takes time and care, but it can be done easily, with relatively little mess, if a few precautions are taken.

All birds are plucked in the same way. Work in a draught-free area to prevent feathers flying about. It is easiest to start plucking the breast of the bird; when the breast is completely clean, move on to the sides, back, legs and wings. To prevent the skin from tearing, hold it taut as you remove the quills, and pull them out in the direction of their growth. Withdraw a few feathers at a time; press down on the flesh at their base with your other hand.

Once most birds are plucked, their innards are removed; the exceptions are snipe and woodcock, whose innards are cleaner than other birds – and are delicious enough to be cooked and eaten. Only the gizzard – the grit sac – should be removed. Wild ducks require an extra step: the oil glands on their tails should be removed or they impart a musky flavour.

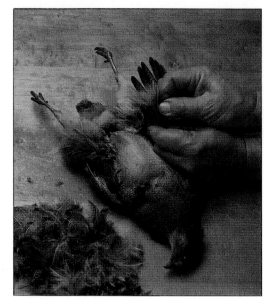

1 Plucking the body and legs. Lay the bird – a partridge is shown here – on its back. Pluck the breast first: hold the skin taut at the base of the feathers and pull out only two or three feathers at a time. When the breast is clean, pluck the sides and back, then pluck the legs (above).

2 Plucking the wings and neck. Grasp a wing, opening it out away from the body to spread the feathers. Pluck the inside of the wing as for as the wing tip joint; leave the feathers on the wing tips as the tips will be cut off. Turn the bird over to pluck the back of the wing. Pluck the feathers from round the neck and finally pull out the tail feathers.

6 Opening out the tail end. To make an incision in the skin without piercing the bird's intestines, pinch the skin below the end of the breastbone to draw the skin away from the carcass. Use a knife to cut through the skin just above the vent; make an opening that is wide enough for you to insert your forefinger.

7 Removing the bird's innards. Insert your forefinger through the slit and use it gently to free the membranes that attach the innards to the cavity walls. Pull the loosened innards free with your thumb and forefinger; the innards should come out in one mass. Feel inside the cavity to make sure that all the innards have been removed.

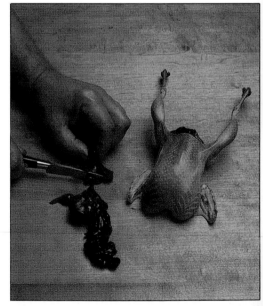

8 Dividing the innards. Spread out the innards and find the membranous tube that separates the heart, lungs and liver from the intestines. Cut through it, taking with it the section of liver with the greenish gall bladder – wood-pigeons, however, have no gall bladder. Do not puncture the bladder; its juice is bitter. Discard intestines and gall bladder.

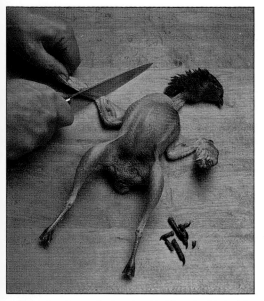

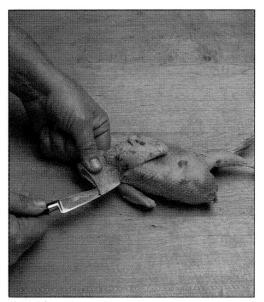

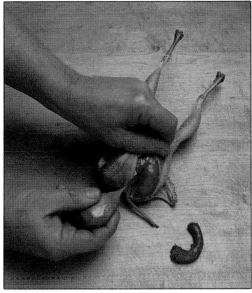

3 Singeing and trimming. Holding the bird with its head and wing tips in one hand and its legs in the other, swing it over a gas flame to singe away down. Lay the singed bird on its back; cut off the hind toe then cut across the front toes to trim them level. To remove the wing tips, sever them at the joint (above).

4 Opening the neck. Cut the bird's head at the top of the neck. Turn the bird on its side and use a small sharp knife to slit the skin down the back of the neck as far as the shoulders. With your fingers, peel back the flap of skin to expose the neck. Leaving the flap of skin, sever the neck at the point where it joins the body – reserve neck for stock.

5 Removing the crop. With the bird on its back, feel inside the neck cavity to loosen the tube-like windpipe and gullet and the ball-shaped crop. Gently pull away the windpipe, gullet and the attached crop and discard them.

Removing Duck Glands

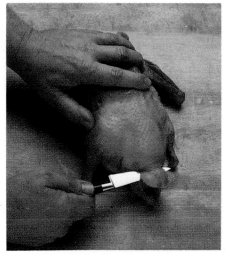

Cutting out the oil glands. Pluck and draw a wild duck – here, a mallard – before removing the oil glands: two small nodules located on the upper side of the bird's tail. Lay the bird on its front and use the tip of a sharp knife to cut out the section of tail flesh that contains the two oil glands (above)

Special Treatment for Snipe and Woodcock

1 Removing the gizzard. Pluck the bird – here, a woodcock. Remove its wings and reserve for stock. Use a knife tip to make a slit in the bird's abdomen, slightly to the right of centre. Insert a trussing needle and locate the hard lump of the gizzard. Pull it out and sever it from the innards; push these back inside the bird.

2 Skinning the head. Use a small knife to cut through the membrane attaching the skin to the flesh at the top of the bird's neck. Grasp the loosened skin at the back of the neck and pull it gently right over the bird's head and off at the tip of the beak. Use a sharp knife to trim the toes in the same way as for partridge (Step 3, above).

Trussing Game Birds

The exact method of trussing a game bird will vary according to the type of bird and the way you intend to cook it.

Quail, partridges and other relatively small birds intended for sautéing or grilling can be split and flattened before being trussed (right). A slit is cut in the skin below the flattened breastbone and the bird's legs tucked through the slit – a technique described as self-trussing.

The most usual method of trussing – with a needle and string – is suitable for all game birds, large and small, that are to be roasted, poached or braised. String is threaded once or twice through the extremities to pin them to the body (below). A large bird will be easier to carve if its wishbone is removed before trussing.

The long beaks of woodcocks and snipe provide a unique means of self-trussing (opposite page). The bird's legs are entwined in a knot and the beak passed through the body to act as a skewer.

Splitting and Flattening Small Birds

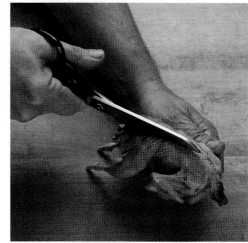

1 Splitting the bird. Pluck the bird – a quail is shown here – and cut off the feet, wing tips and head (see previous page). Using kitchen scissors, split the bird lengthwise, cutting to one side of the backbone from the tail to the neck.

2 Removing the innards. With scissors or a knife, cut off the neck. Open out the bird and pull away the innards, starting at the neck. A female bird may contain, as here, yellow and green eggs. Discard the eggs and the rest of the innards, unless the liver and heart are needed for a stuffing. The neck may be used in a stock.

Securing with String

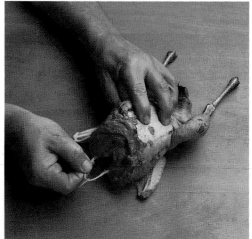

1 Removing the wishbone. Pluck and draw the bird (previous page) – here, a pheasant. Pull back the flap of skin at the neck to expose wishbone. Cut through the flesh along the sides of the wishbone and sever the tip of cartilage that attaches the wishbone to the breastbone. Pull away the wishbone. Fold back the flap of skin over the neck.

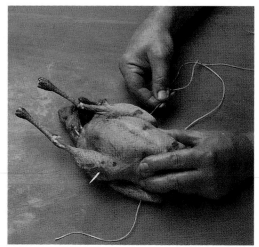

2 Securing the wings and legs. Thread a trussing needle with string. Pull the needle through the upper part of wings to fix them to the body, and then pass the needle in opposite direction through the thighs. Tie the two ends of string together and trim the excess; small birds such as partridges, grouse and quail are now ready for cooking.

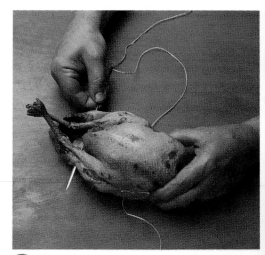

3 Threading the second string. For larger birds, thread the needle with a second length of string. Pass the needle through the wing where it bends, catching the folded flap of neck skin. Pull the needle out through the other wing, then pass it back through the legs and body.

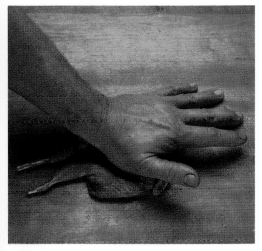

3 Flattening the bird. Lay the bird on a flat surface with the breast upwards. Place the palm of your hand over the breast and press down firmly with the flat of your hand to break the breastbone.

4 Slitting the skin. Keeping the flattened bird breast side up, pull up and hold on to the loose skin between the legs of the bird. Using a small knife, make a horizontal slit in this flap of skin.

5 Completing the trussing. Gently bend the legs of the bird inwards so that they meet in line with the breastbone. Insert the tip of one leg, and then the other, through the slit in the skin. Pull the legs through together (above). Fold the flap of neck skin to the underside of the bird; the bird is now ready for cooking.

4 Completing the trussing. Remove the needle. Turn the bird on its side and pull the two free ends of the string together. Tie them firmly and trim the ends. The bird is now ready for cooking

Skewering a Bird with Its Own Beak

1 Twisting the legs. Pluck a long-beaked bird – here, a woodcock – and remove the gizzard (page 144). Skin the head. Bend the legs gently outwards to loosen the joints. Cross one thigh over the other and twist the tips of the legs together. Bend the tips back and tuck them into the space between the crossed thighs.

2 Skewering with the beak. Bend the neck of the bird downwards towards the legs. With the sharp point of the beak, skewer the flesh of the legs and body. The bird is now ready for cooking.

Jointing Hare and Rabbit

Rabbits and hares can be cut into neat portions that are an ideal size for sautéing or grilling, or for fitting into the pot. You can, of course, buy ready-cut portions, but it is easy and more economical to joint an animal yourself. By starting with a whole skinned animal you will also acquire the offal and trimmings for the stock-pot. In the demonstration here, a hutch rabbit is jointed. Wild rabbits and hares are treated in the same way.

The animal is ready for jointing after it has been skinned and gutted. Always use a large, sharp knife on which you can exert firm pressure. If you find it difficult to cut through the joints, score the flesh, then position the knife on the cut and tap the blade with a mallet.

The two kidneys are often left in place in the animal's middle section – known as the saddle – and cooked with these portions. You should be supplied with the rest of the offal separately: the liver will make a delectable garnish, sliced and tossed in butter, or it can be used with the heart and lungs in a stuffing.

1 Removing the forelegs. Place a skinned and gutted animal – a hutch rabbit is shown here – on its back on a work surface. If necessary, take out the liver and remove the gall bladder. Turn the animal over. Pulling one foreleg away from the body, sever the connective tissue joining the leg to the body. Cut off the other foreleg.

2 Cutting off the hindquarters. Set the two foreleg joints aside. Steady the animal's body with one hand, and start to cut across the body at the point where the hindquarters join the saddle. Continue to cut, applying firm pressure, until the hindquarters are detached.

3 Separating the hind legs. To separate the hind legs, cut lengthwise through the hindquarters, cutting to one side of the backbone or the other. Set the two hind leg joints to one side.

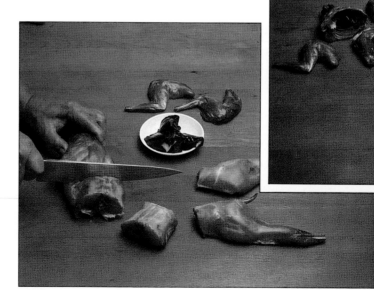

4 Dividing the saddle. Starting at the hind end, cut across the saddle to divide it into two or three pieces, depending on the size of the animal. The two lower portions of saddle each contain one kidney; leave these in place. The last cut separates the saddle from the ribcage (above). If necessary, you can leave the heart and lungs in the ribcage. Here, jointing has yielded two hindquarter portions, three pieces from the saddle, two forelegs, the ribcage and the liver (inset).

Larding and Barding Game

Game meat, naturally lean, always needs supplementary fat to keep it moist during cooking. Mild-flavoured pork fat is the usual choice. The fat is used either in the form of caul, a membrane that surrounds a pig's stomach, or back fat.

Available either dry-salted or fresh, caul is the easiest fat to use: it clings to the meat and can be simply wrapped round a hare, rabbit or piece of venison.

Fresh back fat can be used in several different ways. Cut into slices known as bards, it can be tied over a bird's breast before roasting (far right). The bard of fat will partly melt, basting the meat as it cooks, and can be removed towards the end of cooking to let the meat brown.

Back fat can be cut into strips called lardons, used to nourish meat from within during long roasting or braising. Lardons may be threaded through large pieces of meat with a larding needle (below). For smaller joints, the lardons can be pushed into slits (below, right).

Wrapping in Caul

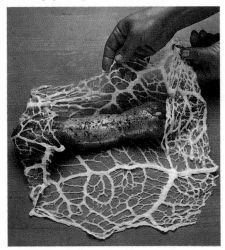

Wrapping a rabbit. Season a skinned and gutted rabbit and sprinkle it with herbs. If using dry-salted caul, soak it in tepid water for 30 minutes then rinse it. If using fresh caul, rinse it. Spread the caul out and blot it dry. Lay the on the caul and fold it over the rabbit to enclose the meat completely.

Draping with Back Fat

Tying the fat in place. Ask the butcher for back fat sliced 3 to 5 mm ($^1/8$ to $^1/4$ inch) thick. Trim each slice into a rectangular shape large enough to cover a bird's breast – here, a grouse. Truss the bird (page 116). Cover the breast with the bard and secure it by tying two pieces of string round bird and bard.

Using a Larding Needle

Larding a venison haunch. Cut back fat into 5 mm ($^1/4$ inch) wide strips. Insert a strip in a larding needle. With the haunch rounded side up, draw the lardon through the meat to make a stitch; trim end. Repeat stitches at 2.5 cm (1 inch) intervals to make horizontal rows, positioning rows about 1 cm ($^1/2$ inch) apart.

Studding Meat with Seasoned Lardons

1 Piercing the meat. Joint a hare (opposite). Cut chilled back fat into lardons roughly 4 cm (1$^1/2$ inches) long and 5 mm ($^1/4$ inch) wide. Season the lardons by tossing them in *persillade*, a mixture of garlic and coarse salt pounded together in a mortar and mixed with chopped parsley. Use a small sharp knife to cut a slit in the meat.

2 Inserting the lardons. Insert your finger in the slit to widen it. Push a lardon into the opening. Continue to make slits in the meat, filling them with lardons until each joint is larded in several places. To lard the back of the saddle and the hindquarters of a hare for a more formal presentation, use a larding needle.

Preparing Haunch of Venison

Unlike game birds and smaller animals, large game, such as deer, is almost never roasted whole. If venison is to fit into a domestic oven, it must be cut into joints. The most suitable cuts for roasting are those from the tender hindquarters, such as leg (right), or saddle.

The length of a leg of venison will vary depending on how far above the pelvic joint the cut has been made – here, a 'long leg' or haunch is shown. But whether cut long or short, the leg will be easier to carve if the section of pelvic bone is removed before cooking (Step 1, right). The lower end of the leg also needs some attention. Sawing off part of the shank bone (Step 3, right) will enable you to attach a carving handle – a *manche à gigot* – to the shaft of bone that remains, making it easy to hold the leg steady during carving. If you have no *manche à gigot*, leave the entire shank bone intact to form a natural 'handle' that can be grasped with a napkin.

Because venison is naturally lean, it needs supplementary fat to keep it from becoming dry during cooking. To protect the meat, either lard it, as here, or wrap it in caul. A marinade based on olive oil (page 164) applied to the larded meat a few hours or the day before it is to be roasted will both moisten it and hasten the browning process that helps to seal the surface of the meat. The inclusion in the marinade of aromatic herbs such as thyme or savory will perfume the meat.

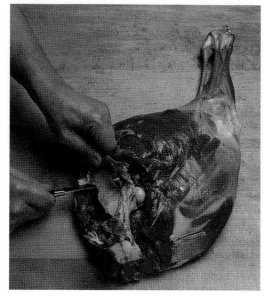

1 Removing the pelvic bone. To remove the section of pelvic bone at the top of the leg, cut round the exposed surface of the bone with a knife. Then cut deeper into the flesh following the contours of the bone until you expose the ball and socket joint connecting the pelvic bone to the leg; cut the ligaments joining the two bones. Lift the pelvic bone free.

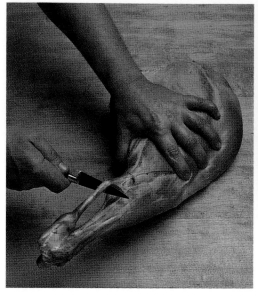

2 Severing the tendon. Turn the venison round. To prepare the shank so that you can later attach a *manche à gigot* for carving, cut through the tendon at its attachment to the upper part of the leg. If you do not have a *manche à gigot*, leave the leg as it is; at serving time, wrap the shank in a napkin so that you can hold it firmly for carving.

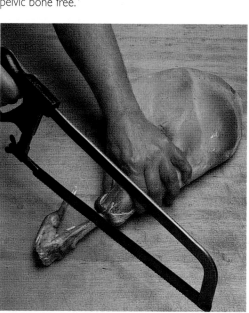

3 Sawing through the shank bone. To expose the shank bone, use a knife to pare the flesh away, scraping towards the top of the leg so that the flesh remains attached to the rest of the meat. Fold back the loosened lobes of flesh; saw off the bone just above the knuckle. To neaten the end, tie back the lobes of flesh with string.

4 Marinating the meat. Lard the surface of the meat (page 82). Put the leg on a tray and sprinkle it with dried herbs. Coat the leg on both sides with olive oil (above); pat the oil on to the surface of the meat. Pour over white wine, pat it on to the meat. Cover the meat with foil and place in the refrigerator to marinate overnight.

Preparing Saddle of Venison

In a perfectly roasted saddle of venison the meat is rose-coloured – neither rare nor overdone – juicy, tender and finely flavoured. Achieving these results requires meticulous preparation.

First, the layers of fat and tough membrane that cover the rounded side of the saddle must be cut away to expose the tender meat beneath. Once trimmed, the saddle must be arranged so that its three types of meat will cook to the ideal stage.

On either side of the backbone, on the underside, lie the two fillets, strips of particularly delicate meat. Above them are the two sections of the eye of the loin – also prized for tenderness. On the outer edges of the joint are two flaps of tougher meat called the aprons. To protect the two delicate fillets and form a barrier between them and the roasting pan, the aprons are folded or rolled under the joint. Finally, to keep the venison moist, the saddle is wrapped in caul.

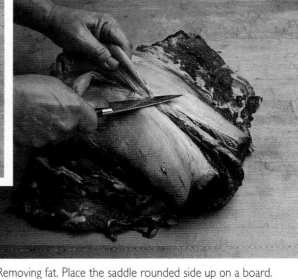

1 Removing fat. Place the saddle rounded side up on a board. Starting at an apron, pull back the fat from one side of the saddle towards the spine. To detach the fat, work inwards with a small sharp knife as you pull (inset). When you reach the backbone, free the fat on the other side. Cut away the whole sheet of fat from the backbone (above) and discard it.

2 Stripping away the membrane. Using a sharp knife, cut away the tough membrane that runs along the back of the saddle. Holding the knife at a slight angle, pare away strips of membrane from the surface of the meat (above), taking care not to cut into the meat.

3 Larding the saddle. Tuck the aprons underneath the saddle. Place the saddle on a sheet of caul and wrap the caul round it so that the meat is completely enclosed.

Preparing Offal

The aim of the techniques shown on pages 122–5 is to ensure the offal is thoroughly cleansed, to remove any parts that would spoil the taste or appearance of the meat, and – in some cases – to make the offal easier to handle during cooking.

Some offal, such as hearts, lungs and tails, need only be trimmed to remove large tubes and fat. Other meats are covered with a membrane that contracts during cooking, causing the offal to buckle. In the case of liver and kidneys, the whole membrane is peeled off. Spleen, however, has a pulpy texture and any membrane that clings tightly should be left to hold the spleen together.

The fat, tubes and superficial membrane that covers sweetbreads must be peeled off carefully, leaving in place the connective tissue that holds the sweetbreads together. Blanching firms the sweetbreads and makes them easier to peel. Calves' sweetbreads may be pressed to compact them; lamb's sweetbreads are usually cut up to make stews, and there is no need to press them.

Intestines and most tripe (page 124) are soaked or rinsed to ensure they are clean; salted caul is soaked to remove excess salt and to make it more pliable. Tripe should be scrubbed free of fat and soaked to dissipate its strong odour. Reed tripe is sold raw and must be soaked and pre-cooked to remove impurities and tenderize it.

The large bones in calves' and pigs' feet (page 125) are usually removed so that the feet can be split for cooking to aid release of their gelatine, and so that they will fit more easily into the cooking vessel. Poultry feet are held over a flame to blister their skins and make them easy to peel.

Cutting Tubes from Heart

Removing connective tissue. Using a sharp knife, remove the fat from round the heart – here, an ox heart. Cut out any remaining fibrous tissue and remove all the large tubes.

Peeling Liver

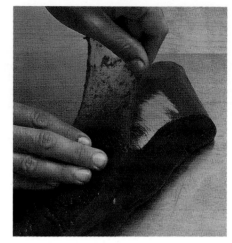

Removing the membrane. With a knife, cut out any fibrous connective tissue from the liver – here, a large piece of calves' liver – taking care not to damage the flesh. To remove the surface membrane, ease a corner loose and gently pull the membrane off the liver, holding the flesh down to prevent it from tearing.

Trimming Poultry Livers

Removing the gall bladder. To remove the gall bladder without piercing it and releasing its bitter fluid, cut round the liver – a goose liver is shown here – at the base of the gall bladder and remove the small section of liver with the intact gall bladder attached to it. Discard the gall bladder. Trim any green-stained flesh from the liver and discard it.

Cleaning Tripe

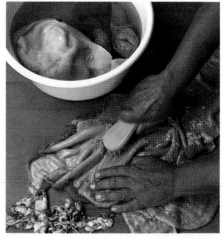

Scrubbing a stomach clean. To clean ox stomachs – shown here – split them open. Sheep's and pigs' stomachs can be left whole and turned inside out. With your fingers, pull of fatty membranes from the inside of the stomach. Scrub the stomach clean with a stiff-bristled brush and leave it to soak in vinegar and water until it is ready for use.

Coring Calves' Kidneys

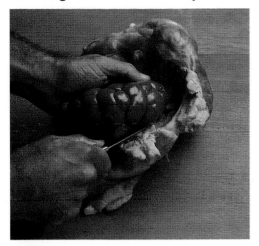

1 Exposing the kidney. Make an incision in the covering of fat round a calves' kidney. Ox kidneys are similarly formed. With your fingers, pull the casing of fat apart, then cut through it where it is attached to the kidney

2 Halving the kidney. Remove the kidney from its fat. Make a slit in the surface membrane and peel it off with your fingers. Cut the kidney in half lengthwise, slicing through its fatty core.

3 Removing the core. Cut out as much of the kidney's core fat as possible.

Trimming Lambs' Kidneys

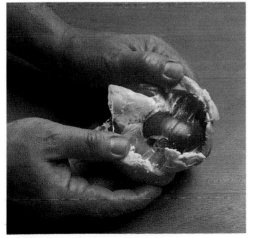

1 Pulling away fat. With a knife, slit the white fat – known as suet – that encloses the kidney. Here, a lamb's kidney is shown; pig's kidneys are formed in the same way. With your fingers, prise open the suet, revealing the shiny membrane that covers the kidney.

2 Cutting off the fat. Peel the fat away from the kidney. Hold the kidney away from its covering of fat and, with a sharp knife, cut through the fat where it is attached to the kidney's core. Discard the fat.

3 Removing the membrane. With a knife, make a slit about 3 mm ($^{1}/_{8}$ inch) deep in the rounded side of the kidney to split the membrane. Pull the membrane off the kidney and cut it free where it is attached to the kidney's core.

Extracting the Flesh from Gizzards

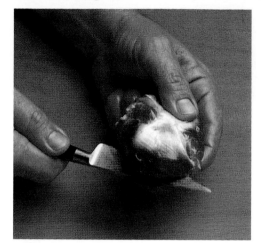 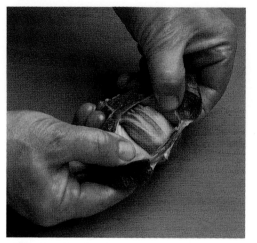 

1 Slitting the gizzard. Remove any fat that surrounds the gizzard – here, a turkey gizzard. Make a slit in one side of the gizzard, cutting through the dark red flesh and the white fibrous membrane that lines it. Take care not to pierce the white gravel sac at the centre.

2 Opening the gizzard. With your fingers, pull the flesh on either side of the slit, exposing the gravel sac in the centre of the gizzard and remove the gravel sac with your fingers.

3 Paring off the flesh. Pare a quarter of the flesh free from the tough membrane. Pare off a second quarter in the same way. Turn the gizzard over and slice off the rest of the flesh. Discard the fibrous membrane and the gravel sac.

Cleaning Raw Tripe

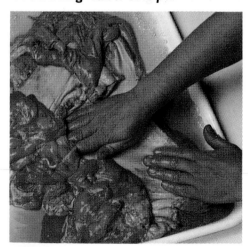 

1 Soaking tripe. Soak the tripe for 1 to 2 hours in several changes of water, spread it out on a tray, rub it all over with vinegar and coarse salt, then leave the tripe to soak in fresh water and vinegar for a couple of hours.

2 Parboiling tripe. Put the tripe in a large saucepan and cover it with cold water. Bring it slowly to the boil, reduce the heat and simmer for a few minutes. Drain in a colander and refresh under cold running water.

De-Salting Caul

Soaking caul. To soften dry-salted caul and to remove excess salt, soak the caul – in this case, pig's caul – in cold water for 10 to 15 minutes. When it is soft, lift it out and pat it dry. Fresh caul does not require soaking.

Boning a Foot

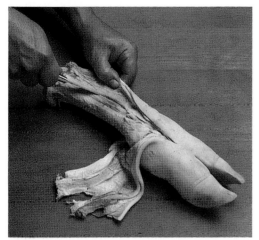 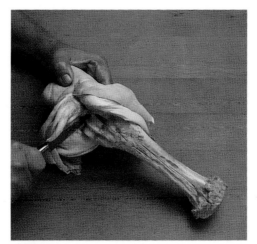 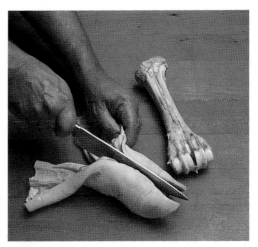

1 Exposing the bone. Scrape between the toes of the foot – here, a calf's foot – to remove any clinging tufts of hair. Scrape or singe off any other hairs on the foot. Starting at the point where the large bone joins the toes – just above the cleft of the foot – cut the skin and flesh lengthwise down the centre to expose the bone.

2 Removing the bone. Turn the foot over and make a lengthwise cut along the centre of the underside. Cut the skin and flesh away from both sides of the large bone, scraping downwards against the bone with the knife blade. Sever the tendons that attach the bone to the foot (above) and remove the large bone.

3 Splitting the foot. Trim away ragged edges of skin, leaving neat flaps above the toes. If you like, split the foot in two (above); the halves will fit more easily into a pan for braising or stock-making.

Skinning Poultry Feet

Singeing the foot. To loosen the skin, pass the foot – in this case, a turkey foot – through a flame until the skin has blistered all over. Using a piece of kitchen paper, pull off the pieces of skin (above) and discard them. If you are cooking the feet in a stew rather than using them for stock, trim the nails.

Extracting Bone Marrow

Prising the marrow free. Buy beef bones sawn into manageable lengths – about 10 to 12.5 cm (4 to 5 inches) long. To loosen the soft marrow that fills the centre of each bone, slide the tip of a knife between the marrow and the bone. Work from both ends of the bone. When the marrow is free, prise it out.

Trimming Oxtail

Cutting off fat. With a knife, remove most of the excess fat that is deposited round an oxtail – particularly at the base of the tail. Some of the fat may be left to nourish the meat during cooking.

Cleaning and Trimming Fish

However fish are to be cooked, they are usually first cleaned and trimmed. Most fish netted by deep-water fishermen are eviscerated before being brought ashore; fish caught inshore or in fresh water are usually sold intact. With rare exceptions, the viscera (internal organs) of the latter should be taken out, and the fins and scales removed. These chores will be performed on request by your fishmonger, but you should, nevertheless, learn to do them yourself: how else will you be able to deal with a freshly caught fish presented to you by an angler friend?

Finning (box, below, left) is done mainly for aesthetic reasons; fish that are to be served whole look tidier and more attractive if their fins and tails are trimmed, and they are easier to serve and eat. If you are dealing with a spiky-finned species, such as the sea bream shown

below, it is wise to trim the fins before going on to other preparations, since the spikes can cause painful punctures if handled carelessly.

Some fish – sharks, eels, anglerfish, for instance – have no scales. Others have tiny scales which may be removed by scraping. The scales of sardines, pilchards and anchovies are so loosely attached to the skin that they may be removed by gently rubbing the fish from head to tail under running water. Most fish are protected by a sheath of firmly attached overlapping scales which can be scraped free with the edge of a knife (box, below, right) or a fish scaler.

There are two principal ways to eviscerate a fish – through the belly and through the gills (box, right). Eviscerating through the belly is a quick and convenient method if you have to bone or fillet a fish; eviscerating through the gills

– which preserves the shape of the fish – is the preferred method for fish that are to be stuffed and cooked whole or served whole in aspic. To clean flat fish, whose viscera occupy a small area directly below the gills, simply make a small incision below the gills and pull out the viscera.

Once fish have been eviscerated and trimmed, you can go on to fillet or bone them (pages 128-131). If you are filleting small flat fish, such as sole, it is convenient to skin them at this stage (box, opposite page, below). Flat fish that are to be filleted should be skinned completely; flat fish that are to be cooked whole should be skinned only on their dark upper side since the white lower skin helps hold the whole fish intact during cooking. Round fish – and large flat fish, such as turbot – are easier to skin after they have been filleted or cooked.

Removing Fins and Scales

Trimming a spiky-finned fish. Lay the fish – here, a sea bream – on a cutting board. With a pair of heavy scissors, cut away the dorsal fin down to the back. Cut off the pectoral, ventral and anal fins.

Remove scales. Grip the fish by the tail and, using the edge of a knife or a fish scaler, scrape towards the head – against the direction in which the scales lie. Work carefully round the head and the base of the fins. (To prevent scales from being scattered around the kitchen, you can scale the fish in a large basin of water.) When the skin is free of scales, rinse the fish thoroughly.

Methods for Gutting

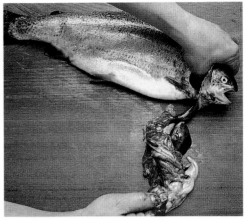

Eviscerating through the belly. Where a recipe calls for the head to be removed, cut off the head behind the last gill opening: here, a herring is being prepared for boning before it is fried. Using heavy scissors or a sharp knife, cut down the belly

as far as the vent (above). Pull out the viscera (above, right). Run a knife-point down both sides of the backbone to release any pockets of blood. Rinse the fish briefly in cold water.

Eviscerating through the gills for stuffing whole. Hook a finger through the opening and pull out the viscera in one piece, together with the gill. Reach into the cavity to be sure you have removed all the organs, then rinse out the fish in cold water.

A Rapid Way to Skin Flat Fish

1 Starting the operation. Lay the fish – here, a sole – dark side uppermost on a cutting board. With a sharp knife, cut across the skin where the tail joins the body (above). Starting at the cut, use the point of the knife or your fingernails to prise a flap of skin away from the flesh until you can obtain a firm grip on it.

2 Peeling off the skin. Grasp the flap of skin in one hand; with the other hold down the tail, using a cloth to prevent your fingers from slipping. Firmly and decisively, pull the skin towards the head (above). On reaching the jaws, turn the fish over and, holding the fish by the head, continue pulling the skin until you reach the tail (inset, right).

Filleting **F**ish

Fillets – full-length sections of fish separated from the bones – are called for in most dishes where fish are to be served in a sauce or deep-fried in batter. Fillets are also the raw material for mousselines, quenelles and fish pâtés. Most fish can be filleted, but best results are obtained with fish that have a well-defined bone structure – such as the sole and whiting shown here.

To separate fillets cleanly from the bones, you need a knife with a long sharp blade that is flexible enough to ride over the fish's bones. The basic technique is the same whatever fish you are handling, but flat fish and round fish call for slightly different methods of working. Flat fish, which are usually skinned before filleting (previous pages), yield four fillets – two from the upper side of the body and two from the lower side. Round fish, which are skinned after filleting, yield two fillets – one from each side of the backbone.

Cook fillets as soon as possible after they have been prepared; since they are not protected by skin, they will dry up if exposed directly to the air. For the same reason, do not grill fillets. They should be fried gently in butter, or poached briefly in a rich stock or sauce; or they can be coated with batter and deep-fried, or covered with a sauce and baked.

Fillets also lend themselves to decorative presentations. They can be rolled around a stuffing and poached, for example, or used to line a mould filled with a mousseline or other stuffing.

Filleting Flat Fish

① Freeing the flesh from the backbone. Lay the skinned fish – here, a sole – on a cutting board with its eyes facing up and its tail towards you. With the tip of a sharp flexible knife, cut down to the backbone, following the median line, from the head to the tail. Insert the blade at a shallow angle between the head end of the fillet and the ribs. Pressing the blade firmly against the ribs, slide the tip between the fillet and ribs the length of the body.

Filleting and Skinning Round Fish

① Cutting down the backbone. Lay the cleaned fish – here, a whiting – on one side, with its tail towards you. Holding the fish steady with one hand, slice along the back from head to tail, cutting deep enough to expose the backbone.

② Removing the upper fillet. Separate the fillet from the head by cutting down to the backbone behind the gills. Holding the head end of the fillet insert the knife between the fillet and ribs. With the blade of the knife parallel to the ribs, cut down the length of the fillet to detach it completely.

2 Removing the first fillet. When the head end of the fillet is detached, lift it clear of the ribs with your free hand and continue sliding the knife tip the length of the fish to free the fillet from the fins and tail. Trim off any clinging fin fragments.

3 Removing the second fillet. Cut away the right-hand fillet. If the fish has been caught in the spawning season, it will probably contain a sac of orange roe beneath the right-hand fillet, as shown here. You can save the roe for a fish stock, or it can be served poached or fried as a delicacy.

4 A bonus for the stock-pot. When the upper side of the fish has been filleted, turn the fish over and repeat the process on the under side. You will be left with four fillets and a cleanly picked skeleton. Save the skeleton for inclusion in a fumet (page 244).

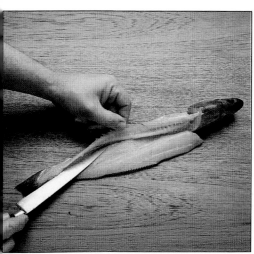 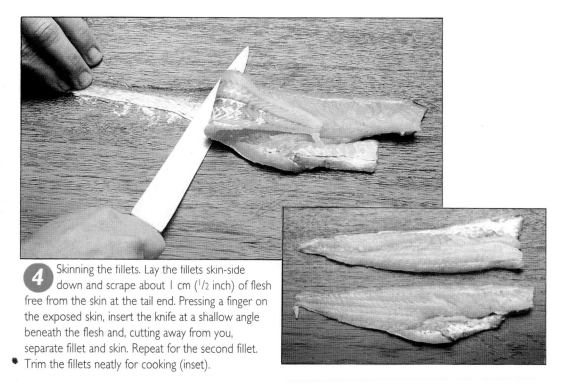

3 Removing the lower fillet. Holding the fish by its exposed backbone, use the flat of the knife to separate the lower fillet from the ribs. If you are filleting a fish with a delicate skeleton – a herring, for example – some bones may remain attached to the flesh. Carefully pull them out with your fingers or tweezers.

4 Skinning the fillets. Lay the fillets skin-side down and scrape about 1 cm (1/2 inch) of flesh free from the skin at the tail end. Pressing a finger on the exposed skin, insert the knife at a shallow angle beneath the flesh and, cutting away from you, separate fillet and skin. Repeat for the second fillet. Trim the fillets neatly for cooking (inset).

Boning Round Fish via the Belly

Bones in cooked fish can be a nuisance – but they are easy to remove beforehand. One method is to fillet the fish, but then you will not be able to serve it whole. Another method, which permits you to bone the fish yet preserve its shape, is demonstrated here. You can then cook the whole fish au gratin, fill the body cavity with stuffing, or poach it and cover it with sauce. This method should only be used for round fish; when flat fish need boning, the bones should be removed by the method described on the previous pages.

Most round fish have simple skeletons consisting of a backbone with 'ribs' branching off it. Removing the bones simply involves opening the underside of the fish from head to tail and freeing the skeleton from the surrounding flesh. In the case of sea bass – shown here – and other large-boned fish, you can use a knife to help free the 'ribs' from the membrane that covers them, and then pick each one out individually.

The skeleton of finer-boned fish, such as herrings, should be prised loose with your fingers alone, since a knife could damage the flesh. Very small fish, such as anchovies, can be boned by slitting the belly with your thumb and peeling away the skeleton.

Alternatively you can – with more finesse than this method requires – bone round fish through the back.

1 Gutting and finning. Check that the fish has been cleanly gutted; if not, first rinse out the gut cavity and wipe away any dried blood. Cut away the dorsal fins together with the underlying bones that support them. Then slice off the pectoral fins (above), cutting forwards, towards the gill apertures.

2 Opening the fish. The fish's belly will already have been opened for gutting. To remove the bones, the opening should be extended along the length of the fish. Using a sharp knife, slit the underside from the vent to the tail.

3 Cutting out the ribs. Hold the fish open to expose the backbone and ribs, which are embedded shallowly in the flesh and covered by membrane. Working down the fish from rib to rib, nick the membrane, and with your fingers – and a small knife – pull the rib free (above). Snap each rib away from backbone with your fingers (right).

4 Freeing the backbone. The backbone of the fish is still partly embedded in flesh. To free it, open the fish as wide as possible without tearing the flesh, and run the knife down both sides of the spine. Take care not to press too hard so as not to cut through the skin.

5 Removing the backbone. With a pair of kitchen scissors, sever the backbone as close to the head as possible. Grasp the severed end and pull out the bone, working back towards the tail. Snip it free. The backbone can be included in a fumet (page 244), if you like.

Cutting up Uncooked Lobster

To prepare lobster for grilling or for braising, the crustacean should be killed not by poaching it live, but by halving it from head to tail, then cutting it into pieces. This ensures that the flesh will stay moist and tender during braising, and that the sauce will pick up additional flavour from the shell and juices.

Many well-known lobster dishes call for raw cut-up pieces. Among these braises are lobster à l'américaine and lobster Newburg, which is served in a sauce of brandy, sherry and cream. The technique of splitting a lobster in half is used in the preparation of lobster thermidor. The spiny lobster and flat

lobster are prepared in the same way as the larger European species. All three contain a greenish tomalley, or liver, which can be used to enrich an accompanying sauce. Some female lobsters also contain undeveloped eggs, the coral, that can be incorporated in a sauce to add flavour.

1 Severing the spinal cord. Keeping your hands clear of the claws, hold the lobster underside down on a work surface. With the tip of a heavy knife, pierce the shell firmly in the centre of the cross-shaped mark behind the head. Save any liquid that runs out for cooking.

2 Halving the lobster. Exerting a firm pressure on the knife, cut along the body and tail to divide the lobster into two. You will see the white gravel sac near the head, the thread-like intestinal canal, the grey-green tomalley beneath the canal, and – if you have a female lobster, as here – the blackish coral.

3 Cleaning the lobster. Pull out and discard the gravel sac (above), and the intestinal canal. With a spoon, carefully remove the tomalley and coral, and reserve them; they can be added to a sauce, as demonstrated opposite.

4 Dismembering the lobster. Twist off the claws and reserve them. With the heavy knife, split each lobster half crosswise between the tail and body sections. Twist off the legs and reserve them.

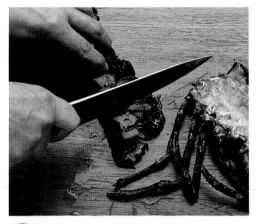

5 Dividing up the tail. Cut the lobster's tail between every two segments of the shell. Do not remove the meat, which will be protected and flavoured by the shell during cooking. Save any liquid from the carcass for incorporation into a braising liquid.

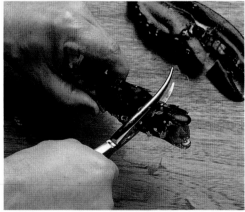

6 Cracking the claws. In order to extract the meat more easily when the lobster is served, crack the claws with a wooden mallet or – as demonstrated here – a pair of pincers. Do not extract the meat.

Dressing Squid etc

Squid, cuttlefish and octopus can be prepared for cooking in no more time than it takes to gut and fillet a fish. Only the tentacles and the fleshy body sac of these species are eaten. The other parts are discarded, starting with the translucent, quill-shaped 'pen' of the squid (right) and the hard white cuttlebone of the cuttlefish. The octopus's body does not have a bony support.

The eyes, viscera and mouth, or 'beak', of all these cephalopods are always removed. Among the viscera lies an ink sac, which contains the black fluid the cephalopods secrete when threatened. If they are to be cooked 'in their ink' – a practice traditional in Mediterranean cookery – the sac must be removed intact. In specimens that have been frozen, the ink will have coagulated; to restore fluidity, remove the frozen granules from the sac and dissolve them in a little hot water.

The flesh of all these cephalopods is firm, rubbery and resilient to the touch. The skin is often removed for cosmetic purposes, but if left on will add flavour. Squid pouches are ideal receptacles for stuffing, in which case the tentacles are usually chopped up and sautéed, to be incorporated in the stuffing. When the pouch of a squid or cuttlefish is cut into rings or squares and the tentacles left whole or split, they are tender and delicious cooked rapidly, either dipped in batter and deep-fried or sautéed over high heat for no more than a minute. The flesh toughens after several minutes' cooking and they must then be stewed for about 40 minutes to become tender again.

Octopus is prepared by cutting away the tentacles in one piece, then emptying the body sac of viscera and finally taking out the beak. It is usually cut into small pieces to be stewed and requires longer cooking than either squid or cuttlefish, from one hour for an octopus weighing less than 500 g (1 lb) to three or four hours for larger specimens. Small octopus can be tenderized by deep-freezing.

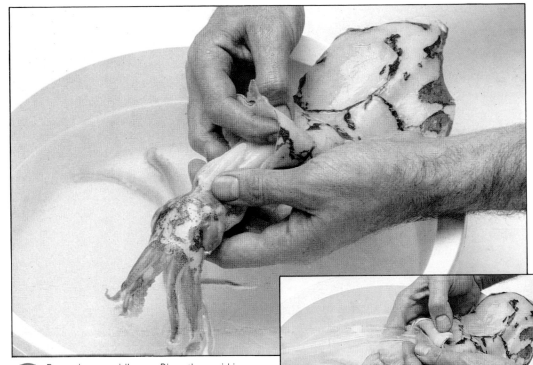

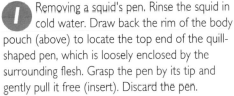
Removing a squid's pen. Rinse the squid in cold water. Draw back the rim of the body pouch (above) to locate the top end of the quill-shaped pen, which is loosely enclosed by the surrounding flesh. Grasp the pen by its tip and gently pull it free (insert). Discard the pen.

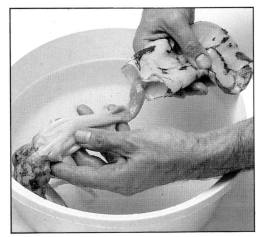
Separating tentacles and body. Hold the body pouch in one hand; with the other, grasp the head just below the eyes. Pull the two sections gently apart. The viscera, including the ink sac, will come away with the head. The body pouch will be empty except for a mucous membrane. Pull the membrane away under cold running water.

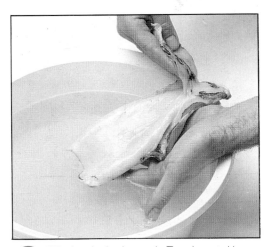
Skinning the body pouch. Translucent skin, irregularly patterned with mauve patches, covers the white flesh of the squid's body pouch. Slip a finger under the skin and peel it off the pouch. Carefully pull off the edible triangular fins which are on either side of the pouch. Skin the fins.

Preparing Molluscs

Because molluscs are cooked only briefly or eaten raw, they must be absolutely fresh. If you gather your own supply, check with local fishermen or the district fishing authority that the area in which the molluscs live is not polluted, since specimens that come from contaminated waters may contain toxic substances.

Most bivalves – mussels, oysters and cockles, for example – are sold live. Their shells are usually closed. Sharply tap any specimens whose shells are open; if they remain open, the shellfish inside are probably dead, and should be discarded.

Univalves such as winkles and whelks are generally sold pre-cooked. Buying from a dealer you trust is the best guarantee of freshness.

Because mussels inhabit the sandy regions of the tide line, they tend to ingest sand or other particles when they feed. When you bring a batch home, scrape any growths from their shells under water with a knife or stiff brush, then place them in a basin of cold water with a handful of sea salt. They will stay alive for several hours and expel any sand or grit they contain.

There are two principal ways to open bivalves to extract their flesh: prising them open, which sometimes involves cutting the muscles that hold the shells together, or applying heat, which causes the shells to open automatically. Oysters should always be prised open (box, right), since heat tends to toughen their flesh. Scallops can either be prised open, or placed in a hot oven for a few minutes; in either case, you then have to separate the edible parts from the inedible (box, opposite page, above). Mussels are usually steamed open in a pan as part of their cooking (page 179); but a few dishes call for them to be prised open.

Winkles and whelks are almost always steamed or boiled until cooked. Their flesh can then be extracted with a pin or a skewer (box, above, right).

De-bearding Mussels

A mussel has a bunch of thin, hair-like strands attached to the hinge of its shell. The strands, known as the beard, serve to anchor the live mussel to rocks. Before cooking, pull the beard off.

Pinning Whelks & Winkles

Whelks, shown here, are cooked in boiling water for 10 to 20 minutes; winkles only 5 to 10. Drain. When the shells are cool enough to handle, extract the flesh by pinning it with a small skewer and levering it free.

A Safe and Efficient Way to Shuck an Oyster

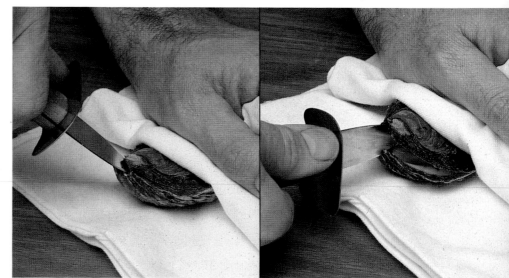

1 Separating the shells. Place the oyster, wrapped in a folded napkin, on a firm surface with the flatter shell uppermost and the hinged end towards you. Holding the oyster firmly in place with one hand, take an oyster knife in the other and insert the tip into the small gap in the hinge (above, left). Twist the blade to snap the shells apart (above, right).

Opening and Cleaning a Scallop

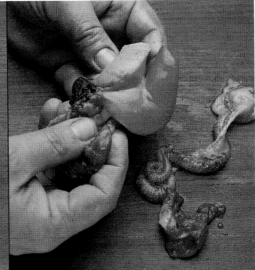

1 Opening the shells. Hold the scallop in a cloth, with the flat shell up. Probe between the shells with a short knife to find a small opening. Insert the blade and run it across the roof of the shell to sever the internal muscle

2 Separating the flesh. Pull the shells apart. Slide the blade of the knife under the greyish outer rim of flesh – the skirt – to free the scallop (above, left). Remove the flesh from the shell and separate the white muscle and pink coral from the other organs (above, right). The muscle and coral are the best parts; the skirt can be used in a stock-pot; the rest should be discarded.

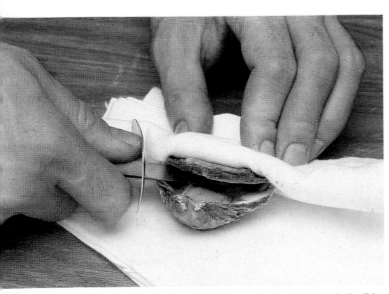

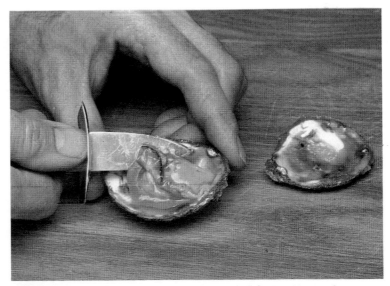

2 Severing the muscle. Continuing to hold the oyster firmly in the cloth, slide the knife blade along the inside of the upper shell to sever the muscle that holds the shells together. Discard the shell, and lift the rounded, lower shell off the napkin, making sure the liquid in it does not spill. Clean out any bits of broken shell with the point of the knife.

3 Cutting the oyster loose. Grip the lower shell firmly with your fingers. Cutting towards yourself, run the blade under the oyster to sever the muscle attaching it to the lower shell and so to free it. The oyster can then be swallowed raw directly from the shell, together with its juices, first seasoned to taste with a little lemon juice or freshly ground pepper.

Vegetable Preparation Techniques

At some time almost every kind of vegetable has to be sliced, diced or chopped to suit it to a particular cooking method or to a recipe. The best all-round cutting implement for these tasks is the classic 'chef's knife': a well-balanced tool with a sturdy handle and a keen, gently curved edge on its rigid blade. Used in conjunction with a hardwood cutting board, such a knife will cut up any vegetable with dispatch.

For maximum control, always hold the knife in the same way. Grip the handle near the blade. Firmly brace your thumb against one side of the butt end of the blade, and the middle joint of your forefinger against the other side. Wrap your other fingers around the handle. The knife's broad blade ensures that all the fingers on the handle stay comfortably clear of the work surface.

Your free hand plays an equally important role. For slicing and dicing, the knuckles act as a guide for the side of the knife blade, helping to determine the width of the cut pieces. For chopping, the hand steadies the blade, enabling you to work with a regular and controlled rocking motion for maximum efficiency.

With experience, you can perform any of these actions accurately and quickly, no matter what vegetable you are preparing. However, if you have to prepare a large batch of vegetables, cutting with a knife may take a good deal of time. Machines — manually operated or electric (see opposite) — speed the process, although none can offer quite the same precision as a deftly wielded knife.

Fine chopping. Herbs – here, parsley leaves – that must be finely chopped to release their flavour are quickly prepared by the rocking technique. Heap the parsley together. Place the blade across the pile, with your free hand resting on its tip to steady it. Using the tip as a pivot, rock the knife up and down. Shifting the butt of the blade after each cut, sweep back and forth over the pile.

Slicing a cylindrical vegetable. Steady the vegetable – here, a courgette – with your free hand, curling your fingertips inwards as shown above. Resting the side of the knife blade on the work surface, guide the knife blade with your knuckle as you slice. Do not raise the cutting edge of the blade above your knuckles.

Gadgets that Speed Slicing

The task of slicing, dicing or chopping a large quantity of vegetables goes quickly with a hand- or electrically operated device designed for the purpose. Two of the most useful hand devices are the mandoline and the rotary shredder. Provided their cutting edges are sharp, they will perform most of the functions of a knife with little loss of quality.

A mandoline (demonstrated on page 239) – so named because of a fancied resemblance to the stringed instrument – is a slicing tool. A vegetable is moved along its flat surface and across its blade, which can be adjusted or changed to provide plain or waffled slices of different thickness.

Rotary shredder, which are fitted with interchangeable cutting discs or drums, quickly produce vegetable strips of several widths. If required, the shreds can then be chopped finely with a knife.

Electric food processors, such as the one illustrated on the right, can perform many of the functions of a knife in a fraction of the time. Depending on which cutting tool is inserted into the bowl of the machine, it will slice, shred or chop raw vegetables; or it will reduce cooked vegetables to a purée, make breadcrumbs or grate cheese for stuffed vegetables and gratins, or mix batters for deep-frying.

Unfortunately, food processors have disadvantages. Vegetables that are to be sliced must first be cut small enough by hand to fit inside the tube that gives access to the cutter in the bowl. And because a processor's blades are never as sharp as that of a good knife, they will never cut quite so cleanly. Finally, the high speed of the electric processor adds to the bruising caused by its blades.

Inside the plastic processing bowl of this electric food processor is a serrated metal blade for chopping and puréeing. The food is fed into the bowl through the oval tube. Beside the machine, from left to right, are a plastic mixing blade and cutting discs for shredding, grating and slicing.

The Way to Dice

1 Cutting slices. Steady the vegetable with your free hand, keeping your fingers as far away as possible from the blade. Then slice the vegetable – a swede is shown here – to the required thickness.

2 Cutting strips. Stack a few slices at a time and steady the stack with your free hand, curling your fingers towards your palm. Using your knuckles to guide the blade, slice through the stock to make equal strips of the required width.

3 Cutting the dice. Gather together several strips at a time under the curled fingers and thumb of your free hand. Now slice across the strips at regular intervals to finish making the dice.

To ensure that the firm stems of broccoli are cooked in the same time as the tender buds, the stems should be peeled (see below, right) and thicker lower parts then cut into 2.5 cm (1 inch) slices.

Low-growing leaves, particularly spinach, require a thorough washing before cooking. With spinach and sorrel, the tough stems should be removed first and discarded (see right). Chard leaves, too, must be separated from their long stalks; but in this case, the stalks – or ribs, as they are called – are reserved and cooked as a delicacy in their own right.

Except for beetroot, mature roots and tubers are usually peeled before cooking. New potatoes, however, need be only scrubbed. To preserve the vitamin content of any root or tuber, prepare it as close to cooking time as possible. Submerge peeled potatoes in water to prevent them from discolouring; place peeled salsify, scorzonera, celeriac and Jerusalem artichokes in acidulated water (see opposite) to stop them turning black.

Stemming and Washing Spinach

Fold each leaf in half so that its glossy upper surfaces touch. Grasp the stem and pull it towards the leaf tip (left); discard the stem. Wash the leaves vigorously in cold water (right). Lift them out with splayed fingers; do not pour them into a colander to drain, the grit will resettle on to the leaves. Wash the leaves in fresh water twice more, then shake off the excess water.

Coring Chicory

The conical core formed by the central leaves is more bitter than the rest. Remove the base of the core by inserting the point of a small knife about 2.5 cm (1 inch) into the base and cutting with a circular motion.

Removing Cabbage Core

Before a cabbage is shredded, the solid core – the inner stem of the plant – should be removed so that the leaves can be cooked more evenly. Slice the cabbage in two, then cut the white central wedge from each half, working diagonally from the centre of each.

Peeling Broccoli Stems

Begin peeling from the base of each broccoli stem. After the first 1 cm ($^1/_2$ inch), grip the skin firmly between the knife and your thumb, and strip it from the stem. Turn the stem and repeat the process until all of the outer skin has been removed – up to the buds.

Three Peeling Techniques

Thin peeling. Use a vegetable peeler to pare vegetables with smooth, thin skins – such as parsnips (shown here), carrots, potatoes (including sweet potatoes), salsify and scorzonera.

Thicker peeling. Use a small sharp knife to slice through the stem end of a swede, as shown here, or a turnip. Continue to remove the remainder of its surface in strips 6 mm ($^1/_4$ inch) thick.

Peeling celeriac. Use a knife with a sharp medium-length blade to pare off thick strips of the gnarled surface of celeriac, making sure to cut out any places where the skin is deeply pitted.

Cutting Out Carrot's Woody Core

Trim and peel all carrots. Slice old specimens in half lengthwise with a sharp knife (above, left) to reveal the tough flavourless core: it is paler than

the rest of the carrot. Insert a small knife beneath the core at the thick end and prise it free along its length (above, right).

Preventing Discoloration

Make acidulated water by adding the juice of 2 lemons to 1 litre ($1^3/_4$ pints) of cold water. Immerse vegetables prone to discoloration – here scorzonera – after peeling.

Trimming Pods

Cut part-way through the stem end – a mange-tout pod is shown here – leaving the stem attached at one edge. Pull off string along pod. Repeat at tip to string other edge.

Shelling and Peeling Broad Beans

Press down on the curved edge near one end to pop the pod open. Run your thumb down its length (above left) to expose the beans, then pull them out. To peel each bean, use your

thumbnail to split the opaque skin at the bean's indented eye. Pull the skin carefully away from the bean (above right).

Husking and Preparing Sweetcorn

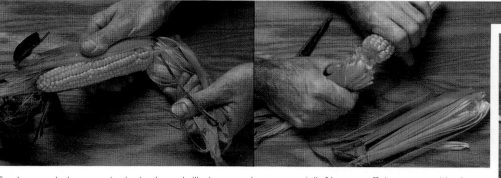

To clean a whole ear, strip the husks and silk down to the stem end (left); snap off the stem and husks together (centre); pick away any remaining silk. If you intend to remove the kernels, snap off only the husks; grip the stem firmly and use a sharp knife to slice away the kernels (right) close to the woody cob.

Trimming Okra

If okra is to be cooked whole, slice off the tip and tough stem end; cut away as little as possible, so that your knife does not pierce the fruit's internal sac containing gummy liquid.

Seeding Peppers

Cut pepper in half vertically and snap out white pithy core with its attached seeds. Trim away the ridges of whitish membrane that line the pepper, and pick out stray seeds.

Skinning and Seeding Tomatoes

1 Removing the core. Cutting at an angle into the centre of the stem end of the tomato, loosen a small column of flesh around the core and lift it out.

2 Loosening skin. Cut a small cross in the bottom of the tomato, barely piercing skin. Drop tomato into boiling water: about 2 or 3 seconds for a ripe tomato, slightly longer for a firm one.

3 Peeling. Starting at the cross cut in the base, catch the skin between your thumb and the knife blade and strip it off in sections, working towards the stem end where the skin adheres more firmly.

4 Seeding. Divide the tomato horizontally to expose the seed pockets. Gently squeeze the seed clusters of each half then shake it sharply to remove any remaining seeds. The halves are now ready for use in sauces or stews.

Turning Artichoke Bottoms

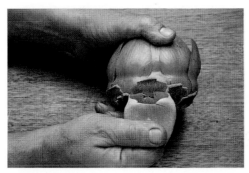

1 Breaking the stem. Hold the artichoke globe firmly and bend back the stem until it snaps from the base. As it breaks, it will pull the tough stem fibres out of the base of the artichoke.

2 Removing the outer leaves. Pull each leaf away from the globe and then downwards to break the tough upper part from the leaf's fleshy base. Continue until you reach the tender inner leaves, that are distinguished by their lighter colour.

3 Topping the artichoke. Cut off one to two-thirds of the plant's top, depending on how pale – and thus how tender – the leaves are. To prevent discolouring, use a stainless steel knife and rub the cut surfaces with lemon juice.

4 Paring the bottom. Starting at the stem and peeling in a spiral, use a small sharp stainless-steel knife to pare away the tough dark-green exterior of the artichoke's bottom. Moisten the cut surfaces with lemon juice or acidulated water.

5 Trimming the top. Trim any remaining dark green parts of the leaves from the top of the artichoke to expose the tightly packed central leaves that conceal the choke. Pull away these leaves until the whole choke is visible.

6 Removing the choke. Scoop out the raw choke with a teaspoon. Rub the artichoke bottom with lemon juice or put it in acidulated water. When an artichoke bottom is parboiled as a preliminary step, it is easier to remove the choke after it has been parboiled.

Peeling Asparagus: for Tenderness

Use a small knife to peel off the tough skin from each asparagus stalk. The paring should be thickest at the stem base, tapering away as the skin becomes progressively more tender. You will be better able to control how thickly you peel if you cut, carefully, towards yourself. Once their skin has been removed, the stalks will cook evenly – and as quickly as the tips.

Peeling Garlic Cloves

Place the clove beneath the blade of a broad heavy knife. Thump the blade lightly with your fist or the heel of your hand to split the tightly clinging skin, which then slips off easily.

Stringing Fennel and Celery

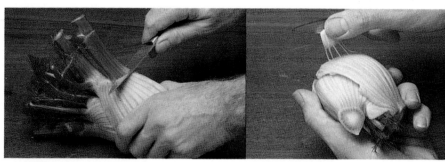

Cut off the upper stems and leaves of fennel (above, left); only the leaves of celery. Cut part-way through the top of the fennel bulb or celery head at the inside edge of each stalk, leaving the strings uncut and still attached to the outside edge. Remove the strings by pulling the partly detached piece towards the root (above, right).

Peeling Shallots

Trim the tops and tails from the shallots. Pull away the first layer of flesh with the skin; it is usually impossible to separate the paper-thin skin from the flesh.

Preparing Pulses

The first step in preparing pulses is to spread them out on a tray or a large plate and pick them over for foreign matter. When you have checked all of the pulses, rinse them under running water.

Once clean, most pulses must be soaked in water to rehydrate and swell. Most large beans and peas need up to 8 hours' soaking; some smaller types require only about an hour. Split pulses, with no hard outer skin to slow down absorption of water, need a similarly short time; lentils require no soaking.

The chart on the right gives soaking times, in cold water, for the pulses illustrated on pages 48-9. If you soak the pulses in hot water (Step 1, below) they will need less time to swell. Both methods produce equally good results. A pinch of bicarbonate of soda can be added to the water to speed up the swelling process.

Because soaking draws indigestible substances from the pulses, discard the water after soaking and replace it with fresh for cooking. Beans of the kidney bean family, particularly red and black ones, contain a potentially dangerous toxin rendered harmless by boiling. After soaking, these beans should be cooked for 10 minutes at a light boil, rinsed and covered with fresh boiling water, before simmering with aromatic ingredients. The chart gives approximate simmering times; precise timing depends on age and variety and some recipes call for simmering for an hour or more after pulses become tender for a more velvety texture.

The cooking time will be longer and the result less perfect if there are minerals – including salt – in the water. Cooks who live in hard-water areas often use bottled spring water for cooking pulses (in the past they collected rain water in barrels, but today people worry about air pollution). Add salt only after the pulses are tender. Acid foods, such as tomatoes, also slow down the cooking and should be added towards the end.

Soaking and Cooking Times

Pulse	Soaking time in cold water	Boiling time	Simmering time
Adzuki beans	1 hr	10 mins	1-1½ hrs
Black beans	7-8 hrs	10 mins	1-2 hrs
Black-eyed peas	7-8 hrs	10 mins	1-1½ hrs
Borlotti beans	7-8 hrs	10 mins	1-2 hrs
Broad beans	7-8 hrs		1-2 hrs
Butter beans	7-8 hrs		1-2 hrs
Cannellini beans	7-8 hrs		1-2 hrs
Chick peas	7-8 hrs		1½-3 hrs
Dutch brown beans	7-8 hrs		1-2 hrs
Field beans	7-8 hrs		1-2 hrs
Flageolet beans	7-8 hrs		1-2 hrs
Haricot beans	7-8 hrs		1-2 hrs
Lentils:			
Puy			45 mins
Large beige			1 hr
Red			20-30 mins
Mung beans	1 hr		40-60 mins
Green or yellow peas			
Whole	7-8 hrs		1-1½ hrs
Split	1 hr		45-60 mins
Pigeon peas	7-8 hrs		45-60 mins
Pinto beans	7-8 hrs		1-2 hrs
Red kidney beans	7-8 hrs	10 mins	1-2 hrs
Soya beans	7-8 hrs	10 mins	1-2 hrs

1 Soaking pulses. Pick over and wash pulses – here, black-eyed peas. Put the peas in a heavy pan with about double their volume of cold water. Bring the water to the boil slowly: gentle treatment helps to tenderize them evenly. Turn off the heat, and leave the peas to soak for about 1 hour. Drain the peas in a colander.

2 Adding aromatics. Return the peas to the pan and cover them with at least twice their volume of fresh water. Stud an onion with 1 or 2 cloves and place it in the water, with a few unpeeled garlic cloves and a carrot. Tie parsley, thyme and a bay leaf in a bundle with a stick of celery; add this bouquet garni to the pan.

Preparing Couscous

When couscous – semolina formed into tiny pellets – cooks in steam, the pellets become tender and light but remain separate. In North African countries, couscous is often cooked in the steam that rises from poaching meat and vegetables; the whole dish – including the meat and vegetables with their broth – takes its name from the grain and is also known as couscous. This technique can also be used to cook cracked grains or grits, although such grains will not acquire the light, fluffy texture characteristic of the steamed couscous.

To become tender, the couscous must absorb water before cooking: the pellets are dampened and left to swell. The damp pellets will form lumps, so you should rub them gently at intervals and shake them through a sieve before cooking.

1 Dampening the couscous. Spread the couscous on a tray or roasting tin and sprinkle it with just enough water to dampen all the grain. Here, the couscous used is made from semolina formed into pellets the size of millet grains.

2 Stirring the couscous. Rake through the couscous with your fingers so that all the pellets are moistened (above). Leave the pellets to absorb the water and swell for about 15 minutes, then sift them through your fingers again.

3 Separating the grains. Roll the grains of couscous gently between your palms to break up any lumps. Sprinkle the couscous with more water, a little at a time, and gently roll the pellets between your palms after each addition. Continue adding water and rolling until pellets are saturated, and have swelled to about twice original size.

4 Sieving the couscous. Put the damp couscous pellets in a coarse-meshed sieve, and shake the sieve over the tray so the couscous passes through. If some of the pellets have lumped together and will not pass through, sprinkle them with a little more water and roll them between your palms again, then re-sieve.

Preparing Polenta

Porridges, made by simmering ground, rolled or flaked grains to a thick, smooth mush, are staples regarded with deep affection by many people. The Scots hold dear their oatmeal porridge, the Italians their polenta made from cornmeal. Polenta can be served quite plain or can be enriched by being baked, grilled or fried with other ingredients.

To make plain polenta, sprinkle the grain into about twice its volume of boiling water, then stir continuously as it cooks to prevent it from sticking to the pan. As the mixture becomes solid, thin it with boiling water.

In this demonstration, the polenta is spread out to cool and set, then cut into shapes and baked with cheese or a tomato sauce. Alternative accompaniments include salt cod or any of the sauces served with pasta. If you choose to fry the polenta, you can incorporate pre-cooked, finely chopped vegetables or meat into the mixture.

1 Sprinkling in the cornmeal. Bring a large pan of salted water to a rolling boil. Strew in coarse cornmeal from a height to distribute the grain evenly in the water. Add the grain fairly slowly, so that the water remains on the boil; otherwise the grains will form lumps. As soon as you have added the grain, lower the heat and begin stirring with a wooden spoon.

2 Thinning the polenta. Stir the polenta continuously. Each time it becomes too thick to stir easily, add a ladleful of boiling water. Cook the polenta for at least 30 minutes, until it acquires an elastic texture and comes away from the sides of the pan. A full hour's cooking will give a softer-textured porridge.

3 Turning out the polenta. Serve the polenta at once, if you wish – either with a sauce or quite plain, as a garnish for meat or fish. If you prefer to bake or fry the polenta, turn it out on a smooth work surface. With a spoon or spatula, flatten it out to an overall thickness of about 1 cm (1/2 inch) and smooth the surface. Leave the polenta to cool and set for at least 20 minutes.

4 Shaping the polenta. Use a knife or a pastry cutter to make shapes from the cold slab of polenta: in this case, the polenta is stamped into circles with a pastry cutter. Collect the trimmings and knead them into a ball. Flatten the ball and cut out more shapes.

5 Arranging the polenta shapes. Lay the polenta shapes in an overlapping pattern in a gratin dish, to form an even layer. Generously sprinkle the polenta with grated Parmesan. If you like, you can bake the polenta simply with its sprinkling of cheese – or cover it with a tomato sauce.

Making Fresh Pasta

Making pasta by hand demands only a little time and effort, and no specialized equipment at all. Flour is moistened to produce dough, and the dough is kneaded. Usually, the dough is rolled out (below) then cut into various shapes (page 150). But to make Hungarian-style pasta shreds, used to garnish soups, the dough is grated (right).

While any type of flour can be used in pasta-making, a flour rich in gluten is best for an easily rolled dough that will yield firm, springy pasta. Gluten is a protein that, when moistened, forms an elastic network that strengthens the dough. Fine semolina made from durum wheat, the variety with the highest proportion of gluten, is used for most commercial pasta – but it produces a hard dough that requires fairly lengthy kneading. Strong

flour sold for bread-making is a good choice for hand-made pasta because it is rich in gluten, but requires less kneading and rolling than semolina. The '00' (*doppo zero*) type of flour used by Italians for the purpose is now more readily available in better food shops.

Although the flour can be made into a dough with water, egg confers a richer flavour. If you are making pasta for rolling out, use about one egg for each 100 g (3^1/$_2$ oz) of flour; the exact proportion will depend on the size of the eggs and the type of flour you use. The addition of a little oil or melted butter softens the dough, making it easier to handle.

Large quantities of dough are most easily mixed on a flat surface, smaller quantities in a bowl. On a flat surface, heap up more flour than you will need,

place the liquids in the centre and gradually mix in flour from the perimeter, stopping when the dough forms a coherent mass. In a bowl, it is more difficult to incorporate the flour progressively, so start with less flour than you think you will need. A little more flour can easily be added, whereas liquid could not readily be blended into a dough that is too stiff.

Once the dough is mixed, it should be kneaded for a few minutes. Kneading is a repetition of two steps – flattening and folding the dough – which develop the gluten network. Kneading should leave the dough smooth and silky – neither dry nor sticky. At this point, the dough is so elastic that it springs back on itself if you try to roll it. If it is left to rest for an hour, however, the gluten relaxes so that

Basic Egg Pasta Dough

1 Adding eggs to flour. Form a mound of flour on a smooth surface. Make a well in the centre of the mound. Break whole eggs into the well, or lightly beat them and pour in the beaten egg. Add salt and, if you like, pour a little olive oil into the well to soften the dough and make it easier to manipulate.

2 Mixing the dough. With one hand, gradually push the flour from around the edge of the well into the egg mixture. Stir with your fingers to form a batter in the well. To prevent the eggs from flowing out, support the perimeter of the flour with your free hand. Continue to incorporate flour into the egg mixture until the batter has become a firm paste. Gather it into a ball.

the dough can be rolled out thinly.

The dough for shredded pasta must be very stiff. Extra flour is incorporated during kneading and the dough is chilled to firm it before grating.

Basic Egg Pasta Dough

MAKES ABOUT 675 G / 1½ LB

450 g / 1 lb strong flour, plus more for
dusting
4 large eggs
1 tsp salt
little olive oil or melted butter
(optional)

Extra Stiffness for Grated Pasta

1 Incorporating extra flour. Lightly flour the work surface. Knead the dough as Step 3 below. During the kneading process, constantly add more flour; the dough should become as stiff as possible without crumbling. Continue kneading until the dough is smooth and firm.

2 Grating the dough. Wrap the dough in plastic film. Put it in a freezer for about 30 minutes. Using the large holes of the grater, coarsely grate the dough on to a sheet of greaseproof paper. Use the pasta shreds straight away or flour them generously in order to prevent them from sticking together.

3 Kneading the dough. With the heel of your hand, press the ball of dough flat on to a lightly floured surface. Fold the dough double, then press again. Repeat this procedure for 5 to 10 minutes, until the dough is silky and elastic. Leave the dough, covered with a cloth, for 1 hour.

4 Rolling the dough. Divide the dough into portions about the size of your fist. Roll each one out on a lightly floured surface. Turn the dough through 90 degrees at intervals, to produce a round sheet. When the dough is almost translucent, it is thin enough to cut into shapes.

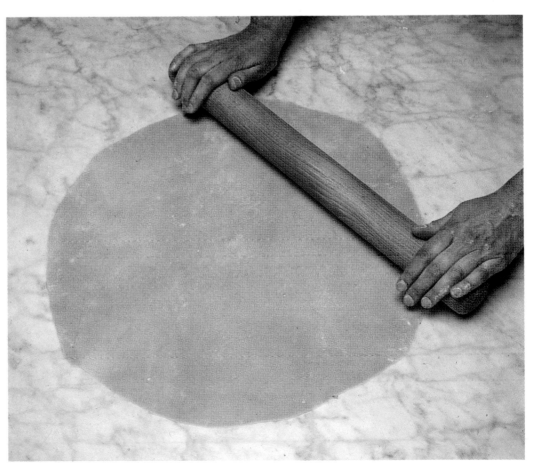

Using a Pasta Machine

Most of the work involved in making pasta at home – kneading and rolling out – can be done by a simple hand-operated machine. There are several types of machine, all of which operate in similar ways. The most common version (right) consists of three pairs of rollers set in a sturdy frame. One pair is smooth, with an adjustable knob at the side of the machine to vary the width of the gap between the rollers. These first knead and then roll out the dough. The other rollers are fitted with cutters to slice the rolled dough into noodles (page 150). Each pair of rollers has a socket for the handle that operates the machine.

The dough itself is mixed from the same ingredients as hand-made pasta, manually kneaded just enough to bind them together. Most of the kneading is done by machine. The dough is floured, to prevent it from sticking to the machine, and then passed repeatedly through the smooth rollers. So that the dough is thick enough to be pressed firmly by the rollers – the essence of kneading – rather than slipping easily between them, it must be folded over between passages. If you are making a large quantity of pasta, tear the hand-kneaded dough into portions the size of your fist, so as to produce sheets of manageable proportions.

The kneading is complete when the dough is very smooth and has attained the exact width of the rollers. During the rolling-out stage, the gap between these rollers is decreased after each passage of the sheet through them. The dough is no longer folded between passages and it becomes progressively longer and thinner as the gap narrows. The sheet of dough is very fragile by this point, and careful handling is necessary to prevent it from tearing. When it has attained the thickness you require, the dough can be cut into different shapes – either by hand or with the machine's cutters.

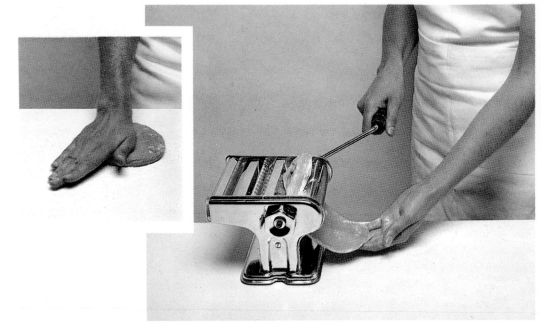

1 Preparing the dough. Mix fresh pasta dough (previous page), knead it and leave it, covered with a cloth, for 1 hour. Divide it into fist-sized portions. Flatten each portion with your hand (inset). Set the adjustable rollers of the machine fully open. Flour the dough and pass it between the rollers. Support the rolled dough with one hand.

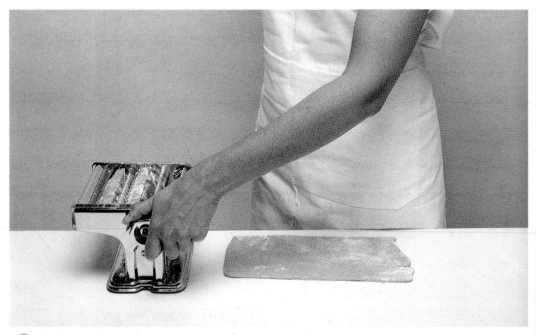

4 Rolling out the dough. Decrease the gap between the rollers by turning the knob at the side of the machine round by two or three notches. Flour the dough and, without folding it, pass it between the rollers. Flour the dough lightly once more.

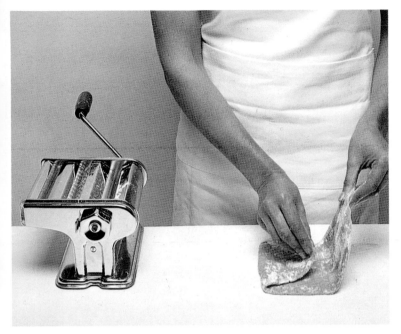

2 Folding the rolled dough. Lightly flour a smooth working surface. Lay the rolled dough out on it. Fold one end of the dough towards the middle and fold the other end on top of it to make three layers of approximately the original size of the portion. Sprinkle on a little more flour.

3 Kneading the dough by machine. Turn the dough 90 degrees, to help produce a neat rectangular shape, and pass it between the smooth rollers again. Repeat the flouring, folding and rolling three or four times – do not work the dough any more than is necessary – until it is very smooth and shaped to the width of the machine.

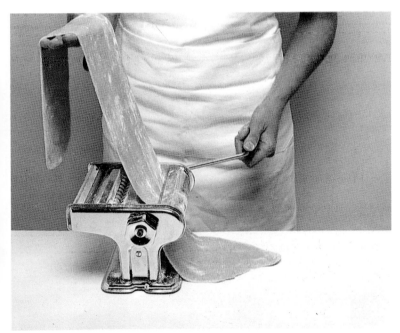

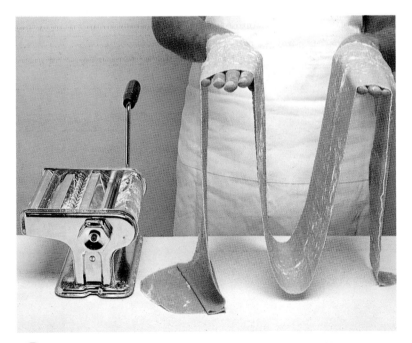

5 Rolling the dough thinner. Decrease the gap between the rollers by two or three more notches. Pass the dough through the machine again. Because the pasta sheet will now be quite long, support it with one hand as you feed it into the machine and, as it emerges, help it to slide along the work surface rather than letting it fall in folds and sticking together.

6 Drying out the rolled dough. Flour the dough and roll it as thin as you require – for most purposes, the machine's next-to-finest setting is the most suitable. Unless you intend to make filled pasta shapes, hang the dough up to dry: an excellent way is to hang it over a broomstick supported by two chair backs. When the dough is no longer sticky, cut it into the lengths you require.

Shaping Fresh Pasta

Homemade pasta can be fashioned into a wide range of flat and rounded shapes, from simple noodles and squares to butterflies. Some of the most rapidly formed shapes are demonstrated here.

Noodles can be made by machine (right) or by hand (below). Small squares are speedily prepared by cutting through several layers of pasta (opposite, bottom left). For decorative effect, a pastry wheel will give noodles and squares serrated edges; you can pinch rectangles into butterflies and press rounds into shapes.

For cutting, the pasta dough should be flexible but not at all sticky. To achieve the right state, you may have to leave the rolled-out pasta to dry for a time – from a few minutes to 1 hour, depending on the temperature of the room and its humidity. Do not leave the pasta so long that it becomes leathery: it would crack when cut. After cutting, sprinkle the shapes liberally with fine semolina or flour to prevent them from sticking together.

Rapid Cutting with a Pasta Machine

 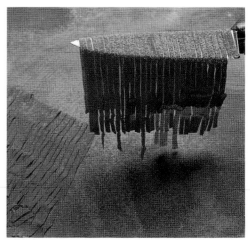

Making noodles. In addition to the rollers for kneading dough, pasta machines have two or more cutters of different widths. To prepare medium noodles, insert the handle beside the wider cutter and crank a length of the rolled-out dough through the machine. Support the noodles with your hand as they emerge.

Cutting fine noodles. If you prefer thin noodles, insert the handle of the machine beside the narrow cutter and pass a past sheet through it. Once the cutter has gripped the pasta, there is no need to touch the uncut sheet; leave it draped over the machine and use your free hand to catch the noodles as they emerge to prevent tangling.

Hand-sliced Noodles

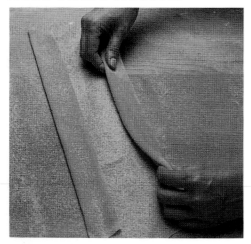  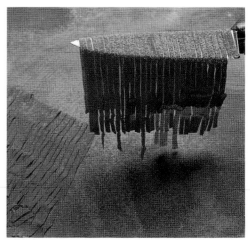

1 Folding the dough: Roll out a piece of dough into a roughly circular shape. Sprinkle with fine semolina to prevent it from sticking. Fold the pasta very loosely over on to itself, working from both sides towards the centre until the two loose rolls meet. Do not press the folded pasta or it may stick together.

2 Cutting the noodles. With a sharp knife, cut the dough into even strips. One advantage of cutting by hand instead of machine is that there is no restriction on the noodles' width: cut them as wide or narrow as you please.

3 Unrolling the noodles. Slide a knife underneath the cut pasta at the point where the two rolls meet. Insert the full length of the blade, then raise the knife, blunt edge uppermost; the rolled-up noodles will unroll, dropping down either side of the blade.

Using a Pastry Wheel

Place a rectangular strip of either hand-rolled or machine-rolled pasta dough on a floured surface. Cut around the outside of the strip with a pastry wheel to make a serrated edge. With the wheel, cut the strips into wide noodles or lasagne pieces 12cm / 5 inches square.

Forming Figures-of-Eight

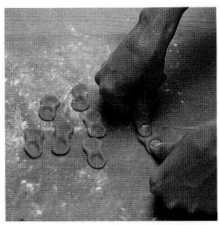

Tear off small, walnut-sized pieces of dough from a larger piece and form them into sausage shapes with your fingers. Flatten the pieces slightly and place them on a floured surface. Using your thumbs, press down firmly at both ends of each shape, leaving an imprint on either side of a central ridge.

Making Mushroom Caps

Roll some pasta dough on a floured surface into a cylinder about 2cm / $^3/_4$ inch in diameter. Cut the cylinder into 3mm / $^1/_8$ inch thick slices. Place a round in the palm of your hand and, with the thumb of the other hand, make a depression in the round while twisting it slightly so that it becomes broader.

Fashioning Butterflies

Cut round the edge of a rectangular sheet of pasta dough with a pastry wheel to give a serrated edge. With the pastry wheel, cut the pasta sheet into small rectangles about 5 by 2.5cm / 2 by 1 inches. Pinch the small rectangles of dough at the centre to form butterflies.

Mass-producing Small Squares

Stacking layers for speedy cutting. Roll out sheets of pasta and cut them into long strips about the width of three fingers (above left). Flour the strips and stack them neatly on top of each other. Cut this stack across into small strips about 2.5cm 1 in wide. Cut the strips in half again to make squares (above right).

Colouring and Flavouring Pasta

Coloured pasta requires no more effort to make than plain pasta, yet the results, especially if you combine several colours in one dish, are spectacular. The colourings – herbs for speckled green pasta, beetroot for red, tomato for orange, spinach or chard for solid green and saffron for yellow – also flavour the pasta subtly.

All the colourings, except saffron, require preparation before they are mixed with the other pasta ingredients. The herbs are chopped, the vegetables are cooked then chopped or puréed so that they will be assimilated evenly into the dough. Spinach is parboiled and puréed if the pasta is to be hand-rolled. If you use a machine, however, it is enough to chop the parboiled spinach finely; the machine's rollers will spread the colour uniformly. For a tomato colouring, simply use a little well-reduced tomato sauce. Beetroot must be boiled and puréed, no matter how you make the pasta; you can pound it in a mortar and pestle, but the easiest way to pulp beetroot is in a food processor.

To distribute saffron evenly through the dough combine it with the flour before the moist ingredients are added. Vegetable purées and herbs can be combined with the other ingredients in a single step.

Once the colourings have been incorporated into the dough, the pasta is kneaded and rolled out. To compensate for the moistness of most of the colourings, add extra flour to the dough during kneading. Some colourings, such as spinach and herbs, release their moisture progressively and, to counter the stickiness, dust the pasta with more flour than usual when you roll it out.

Sheets of pasta in rainbow tones hang to dry over a broomstick. From left to right are herb, beetroot, tomato, spinach and saffron-coloured pasta.

A Muted Green from Spinach

1 Preparing the spinach. Cook trimmed and washed spinach in boiling water for 2 minutes. Drain and refresh it in cold water. Squeeze as dry as possible and chop it finely.

2 Kneading the dough. Mix all of the ingredients for the pasta thoroughly with a fork. Knead the dough by hand, leave it to rest, then use a pasta machine to knead and roll it out.

A Speckling of Fresh Herbs

1 Chopping herbs. Finely chop a selection of fresh herbs – in this case parsley, sorrel, thyme, sage, tarragon and lovage. Basil, marjoram, hyssop and fennel are among other possibilities.

2 Stirring in the herbs. Using a fork, stir the chopped herbs into the other pasta ingredients – flour, olive oil, salt and eggs. Knead the dough, allow it to rest and roll it out.

A Lively Pink from Beetroot

1 Puréeing the beetroot. Boil unpeeled beet-roots in salted water until tender – 40 minutes to 2 hours, depending on size. Peel and chop and purée in a food processor.

2 Stirring in the beetroots. Stir the beet purée with the other pasta ingredients in a mixing bowl or on a flat surface. Knead the dough, allow it to rest and roll it out.

Orange from Tomato

Blending in the tomato purée. Stir a well-reduced tomato sauce into the other ingredients before kneading, resting and rolling out the dough.

Yellow from Saffron

1 Mixing in the saffron. Add a knife-tip of powdered saffron to the dry ingredients – flour and salt – and stir it in well with a fork to ensure the colour is distributed evenly.

2 Kneading the dough. When the saffron is evenly spread through the flour, mix in the liquid – eggs and oil. Knead, rest and roll out the dough.

Savoury Fillings for Pasta Shapes

Puréed or finely chopped mixtures based on meat, fish, vegetables or cheese all make excellent fillings for pasta shapes. Two contrasting stuffings are demonstrated here, both suitable for filling any shape (opposite page and overleaf).

Both stuffings readily lend themselves to improvisation: you can vary the proportions as you please, omit spinach or replace it with chard leaves and use any kind of meat, including leftovers. A little egg helps bind the ingredients, but is not essential because the stuffing will be tightly enclosed.

Since fresh pasta needs such brief boiling, any stuffing ingredient that cannot be eaten raw must be pre-cooked. Leaves must be squeezed dry after boiling, otherwise they will make the pasta soggy and easily torn. Similarly, a braising liquid should be reduced – or strained off and used later as a sauce for the pasta.

A Fresh Cheese Mixture

1 Mixing cheese and egg. Remove the stalks from spinach leaves and wash the leaves well. Cook the spinach in boiling water for 2 to 3 minutes. Drain it, rinse it under cold water, then squeeze and chop it finely. Mix ricotta cheese with eggs and some grated Parmesan cheese.

2 Stirring in the spinach. Add the chopped spinach to the other stuffing ingredients in the bowl. Stir to combine them all thoroughly. Season with salt, pepper and ground allspice to taste.

Braised Meats Allied with Spinach

1 Finely chop onions and meat – here veal and beef with cooked ham. Sauté onions in oil until soft. Stir in meat, turning until brown. Add thyme, bay leaf and glass each of wine and stock. Simmer until meat is tender and liquid reduced.

2 Parboil trimmed spinach for 2 to 3 minutes in plenty of water. Drain, refresh and squeeze dry. Chop finely. Remove thyme and bay leaf from cooked meat. Transfer meat and onions to a large bowl and mash thoroughly with a fork.

3 Mixing in the spinach. Add egg yolks and the chopped spinach to the mashed meat and onions. Use a fork to blend the ingredients thoroughly. Taste the stuffing and, if necessary, season it with salt and freshly ground pepper.

Stuffing Pasta Shapes

Small stuffed pasta shapes are made by one of two methods. The filling is either sandwiched between two sheets of pasta (below), or it is placed in the centre of a small pasta square or circle, which is then wrapped around it (overleaf).

The ravioli here are of the first type and are the quickest shapes to make, since they lend themselves to mass production. A strip of pasta rolled out with a pasta machine, or a hand-rolled sheet of pasta trimmed to a rectangular shape, is dotted at regular intervals with small heaps of stuffing. The pasta between the mounds is moistened, so that it will stick to a second sheet of pasta laid on top. By running a knife or a pastry wheel carefully between the mounds of stuffing, you can quickly separate the dough into individual ravioli.

For the more complex shapes demonstrated on the following pages, the dough is first cut into squares or circles, then, once the stuffing is in place, folded in various ways. A circle of pasta can simply be moistened along the edge, folded over and sealed to give a half-moon; or the half-moon can be curled round to make the compact shapes known as tortellini (overleaf, above). Folded and sealed like an envelope, a circle yields a neat rectangular package. You can make pasta stars from small squares just lightly pinched together at the corners (overleaf). Most stuffings would fall out of such an open container, but if you use a stiff, coherent mixture and smear just a little on each pasta square, the stuffing will cling to the pasta during cooking.

Dough for any stuffed shapes should be rolled to a thickness of 3 mm ($^1/_8$ inch) – a little thicker than dough for unstuffed pasta: the packages must be fairly strong to hold their contents. So that the pasta can be moulded round the stuffing, it should be as moist and flexible as possible: use the pasta sheets immediately when they are ready. For ravioli, roll out just two sheets at a time; for the other shapes, roll and cut out as many circles or squares as you want; flour them well so that they do not stick together and stack them on top of each other to keep them from drying out while you work.

Each pasta shape needs a margin of at least 5 mm ($^1/_4$ inch) of sealed pasta round the stuffing to enclose it securely. You should avoid using too much stuffing or, with ravioli, placing the mounds of stuffing too closely together.

Because of the dough's moistness, stuffed pasta shapes tend to stick to each other and to any surface on which they are laid. To prevent sticking and tearing, place them, well separated, on a floured cloth until you are ready to cook them.

The Knack of Forming Ravioli

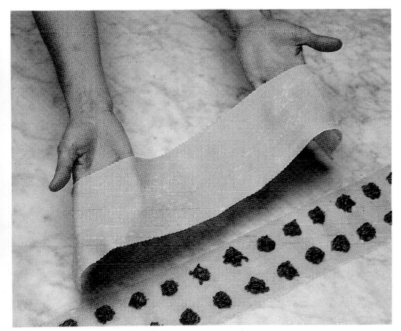

1 Sealing in the stuffing. Roll out two identically sized sheets of pasta; trim their edges with a pastry wheel. Place half-teaspoon portions of stuffing (opposite page) on one of the sheets at 5 cm (2 inch) intervals; leave a 2.5 cm (1 inch) margin round the edge of the sheet. Brush the dough with water between the mounds of stuffing. Lay the second sheet of pasta over the first one.

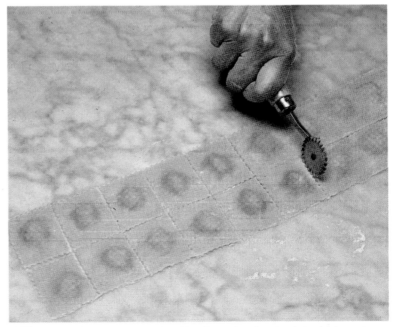

2 Cutting the ravioli. With the side of your hand, press the pasta between the mounds of stuffing, so that the two moistened sheets stick together firmly. Using a fluted pastry wheel, cut along and across the dough, midway between the rows of stuffing to separate the individual ravioli.

Moulding Circles into Tortellini

1 Adding the filling. With a biscuit cutter, stamp circles about 7.5 cm (3 inches) in diameter from a sheet of pasta dough. In the middle of each circle, put a teaspoon of stuffing – here, a spinach and curd cheese mixture (page 154). Using a pastry brush or your finger, moisten the edge of the circle with water.

2 Making the first fold. Fold over the circle of dough to form a half-moon containing the stuffing. To seal in the stuffing, pinch the moistened edges of the dough together between your thumb and forefinger. If you like, you can cook the pasta in this form – or go on to make tortellini (Steps 3 and 4).

Two Ingenious Ways to Form a Wrapping

Folding circles for a trim package. With a biscuit cutter, stamp circles about 7.5 cm (3 inches) in diameter from a sheet of pasta dough. Put a teaspoon of stuffing in the centre of each circle. Brush the rim of the circle with a little water. Fold two opposite sides of the circle over the stuffing. Fold the other two sides over the first two, and press gently to seal the envelope-like container.

Pinching squares for a star-like shape. With a fluted or plain pastry wheel, cut a sheet of pasta dough into squares measuring approximately 7.5 cm (3 inches) across. Place a teaspoon of stuffing in the middle of each square, and brush the edge of the square with water. Pinch together two opposite corners of the square over the stuffing, then fold the other two corners into the centre. To enclose the stuffing securely, pinch the edges together.

3 Bending the half-moon into shape. Take each half-moon in both hands and curve it gently into a ring shape around your index finger, until its ends are almost touching. At the same time, fold the sealed margin of the dough upwards to form a groove around the edge.

4 Fixing the shape. Pinch the ends of the curled half-moon firmly together, so that the shape remains curled round. Lay the completed tortellini on a floured towel; be sure that they are not touching, or they may stick together. Leave the tortellini to dry out for a few minutes before you cook them.

Loosely Enclosing a Finely Ground Stuffing

1 Preparing the stuffing. Trim fat and connective tissue from a piece of lamb shoulder. Chop the meat into small pieces. In a mortar, pound the lamb with peeled garlic, salt and pepper, and herbs – mint, oregano and parsley are used here – until it is a fairly smooth paste. Alternatively, purée the meat and flavourings in a food processor.

2 Pinching the corners. Cut a sheet of pasta dough into 3 cm (1 1/4 inch) squares. Smear a little stuffing on each square. Bring together two opposite corners of each square (above) over the stuffing, then the other two, and pinch all four corners together (right). There is no need to seal all the edges: the stuffing will adhere to the pasta during cooking.

Preparing Fruit

Fresh fruit needs very little preliminary preparation. Once it has been washed or peeled, and freed of any stems, stones or cores, it is ready for use. For the sake of appearance and economy, the cook's aim is to remove these unwanted parts in a way that will leave the precious flesh intact and undamaged. The most effective technique for achieving this end varies from one fruit to another, as shown here.

To strip off the tough coverings of firm fruits such as apples and unripe papayas, many cooks rely on a small sharp knife; others resort to a vegetable peeler. The thin, tight skins of nectarines, plums, peaches and apricots may – depending on ripeness – need to be softened in boiling water before they can be eased off. But some fruits, such as passion fruit, guavas and medlars, are so soft and pulpy that peeling is virtually impossible; the best way to enjoy these varieties is to halve them and spoon out their flesh.

The task of removing cores, stones or pips without damaging the flesh is made easier by implements such as an apple corer – equally efficient for pears and for quinces – or a cherry stoner that will extract the stone while leaving the cherry intact. Grapes can also be seeded without being split by inserting the tip of a small, pointed knife at the stem end. Alternatively, large grapes may be split in half before they are seeded.

The best utensils for any of these tasks are those made of non-reactive metal, such as stainless steel; other metals may react chemically with the acid in the fruit, which would impair the flavour and cause discoloration. Discolouring also occurs when fruits containing tannin – apples and bananas, for example – are exposed to air. Such fruits should be rubbed with a lemon half, rolled in lemon juice or placed in acidulated water – water and lemon juice – as soon as they are peeled. But, since all fresh fruits are vulnerable once they are cut or peeled, every variety is best prepared just before use.

Paring Firm Fruits

To peel the skins of firm-fleshed fruits such as apples, pears or the unripe papayas shown here, hold the fruit firmly in one hand and, using a vegetable peeler or a small paring knife, peel towards yourself to remove the skin in lengthwise strips.

Peeling Soft Fruits

To peel a soft-fleshed fruit such as a mango without bruising, either hold the fruit gently in the palm of your hand or secure one end on the prongs of a fork. With a knife, slit the skin lengthwise to divide it into four sections. Grip each section between your thumb and the knife-flat and strip it off.

Hulling Strawberries

Place strawberries in a colander; briefly rinse them in cold water. Using the tip of a small knife or your thumb and finger, remove the circle of leaves at the top of the fruit; the fibrous white core will come away at the same time. For less ripe berries it may be necessary to twist the hull gently.

Releasing Berries

Stemming currants. Hold a spray of currants – redcurrants are used here – over a dish. Place the prongs of a fork at the top of the spray. Pull gently upwards on the stem (above); the berries will drop away intact and unbruised.

Using a Corer

Coring apples. Put water acidulated with lemon juice into a bowl. Use a small paring knife or a peeler to peel the apple. To core it, hold it steady with one hand and plunge a corer down through the stem end to the base; remove and discard core. Immediately place apple in the acidulated water.

Stoning Cherries

Removing the stones. Place cherries in a colander and rinse them in cold water. Removing the stalks as you work, place each cherry upright on the base of a cherry stoner. As you close the stoner, the plunger will push the stone through the fruit and out at the bottom.

Seeding Melons

Removing the seeds. To remove the seeds from melon or papaya, slice the fruit in half – here, an Ogen melon is shown. With a metal spoon, scoop out the mass of seeds and the attached seed membrane from each melon half.

Segmenting Grapefruit

Loosening the segments. With a sharp knife, halve the grapefruit and cut round the white central core and remove it. With a curved serrated knife, cut through the membrane that separates each of the segments. Run the knife round the flesh of the grapefruit to free the segments of flesh completely.

Stoning Fruit

Removing the stone. To remove the stone from fruit such as peaches, plums, nectarines or, as here, apricots, cut along the natural groove in the fruit with a sharp knife and gently prise apart the two halves. Using the tip of the knife, ease out the stone.

Pulping Passion Fruit

Scooping out the flesh. Use a small sharp knife to slice off the top of each passion fruit. With a small spoon, scoop the flesh and edible seeds into a bowl. Discard the skin.

Hollowing out a Pineapple Shell

1 Trimming the pineapple. Cut the stalk from the base of the pineapple. Using a long sharp knife, trim the base flat so the pineapple will stand upright. Holding the knife at an angle pointing downwards, cut off the leafy top of the pineapple to make a lid for presentation.

2 Cutting into the pineapple. Taking care not to pierce the skin, make a cut all around the inner circumference of the pineapple, reaching about halfway down into it. Make another circular cut through the flesh around the central core.

3 Cutting wedges. To divide the flesh into wedges that will lift out easily, make spoke-like cuts in the flesh radiating from the inner to the outer circular cut. Use your other hand to steady the pineapple as you cut.

Making Julienne Strips of Citrus Rind

1 Paring the rind from oranges. Using a vegetable peeler, carefully pare off the rind of each orange working in sections from the base to the top to get long, thin, unbroken strips. Leave any rind that will not come off in one piece.

2 Cutting the julienne. Place the long strips of orange rind on a wooden surface or chopping board. Take a small sharp knife and, using your fingers to guide the blade, slice each strip of rind lengthwise into fine julienne.

Peeling Chestnuts

4 Scooping out the flesh. Using a tablespoon, scoop out the chunks of pineapple. Make circular cuts around the edge and core of the lower half. Cut and scoop out the chunks of flesh as before. Then scrape out the flesh round the shell until empty except for core. Cut base of core with tip of knife and break off.

1 Preparing chestnuts. Sort through the chestnuts, discarding any that are rotten or broken. With a small sharp knife, carefully cut a cross shape in the rounded side of each chestnut shell. Avoid slicing into the flesh of the chestnut.

2 Peeling the chestnuts. Put the chestnuts into a saucepan of boiling water for a couple of minutes. Lift them out in small batches with a perforated spoon. Using a sharp knife, or your finger and thumb if this is easier, peel off the outer shell of each nut and then the brown inner skin.

Peeling and Seeding Grapes

Peeling grapes. One by one, pick grapes – seedless grapes are used here – off their stems. Starting at the point where the stem was removed, lift the skin of each grape with the tip of a small knife and peel the skin back in sections (above). If you are using grapes with pips, halve them lengthwise and remove the pips with the point of the knife. Set the peeled grapes aside on a plate.

Skinning a Prickly Pear

To avoid touching the outside of the fruit – which is covered with spines – steady it with a fork and use a sharp knife to top and tail it. To skin the fruit, cut a lengthwise slit down one side. Keep the fruit steady with the fork and use the knife to work underneath the skin and ease it away from the flesh beneath.

Removing Clinging Skins

Blanching a nectarine. To loosen the skins of plums, peaches or, as here, nectarines, immerse the fruit in boiling water for a few seconds; drain, then cover the fruit with cold water. With a knife, nick the fruit at the stem end to detach the skin from the flesh, then peel off the loosened skin in strips.

Peeling a Kiwi Fruit

Stripping off the skin. Use a sharp knife to top and tail the kiwi fruit. With your fingernail or a knife tip, nick the brown skin and peel it away in lengthwise strips. Remove the buff-coloured, papery skins of lychees in the same way.

Stringing Rhubarb

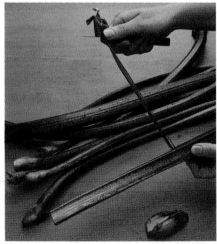

Removing fibrous strings. Cut off and discard the leaves and the base of a stick of rhubarb. Starting at one end, grip the tough outer skin between your thumb and the flat of a knife and pull off the skin in strips.

Dividing a Pineapple

1 Removing skin and spikes. With a sharp knife, cut off the top of a pineapple. Trim the base so that it stands flat on a work surface. Push a fork into the top of the fruit to steady it. Use the knife to slice off the skin in vertical strips. With the tip of the knife, remove the spikes embedded in the flesh.

2 Coring and cubing. Position the knife to one side of the central core and slice lengthwise through the pineapple. In the section of pineapple containing the core, make a second vertical cut, also to one side of the core. Cut away the core from the remaining third section. Cut the sections of flesh into even-sized chunks.

Simple Steps to Smooth Purées

Fruit crushed or sieved to a purée is both a sauce and a versatile ingredient for all kinds of savoury dishes and desserts, from soups to sorbets.

Fruits can be puréed with a sieve, a food mill or a processor, but the best tool for the job will depend on the character of the fruit. Whole currants or berries, and peeled, soft-fleshed fruits – passion fruit and bananas, for example – are puréed raw. Because they are so soft, these varieties break down easily if simply pressed through a nylon sieve that will hold back any skins or seeds (right). Crisp-textured pineapple flesh can also be puréed raw, but requires more vigorous treatment to crush it – the best device is a blender or processor (far right). To give it a finer texture, strain the resulting purée through a food mill or a sieve.

Many fruits are either too firm or too fibrous to purée raw. Apples, quinces, pears and rhubarb, sliced or halved as necessary, must be softened first by brief poaching. The fruits will release their own juices as they cook, so the only additional moistening needed is a spoonful of water or a knob of butter, to prevent the fruits from sticking to the pan. You can add sugar to taste, along with a cinnamon stick, cloves, or any other flavouring that will complement the fruit.

After the fruit is cooked, any liquid that has collected in the pan should be drained off; you can reserve these juices, if you like, to thin the purée. Softened apples, pears and quinces are easily puréed by passing them through a sieve or a food mill. Rhubarb, because of its stringy fibres, is puréed most efficiently by forcing it through the medium disc of a food mill (far right). The action of the blades, pressing the rhubarb through the metal disc, will break down the strings to produce a smooth-textured purée.

Sieving Berries

Sieving raspberries. Pick over berries – here, raspberries. Remove any stalks and leaves from strawberries or from gooseberries. Place the fruit, a small batch at a time, in a nylon sieve set over a bowl. Using a wooden pestle, push the fruit through the sieve to purée it.

Pulping a Pineapple

Processing pineapple chunks. Peel and core pineapple and cut the flesh into even-sized chunks (opposite). Put the chunks into a food processor or blender, a batch at a time. Process the fruit in short bursts until evenly puréed.

Softening Firm Fruit

Puréeing apple. Peel and core apples (pages 158-9); slice thinly. Put in a heavy pan with a knob of butter or a spoonful of water. Cook until tender. Drain off any liquid. To make a smooth purée, pass through a fine-meshed drum sieve. For a coarser purée, use a nylon sieve or a food mill fitted with a medium disc.

Puréeing Rhubarb

Trim rhubarb (opposite); cut the stalks into 5 cm (2 inch) pieces. Put in a heavy pan with half their weight of sugar and a knob of butter. Cook, covered, over a low heat for 20 to 30 minutes, or until tender. Drain the rhubarb and pass it through a food mill fitted with a medium disc set over a bowl.

Marinades and Stuffings

Marinades and stuffings both give extra flavour to meat, but in quite different ways. A marinade is a fragrant mixture in which the meat is steeped before cooking. A stuffing exchanges flavour with the meat during the cooking, and then is served as a garnish to the meat.

Marinades usually contain herbs and aromatic vegetables such as onion. Olive oil – which helps to distribute flavours and moistens the meat – is often added. An acidic liquid such as wine is also common: it helps to break down muscle fibres, making the meat more tender.

A 'dry' marinade (right, below) contains oil, but very little other liquid, or none at all. It is used principally before dry cooking meats by methods such as roasting or grilling, for which the surface of the meat must be dry to sear quickly. A 'wet' marinade (far right, below), which has enough liquid to cover the meat, is valuable before braising – the marinade then serves as part of the braising liquid.

Stuffings are used frequently for boned joints or poultry, whether intended for roasting, braising or poaching. The stuffing is enclosed in the space left by the bones, or for poultry, boned or not, in the body cavity. You can also stuff between the flesh of, say, a leg of lamb and the membrane covering it (page 96) or between the flesh and the skin of poultry or game birds (page 111, 167).

The persillade on the right, above – a combination of crushed garlic cloves and chopped parsley – is a highly flavoured mixture that may be used in small quantities on its own, or serve as one element in a bulkier stuffing. Other flavouring elements include leaf vegetables, mushrooms, spring onions, ham and bacon. To make a substantial stuffing, you can combine flavouring elements with such ingredients as breadcrumbs, cooked rice and soft cheese. Added fat will keep the stuffing moist, and eggs will bind it.

Persillade: a Versatile Stuffing Element

Combining parsley and garlic. Press garlic cloves lightly with the flat of a knife to split the skin. Peel the garlic cloves and put them in a mortar with some coarse salt – it will help you to grind the garlic to a paste. Pound with a pestle until

the garlic is puréed (above, left). Finely chop some flat-leafed parsley. Blend the chopped parsley into the garlic purée with your fingers (above, right).

A Dry Herb Marinade

Making a dry marinade. Rub olive oil into the joint. Rub in dried herbs or chopped fresh herbs – such as thyme, savory, marjoram and oregano. Here, slashes are made in the meat so that it will grill evenly, and rosemary twigs are placed in them. Partly enclosed, the rosemary will flavour the meat more effectively than on the surface. Cover the meat and leave it at room temperature for 2 to 3 hours or for a day in a refrigerator.

A Wine Marinade

Making a wet marinade. Cut the meat into chunks and place it in a bowl with the ingredients for the marinade: here, thin slices of onion and carrots, unpeeled crushed garlic cloves, a bay leaf and sprigs of rosemary, thyme and oregano. Pour over a spoonful or two of olive oil and enough red or white wine to immerse the meat. Leave the meat, covered, for 2 to 3 hours at room temperature or for a day in a refrigerator.

Ham and Cheese

1 Preparing the ingredients. Cut boiled ham into small cubes. Make a persillade (opposite page, above). Put these ingredients in a bowl together with ricotta cheese, eggs and fresh breadcrumbs.

2 Seasoning the mixture. Add some softened butter to the ingredients. Season with salt, freshly ground pepper, mixed dried herbs and, if you like, grated nutmeg.

3 Mixing the stuffing. With your hands, mix the ingredients, kneading lightly until they are amalgamated. The finished stuffing should be of a firm consistency.

Pork Forcemeat

1 Mincing the meat. Cut lean and fat pork – here, leg and belly – into cubes and pass it first twice through the medium disc, then once through the fine disc of a mincer.

2 Adding the other ingredients. Finely chop parsley and garlic. Place in a bowl with the meat, fresh breadcrumbs, an egg and herbs. Finely chop an onion, sauté it until soft and add it to the mixture.

3 Mixing the stuffing. Season with salt and pepper. Work the ingredients together until the seasonings, egg and the different meats are evenly distributed. The mixture should be moist but firm-textured.

Bacon and Vegetables

1 Chopping the ingredients. Finely chop spring onions, mushrooms, fresh herbs and any meat trimmings. Put them in a bowl with salt and some butter. Remove the rind from rashers of green bacon; chop the bacon

2 Combining the ingredients. Add the bacon to the mixture; season to taste with ground spices such as mace, nutmeg and allspice. Using your hands, mix the ingredients together.

3 Kneading the stuffing. Thoroughly amalgamate all the ingredients to make a loose, fairly light mixture. If you want a firmer consistency, add fresh breadcrumbs and an egg to bind the stuffing.

Stuffings for Poultry

One of the simplest ways to vary poultry is by resorting to different stuffings.

One kind of stuffing for roast poultry is based on dry bread cubes that have been baked or fried in butter until crisp (right). Although no moisture is added before the bird is stuffed, this rough-textured stuffing is anything but dry after roasting; it absorbs cooking juices and becomes moist and flavourful – yet retains its crispness.

A softer, more even-textured stuffing can be made by combining bread and other ingredients with a liquid. To give extra flavour, substitute a simple stock for the usual water or milk by simmering for half an hour the bird's giblets, together with herbs, sliced onion and carrot. Strain and skim the stock before mixing it into the stuffing.

Vegetable-based stuffings (third panel) offer an interesting change from the familiar bread mixtures. Prepare and chop different vegetables according to their various needs. You can mix them with a white curd cheese, such as Italian ricotta, for body and a smooth texture. Boned chicken or guinea fowl (pages 106-7) can be stuffed with mousseline forcemeat made from chicken breast, often combined with duxelles, mirepoix, chopped truffle, tiny petits pois, peeled young broad beans, etc., and poached in stock, which may be made into a sauce.

Whatever kind of stuffing you make, you can enrich it economically by mixing with it the bird's giblets – its liver, heart and gizzard (fourth panel). Clean, chop and quickly sauté the giblets before adding them to the stuffing.

Chicken and turkey always benefit from being smeared with butter before roasting; but if you feel like trying something slightly more ambitious, stuff additional butter – seasoned with herbs or other flavourings – beneath the skin of the breast (fifth panel). Slices of truffle are often slipped between the skin and flesh of the breasts and legs of a chicken the day before roasting or poaching.

A Dry Bread Stuffing

Make the croutons for a dry bread stuffing from a firm loaf about two days old. Choose other ingredients that will complement poultry: here, chopped celery, parsley and mixed herbs are combined to complete a stuffing for the roast turkey.

1 Browning the croutons. Cut the bread into chunks. Melt the butter in a pan. Fry the bread over a low heat, stirring. Add more butter as it is absorbed, and continue frying until evenly browned. Or, cook the cut bread for half an hour in a buttered baking tin in a moderate oven.

2 Mixing the stuffing. Place the croutons with the other ingredients in a bowl. The best way to mix any kind of stuffing is with your hands: this combines all elements thoroughly and produces a light, airy mixture.

A Moist Bread Stuffing

Although you can season moist bread stuffing in many ways, one of the oldest flavour combinations is sage and onion. The pungency of the herb and the sweetness of the pre-cooked onion give the stuffing an appetising perfume that improves with roasting.

1 Preparing the ingredients. Parboil an onion for about 10 minutes. Chop it coarsely. Use fresh sage if possible – dried sage always has a musty odour. Mix the chopped sage and onion with fresh coarse breadcrumbs, chopped parsley, salt, pepper, butter and an egg yolk for binding.

2 Moistening and mixing. Add just enough liquid – here, chicken stock – to moisten the ingredients completely. Mix the stuffing together gently but thoroughly, using a spoon, a fork or your fingers.

Pre-cooking Vegetables

Leaf vegetables such as chard and spinach are prepared by parboiling them, pressing them dry and chopping them. Moist vegetables such as courgettes, turnips or swedes should have their high water content reduced before they are combined with other ingredients.

1 Drawing out moisture. Coarsely shred courgettes with a flat or rotary grater. (Treat turnips and swedes the same way.) In a deep bowl, arrange the shreds in 2.5 cm (1 inch) layers, each liberally salted. Leave them for 30 minutes to allow the salt to draw out their water. Then squeeze out the salty water.

2 Cooking the vegetables. Sauté the courgettes in butter for 7 to 8 minutes over a moderate heat. Toss or stir regularly, so that they cook evenly. When they are dry and lightly coloured, take the pan off the heat. Let them cool before mixing the stuffing.

Preparing Giblets

Reserve the bird's gizzard, heart and liver to add to most bread-based stuffings. Wash them in cold water to rinse away any blood before you cut them up, and cut away any white connective tissue. Goose giblets are shown here; but treat those of other birds in the same way.

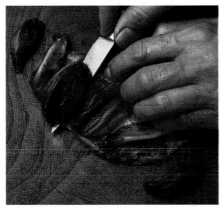

1 Cutting up the giblets. Pare away the dark red flesh from the thick hard membrane that lines the gizzard. Slice the gizzard, heart and liver.

2 Cooking the giblets. Melt butter in a saucepan and add the giblet pieces. Sauté them briefly over a moderate heat: when they have changed colour from red to a pinkish grey, add them to the other stuffing ingredients. They will cook through as the bird roasts.

Buttering Under the Skin

Flavourings and a generous quantity of butter placed underneath the breast skin will blend together to nourish the breast meat of a roasting bird. Anchovies and almonds are used below, but you could substitute pistachios and slivers of grilled peeled sweet pepper.

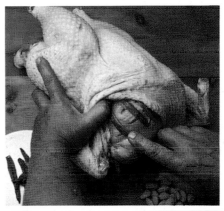

1 Inserting the flavourings. Pull back the skin at one side of the neck to expose half the breast flesh. Still holding back the skin, use a small sharp knife to cut little slits all over the breast; insert an almond into each pocket. Lay anchovy fillets on the surface. Repeat an the other side of the breast.

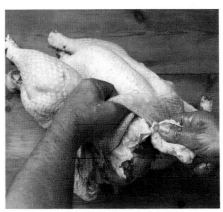

2 Buttering the breast. Soften the butter to room temperature. With your hand, spread it beneath the breast skin, generously covering the anchovies and almonds.

Gravlax

Layered with a dry marinade of salt, herbs and spices; fillets of raw fish gradually acquire a firm yet tender texture as the salt draws out their juices. At the same time, the flavours of the herbs and spices are absorbed by the fish; after a few day's curing; it need only be sliced thinly to make a cold *hors-d'oeuvre* that finds a place of honour in many cuisines.

Swedish *gravlax* flavours salmon with dill and a mixture of white and black peppercorns. You can vary the proportions of the pepper to suit your tastes, or add a few allspice berries – or even some vodka – for a more aromatic result.

The dish's name comes from *gravad lax* – buried salmon – which may describe how, in times past, the fish was kept cool under a covering of earth while it cured. Nowadays a refrigerator is a more convenient storage place and a wrapping of plastic film or aluminium foil prevents the surface of the fish from drying. A weighted board compresses the wrapped fish and accelerates the marinating process. Periodically, the fish must be unwrapped, turned and basted, so that the seasonings penetrate evenly and no part of the flesh dries out.

The whole treatment will take 2 to 3 days, depending on the size of the piece of fish you are curing and how highly seasoned you want it to be.

FOR 8-10

1 kg / 2¼ lb salmon, centre cut, cleaned and filleted with skin left on

FOR THE MARINADE:
10 black peppercorns
10 white peppercorns
3 or 4 allspice berries (optional)
about 6 tbsp coarse salt
about 4 tbsp caster sugar
about 50 g/2 oz fresh dill, finely chopped

1 Removing the upper fillet. Lay a long piece of salmon – here, a tail section – on its side. With a long flexible knife, cut a deep slit along one side of the backbone to expose the rib bones. Then, keeping the edge of the knife against the fish's rib bones, gradually cut and lift away the upper fillet.

2 Removing the lower fillet. Insert the blade of the knife horizontally under the backbone and ribs; carefully pare the bones away from the lower fillet as shown above. Then cut the fillet free at the tail end and discard the bones and tail. Use tweezers or your fingers to remove any tiny 'pin' bones remaining on the fillets.

6 Sealing and weighing the fish. Cover the salmon with plastic wrap or foil. Stretch the wrap around and under the edge of the plate to form an airtight seal around the fish. Place a board or another large plate on top of the fish. Distribute kitchen weights evenly along the board. If you have no weights, improvise with large cans of food.

7 Basting the fish. Refrigerate the salmon or leave it in a cool larder for 2 to 3 days. Every 12 hours or so, unwrap the plate and turn over both fillets; separate them and spoon over their flesh the juices that have collected in the plate as shown. Then reassemble the fillets, reseal the plate and return to the refrigerator.

3 Preparing the dry marinade. With a mortar and pestle, crack black and white peppercorns into small pieces; if you like, you can incorporate a few allspice berries. Stir coarse salt and caster sugar into the spice mixture.

4 Coating the fish. Place one of salmon fillets skin side down on a large plate. Coat the fish evenly with half of the dry marinade mixture. Coarsely chop fresh dill and spread a generous layer on top. (If dill is not available, you can achieve a different but equally good effect by substituting fennel leaves.)

5 Layering the fish. Distribute the remainder of the dry marinade on top of the dill. Place the second salmon fillet, skin side up, on top of the dry marinade.

8 Scraping off the marinade. Before serving, unwrap the fish and place it on a kitchen towel to drain. Separate the fillets and scrape of the dry marinade with a knife as shown. Then wipe the fish clean with paper towels.

Serving the gravlax. Place each fillet, skin side down, on a carving board and slice it thinly, as you would smoked salmon. Arrange the slices on a serving platter; serve with dill mustard sauce.

Cooking Food

Although we still eat many things raw – especially fruit, vegetables and nuts, even meat on occasion – perhaps nothing marks us out more from other creatures than that we chose to cook our food. We apply heat to food for several reasons: to make it more tender, to render it more digestible, to preserve it, or even to remove unpleasant tastes and textures – but most of all we do it because it improves its flavour, especially when several foodstuffs are cleverly combined.

There are basically two different ways of classifying the methods we use to cook food: whether wet or dry and whether slow or fast. Fast cooking, like grilling or boiling, is generally used when we want to keep as much of the natural flavour and texture of the – usually fairly tender – food. Rapid boiling of green vegetables fixes their brilliant colour (as well as preserving more of their nutrients and flavour) and fast grilling of a steak, say, keeps the meltingly tender texture of the beef while adding a delicious caramelized coating that further enhances the flavour. Slow-cooking, on the other hand, is usually applied where we want to effect some transformation, as in braising for example, where the gristly connective tissue of tough cuts of meat breaks down over several hours on a gentle heat to produce meat that gives to the spoon and a magically rich and deep flavour.

Long slow cooking in a moist environment allows us both to draw out the flavours inherent in the food and to combine these with added flavours like those of herbs and spices. When fast-cooking with dry heat, if we want to add flavour we usually either marinate the food first or give it a flavoured coating, which as in the case of deep-frying can also serve to protect fragile food from the intensity of the process.

Often the preparation of some dishes requires a sequence of different techniques. For example, many vegetable dishes require initial blanching to fix the colour or soften texture before any further cooking. Many roasted, stewed or braised dishes require that the meat is first quickly fried over a fairly high heat to brown the exterior, and innumerable recipes begin with the gentle sweating of onions to soften them and develop their flavour.

Of course, not all 'cooking' requires the application of heat. We do apply the term to dishes like ice-creams, sorbets and refrigerator cakes where 'cold' is applied instead. Food is also cured with salt or cold smoke, or even air-dried, and in the South-American *ceviche* fish is actually 'cooked' by the action of lime juice on the flesh.

Boiling Eggs

Of course, eggs in their shells are not actually 'boiled', in the true vigorous sense – as vegetables and pasta are – or they would be smashed; instead they are simmered gently. The same is true of 'boiled rice' and indeed 'boiled beef', which more rapid cooking toughen.

Soft-boiling Eggs

This simplest way of cooking an egg – in hot water – presents the cook with only one variable: the time it spends in the water. Nevertheless, timing must be exact, for even gentle simmering results in rapid cooking of the egg, and half a minute will make a significant difference.

Obviously, the correct cooking time will depend partly on the size of the egg. A large egg is perfectly soft-boiled after 4 minutes of cooking, while small eggs are ready in 3 minutes. Freshness also plays a part; the compact white of a new-laid egg will take up to a minute longer to set than the thinner, more alkaline white of an older egg. Remember, too, that eggs still partly chilled from the refrigerator will take a minute or two longer to cook. (Eggs should ideally not be boiled directly from the refrigerator – the sudden change of temperature may crack them.)

Although it is possible to start eggs in cold water, precise timing is easier if they are placed in water that is already simmering (Step 1, right). If you are preparing several eggs at once, you can synchronize the moment at which they start cooking by lowering them in a wire basket. If you do not wish to cook all the eggs for the same length of time, remove them individually with a slotted spoon.

The water should be simmering gently. Vigorous boiling will overcook the outside of the white, making it leathery, while the agitation increased the danger of cracking.

When ready, the eggs should be opened immediately; otherwise their internal heat will continue to cook them.

1 Boiling the eggs. Bring a saucepan of water to the boil. Reduce the heat so that the water is gently bubbling. Place the eggs in a wire basket, and lower them gently into the water. Time the eggs from the moment they enter the water.

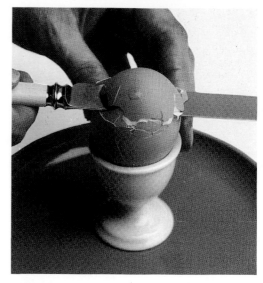

2 Opening the eggs. Remove the eggs when they have cooked for the time required. Set each egg in an egg cup. Holding the egg in its cup, strike it firmly with a knife blade at the point where it becomes wide enough to admit a small spoon, and slice off the top. Lift the top away from the egg, and clear away any pieces of broken shell.

Gradations of Boiling

After 3 minutes. Started in cold water and cooked for 3 minutes from the moment the water comes to the boil, whites that have only partially set and yolks that are still liquid. These are the *mollet* eggs of French cooking. Allow 6 minutes to cook *mollet* eggs if they are started in boiling water.

After 4 minutes. The white is firmly set, as is most of the yolk, though the centre is still soft. This egg is easier to handle and to shell than the *mollet* egg; it can be used in the same way as a hard-boiled egg. To attain this consistency from a boiling-water start, the egg should be cooked for 8 minutes.

Boiling for Shelling

Shelled boiled eggs are useful garnishes as well as essential in many assembled dishes. The eggs may be soft-boiled or hard-boiled, depending on intended use.

The best eggs for shelling are three to four days old. The whites of new-laid eggs adhere firmly to the shell membrane.

Instead of plunging the eggs into boiling water, you can start them in cold water, which should be brought to a simmer over a medium heat. Though it permits less precise timing, this method reduces the risk of the shells cracking through a sudden change of temperature, while the relatively gentle heat makes for more tender whites. The timings below are for size 2 eggs. Deduct a minute from the times shown when using size 3 or 4 eggs, and up to 2 minutes for smaller sizes.

It is best to shell eggs just before use, as the shells protect the whites from drying out.

Arrange eggs loosely in a pan. Cover generously with water, and place over medium heat. Time from moment bubbles begin to rise from the bottom of pan. Maintain a bare simmer. When eggs have cooked for the time required, remove from pan and immediately plunge into cold water to stop cooking.

Crack shell of each egg by gently tapping it all over with back of a spoon or knife handle. The finely cracked shell will adhere to inner membrane and can easily be peeled away from tsurface of white. Gently strip shell away from white of the egg, peeling off the underlying membrane at the same time.

After 6 minutes. Both yolk and white are firmly set, although the centre of the yolk remains tender. This egg can be cut into quarters, sliced or chopped, but retains enough natural moisture to be briefly cooked as part of a further presentation. Equivalent timing for an egg started in boiling water is 10 minutes.

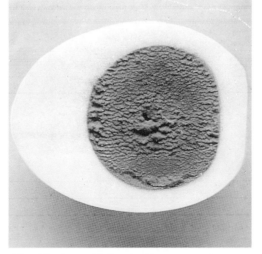

After 10 minutes. Yolk and white are both firmly set. This is the classic hard-boiled egg used for stuffing and as a garnish in cold dishes. Chopped or sliced, it can also be reheated in a sauce. Eggs require 12 minutes' cooking to hard-boil from a boiling-water start.

The effect of overcooking. If boiled for more than 10 minutes from a cold-water start – or 12 minutes if started in boiling water – egg whites turn rubbery and the yolks become dry and crumbly. Elements in the yolk and white interact to produce a green ring around the yolk – a sure sign of overcooking.

Boiling Vegetables

There are two schools of thought about the best way to boil vegetables. On the one hand, most of the professional chefs use the classic French method of plunging the vegetables into a large quantity of rapidly boiling water; on the other hand, cooks informed by the findings of modern food science employ a boiling method that uses as little water as possible.

The merit of boiling vegetables in a lot of water lies in its speed. A large volume of boiling water will heat the vegetables through very quickly – and the faster a vegetable cooks, the more of its colour, texture, flavour and nutritional content remains.

Boiling in minimal water takes longer and diminishes flavour and texture, but the method is defended on nutritional grounds. Vegetables lose slightly less vitamins and minerals when they are boiled in a small amount of liquid; and those nutriments that do leach out are easily reclaimed by adding the liquid to soups or stews. Some cooks, carrying this principle to the extreme, cook leaf vegetables in no more liquid than the drops of water that cling to them after rinsing. However, large quantities of vegetables boiled in very little liquid may not cook evenly; the parts in contact with the pan can soften and discolour before the rest cooks through.

When cooking green vegetables by either method, the pan should be uncovered. In a closed pan, they will take on a grey tinge, caused by a heat-triggered chemical reaction between the vegetables' chlorophyll and acids that would otherwise escape with the steam.

1 Starting in boiling water. Bring a pan of liberally salted water to a vigorous boil. Because the vegetable will cook briefly, it will not have time to absorb too much salt. Slip the vegetables into the water quickly. Broccoli (above) should first have its stalks peeled (page 138) so that the stalks cook through at the same rate as the tops; if the stalks are very thick, trim them before cooking.

2 Testing for doneness. Boil, uncovered, until the vegetable is tender but not soft. Young, peeled broccoli will take about 5 minutes to cook, depending on the thickness of the stalks. Test broccoli by piercing the thickest part of the stalk with the tip of a sharp knife, the point of the knife should enter the stalk easily.

3 Draining and serving. Drain the vegetable in a colander set in a sink – or a bowl to save the liquid. Shake the colander gently to remove as much water as possible. Serve immediately. Many cooks 'refresh' green vegetables by plunging them into cold water to stop their cooking. But they must then be reheated briefly and may end up overdone.

Times and Hints

The alphabetical guide below gives boiling and steaming instructions for individual vegetables suited to these methods of cooking and suggests approximate cooking times, counting from the moment when the water returns to the boil. Most of the timings are given with both a minimum and a maximum to reflect how vegetables vary in age, size and even variety; obviously, small and young vegetables require fewer minutes of cooking than large or old ones of the same type. For perfect results, always test for doneness by probing the thickest part with a knife or simply by tasting.

If you cut up vegetables for cooking, make sure all the pieces are the same size, so that they will be ready at the same. Do not cut them up too finely: too much surface area exposed to the water causes loss of nutrients and flavour.

The amount of salt you should add usually depends on the cooking time; as a general rule the longer a vegetable boils, the less salt is needed to season it.

Some vegetables react chemically with iron and aluminium. To prevent discoloration, cook them in non-reactive stainless steel, enamelled or glass pans. Other vegetables discolour rapidly in plain water; boil them in acidulated water (page 139) or a *blanc* – water to which flour, oil and lemon juice are added in the proportion of 1 tablespoon of each per litre (1 3/4 pints) of water.

Artichokes. Immerse in a large pan full of lightly salted, rapidly boiling water. Simmer, covered, for 20 to 40 minutes. Drain upside-down. Use a non-reactive pan.

Asparagus. Immerse in enough lightly salted boiling water to cover. Simmer gently for about 8 minutes.

Beans. Immerse in a large pan full of salted, rapidly boiling water. Boil whole green or wax beans for 2 to 10 minutes over a high heat; boil sliced runner beans for 5 to 10 minutes; boil young peeled broad beans for about 1 minute. For older broad beans, reduce the heat and simmer for 5 to 15 minutes; simmer fresh haricot beans for 40 to 60 minutes.

Beetroot. Immerse in enough unsalted, rapidly boiling water to cover. Simmer, covered, for 40 minutes or until tender when tested with a skewer.

Broccoli. Immerse in a large pan full of lightly salted, rapidly boiling water. Boil for 3-5 minutes. (Demonstration opposite).

Brussels sprouts. Immerse in a large pan full of generously salted, rapidly boiling water. Boil uncovered until they turn a brighter green, from 3 to 5 minutes.

Cabbage. Immerse in a large pot full of generously salted, rapidly boiling water. Boil cored, shredded cabbage for 5 to 7 minutes; cabbage quarters for 10 to 15 minutes. To preserve the colour of red cabbage, add 1 to 2 tablespoons of vinegar to the water.

Cardoons. Immerse in enough simmering *blanc* to cover. Cover the pan – leaving the lid ajar – and cook for 25 to 30 minutes.

Carrots. Immerse in enough boiling, lightly salted water to cover. Simmer young carrots for 5 to 10 minutes; simmer older, cored carrot pieces for up to 30 minutes. Carrots may be started in cold water.

Cauliflower. Immerse florets in a large pan full of moderately salted boiling water. Simmer for 3 to 5 minutes. Steam for 15 minutes.

Celeriac. Immerse in enough lightly salted, boiling water to cover. Simmer for 30 to 40 minutes. Use a non-reactive pan.

Celery. May be parboiled far about 10 minutes before braising.

Chayotes. Immerse in enough moderately salted boiling water to cover. Boil chayote pieces for 5 to 10 minutes; boil small whole chayotes for 10 to 15 minutes.

Courgettes. Immerse very small unpeeled courgettes in generously salted boiling water. Boil for 3 to 4 minutes. Peeled or large courgettes are unsuitable for boiling.

Cucumbers. Immerse in generously salted, rapidly boiling water. Boil for 2 minutes or less.

Endive and Batavian endive. Immerse in a large pan full of generously salted, rapidly boiling water. Boil for 1 to 2 minutes.

Fennel. May be parboiled for about 10 minutes before braising.

Garlic. Boil only with other vegetables as a flavouring.

Jerusalem artichokes. Immerse in enough moderately salted boiling water to cover. Boil peeled slices for 5 to 10 minutes; boil whole and unpeeled for 15 minutes, or steam for 20 minutes. Use a non-reactive pan.

Kale. Immerse in a large pan full of lightly salted boiling water. Boil for 5 to 7 minutes.

Kohlrabi. Immerse in enough lightly salted boiling water to cover. Simmer whole kohlrabi for 30 to 40 minutes, quarters for 20 minutes.

Leeks. Immerse in enough moderately salted, rapidly boiling water to cover. Boil sliced leeks for 1 to 2 minutes, whole thin leeks – bundled like asparagus – for 8 to 10 minutes.

Onions. Immerse in enough lightly salted boiling water to cover. Simmer for 15 to 45 minutes, depending on size.

Parsnips. Immerse in enough lightly salted boiling water to cover. Simmer for 10 to 15 minutes. Steam for 20 to 30 minutes.

Peas. Immerse in a large pan full of lightly salted, rapidly boiling water. Mange-tout are ready as soon as the water returns to the boil; boil shelled peas for 2 to 10 minutes.

Potatoes. Immerse in enough lightly salted boiling water to cover. Simmer for 15 to 40 minutes depending on size and variety. Or steam for 20 to 50 minutes. Potatoes may be started in cold water.

Pumpkin. Immerse in a large pot full of generously salted, rapidly boiling water. Boil for 10 to 15 minutes.

Salsify and scorzonera. Immerse in enough simmering acidulated water, or *blanc*, to cover. Simmer for 20 to 30 minutes. Use a non-reactive pan.

Sea kale. Immerse in enough simmering acidulated water or *blanc* to cover. Simmer for 10 to 12 minutes. Use a non-reactive pan.

Spinach. Immerse in a large pan full of generously salted, rapidly boiling water. Boil for 1 or 2 minutes, pushing the leaves back under the water with a wooden spoon when they rise to the surface. Tender young spinach is cooked as soon as the water returns to the boil.

Squash. Immerse in a large pot full of generously salted, rapidly boiling water. Boil for 10 to 15 minutes.

Swedes. Immerse in a large pot full of lightly salted, rapidly boiling water. Simmer sliced or cubed swedes for 15 to 20 minutes; whole swedes for 30 to 40 minutes. Or steam swede pieces for 30 minutes, whole swedes for 45 to 50 minutes.

Sweet potatoes. As a preliminary to puréeing, immerse in a large pot full of lightly salted, rapidly boiling water, Simmer for about 25 minutes.

Sweetcorn. Immerse in a large pan full of unsalted, but lightly sugared, rapidly boiling water. Boil for 2 to 5 minutes.

Swiss chard. Cook leaves and ribs separately. Immerse leaves in a large pot of generously salted, rapidly boiling water. Boil for 1 to 2 minutes. Immerse ribs in enough lightly salted boiling water to cover. Boil ribs for 10-12 minutes.

Turnips. Immerse in enough moderately salted boiling water to cover. Simmer for 5 to 10 minutes. Turnips absorb water. to dry them out, finish cooking by stewing them in butter.

Vine leaves. Not suitable for boiling. Parboil for a few minutes before stuffing and braising.

Cooking Rice & Grains

Cookery books abound with detailed – and contradictory – descriptions of the perfect technique for cooking rice and other grains. In fact there are many ways to achieve a good result: the two techniques demonstrated here are the most commonly used.

The simplest method is to boil the grains in an unlimited amount of water. To keep the grains from sticking to each other or the base of the pan, bring the water to the boil before adding the grains and give them a good stir at the start of cooking. Because more water is used than the grains can absorb, they will need to be drained after being cooked, then allowed to dry and swell in their own steam, either in the oven or over a very low heat. Approximate cooking times for each type of grain are shown on the chart opposite.

The chart also indicates the volume of water required by each type for the second method – boiling in a measured amount of liquid (right, below). With this method, all of the water is absorbed by the grains as they cook, leaving them ready to serve without drying. The wild rice used in the demonstration is soaked raw for a few hours in cold water or for about an hour in hot water to soften the grains. Soaking gives a fluffier, more tender result, but it does not affect either the volume of water required for cooking or the cooking time.

Whichever method you use, do not regard the times in the chart as immutable. Such imponderables as the variety and age of the grain affect the timing, and different people prefer different degrees of doneness. Try the grains – by pressing them between finger and thumb – about 5 minutes before the earlier time given on the chart and serve them when tender.

Boiling in Unlimited Water

1 Boiling long-grain white rice. Fill a large saucepan nearly full of salted water and bring it to the boil. Adjusting the heat to keep the water on the boil, gradually sprinkle in the rice (above). Stir once to separate the grains. Hold at a light boil, uncovered.

A Measured Mode of Boiling

Measure out a volume of water three times that of the rice before soaking (see chart) and pour into a pan. Add salt and drained rice. Bring to the boil, stir once, then reduce the heat. Cover and simmer for about 45 minutes (for wild rice), or until all of the water has been absorbed and the grains feel soft when pinched. Take off the heat; add butter and toss.

2 Draining off the water. To test if the rice is cooked, pinch a few grains with your fingertips. Drain when the rice still has a slightly resilient core; it will finish cooking during drying-out. Either tip rice into a large, flat, ovenproof dish and spread it out evenly, then cover and put in a low oven for 10 to 15 minutes. Alternatively, just return rice to pan and place over a very low heat. Either way, add a few small pieces of butter and fluff with forks.

Boiling Grains

The chart below gives the approximate amount of liquid that each type of grain absorbs when cooking, and the time each takes to cook.

You may have to add more liquid as the grains cook, or extend the cooking time. However, do not uncover the pan too often, or steam will escape and the grains will not cook properly.

Grain	Proportion of liquid to grain	Approximate cooking times (minutes)
Brown rice	2:1	50-60
Buckwheat	2:1	15-20
Millet	3:1	15-20
Oats	2:1	60-90
Pearl barley	2-2^1/$_2$:1	90
Pot barley	2-2^1/$_2$:1	90
Rye	2:1	60-90
Wheat	2:1	60-90
White rice	2:1	18-20
Wild rice	3:1	45

Steps in Boiling Pasta

The most basic way of preparing pasta is to boil it in salted water, drain it and then mix it with a sauce in its serving dish. Both fresh and dried pasta are boiled in the same way; the only difference is the cooking time. To keep the pasta from clumping together as it cooks, use plenty of lightly salted water – at least 4 litres (6 pints) for every 500 g (1 lb) of pasta – and you can add a spoonful of olive oil to the water if you like. Make sure the water is boiling vigorously when you add the pasta: the water's movement will help to keep the pasta separate. Stir the pasta gently at the beginning of cooking to unravel any tangled strands.

Pasta should be boiled until it is tender but not flabby. The Italian expression for perfectly cooked pasta *al dente* – 'to the tooth' – means that the pasta should still have a firm, faintly chewy core. Fresh pasta shapes – whether unfilled or filled – reach the *al dente* stage after anything from 2 to 5 minutes of cooking. Dried pasta requires at least twice as long. The precise time depends on the thickness and dryness of the pasta, and its constituents: pasta made from semolina, for example, needs more cooking than pasta made from flour. To time the cooking accurately, remove a sample of pasta at regular intervals and pinch it.

Once it is ready, the pasta should be removed from the water immediately so that it stops cooking. You can use a wooden pasta fork (Step 2, above) to lift out and drain long pasta shapes, such as noodles and spaghetti, before transferring them to a warmed serving dish. Alternatively, long shapes can be drained in a colander – the most appropriate method for draining small pasta shapes. Unless dressing it with oil, it is generally important not to drain pasta too well; indeed Italians often reserve a cupful of the cooking water to loosen a thick sauce before adding it to the pasta.

Fresh Pasta

1 Adding pasta to water. Bring plenty of water to the boil in a large saucepan. Add salt and a spoonful of olive oil if you wish. When the water is boiling rapidly, put in the noodles. Stir them to make sure the strands are not stuck together. Keep the water at a steady boil.

2 Draining the pasta. With a pasta fork, lift out some of the pasta from the pan every 30 seconds or so. Test whether a strand is cooked by pinching it. When the noodles are done, lift them out with the fork. Hold each forkful above the pan for a few seconds to drain, then transfer it to a warmed bowl or individual plates.

Dried Pasta

1 Cooking the pasta. Here the pasta is cooked in a traditional Italian manner with vegetable accompaniments (potatoes and green beans). In a large pan, bring plenty of lightly salted water to the boil. Put in the potatoes; 5 minutes later, add the beans. When the water returns to a rapid boil, add the pasta, pushing the strands gently against the base of the pan until they soften and bend into the pan.

2 Testing for doneness. About 7 minutes after adding the pasta, begin testing for doneness. At 30-second intervals lift out a few strands with a pasta fork and pinch one (above). When the pasta is done, empty the remaining contents of the pan into a colander.

Some vegetables can be cooked inside a covered pan in the steam rising from water, rather than in the water itself. Steaming is a gentler process than boiling, but it takes longer. Steaming suits vegetables, such as cauliflower and most of the roots. Green vegetables are better boiled: a lengthy steam bath sweats out more of their colour and flavour.

To hold vegetables above the water for steaming, you can use a special pot with a perforated insert or a collapsible metal basket (right). You can even improvise with a colander inside a saucepan, so long as the lid fits tightly.

Here new potatoes are cooked in a metal basket steamer that expands or contracts to fit inside different sizes of pan. When using any kind of steaming device, first bring a little water to the boil in the pan, then set steamer and its load above the water and cover pan until the vegetables are done.

Steaming takes longer than other methods, and is thus less practical for long-cooking grains such as barley and brown rice. Indeed, this method is usually restricted to white rice. To ensure that the rice will be tender, soak it for about an hour beforehand. Most steamers have two sections: a lower one for the water and a perforated upper section – fitted with a lid – for the food. To prevent any grains from dropping into the water, line the upper section with muslin.

Steaming Rice & Grains

Steaming rice in muslin. Soak rice in cold water for at least an hour, then drain it through a strainer. Half fill the bottom of a steamer with water and bring it to the boil. Put the top section of the steamer in place; lay a single piece of muslin in it. Tip the rice into the steamer; fold the muslin over the rice. Cover and steam the rice for 25 to 30 minutes, or until it is tender.

Steaming Shellfish

With bivalves (page 33) the main steaming medium is their own abundant liquid, which they release as they are heated. You can, in fact, steam them without supplementing this liquid; simply place the shellfish in a deep, heavy-bottomed pan, cover it, and heat. However, adding a little white wine, together with some aromatics, flavours the liquid and transforms it into a fragrant broth that can be served with the shellfish – either as it is or reduced by boiling, enriched with butter chunks and flavoured with lemon.

Steaming with a little wine – a style termed à la marinière – is demonstrated below with mussels. The steaming serves to open bivalves as well as to cook them. They are ready to eat when the shells gape apart; longer cooking would wither and toughen them. They should be steamed over a high heat and shaken vigorously in the pan so that all the shellfish cook evenly. Before cooking, always check that the bivalves are alive by tapping open ones to see if they close (page 134).

Steaming is both a complete cooking process and the first step in the preparation of more elaborate dishes. The liquid can be added to a velouté sauce for example, or used to supplement a fumet for poaching fish, when the shellfish themselves are used as a garnish. The steamed bivalves can be dipped in batter and deep-fried; or you can bake them in a gratin.

Moules à la Marinière

FOR 4

2 litres / 3$^1/_2$ pints mussels
1 onions or 2 shallots, chopped
2 garlic cloves, crushed
2 bay leaves
small bunch of parsley, chopped
few sprigs of thyme
knob of butter
150 ml / $^1/_4$ pint dry white wine
pepper

1 Steaming. Clean the mussels (page 134). Put them in a large heavy pan with the onions or shallots, garlic, bay leaves, parsley, thyme, butter and pepper. Pour in the white wine, cover the pan and place it over a high heat to cook. At intervals, lift the pan and shake it to redistribute the mussels.

2 Serving. After about 3 to 5 minutes, depending on the size of the mussels and their number, their shells will open. Use a slotted spoon to transfer them to soup plates. Pour the cooking liquid over the mussels. Eat the mussels, prising them from their shells with an empty shell, then spoon up the broth – with a mussel shell instead of a spoon if you like.

Steamed Steak and Kidney Pudding

Meats cooked in pastry are common to many national cuisines. By steaming, the pudding is cooked in the gentlest possible way. The pastry seals in the meat and its cooking liquid so that the flavours intermingle and intensify; in addition, the pastry absorbs the meat's rich essences, until it has a savour of its own.

The traditional English steak and kidney pudding demonstrated here uses time-honoured techniques to ensure that meat and pastry cook perfectly together. The ingredients are packed in a pudding basin and carefully covered (usually with a large clean cloth, damped and floured). The basin is then immersed to two-thirds of its depth in boiling water in a large, covered pot and simmered for several hours. The water below and the steam above join to provide a well-tempered, moist heat that braises the meat while it keeps the pastry soft and springy. The pudding can cook in about 4 hours, but longer steaming – up to 8 hours – will greatly enrich the flavours without over-cooking it.

FOR 6

1 kg / 2-2¹/₄ lb piece of chuck steak, coarsely cubed
2 ox kidneys
about 850 ml / 1¹/₂ pints water or beef stock
2 tablespoons Worcestershire sauce
salt and pepper

FOR THE SUET CRUST:
500 g / 1 lb flour
pinch of salt
250 g / 8 oz suet (see overleaf), finely shredded
150-300 ml / ¹/₄ -¹/₂ pint water

1 Preparing the kidneys. Peel off any fat or membrane clinging to the kidney's surface. Divide the kidney in half lengthwise, cut away the fat from inside and slice the halves into sections. If you prefer to attenuate the strong flavour of the pieces, plunge them into boiling water for 1 minute and drain them for 15 minutes.

2 Lining the basin. Make the crust: sift the flour into a mixing bowl and add the salt and suet. Combine by rubbing lightly with the fingers. Add water a tablespoon at a time, stirring with a fork, until dough holds together in a firm mass. Knead well until smooth and workable. Roll out to a thickness of about 2 cm (³/4 in). Cut a wedge of about quarter for the lid and fit remaining piece into basin. Press the dough firmly against bottom and sides, letting its edges hang over the rim.

3 Packing the pudding. Compactly fill the lined basin with the beef and kidney, seasoning each layer as you go. Add the Worcestershire sauce and water or stock to within 5 cm (2 inches) of the top of the basin. Re-roll the remaining dough to form a circle slightly larger than the top of the basin, and lay it over the pudding.

4 Sealing the lid. With water, moisten the edges of the dough lining the basin and fold them up over the edges of the lid. Crimp the dough together by pressing down all round the rim with your thumb, or with the tines of a large fork.

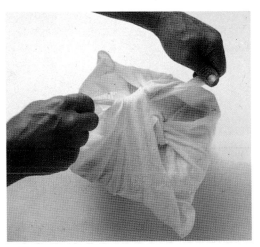

5 Covering the basin. Moisten a cloth and lightly flour one side. Lay it floured side down over the basin and tie it on securely, using a piece of string passed round the basin below the rim. Alternatively, use aluminium foil, pleated to allow room for the dough to expand.

6 Tying the cloth. Draw up two opposite corners of the cloth on top of the basin and tie them together with a double knot. Repeat with the other corners. Rest the pudding on a trivet or grill rack in a large deep pot. Pour boiling water into the pot to two-thirds of the basin's depth.

7 Steaming the pudding. Cover the pot and simmer over gentle heat for 4 to 8 hours. Add boiling water from time to time to maintain the water level. To lift out the pudding, slip the tine of a carving fork beneath the knots in the cloth.

8 Serving the pudding. Untie the knotted corners of the cloth and snip the string. Serve the pudding steaming, directly from the basin, scooping out the suet pastry and meat with a large spoon or a ladle .
Your can make this pudding even tastier by adding some chopped onions and sliced mushrooms to the beef and kidney mixture.

A Steamed Winter Fruit Pudding

Steamed puddings of dried fruits incorporated into a batter are traditional to English cookery. Christmas pudding – containing generous quantities of dried and crystallized fruits – is perhaps the best known example; the fig pudding shown here is a simpler version. Many other fruits might be used, in combination with tangy flavourings such as lemon peel or ginger. Dried dates and apricots, currants, raisins, sultanas, and slices of dried apple or pear are readily available in the winter, but you could also make a successful steamed pudding with fresh cherries or plums.

The batter for a steamed fruit pudding usually contains suet. Suet is the hard, white fat that surrounds beef kidneys; it is available fresh from the butcher. Pick the suet clean of membranes and fibres before shredding it with a grater. With long, slow cooking, the suet melts and helps to give the pudding its moist texture.

The pudding basin, classically of heatproof, glazed porcelain, should first be buttered generously so that the pudding will come out cleanly at the end of cooking. To make doubly sure, line the bottom of the basin with greaseproof paper (Step 4) or, if you like, spread the bottom of the basin with a little jam or treacle. As well as a basin, you will need a dampened cloth to protect the top of the pudding from splashes while it steams.

For steaming, the bottom two-thirds of the basin is immersed in boiling water, to surround the pudding with moist heat. Some steam will pass through the protective cloth, helping the pudding to rise slightly and the dried fruits to plump and swell. Although the pudding is ready to eat after an hour or so, longer boiling will enable the flavours to blend more fully. During cooking, make sure the water boils steadily, and if you need to top up the water level, use boiling water.

FOR 6

250 g / 8 oz dried golden figs
125 g / 4 oz flour, sifted
1 teaspoon baking powder
pinch of salt
125 g / 4 oz caster sugar
125 g / 4 oz fresh breadcrumbs
grated zest and juice of 2 lemons
pinch of nutmeg
125 g / 4 oz finely shredded suet
2 eggs, beaten
about 200 ml / 7 fl oz milk
butter for greasing
flour for dusting

1 Preparing the fruit. Wipe the figs with kitchen paper. Squeeze the top of each fig between your fingers and thumb and break off the woody stalk. Using a sharp knife, cut the figs into strips about 1 cm (½ inch) wide. Gather the strips together with one hand and cut across the strips to produce coarsely chopped pieces.

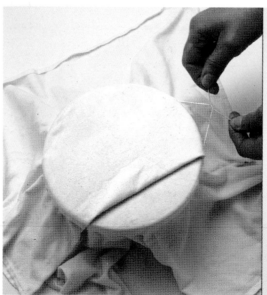

5 Sealing the pudding. Flour a dampened cloth and place it over the pudding, floured side down. Pleat the cloth to allow the pudding to expand, then tie the cloth with string beneath the ridge of the basin (above, left). Tie two opposite corners of cloth over the basin (above, right). Tie the other two corners over the first knot, forming a convenient lifting handle for the pudding basin.

2 Assembling the ingredients. Place the chopped figs in a large mixing bowl with sifted flour, baking powder, salt, sugar, lemon zest, breadcrumbs and nutmeg. Add the finely shredded suet. Mix the ingredients thoroughly and add the lemon juice and beaten egg diluted with a little milk. If the mixture is too stiff, gradually add more milk to moisten it.

3 Greasing a pudding basin. With your fingertips, rub the inside of a pudding basin liberally with butter. To make the pudding easier to turn out, cut a circle of greaseproof paper and place it in the bottom of the basin.

4 Filling the basin. Use a spoon to transfer the pudding mixture to the basin. Since the fig pudding will swell only moderately during cooking, you can fill the basin right to the top.

6 Steaming the pudding. Place the basin on a trivet in a pan of hot water; the water should reach two-thirds of the way up the basin. Cover the pan and boil for 2¹/₂ hours. Lift the basin out and remove the cloth. Place a warmed plate over the basin and invert them, shaking gently. Slice the pudding (right) and serve at once, with a custard sauce (crème anglaise, page 256) if you wish.

Poaching Eggs

Poaching is a method of very gentle cooking in barely simmering liquid. It suits fragile foods like eggs, fish and fruit which are easily overcooked and prevents meat and poultry from drying out.

Fresh eggs are prerequisites for successful poaching. Immersed in hot liquid, the whites of eggs that are several days old will spread out thinly and overcook, whereas the bulk of the whites of new-laid eggs will gather compactly around the yolks and poach neatly.

No special equipment is needed for poaching eggs other than a shallow heavy pan with a lid. Most so-called 'poaching' pans, built with small cups to contain the eggs, do not actually poach: the eggs are cooked by steam rather than immersion.

The temperature of the poaching liquid will drop when the eggs are broken into it, so the larger the pan you use, the better. To avoid slowing down the process unnecessarily, it is also best not to poach more than four eggs at a time.

The usual poaching liquid is water, although eggs can be poached in milk, stock or wine. Such flavourful liquids may then be thickened with butter and flour and transformed into sauces. Whatever the liquid, it should be kept below a simmer while the eggs cook; stronger heat would turn the whites rubbery. An easy way of controlling the temperature is to bring the liquid to the boil, turn off the heat before adding the eggs, then cover the pan to retain the liquid's heat.

Ensuring a Compact shape

1 Breaking the eggs. In a shallow sauté pan, bring 5-7 cm (2-3 inches) of unsalted water to the boil. Turn off the heat and add the eggs at once. To minimize the spreading of the whites break the eggs directly into the water: carefully open the two halves of the shells at the water's surface, so that the eggs slide into the water compactly.

2 Poaching the eggs. Cover the pan with a tight-fitting lid in order to retain the heat. Leave the eggs to cook undisturbed in the water for about 3 minutes, then lift off the lid. If the whites are opaque and the yolks covered with a thin translucent layer of white, the eggs are ready.

3 Lifting out the eggs. Remove the eggs from the pan with a perforated spoon. Place the eggs immediately in a shallow dish filled with cold water to arrest their cooking. The dish should be big enough to hold all the eggs without crowding.

4 Draining and trimming. Lift the eggs out of the water and place them to drain on a damp tea towel. Using a small knife, trim the eggs by cutting away the thin outer layer around the edges. If you do not intend to use the trimmed eggs immediately, transfer them to a second dish of fresh cold water to keep them moist. Just before use, reheat them by dipping them briefly in hot water.

Poaching Whole Fish

Poached and skinned, a large fish such as the salmon shown here makes a splendid dinner or buffet dish. It does, however, require a special fish kettle – a long, narrow pan that accommodates the shape and size of the fish, and which is fitted with a removable rack that makes it possible to lift the fish in and out with ease.

A large fish that has been cleaned through the belly should first be trussed to ensure that it retains its shape as it cooks. A fish that has been eviscerated through the gills does not need trussing. Large fish should always be started in a cold court-bouillon and warmed through gradually – otherwise the surface flesh will be cooked before the inside is done.

A small fish – like the whiting shown below – will cook more quickly, and so can be covered directly with warm poaching liquid. It can also be cooked without a fish kettle: by curling it as shown.

1 Trussing the fish. Gut and clean the fish, but do not remove its fins and scales; keeping the skin intact will help hold the fish together. For a neat presentation at table, tie up the fish's mouth: push a trussing needle, threaded with about 30 cm (12 inches) of cotton string, through the gills (above, left), then cross the two ends of the string over the snout and tie them under the mouth. If the fish has been gutted through the belly cut a piece of string long enough to encircle the fish's girth. Tie it round loosely (above, right).

A Neat Fitting Trick

Eviscerate and scale the fish – here, a whiting – but do not truss it. Curl it into a ring shape, fixing its tail in its mouth. Place it in a shallow, straight-sided pan just large enough to maintain this position. The fish should be put in the pan belly-up, so that it will lie on its underside when it is tipped out. Cover it with hot, but not boiling, court-bouillon and poach it, covered. Cook until tender when tested with a needle (Step 2, right). Pour out the liquid and turn the fish on to a warmed serving dish.

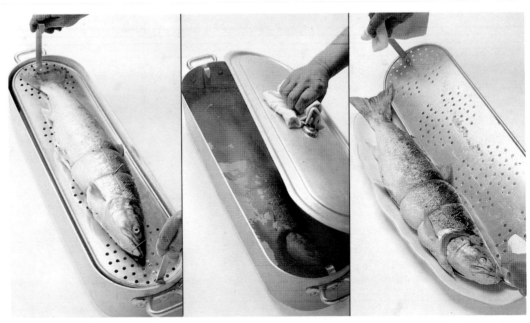

2 Using a fish kettle. Place the fish on the rack of the kettle and lower it into the empty pan (above, left). Cover with cold, strained court-bouillon (page 244). Put the lid on the kettle (above, centre), and heat the court-bouillon until the liquid begins to stir, but not boil; in boiling liquid the fish would overcook and begin to fall apart.

Poach the fish, allowing 10 minutes' cooking time for every 2.5 cm (1 inch) of its thickness. The fish is done when a trussing needle, inserted in the thick flesh behind the gills, meets almost no resistance. Carefully lift out the rack and slide the fish on to a platter. Remove the skin and any stray scales from the upper surface of the salmon before serving.

Poule au Pot

A whole chicken poached with vegetables is a complete meal in itself. The chicken and vegetables provide a satisfying main course, and the long cooking transforms the poaching liquid into a delicious clear broth; it can be served as a first course with a slice of bread and, if you like, a generous sprinkling of Parmesan cheese.

This poaching method was evolved to prepare a tough old hen for a peasant's dinner table, but you can substitute a large roasting chicken. Such a bird will be cooked in about an hour – approximately half the time required for an older boiling fowl. And although the gelatine-rich meat of the older bird produces a more savoury broth, it cannot match the younger roasting chicken for juicy tenderness.

After the bird is trussed, placed in just enough water to cover and brought slowly to a boil, the liquid must be skimmed. Only then is it time to add the vegetables and flavourings. Usually, the vegetables are served with the chicken; but if you are poaching an old bird, the 2 or more hours needed to render it tender will leave the vegetables limp and tasteless, their flavour transferred to the broth. For a garnish with taste and texture, replace the old vegetables with fresh ones about 30 minutes before the chicken is ready.

FOR 4-6

I oven-ready chicken, weighing about
  2 kg / 4 lb
500 g / I lb leeks, trimmed and rinsed
500 g / I lb carrots
2 onions, one stuck with 3 cloves
bouquet garni
I whole head of garlic (optional)
coarse sea salt

TO SERVE:
4-6 slices of day-old white country-style
  bread
Parmesan cheese and grater
gherkins
coarse sea salt and pepper grinder
fresh creamed horseradish or Dijon
  mustard

1 Immersing the chicken. Stuff and truss the chicken as you would for roasting (page 108). Place it in a pot and add enough water to cover the bird. Add salt and bring slowly to the boil, spooning off any scum that comes to the surface.

2 Adding vegetables. When no more scum forms, reduce the heat so that the liquid barely trembles. Add the vegetables and bouquet garni – and, if you like a whole head of garlic. If you add leeks, as shown here, trim off the tough leaves and tie the stems in a bundle to prevent them from falling apart.

3 Poaching the chicken. Regulate the heat so that hardly a bubble breaks the surface of the liquid. Test a young bird for doneness after about an hour of cooking by pushing a skewer into the thickest part of a thigh; if the juices run clear the bird is cooked. Older birds would show clear juices after the same cooking time but will require up to 2 hours more to reach tenderness.

4 Serving the broth. When the bird is done, skim off any surface fat. Put a slice of bread in each soup plate, garnish with a slice of cooked carrot, and ladle the broth on top. Grate cheese over the soup. Leave a little poaching liquid in the pot with the chicken and vegetables to keep them warm and moist. Cover the pot until the chicken is ready to serve.

5 Serving the chicken. Remove the bird from the pot and cut the trussing strings. Place the chicken on a warm serving platter and surround it with the vegetables for the table. Traditionally, poule au pot is accompanied by pickles and coarse salt. Fresh creamed horseradish or Dijon mustard and Parmesan cheese may also be served.

Poaching fruit for a compote

Fruit poached in a sugar syrup (page 254) gains in sweetness and flavour; the syrup itself, reduced after cooking, provides a translucent sauce for a complete dessert.

Ripe fresh fruits should be poached only briefly or they will break up: peaches become very soft after 10 minutes, and currants disintegrate after more than 2 to 3 minutes. If the dessert consists of a mixture of fruits, poach different types of fruit separately so that none is overcooked.

In place of syrup, you can use wine sweetened with sugar or honey to poach fresh or dried fruit (see below).

FOR 6-8

1kg / 2lb prepared fresh fruit, such as sliced apples, pears, apricots, peaches, and whole gooseberries, redcurrants and cherries
600ml / 1 pint medium sugar syrup (see page 254)
squeeze of lemon juice

1 Poaching the redcurrants. Make the syrup and bring it to a simmer. If possible, use an unlined copper pan as shown as a harmless chemical reaction caused by the metal will intensify the colour of red fruits. Gently tip the redcurrants into the syrup as above left and cook them for about 2 minutes. Remove them with a strainer as shown above right. The syrup will absorb colour and flavour from the berries; use it as a poaching liquid for other fruit (see right).

Figs in a Wine Syrup (for 4-6)

1 Simmering the figs. Put 500g/1lb whole dried figs in a pan with enough red wine to cover (about 450ml / ³/₄pt). Add 3 tablespoons of honey, 2 or 3 small sprigs of fresh (or ¹/₂ tsp dried) thyme, wrapped in muslin. Bring to a simmer, cover and cook the figs gently for about 1 hour, until they are tender, turning them occasionally.

2 Reducing the wine. Use a slotted spoon to remove the figs from the pan to a serving dish and discard the thyme. To make a sauce for the figs, turn up the heat a little and boil the wine until it has reduced to a syrupy consistency as above.

3 Serving the figs. Pour the wine syrup over the figs. Serve the figs tepid, or else chill them in the refrigerator. Accompany them, if you like, with cream and crisp sweet biscuits.

2 Poaching firmer fruit. Peel, halve and stone the other fruits, reserving the peels. To prevent discolouring, keep the fruits in a bowl of water acidulated with a squeeze of lemon juice. Simmer the fruits together in syrup. Use a toothpick to gauge tenderness, and remove each fruit as it is ready.

3 Simmering fruit peels. Top and tail the gooseberries and simmer them in the syrup for 2 to 3 minutes. Transfer them to a serving dish with the other fruits. Add the fruit peels to the syrup and boil the syrup rapidly to extract colour and flavour from the peels and to reduce the volume of the syrup by about one-third.

4 Serving the poached fruit. Allow the syrup to cool a little and then strain it over the poached fruit in the serving dish. Discard the fruit peels. Serve the compote either warm or chilled.

Lamb with Haricots

Like poaching, stewing involves the slow gentle cooking of food in liquid. The borderline between the one and the other may not always be clear, but stewing normally requires a mixture of ingredients and a smaller amount of liquid which, in the cooking process, is transferred into a sauce and becomes an integral part of the dish.

Lamb and Haricot Stew

FOR 6

500 g / 1 lb dried haricot beans
3 carrots
1 onion studded with 2 cloves
2 bouquets garnis
2 tablespoons olive oil
1.5 kg / 3 lb lamb shoulder, cut into pieces
3-4 garlic cloves, crushed
2-3 tomatoes, quartered
flour for dusting
salt

1 Softening the beans. Pick over beans to remove any imperfect ones and grit. Rinse the beans and soak them in water overnight, or bring them to the boil in water and let them soak for 1 hour in the same water. Drain the soaked beans; pour them into a saucepan. Add enough fresh water to come about 2.5 cm (1 inch) above the top of the beans.

2 Cooking the beans. Add one of the carrots, the onion studded with cloves and one of the bouquets garnis. Cook over a low heat for 1-1½ hours, until the beans can easily be crushed between the fingers. While they are cooking, heat the oil in a sauté pan and brown the lamb, then dust with flour, turning them around and over, until the floured surfaces are lightly browned.

3 Moistening the stew. Ladle over enough of the beans' cooking liquid enough to keep the beans submerged. Scrape the bottom of the pan with a wooden spoon to dissolve any sediment. Add the tomatoes, garlic, remaining carrots chopped into pieces and the other bouquet garni to the stew.

4 Simmering meat and beans in sauce. Simmer with the pan lid slightly ajar, for about 1¼ hours. Remove meat to a plate, discard carrots and bouquet garni and with a pestle, press contents of pan through a sieve into a small saucepan. Return meat to sauté pan. Hold saucepan half off heat, maintaining a light boil to one side. Skim quiet side periodically until no more fat rises to surface. Drain the beans and add them to the meat. Reserve the cooking liquid. Pour the cleansed sauce over the meat and beans. If necessary, add some of the beans' cooking liquid. Adjust the seasoning and cook gently for about 30 minutes to allow the flavours to mingle.

Coq au Vin

Chicken cooked in wine is a classic dish – or rather, many classic dishes; scores of recipes develop the theme with variations that depend on the country of origin and the imagination of the creator. One of the most celebrated is coq au vin, a speciality of France's Burgundy region that combines chicken with the full-bodied red wine of that province.

Like most fine stews, coq au vin is an assembly of ingredients that are first prepared individually to bring out their flavours. While the chicken is simmering on the stove or in the oven, the garnish vegetables are partly cooked and then set aside. To prevent them from losing their shape, texture and flavour, they are not added to the stew until the last few minutes of cooking.

When the chicken is done, the liquid is cleansed of fat and impurities to produce a rich, yet pure and digestible sauce.

FOR 6

2 slices of lean green bacon, cut into
   pieces
about 2 tablespoons oil
3 large onions, coarsley chopped
6-7 small carrots, cut into bite-sized
   pieces
6 large chicken leg portions
2 tablespoons flour
2 tablespoons brandy (optional)
1 (750 ml) bottle of good red wine
bouquet garni
about 24 small pickling onions
50 g / 2 oz butter
250 g / 8 oz button mushrooms
salt and pepper

FOR GARNISH:

3-4 slices of slightly stale bread, crusts
   removed and cut into cubes
50 g / 2 oz butter
2-3 tablespoons finely chopped parsley
1 garlic clove (optional)

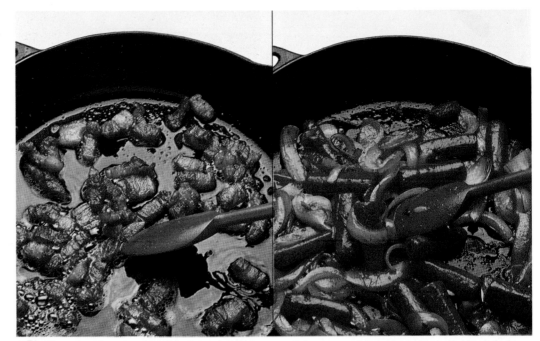

1 Preparing the aromatics. Melt down the pieces of bacon by frying them in a little oil (strongly cured bacon should first be parboiled, to rid it of excess salt, and then dried). When the pieces are golden-brown, remove them and set them aside to drain: they will form part of the garnish for the finished dish. In the same pan, gently fry onions and carrot pieces (above, right). Cook the onions and carrots for about 20 minutes, stirring frequently to prevent them from burning. Remove them from the pan and reserve.

2 Colouring the chicken. Season the chicken pieces with salt. Add more oil to the pan if necessary, and cook the pieces over a moderate heat turning them until they are lightly browned all over. Sprinkle flour on the chicken (above, right) and turn the pieces until the flour is lightly coloured. The flour will help thicken the cooking liquid. Return the onions and carrots to the pan.

3 Flaming with brandy. Brandy is not an essential ingredient, but it does add depth of flavour. Flaming burns off the alcohol so that only the flavourful essence remains to enrich the finished dish. Pour over the brandy, carefully set it alight and stir the contents of the pan until the flames die.

4 Deglazing with wine. Pour the wine into the pan and bring to a boil. Scrape the bottom of the pan (above, right) with a wooden spoon to loosen all the residues – they are important flavouring elements. The next stage of slow cooking can be done in the same pan or in an earthenware or metal casserole. (Earthenware can be used on top of the stove if protected by a fireproof mat.) Pour in sufficient hot stock to cover the chicken. Add a bouquet garni. Whether you cook in the oven or on top of the stove, regulate the heat so the liquid barely trembles. If the bird is old, simmer for about 1½ hours; a young chicken will cook in 45 minutes or so.

5 Preparing the garnish. While the chicken is cooking, peel the small onions. Drop the onions into butter, cover the pan, turn the heat low, and cook for 20 to 30 minutes. Stir or shake the onions frequently to prevent them from colouring unevenly. Wash and dry the mushrooms and trim their stems. When the onions are done, remove and set them aside. Using the same pan, toss the mushrooms in butter for a few minutes – over a high heat so that the moisture they exude evaporates quickly (above, right), thus preventing the mushrooms from stewing.

6 Straining the cooking liquid. When the chicken pieces are tender, transfer them to a warm dish. Pour the cooking liquid through a strainer into a saucepan. Discard the remains of the bouquet garni and return the carrots and the chicken to the pot. The onions, unlike the carrots, will have lost most of their texture, but do not discard them: press them through the strainer with a pestle (above, right) or a wooden spoon to give more body to the sauce. Skim the surface fat off the sauce, using first a spoon and then absorbent paper.

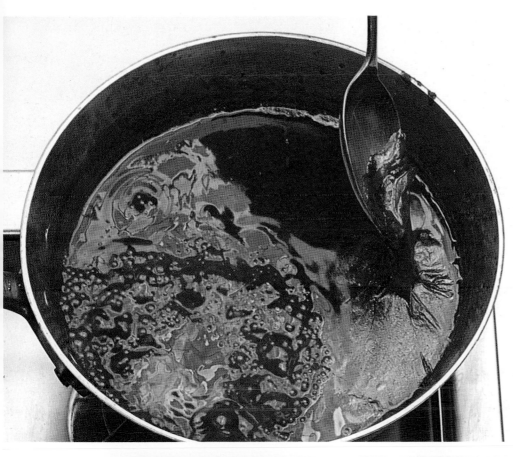

7 Cleansing the sauce. Bring the sauce to the boil, then reduce the heat and place the pan half off the heat so that only one side continues to boil. On the still side, a skin of fat and impurities will form; when it is thick enough, remove it with a spoon. Repeat until the skin that forms is free of fat and the sauce has reduced to a consistency that will coat a spoon.

8 Assembling the dish. Add the onion, mushroom and bacon garnish to the chicken and carrots and pour over the sauce. Adjust the seasoning, if necessary and heat the dish through by simmering for 15 to 20 minutes.

9 Finishing the dish. Gently fry the cubes of bread – croutons – in butter until they are golden-brown. Sprinkle the croutons with a little chopped parsley or with a persillade, made by mixing chopped parsley and pounded raw garlic (above). Cook the parsley or persillade with the croutons for a minute, then scatter the garnish over the finished dish (right).

Mediterranean Fish Stew

All Mediterranean fish stews share certain distinctive characteristics. The fish – and sometimes shellfish as well – are boiled in olive oil mixed either with water or a fumet flavoured with onions, garlic, and the local herbs and spices.

The stew shown here is one variation on this theme. The inclusion of pastis, orange peel, fennel and thyme, distinguish the dish as peculiar to Provence.

A Mediterranean stew mixes both delicate and firm-fleshed species. Delicacy is provided here by John Dory and red mullet; you could substitute whiting and brill. Baby squid, conger eel, angler-fish and wrasse have been chosen for their compact flesh; among the alternatives are sea bass, weaver, gurnard and the sea breams. Include shellfish – mussels, prawns and spiny lobster, for example – if you like. Avoid oily fish, such as sardines, whose strong flavours would dominate. Large, firm-fleshed fish are added first, then the smaller, delicate fish.

FOR 8-10

3 kg / 6 lb assorted fish (see above)
500 g / 1 lb leeks
2 onions, finely chopped
2-3 tablespoons olive oil
500 g / 1 lb tomatoes, halved and seeded
large pinch of saffron threads
strip of dried orange peel
500 g / 1 lb potatoes, thickly sliced
dash of pastis
salt and pepper

FOR THE FUMET:

2 or 3 bay leaves
1 branch of fennel leaves
sprig of thyme
strip of dried orange peel
1 large onion, chopped
3-4 garlic cloves

TO SERVE:

8-10 thin slices of bread
2-3 garlic cloves
rouille (see box opposite)

1 Preparing the fish. Clean, trim and marinate a selection of fish. Keep the small fish whole; cut up the larger ones, saving their heads and tails for the fumet. Here, clockwise from top right, are an angler-fish, being beheaded, conger eel steaks, wrasse, red mullet and some small squid, another wrasse and two John Dory.

2 Making the fumet. Remove the outer leaves of the leeks for the stew, wash and chop the green parts of the stems, and put them in a large pan of water with the bay leaves, fennel and thyme. Add the fish trimmings and heads (above), the strip of orange peel, chopped onion and garlic cloves. Add salt and simmer, covered, for about 30 minutes.

3 Straining the fumet. Pour the fumet through a colander, pressing the solids with a pestle to extract flavour (above). Meanwhile, gently stew the chopped whites of the leeks and finely chopped onions in olive oil for 10 minutes; add skinned, halved and seeded tomatoes, saffron and a strip of dried orange peel and cook for 5 minutes more.

4 Combining vegetables and fumet. If you like, add thickly sliced raw potatoes to the vegetables, adding a welcome contrast to the highly flavoured fish. Season with salt and pepper. Pour on the fumet (above) and a dash of pastis.

5 Stewing the fish. Bring to the boil and add the firmer fish: squid, conger eel (above, left), angler-fish and wrasse. Boil, uncovered, for 5 minutes. Add the delicate-textured John Dory

(above, right). Cook for another 5 minutes. Then add the even more delicate red mullet and cook for 5 minutes more. Depending on the fish used, the total cooking time will vary from 15 to 20 minutes.

Rouille: a Fiery Sauce

Prepare the rouille by pounding 1 or 2 seeded red chilli peppers to a paste with 2 or 3 peeled garlic cloves, salt and pepper (above, top). Gradually stir in about 150 ml / ¹/4 pint of olive oil, and add 85-115 g / 3-4 oz breadcrumbs as necessary to give a light-bodied sauce. Serve in a bowl so that guests can spread it on the garlic bread or put it into their soup.

6 Serving the stew. While the fish are cooking, dry some thin slices of bread in an oven set at a low heat, rub them with garlic, and place a bread slice in each soup bowl. When the stew is

ready, arrange the fish and potatoes on a hot serving platter. Moisten the fish with some broth; pour the rest into the soup bowls.

Vegetable Stews

Most mixed vegetable stews need no braising liquid: the vegetables cook in their own juices with only a knob of butter – and perhaps a few drops of water added during cooking to prevent burning.

In a ratatouille (bottom), the main ingredients are vegetable fruits, which exude so much juice that the liquid must be reduced separately before serving. In the stew of firm young vegetables (top), less liquid is rendered; lettuce leaves are added to provide moistening, as well as texture and flavour.

Spring Vegetable Stew

FOR 4-6

85 g / 3 oz butter

500 g / 1 lb small whole onions

6 artichoke hearts, quartered and
   chokes removed

1 head of garlic, cloves separated but
   unpeeled

bouquet garni

1/2 tender-leaved lettuce

225 g / 8 oz mange-tout peas

3-4 thin young courgettes

salt

2 tablespoons chopped parsley, to
   garnish

Ratatouille

FOR 4-6

500 g / 1 lb onions, coarsely chopped

about 5 tablespoons olive oil

3-4 ripe tomatoes

bouquet garni of parsley, thyme, leek,
celery and a bay leaf

2-3 garlic cloves, sliced

500 g / 1 lb aubergines

3-4 red and green sweet peppers,
trimmed and seeded

500 g / 1 lb courgettes

salt and pepper

fruity extra-virgin olive oil, to serve

1 Cooking in butter. Melt one-third of the butter in a shallow vessel that holds heat well. If you use an earthenware pot, as here, protect it from direct heat with a flameproof mat. Add the vegetables that need most cooking – here, the small whole onions, quartered artichoke hearts and garlic cloves. Other firmer vegetables, such as young turnips, carrots and cauliflower could be added here.

2 Stewing with lettuce. Turn all the vegetables in the butter, bury a bouquet garni among them and cook them slowly, covered, while you shred the lettuce. Add the lettuce to the cooking pot. Salt lightly, cover and stew gently for about 30 minutes. Shake the pot occasionally; add a little water if the lettuce's liquid evaporates.

1 Cooking the onions. Cook the chopped onions gently in the olive oil until they soften; do not let them brown. Skin, seed and quarter the tomatoes and add to the onions. Cook for a few minutes more until the tomatoes disintegrate and form a liquid in which the other vegetables will stew.

2 Adding aubergines and peppers. Put the bouquet garni into the pan, together with the garlic slices. Cut up the aubergines and peppers and tip them into the mixture (above). Salt lightly, cover the pan and cook over a low heat for about 45 minutes.

3 Adding mange-tout. Plunge mange-tout peas into a pan of boiling salted water, cooking them only until the water returns to the boil. Drain them well. Slice the courgettes thinly and sauté them in hot butter for 3 to 5 minutes until they begin to colour. At this point, stir the mange-tout into the stew (above).

4 Adding the remaining vegetables. As soon as you have mixed in the mange-tout, add the courgettes (above). Other more tender vegetables that might be added at this stage include pan-fried mushrooms, parboiled asparagus tips and very young raw peas or broad beans. Pour a little water into the stew if you include peas or broad beans; they will cook in the steam that rises from it.

5 Finishing the stew. Continue to stew very gently for a few minutes, to enable the flavours to mingle and to complete the cooking of the last vegetables added. Remove the bouquet garni and add pepper and salt, if necessary. Turn off the heat and add the remaining butter, cut into pieces. Shake and tilt the pot until it has melted and mixed in. Serve garnished with chopped parsley.

3 Adding courgettes. Cut the courgettes into large chunks and add them to the other vegetables. Cook for another 45 minutes or so. Do not add any liquid; the vegetables themselves will provide more than enough moistening.

4 Straining off the liquid. Turn the vegetable mixture into a colander and allow the juices to drain through. In a sauté pan, reduce the drained liquid to a syrup; meanwhile, discard the bouquet and return the vegetables to the pan.

5 Preparing to serve the dish. Pour the reduced liquid back over the ratatouille. You can serve the dish hot, cold or barely warm. If the ratatouille is to be eaten cold, let it cool and then pour some good, fruity extra-virgin olive oil over it. Stir with a wooden spoon to blend in the oil without mashing the vegetables. Season to taste.

Osso Buco: Braising a Bony Cut

Braising can turn the sinewy toughness of the less expensive cuts of meat into an asset: the long, slow cooking softens tendons and cartilage, melting their gelatine into the braising liquid to make a luxurious sauce. Cuts from leg, neck and shoulder are all good braising material. But knuckle or shank, if sawn crosswise into sections, has an advantage: the bone is filled with delicious and nutritious marrow. When the meat is done, you can scoop this out and eat it.

As in most braises, preparation begins with a preliminary browning of the veal in fat or oil. Before cooking shanks, however, slit the thin membrane that surrounds each slice; otherwise, the skin may shrink and distort their shape. For the braising medium, stock or even water will serve. The north Italian dish known as *osso buco* ('hollow bone') demonstrated here relies on tomatoes for part of the liquid. Summer-ripe tomatoes are best, but when out-of-season, you can substitute tinned Italian plum tomatoes.

FOR 8-9

8-9 cross-section slices of veal knuckle, cut about 4 cm / 1¹/₂ in thick, membranes slit (as above)
about 2 tablespoons olive oil
1 onion, finely chopped
2 carrots, finely chopped
1 celery stalk, finely chopped
3-4 garlic cloves, finely chopped
1 tablespoon finely chopped parsley
250 ml / 8 fl oz dry white wine
2-3 large tomatoes, skinned, seeded and chopped
about 300 ml / ¹/₂ pint veal stock or water
salt

FOR THE GREMOLATA GARNISH:

1 tablespoon chopped parsley
1 garlic clove, finely chopped
grated zest of 1 lemon

1 Browning the veal. Salt the veal. Heat enough oil to cover the bottom of a heavy pan. Over moderate heat, brown the veal, turning the pieces so that they colour evenly on both sides but keeping them upright to prevent the marrow falling out. Reduce the heat and stir in finely chopped onion, carrots, celery, garlic and parsley.

2 Deglazing the pan. When the aromatics have softened and coloured, add the white wine and scrape up meat residues from the bottom of the pan with a wooden spatula (above). Continue scraping until the wine has almost completely evaporated.

3 Adding tomatoes. Stir the tomatoes into the pan and cook gently for 5 to 6 minutes. When the tomatoes soften and begin to liquefy, add veal stock or water almost to cover the veal pieces. Then put a lid on the pan and simmer gently for about 1¹/₂ hours, until the veal is tender and ready to fall from the bone. Adjust the salt.

4 Finishing the dish. When the veal is cooked, degrease the sauce by skimming off the fat with a spoon or blotting with kitchen paper and mix the ingredients for the gremolata garnish. Sprinkle the garnish on top of the veal. Replace the lid for a minute or two before serving: the heat in the pan will release the full flavour of the garnish.

Beef Olives

A practical and attractive way of making meat go further is to cut it into thin slices, roll each one around a stuffing and then braise the rolls. These neat parcels go by many names: *paupiettes* in France, *rollatini* in Italy, 'olives' or 'birds' in Britain.

Stuffings may range from economical bread mixtures to imaginative combinations of meats, cheeses, sour pickles and seasonings; they should always include some element of fat – chopped bacon or ham for example, or simply a little butter to baste the meat from within.

FOR 6

about 1 kg / 2½ lb silverside, topside or
   rump of beef, cut into 12 thin slices
salt
2 tablespoons olive oil
about 300 ml / ½ pint veal stock

FOR THE STUFFING:

3 slices of green bacon, chopped
3 hard-boiled eggs, shelled and
   quartered
about 36 capers
3-4 tablespoons finely chopped parsley
12 anchovy fillets, rinsed, drained and
   patted dry

1 Stuffing the rolls. Flatten each slice of meat slightly with a mallet or meat bat. Near one end, arrange a neat pile of the stuffing ingredients: some chopped bacon, parsley and capers, an egg quarter and an anchovy fillet.

2 Rolling the slice. Start folding at the end nearest the stuffing. To help hold the stuffing in place, tuck in the edges of the meat on both sides as you roll up the meat into a compact package.

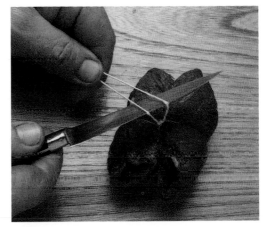

3 Trussing each roll. Cinch the centre of a piece of string about 30 cm (1 foot) long around the middle of the rolled meat. Cross the string and loop it lengthwise around the roll, finishing with a double knot. Trim off the excess string.

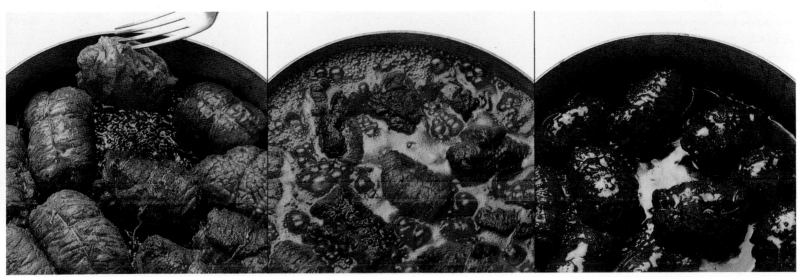

4 Braising the olives. In a pan just large enough to hold all the rolls snugly, heat a thin coating oil. Put in the rolls and brown them over a moderate heat, turning them with a fork (above, left). Add just enough veal stock so that the meat is about two-thirds covered. Bring the liquid to a rapid boil (above, centre), then reduce the heat to a bare simmer and cover the pan. Cook until tender, basting regularly and turning the meat several times; leisurely braising and basting – for about 3 hours or even longer – will concentrate the juices and give the rolls a rich glaze (above, right). Cut away the strings before serving.

Boeuf à la Mode: a Grand Braise

When a large whole cut of meat is simmered with pork rind, calves' feet or pigs' trotters, which gradually surrender their gelatine to the cooking liquors, the meat can be eaten hot or cold in its own jellied sauce. A classic example of such a braise is the beef à la mode.

Beef à la mode does not necessarily require advance browning, and the vegetables for the braise, instead of being softened in fat, can be 'pinched' – that is, baked covered for 30 minutes or so in a hot oven without any added fat or moisture, until they begin to caramelize at the edges. Their flavour will be purer, and there will be less fat to cleanse from the sauce.

An excellent feature of beef à la mode is that leftovers (or the whole braise) can be moulded in the jellied sauce. But the need for a limpid jelly calls for one last refinement: a scrupulous cleansing of the braising liquid (box, opposite).

FOR 6-8

3 kg / 6 lb silverside or rump of beef
10-12 long strips of fresh pork back fat
large piece of fresh pork rind
2-3 pigs' trotters or 1 split calf's foot
2-3 large carrots, diced
3 onions, chopped
about 450 ml / ³/4 pint beef or veal stock
bouquet garni
salt

FOR THE MARINADE:
2 onions, halved and sliced
2 celery stalks, chopped
1 bay leaf
3-4 parsley sprigs with stalks
3-4 garlic cloves, sliced
2-3 sprigs of thyme
few black peppercorns
2 tablespoons olive oil
about 450 ml / ³/4 pint white wine

TO SERVE:
braised carrots, baby onions and celery
(see overleaf)

1 Trussing. After larding the beef with the long strips of pork fat, as shown on page 82, form it into a compact shape. Using a single piece of kitchen string approximately 1 metre (3 feet) long, tie up the meat securely just as you would a parcel. Knot the string and snip off any excess.

2 Marinating the meat. In a bowl, mix the dry ingredients of the marinade with the olive oil. Add the meat, coat it with the mixture then add white wine to cover. Marinate for several hours at room temperature or overnight in the refrigerator.

3 Preparing the gelatinous elements. Cut the pork rind into 2.5 cm (1 inch) squares. Put them in a pan with 2.5 cm (1 inch) of cold water. Add the pig's trotters or calf's feet. Bring to the boil, and boil for 2 to 3 minutes to extract some of the albumin that rises from the meat as foam. Rinse the rind and trotters or feet in cold running water.

4 Preparing the aromatics. Spread the carrots and onions evenly in the bottom of a casserole that is just larger than the trussed meat. Cover the casserole and place it in a hot oven for 30 minutes until the vegetables begin to stick and turn golden at the edges. Uncover for the last 5 minutes to let moisture evaporate.

5 Deglazing with the marinade. After removing the meat, pour the marinade through a strainer into the casserole with the aromatics. Discard the marinade seasonings left in the strainer. Then use a wooden spoon to scrape any residue from the bottom of the casserole.

6 Assembling the braise. Centre the meat on the vegetables in the casserole, arrange the bouquet garni, pork rinds and trotters or split foot around it. Salt lightly and add stock until the meat is barely covered. Slowly bring liquid to boil on top of stove. Cover casserole and cook in a low oven (160°/325°F/gas 3) until tender (about 3 hours) basting often and turning meat once or twice.

A Simple Procedure for a Pure Sauce

While a braise cooks, its liquid draws flavours from the vegetables and meat. But the long cooking also coaxes out fats and impurities, some of which remain dispersed through the liquid, spoiling its clarity and muddying its flavour.

After the meat is done, clean the liquid, as part of the final preparation of the sauce. First strain it into a saucepan and degrease it as by spooning off the fat on the surface or blotting with kitchen paper, then bring to a simmer. The impurities will rise to the surface, where they will be trapped by a skin that will gradually develop. The skin can be spooned off.

Do not hurry the process; give the skin time to form firmly. After removing the first skin let the liquid simmer until another skin forms, and so on. It may take some 30 minutes of repeated skinning before a skin forms that is clear of impurities.

Cleansing the liquid by skinning. Bring the liquid to the boil in a small saucepan. Reduce the heat and move the pan half off the heat. When a firm skin forms on the cooler side of the liquid, draw it aside with a spoon (above), lift it off and discard it. Repeat until only a thin clear skin forms.

7 Serving the hot beef. Remove the meat long enough to empty casserole. Bone the trotters or foot and cut meat into pieces. Hold with the beef and pork rinds in the covered casserole to keep warm while cleansing the liquid (left). Transfer meat to a warmed platter. Cut away trussing string and slice as much as you plan to serve. Surround it with pork rinds, trotter or foot meat and freshly prepared vegetables. Spoon some of cleansed juices over meat and serve the rest separately.

Braised Vegetables

Braising can be adapted to suit any vegetable's characteristics and flavour. Bulb fennel for example, has slightly sweet aniseed taste that is enhanced when the split bulbs are browned in olive oil, the caramelized adherences enriching the braising juices. The unpeeled garlic cloves delicately flavour the fennel and the garlic is transformed into a purée which, when pressed from the skin and spread on bread, is delicious.

Braised Fennel

FOR 6

6 fennel bulbs
2 tablespoons olive oil
12 whole garlic cloves, unpeeled
salt and pepper

Celery Braised in Stock

FOR 6

6 heads of celery
1 large onion, coarsely chopped
2 carrots, cored and coarsely chopped
about 450 ml / ³/₄ pint veal stock
1 tablespoon finely chopped parsley
salt

These braising methods are pretty much interchangeable. Here, celery has been parboiled to attenuate its imposing flavour, before absorbing that of the stock.

Artichoke hearts may be treated by either of these methods. The water in the fennel braise can be replaced by white wine and any of these vegetables can be braised on a bed of mirapoix, with or without unpeeled garlic cloves, in white wine, instead of stock, with a dribble of olive oil added. The mirepoix is often first cooked gently in butter or olive oil until softened but not coloured, or it may be put, covered, into the oven to sweat until it begins to stick to the pan.

1 Preparing fennel. Trim and string the fennel bulbs (page 142), reserving their feathery leaves to sprinkle over the dish at the last minute. Halve the bulbs, as here, or quarter them if they are very large or if you wish to reduce the cooking time

2 Preliminary cooking. Place the fennel pieces, flat-side down, in a heavy pan coated with hot oil. Add the garlic cloves, unpeeled to avoid the risk of the cloves burning and becoming bitter. Sprinkle a little salt over the pan and cook for at least 10 minutes, turning over the fennel (above) from time to time, until the pieces are well browned.

1 Parboiling celery. Trim the celery hearts to a length of about 12 cm (5 inches). Trim only the discoloured surface from the base of each heart: excessive trimming wastes flavour and will cause the hearts to break up. Halve each heart lengthwise. Parboil the hearts in salted water for 8 to 10 minutes and drain well.

2 Adding the flavourings. Strew the onions and carrots over the bottom of a heavy pan and then arrange the celery hearts on top of them, cut sides down.

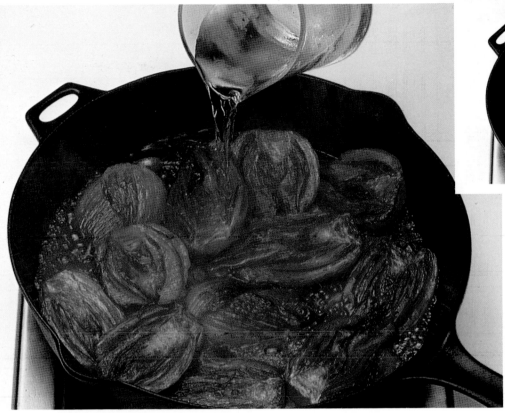

3 Braising in water. Pour over enough water partially to immerse the fennel and gently scrape up all the caramelized deposits on the bottom of the pan. When the water is boiling, cover and simmer for 30 minutes to 1 hour, adjusting the heat so that by the time the vegetables are tender, the sauce has reduced to a thin coating consistency. Turn the fennel sections over in the sauce a couple of times. Shake the pan until the vegetables are glazed with the sauce. Season with pepper and scatter the reserved finely chopped fennel leaves over the cooked bulbs just before serving.

3 Cooking and serving. Pour in enough veal stock just to cover the vegetables; bring it to the boil, then simmer gently, covered, for about an hour, or until the celery is very tender. If, when the celery is ready, the sauce has not reduced to a coating consistency, put all the vegetables on a warm dish and boil down the sauce rapidly. Pour it over the vegetables and sprinkle chopped parsley on top.

Glazing Vegetables

Gentle cooking with sugar and butter in a little liquid produces sweet, moist vegetables coated with a shiny film of syrup that adheres to them as the cooking liquid evaporates. This cooking method, known as glazing, is an excellent way to sauce firm vegetables that have a hint of natural sweetness.

Here, carrots are used to show the basic glazing technique (right). Turnips, parsnips, chayote and beetroot can all be prepared in a similar fashion. Although boiling or braising is enough to bring out the natural flavours of these vegetables, the sugar and butter they absorb when glazed give them added richness.

Small, white onions can be glazed in the same way (box, below) or cooked with only a little additional liquid to produce a rich brown glaze (below, right).

Sugar-coating Carrots

1 Starting the cooking. Leave very young carrots whole; slice larger ones, core and quarter, or slice, older ones. Put the vegetables in a pan with about 30 g (1 oz) of butter and 1 tablespoon of sugar for every 500 g (1 lb). Season with salt and pour in a little cold water until they are partly covered: almost all the water should evaporate as the vegetables cook. Bring the water to the boil, then cover the pan and simmer.

White Glazed Onions

Onions cooked in liquid to which sugar and butter are added emerge pale, with their natural flavour barely altered. To prepare white glazed onions, follow the steps described for glazing carrots (above, right). Add sugar and butter at the beginning of cooking, along with a little liquid – veal stock is used here to give additional flavour. The liquid will prevent the sugar from caramelizing and browning the onions.

Brown Glazed Onions

1 Cooking in butter. Melt a generous amount of butter in a heavy pan, put in the peeled whole onions and season with salt. Cook the onions gently until they are soft and their surfaces are evenly coloured. Allow about 20 minutes for the onions to cook through at this stage. Shake the pan occasionally to prevent them sticking; do not stir the onions in case they fall apart.

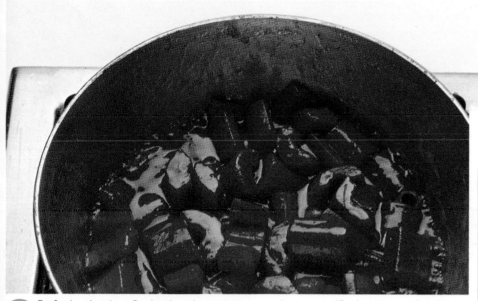

2 Perfecting the glaze. By the time the carrots are tender – up to 45 minutes or so for older ones – there should be little liquid left. Remove the lid and boil hard to evaporate all the remaining water, gently shaking the pan to prevent the vegetables from sticking. Take the pan off the heat. Add a knob of butter to give more body to the glaze, shaking the pan so that each carrot piece is evenly coated. Sprinkle the glazed carrots with finely chopped parsley or fresh lemon juice just before serving.

2 Caramelizing the sugar. Scatter a spoonful of sugar over the onions. Continue cooking for a few minutes over a very low heat. When the butter and sugar mixture begins to turn golden-brown, add a few tablespoons of stock or water to dissolve any caramel sticking to the pan; swirl the pan constantly until the vegetables are thickly coated with a syrupy glaze (above), then serve (right).

G r i l l i n g S t e a k s

Grilling involves the rapid cooking of food by proximity to a searing close dry heat. To avoid the food being dried out by the intensity of the process it has to be done speedily so that the outside of the food, say a steak, rapidly browns and forms a seal to keep in the juices. Obviously then the grill has to be as preheated to be as hot as possible and the grill pan arranged to be as close as can be managed to the heat source. Prior to cooking the food is also usually brushed with a protective coating of oil or melted butter, which also helps the sealing process and adds to flavour.

As grilling times for steaks are so brief, it is imperative that you prepare the meat and the grill well in advance. Remember to remove the meat from the refrigerator well ahead of cooking. Dress it and season it as described on page 85. Also make any accompanying sauces well ahead.

The grill should be carefully preheated. A charcoal or wood fire may take up to 1 hour to reach the right state, depending on the fuel used. Ten minutes should do for a gas or electric cooker. The grills of some stoves are simply incapable of reaching the necessary temperature. If you find that, even after lengthy preheating of the grill, steaks do not sear as they should, you would be well advised to pan-fry

them instead or cook them on a ridged griddle; a heavy frying pan or griddle can easily reach a satisfactory searing temperature even over a moderate heat.

As a general rule, the thinner the steak the closer it should be to the heat as it cooks. For steaks that are less than 4 cm (1 1/2 inches) thick, allow about 7.5 cm (3 inches) distance. If they were grilled farther away, the heat would cook them through before the surface was properly seared, and a rare steak with a crusty brown outside would be an impossibility. Thicker steaks can be given an initial searing at the same distance, but thereafter should be moved farther from the heat – 12 cm (5 inches), or more for a very thick steak – until they reach the right degree of doneness (opposite).

Many people insist on serving steaks sizzling, straight from the grill. But steaks, like roasts, benefit from a few minutes' rest, becoming more tender and delicious if the fibres are allowed to relax and redistribute their juices.

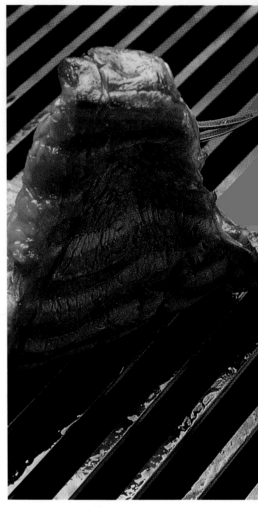

Cooking the steak. Place the steak on the heated grill. When one surface has been seared (about 1 minute) turn the steak and sear the second side. Continue cooking to the prescribed time for the desired degree of doneness. Do not turn the steak more than once again during the remaining cooking time: with each toss, you will lose any juices that may collect on top of the meat.

Grilling Times for Beef and Veal

Total cooking times in minutes

This chart suggests approximate times for grilling steaks and chops to the degrees of doneness illustrated. The figures represent the total cooking times for both sides of the meat, including one minutes' initial searing at high heat on each side. If your steak is a little thicker than the dimensions given here, increase the cooking time by about one minute for each additional 1 cm (1/2 inch) of thickness.

The times show are based on prime-quality meat grilled after searing at a distance of about 7.5 cm (3 inches) above a bed of embers or 7.5–12 cm (3–5 inches) below a gas or electric grill at about 200°C (500°F).

		App. thickness	Very rare	Rare	Medium rare	Medium	Well done
Beef	**Boneless**						
Fillet		2.5 cm (1 inch)	3-4	4-5	5-6	6-7	—
		5 cm (2 inch)	5-6	6-8	8-10	10-12	—
		7.5 cm (3 inch)	7-8	8-10	10-12	12-15	—
Sirloin/entrecôte		2.5 cm (1 inch)	4-5	5-6	6-7	7-9	12+
Rump		2.5 cm (1 inch)	4-5	5-6	6-7	8-9	15+
		5 cm (2 inch)	6-7	7-8	8-9	10-12	18+
Skirt		2.5 cm (1 inch)	5-6	7-8	9-10	11-13	—
Hamburger		5 cm (2 inch)	4-5	5-8	8-12	12-14	—
	On the bone						
Forerib		7.5 cm (3 inch)	12-15	15-18	18-20	20-25	25-30
Porterhouse		2.5 cm (1 inch)	5-6	7-8	10-12	14-16	20-22
		5 cm (2 inch)	7-8	9-10	12-15	16-18	22-25
T-bone (with fillet)		2.5 cm (1 inch)	4-6	6-7	8-10	12-13	15-16
Veal chop		2.5 cm (1 inch)	—	—	—	—	12-15

Judging When a Steak is Done

As heat penetrates from the surface of a steak to the inside, it progressively alters the protein structure of the meat – and so also its colour and moistness. Such terms as 'rare', 'medium' and 'well done' denote informally defined points along the continuous scale from uncooked to completely cooked.

Most people care passionately that their steaks should be done exactly as they prefer. But since mere seconds of cooking can separate rare from medium and medium from well done, success calls for exquisitely accurate timing.

The simplest and most direct way to test your steak for doneness is to press it with your finger. The same principle applies as in testing a roast by pinching (page 212): the more yielding the meat, the rarer the steak. Another way to gauge doneness – provided that you are grilling over, rather than under, the heat source – is by the colour of the meat juices. When red droplets appear on the steak's upper surface while the second side is still cooking, it is medium rare. Pink juices mean the steak is medium; clear juices mean well done, but you must make a tiny slit in the steak to see their colour.

Until you develop confidence in judging a steak's doneness by look or feel, the chart on the opposite page can serve as a guide to approximate times for grilling all the usual steaks. Grills vary greatly in efficiency, so you may have to adapt the figures fairly freely by trial and error.

Plainly the thickness of a steak is the most important consideration for timing: the thicker the steak, the longer the heat will take to penetrate it. But some other factors are reflected in the cooking chart opposite. Boneless steaks (listed first) take a little less time than those that include a bone. Tender meat takes less time than more resistant cuts; for example, fillet, the most tender, needs an appreciably shorter time than rump or skirt.

Very rare (or blue) steak. After a minute's searing and a couple of minutes' cooking on each side, the outermost surfaces of this thick rump steak are browned, but the internal temperature has not yet had time to rise enough to alter the meat's structure or colour.

Rare steak. After about 3 minutes of cooking on each side following the searing, most of the steak is still quite red inside a thin layer of cooked meat. (Skirt steak should always be kept rare; otherwise it will be tough and dry).

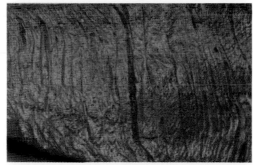

Medium-rare steak. Another minute or two brings the steak to the stage shown here: the outer cooked layer is thicker and the centre, though still very moist, is a paler red than before as the internal temperature continues to rise.

Medium steak. After a total of about 12 minutes' cooking time, only the centre of the steak retains any pinkness; the outside is richly brown but the meat is still running with plenty of pink, almost-clear juices.

Well-done steak. After cooking for about 18 minutes, the steak is evenly done all through; further cooking can only dry it up. Never serve fillet steaks well done: such tender meat would have become dry and flavourless before it was cooked through.

G r i l l i n g F i s h

When subjected to the intense heat of a grill, fattier fish – salmon, mackerel and herring, for example – are kept from drying out by their natural oils. Some firm-fleshed ones, such as tuna, swordfish, bonito and salmon can even be grilled en brochette – cut into chunks and skewered together with vegetables (opposite page, below). Lean fish such as the sea bream (right), however, can also be grilled with excellent results if they are frequently basted with oil or an oil-based marinade. Indeed, basting adds extra succulence and flavour to any grilled fish.

Most fish should be grilled whole and unskinned, to shield the flesh and conserve its moisture. Small fish can be further safeguarded against drying by wrapping in leaves (opposite page, above). Vine leaves, fresh or preserved, make good wrappings, since they do not shrivel quickly when exposed to high heat.

Before grilling fish, preheat the grill and oil its rack (which need not be preheated) to prevent the fish from sticking to it. Cooking time will depend on the size of the fish and the distance it is placed from the heat source. The smaller the fish, the closer it should be to the heat – about 5 cm (2 inches) for sardines. Larger fish should be about 10 cm (4 inches) away, so that they cook through without burning on the outside. To allow heat to penetrate them, score their sides with a knife (above, right). Any fish is cooked if its flesh separates easily from the bone; test whole fish by inserting a knife behind the gills.

To avoid breaking a large fish when turning it, use a double-faced grill of the type shown here, which will allow you to turn the fish without actually touching its skin. Turn smaller fish in a hinged rack or with the aid of two spatulas – one placed under the front of the fish, the other under the tail end.

A Double-Sided Rack to Handle Large Fish

1 Preparing the fish. Place the scaled gutted fish – here, a sea bream – on a dish. Cut two or three diagonal slits in each side (above, left). Rub chopped herbs into the slits and stuff the body cavity with sprigs of herbs (above, centre); fennel – the choice here – complements fish particularly well. Rub the fish with olive oil to coat it thoroughly on both sides (above, right) and, if you like, sprinkle it with a few drops of Pernod or other aniseed-tasting liquor.

2 Grilling and serving. Lay the fish on a well-oiled, double-sided grill and cook until done, turning the grill once and basting the fish frequently with oil. To serve, slip the fish out of the rack on to a hot serving dish. Cut away the fins, and cut the flesh down the backbone to separate the fillets. With a fish slice, cut each fillet into serving portions (right).

Vine-Leaf Jackets for Small Fish

1 Wrapping the fish. Place the prepared fish in a dish; red mullet, used here should not be eviscerated since their livers are a delicacy. Sprinkle herbs – such as chopped fennel, dill or fines herbes – over the fish, then marinate them in olive oil for up to an hour. Lay each fish across the bottom of a vine leaf and roll the leaf around it. Arrange the fish on an oiled grill rack, with the loose ends of the leaves underneath to prevent them from unrolling.

2 Grilling and serving. Grill the wrapped fish for about 3 minutes on each side. When the vine leaves begin to char and the exposed flesh at the head and tail crisps, remove the fish from the grill. Serve the fish immediately in their wrappings, garnished with lemon wedges. Each guest can then peel away the leaves at table.

Skewering Firm-Fleshed Fish with Vegetables

1 Preparing the ingredients. Choose a steak about 4 cm (1¾ inch) thick, cut from a large, firm-fleshed fish, such as the tuna used here. Cut the steak into 4 cm (1¾ inch) cubes. Prepare vegetables to accompany the fish, here, cucumbers have been peeled, halved, seeded and cut into 2.5 cm (1 inch) square segments.

2 Marinating and skewering. Put the cubed fish and vegetable pieces in a dish and pour over them a marinade – here, melted butter, white wine, herbs and lemon juice. Coat the pieces evenly, letting them steep for at least 1 hour. Impale alternate pieces of fish and vegetable on skewers (above) and place them on an oiled pan or grill rack.

3 Grilling the brochettes. Place the pan under a preheated grill. Cook for about 10 minutes, occasionally turning the skewers. Baste the fish frequently with the remaining marinade. Serve from the skewers, pressing the pieces free with the back of a fork.

Grilling Vegetables

Cooking vegetables by exposing them directly to a dry searing heat produces crisp, slightly charred surfaces and a unique flavour. Mushrooms and tomatoes are perhaps the most familiar candidates for the grilling process; however, courgettes, aubergines, artichokes, new potatoes and even whole ears of corn take equally well to this method.

Grilled vegetables taste best cooked outdoors over fruitwood embers instead of charcoal; you can impart extra aroma if you burn a few sprigs of rosemary, bay or thyme as cooking nears completion.

The vegetables should be prepared so that the heat will penetrate them evenly, cooking them through before their outsides burn. Slice aubergines and courgettes in half lengthwise and score their cut surfaces with a criss-cross pattern. Cut artichokes in half. Trim mushroom stems even with the underside of their caps so that they sit level on the grill. Leave new potatoes whole, but pre-cook them by parboiling for 5 to 10 minutes. Leave peppers whole, too, so that the juices given off by their flesh as it cooks collect inside. After grilling, place in a plastic bag for 30 minutes. The steam will loosen their skins. Peel away their blistered skin and seed them, saving the juices.

Oil most vegetables before grilling them; peppers are not oiled. By adding herbs or garlic and perhaps a little fresh lemon juice to the oil, you can make a simple marinade in which to steep the vegetables for 30 minutes beforehand.

Sweetcorn needs special preparation to prevent it from drying out. Peel back the husks and remove the silk; then, with kitchen string, tie the husks back on to reform the protective sheath around the ear. Soaking the raw ear and its husk in cold water for 30 minutes will help to keep the kernels soft; shake off excess water and grill the corn in its wet husks.

Start cooking on a very hot grill close to the heat source, turning the vegetables to sear them quickly on all sides. After a few minutes, move the grill further from the heat, and continue cooking and turning until you can pierce the vegetables easily with the tip of a sharp knife. To keep them moist, baste them with oil or the marinade as they grill.

You can also cook vegetables directly in the embers of a fire. Whole potatoes can be cooked in this way in their skins, unprotected; other vegetables – whole and singly, or cut up and combined – should be wrapped, with butter or olive oil and seasonings, in heavy metal foil.

In preparation for grilling, place the vegetables – here, trimmed mushrooms and scored halves of aubergines and courgettes – in a shallow dish, with their cut surfaces up. Sprinkle with herbs and dribble olive oil over them. Sear their cut sides first on the hot grill, then turn the vegetables over. Raise the grill and continue the cooking over a moderate heat until the vegetables are tender, basting them occasionally. Use a brush to avoid oil dropping on the embers and flaring up.

Tactics for Whole Vegetables

Whole vegetables retain their natural moisture and flavours when grilled over coals or baked in the hot ashes of an open fire. Almost all vegetables can be grilled; those with thick protective skins also lend themselves to baking.

New and old potatoes, sweet potatoes and yams are examples of vegetables that can be grilled or roasted. Here, new potatoes are boiled until almost tender, brushed with oil and seasoned, and then grilled over coals to finish cooking and to develop crisp skins. The boiling is optional, but it shortens the grilling time and also ensures even cooking. To facilitate turning, the potatoes are impaled on skewers; if they are not skewered, pierce them to prevent bursting.

Potatoes for baking in ashes (opposite page, above) should be scrubbed and then pricked. Sweet potatoes and yams do not require piercing since their porous skins allow steam to escape. Onions and heads of garlic can be baked in their skins like potatoes. Beetroots need a wrapping of foil to keep them from losing their juices.

Well-coated with oil, large mushroom caps can be grilled flat on the rack, and they form natural containers for a stuffing (right). Choose a filling that needs little cooking because, once stuffed, the caps cannot be turned on the rack. Here, the stuffing contains chopped sautéed shallots, garlic and red peppers, mixed with breadcrumbs, parsley and lemon juice.

Other whole vegetables that can be simply set on the rack for grilling include courgettes and aubergines, spring onions and sweet peppers. Make long incisions in courgettes and aubergines to prevent them from bursting and to allow the piquant aroma of the coals to penetrate their flesh. Otherwise, the vegetables merely need to be well oiled. Bear in mind that when different vegetables are grilled together the timing must be orchestrated. Slow-cooking varieties should be started first and fast-cooking ones added last so that all of them will be done at the same time.

Potatoes Impaled on Skewers

1 Skewering. Boil unpeeled new potatoes until barely tender – 12 to 15 minutes. Drain them and toss them in oil seasoned with salt and, if you like, crushed dried chilli peppers. Thread five or six potatoes on to each skewer. Pour the remaining seasoned oil over the potatoes and lay the skewers on an oiled rack 10 to 15 cm (4 to 6 inches) above medium-hot coals.

2 Grilling. Turn the skewers frequently, using tongs or a cloth to protect your hand. Grill the potatoes for 3 to 4 minutes in all, until the skins are crisped evenly. To serve the potatoes, use a fork to push them off the skewers and on to plates.

Mushroom Caps with a Stuffing

1 Stuffing mushrooms. Remove the stems from large mushrooms; wipe the caps. Marinate them for up to 2 hours in olive oil and lemon juice. Remove them from the marinade. For the stuffing, combine sautéed chopped sweet red peppers shallots and garlic with parsley, a little marinade and fresh breadcrumbs. Add seasoning and spoon into the mushrooms.

2 Grilling the mushrooms. With a long-handled spatula or tongs, place the stuffed mushroom caps on an oiled rack 10 to 15 cm (4 to 6 inches) above medium-hot coals. Grill them for 8 to 10 minutes. The mushrooms are done when the caps feel slightly soft to the touch and the stuffing is cooked through.

High Heat Roasting of Beef and Vea

The principle of high-heat roasting is to sear the outside of the beef by exposure to very hot air and then to bring the interior of the meat, as rapidly as possible, to the temperature that will give the desired degree of doneness. The cooking process is not complete at the moment the roast emerges from the oven. The meat must 'rest' in a warm place long enough to let the temperature equalize throughout its bulk, and to allow the tissues to relax and reabsorb their juices.

The distinction between high-heat roasting and combined high- and low-heat methods is more one of appropriateness than principle. A bulky roast such as the 4 kg (9 lb) prime rib shown overleaf will need a relatively long cooking time to allow the heat to penetrate to its centre. The oven temperature must therefore be reduced after searing to protect the outside of the roast until the interior is done. A smaller roast, such as a whole fillet, will need little extra cooking after searing, and may therefore be roasted at a high heat throughout. Guidelines for oven temperatures and roasting times are given in the chart opposite.

For either the high- or high-and-low heat method the beef should be the very best of the prime back cuts – ribs, sirloin or rump. Such cuts will be perfectly tender however briefly they are cooked. The meat is juiciest when rare – and really rare beef is best achieved by high heat.

The simplest way to judge when roast beef is done is by feel: give the centre of a lean surface a quick pinch: the more yielding it is, the rarer the meat will be. Or you can use a meat thermometer; insert it into the thickest part of the meat before cooking, keeping the tip away from any bone and fat. Beef is rare at an internal temperature of 60°C (140°F), medium at 70°C (155°F) and well done at 75°C (165°F). The internal temperature will continue to rise by as much as 2 to 3°C (5°F) while the meat rests, so remove the roast from the oven while it is still slightly underdone.

Matching Time and Temperature

The chart below gives approximate oven temperatures and cooking times – calculated in minutes per 500 g (1 lb) – for roasting beef and veal by the methods demonstrated on these pages. Note that the cooking times include any initial period of searing at high heat. Since ovens vary in efficiency and thermostats are not always accurate these figures should be treated as guidelines, not as rules; adapt them freely to suit your taste – and your oven.

Beef

High-heat roasting

Doneness	On the bone	
Rare	10-12 minutes per 500 g (1 lb)	8-10 minutes per 500 g (1 lb)
Medium	12-15 minutes per 500 g (1 lb)	10-12 minutes per 500 g (1 lb)
Well done	18-20 minutes per 500 g (1 lb)	15-18 minutes per 500 g (1 lb)

Sear at 240°C/475°F/gas 9 for first 15 minutes
Roast at 180°C/350°F/gas 4 for remaining time
Note: roast whole fillet at 240°C/475°F/gas 9, allowing 7 minutes per 500 g (1 lb) for rare;
10 minutes per 500 g (1 lb) for medium

Low-heat roasting

Doneness	On the bone and boneless
Medium	20-25 minutes per 500 g (1 lb)
Well done	30-35 minutes per 500 g (1 lb)

Roast at 150°C/300°F/gas 2 for total time

Veal

Doneness	On the bone and boneless
Well done	20-25 minutes per 500 g (1 lb)

Sear at 190°C/375°F/gas 5 for first 15 minutes
Roast at 180°C/350°F/gas 4 for remaining time

Slow-roasting at Moderate Heat

Steady moderate heat makes it possible to roast cuts that would remain tough if cooked more briefly at a higher heat. Roasts from the thick ribs, top or back ribs, or topside (see the chart opposite), although not quite so tender as the back cuts, have an excellent flavour and, with leisurely roasting, yield juicy slices. Because these cuts often have little natural fat, the addition of a bard or sheet of fat (see page 80) can be useful to nourish and protect the meat as it roasts.

When the cooking time is long, the heat must be mild, or the meat will dry out. Some cooks advocate a steady temperature as high as 180°C/350°F/gas 4, and some as low as 130°C/250°F/gas $^1/_2$ for the minimum of shrinkage. About 150°C/300°F/gas 2 is probably a satisfactory average, but you will form your own ideas with experience.

Since slow-roasted beef cooks through at an even rate, this method does not achieve the much-admired combination of a crustily brown roasted exterior with a red and rare interior. But you can produce moist, medium-rare beef if you do not insist on a seared surface – or a temptingly browned exterior if you do not mind relatively well-done beef within.

If barding makes it difficult to test the meat for doneness by pinching (see above and overleaf), you can estimate when slow-roasted beef will be done by calculating the cooking time according to the weight of your roast and the heat of your oven – or by using a meat thermometer. (Suggested times and temperatures are given in the chart opposite.) In slow roasting, small variations in time are not disastrous.

For slow-roasted beef, the resting period after cooking is not an essential part of the cooking process, as it is for quick-roasted meat. Nevertheless, the meat will benefit from a short rest in a warm place before being sliced. It will be easier to carve and will lose less of its juice.

Slow-roasting beef can produce well done meat that is still very moist, with an attractively burnished brown exterior.

Roast Rib of Beef with Yorkshir

This very traditional roast is a classic example of the use of a combination of high- and low-heat methods to cook a bulky roast which needs a relatively long cooking time to allow the heat to penetrate to its centre. After initial searing, the oven temperature is therefore reduced to protect the outside of the roast until the interior is done.

The juicy roast prime rib is served with gravy made from its pan juices, a creamy horseradish sauce and a delicious light version of Yorkshire pudding.

FOR 10-12

4 kg (9 lb) rib of beef
little stock, water or wine (optional)
salt and pepper

FOR THE HORSERADISH SAUCE:
50 g / 2 oz horseradish root, soaked in cold water for 1 hour
150 ml / ¼ pt whipping cream, whipped to stiff peaks
little oil
pinch of mustard powder
generous pinch of sugar
1-2 teaspoons white wine vinegar

FOR THE YORKSHIRE PUDDING:
2 eggs
125 g / 4 oz plain flour
300 ml / ½ pt skimmed milk
generous pinch of salt

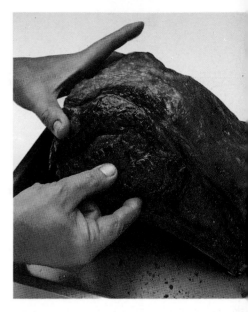

1 Preparing the meat for the oven. If you use a rib roast on the bone, the feather bones (upper spinal bones) must be sawn through, or chined, so that they will be easy to remove before carving. Season and set the meat in a roasting pan on the rib bones with the fat uppermost. As the fat melts, it will baste the meat; the bones will form a natural rack to hold the meat clear of the pan.

2 Roasting the beef. Place the meat in an ove preheated to 240°C/475°F/gas 9. After abo 15 minutes, reduce the heat to 180°C/350°F/gas 4 until the meat is done. Test the meat by pinching a lean surface: if the flesh springs back readily, it is rare; if less resilient, it is medium rare; if firm, the beef is well done.

Fresh Horseradish Sauce

Make this well ahead so that the flavours have time to mingle. First, wash the horseradish, chop off its green top and scrape away the coarse outer skin. Pare tiny shavings with a sharp knife: grating would be quicker but gives the sauce a coarser texture. Blend the parings with whipped cream to make a thick paste (for extra smoothness, you can add a little oil). Add the mustard powder, sugar and season the mixture to taste. Add just enough vinegar to sharpen the flavour.

A Light Yorkshire Pudding

Originally served as a first course before roast beef, Yorkshire pudding has become – in England, at least – its inseparable companion. This simple batter gains its special character by cooking in the fat from the roast.

It is important that the pudding an the beef should be ready at the same time. While the beef is roasting, spoo several tablespoons of fat out of the roasting pan to line a baking tin for the batter. About 15 minutes before the beef is ready to come out of the oven, put the pudding in to bake at the top of the oven, and leave it in when you take out the meat. By the time the roast has finished resting and is ready to carve, the Yorkshire pudding will be puffed and golden.

3 Finishing the roast. Let the meat rest for 15 to 20 minutes. Pour off the fat from the pan and ˙ake a gravy by seasoning the remaining juices ˙emember to pour in any juices. If you like, add a ˙ttle stock, water or wine and boil to reduce. ˙emove the feather bones (above) before carving.

4 Carving the beef. Slice vertically, steadying it with the back of the carving fork: piercing the ˙eat would spoil its appearance and release more ˙ices than is necessary. To let each slice fall free as ˙ou cut it, separate the meat from the bone first by ˙utting horizontally along the contours of the rib.

1 Mixing the batter. Lightly beat the eggs in a bowl. Add the flour, sifting it (above) to ˙corporate air and eliminate lumps. Pour the milk in ˙radually, whisking to keep the batter smooth. Blend ˙e ingredients to the consistency of thin cream and ˙eason the mixture with salt.

2 Preparing the baking tin. Draw off fat from the roasting pan and pour it into a baking tin to a depth of about 1 cm ($^1/_2$ inch). Put the tin in the oven to heat. When the fat is sizzling hot, pour in the batter.

3 Baking the pudding. Put the baking tin in the oven, at 180°C/350°F/gas 4 – the temperature used to cook the roast. After 30 to 40 minutes – or when the pudding is well risen and crisp – remove it from the oven, cut it into squares and serve it from the hot pan.

Roasting Poultry

Oven–roasting is perhaps the simplest – and most satisfying way of cooking poultry: put the bird in the oven (see below for temperatures and roasting times), baste it, turn the bird periodically so that it browns evenly and take it out ready to eat.

Stuffing (see pages 166-7) adds variety of flavour and of texture, and helps prevent the bird drying out in the oven .

After stuffing, the bird must be trussed (see pages 108-9) as this both gives a tidy look and, more importantly, by holding the legs and wings close to the bulk of the body, it gives a compact shape that will cook at about the same rate throughout.

The skin of a lean bird should be generously smeared with fat – here butter – or barded – covered with fat bacon – as a protection against the intense dry heat.

Use a pan that is just big enough to let you turn the bird and baste it easily with a spoon as it roasts.

As with all roasts, it is important to let the bird rest, covered, in a warm place after it comes out of the oven (allow 20 minutes for a turkey, less time for smaller

1 Anointing the bird. To allow the skin to brown crisply without becoming hard, smear the bird all over with the butter. While the bird is roasting, simmer the giblets with the other stock ingredients in water to cover generously in a covered pan for about 1 hour. Drain and reserve.

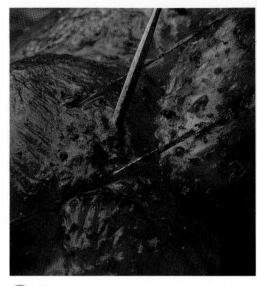

2 Testing for doneness. At the end of the roasting time, push a skewer into the thickest part of a thigh. If the juices that run out are clear, the bird is done; if they are pink, roast it for up to 10 minutes more and test again (see pages 304-5 for carving instructions).

birds) so that the flesh gets a chance to relax and the juices get redistributed.

The turkey is served with a simple but tasty gravy made from the pan juices

deglazed with a stock produced by simmering the bird's giblets with an onion, bay leaf, 2-3 parsley sprigs and a sprig of thyme after the bird has gone in the oven.

A Guide to Oven Temperatures and Roasting Times for Poultry

The chart below suggest the times and temperatures for roasting whole unstuffed birds (add 20-25 minutes to the overall time if the bird is stuffed).

Two methods – quick and slow – are presented. In quick roasting, the bird is started in a hot oven and the temperature is then reduced for the bird to cook until it is done. The initial period of high heat is essential for

drawing off excess grease from fat birds, such as duck and goose; and it will be enough to cook small lean birds such as pigeon completely. Larger lean birds may be roasted by either method.

Whichever method you use, the bird will roast and brown more evenly if you change the way it lies in the pan several times while it roasts. Lay the bird on one side for about one-third of the cooking time; then turn it on its other side

for an equal time, and finally place it breast side up until done.

To keep the flesh from drying and to help the skin brown, baste the bird regularly — every 10-15 minutes — using the pan drippings. If you find that the breast is browning too rapidly before the bird is cooked through, cover it loosely with foil, or reduce the oven temperature.

TYPE OF BIRD	SIZE	QUICK ROASTING		SLOW ROASTING
		Time at high temp	Time at reduced temp	Time at constant temp
Chicken	1-1.5 kg (2-3 lb)	30 min at 220°C/425°F/gas 7	15-30 min	1¼-2 hr at 170°C/325°F/gas 3
	1.5-2.5 kg (3-5 lb)		30 min-1 hr at 170°C/325°F/gas 3	
Capon	2.5-3.5 kg (5-8 lb)	45 min at 220°C/425°F/gas 7	45 min-1¾ hr at 180°C/350°F/gas 4	2½-3½ hr at 170°C/325°F/gas 3
Turkey	3.5-5.5 kg (8-12 lb)	50 min at 220°C/425°F/gas 7	1½-2 hr	3½-4 hr
	5.5-7 kg (12-15 lb)		2-2½ hr	4-4½ hr
	7-9 kg (15-20 lb)		2½-3 hr at 180°C/350°F/gas 4	4½-5 hr at 170°C/325°F/gas 3
Duck	2-3 kg (4-6 lb)	30 min at 220°C/425°F/gas 7	1-1½ hr at 180°C/350°F/gas 4	
Goose	3.5-4.5 kg (8-10 lb)		1¾-2 hr	
	4.5-5.5 kg (10-12 lb)	45 min at 220°C/425°F/gas 7	2-2½ hr at 170°C/325°F/gas 3	
Guinea fowl	0.75-1.5 kg (1½-3 lb)	30 min-1 hr at 220°C/425°F/gas 7		
Poussin/pigeon/squab	0.5-0.75 kg (1-1½ lb)	20-30 min at 220°C/425°F/gas 7		

Roasting Game Birds

To produce perfectly roasted game birds, first choose young plump, tender birds that will cook quickly in the intense dry heat of the oven. Then, prepare the birds in a way that will prevent them drying out in this heat, and, finally, maintain a close watch on cooking times.

When roasting, you can either use birds of a single species, or roast several different game birds together. Here pheasant, partridge and quail are cooked together and presented as a mixed roast. If your roast is to include pheasant, try to obtain a hen pheasant rather than a cock – the hen's flesh is more tender and succulent.

After plucking and drawing the birds (pages 114–5), the pheasants should have their wishbones removed to facilitate carving once they are cooked. All the birds are then trussed (pages 116–7). Game birds are not generally stuffed for roasting; their fine flavour requires little embellishment, and the short time the birds spend in the oven would not suffice to cook a raw stuffing through properly.

Because their flesh is very lean, the birds must be provided with extra fat to keep them from drying out in the oven. Large birds can simply be barded (page 119), small ones such as partridges and quail can be given extra flavour if they are smeared with butter and wrapped in vine leaves – fresh or preserved – before they are barded. If preserved leaves are used, they should be rinsed first in cold water.

The roasting time for game birds is a delicate matter. Because they are usually relatively small, game birds are roasted at a high temperature. By the time the outside of the meat has been seared, the inside will be cooked through. But if you are

1 Wrapping and barding the birds. Truss the birds – here, pheasant, quail and partridge, removing the pheasant's wishbone first. Bard the pheasant. Wash and dry vine leaves large enough to cover the other birds. Twist off the leaf stems.

Smear each bird's breast and thighs with butter and place a leaf on the breast (above, left). Tucking the edges of the leaf underneath the bird, cover the breast with a bard; tie it loosely in place with pieces of string (above, right).

cooking a mixed roast, it is important to remember that different kinds of birds should be roasted to different stages. Both pheasant and partridge, for example, are best eaten still pink; if they are overdone, their flesh becomes tough and stringy. Quail, on the other hand, should always be served well done. Large birds obviously take longer to cook than small ones. To ensure that all the birds are cooked to the desired state at the same time, the largest bird – here, a pheasant – should be put to roast first, and the other birds added to the oven in order of size. Pheasant will require about 25 minutes' cooking time, partridge about 18 minutes. Quail, the smallest of the birds, will require 15 minutes in order to be well done.

2 Roasting the birds. Preheat the oven to 230°C/450°F/gas 8. So that the birds are ready at the same time, put the pheasant, which takes longer to cook, in an ovenproof dish and roast it for about 10 minutes. The smaller birds can be set in another dish (above) and placed in the oven at the end of the 10 minutes. After a further 15-18 minutes, remove all the birds.

Baked Eggs

There is no clear line of demarcation between the terms roasting and baking. The antique definition of roasting – food revolving on a spit before fireplace flames – is now more or less obsolete. Today the term roasting is usually reserved for relatively large meat cuts and whole birds. A chicken is 'roasted', a potato 'baked' – but, of course, cakes, pastries and gratins are also baked. To be baked is to be cooked in an oven.

If eggs are broken before baking, the results are very interesting. To prevent the exposed eggs from overcooking, however, they need some protection from the heat. In the demonstration on the right, the eggs are cooked with cream in small, deep, individual dishes known variously as ramekins or cocottes. To ensure a gentle cooking temperature, the dishes are usually placed in a bain-marie; the water in the bain-marie is kept at a gentle simmer and, with a lid to trap the steam, the eggs are surrounded by a moist and even heat.

Preheat the cream before you pour it into the ramekins; the warmth will start the eggs cooking immediately, thus reducing the time required. You could add herbs or grated cheese to the dish, or replace the cream altogether with melted butter or a spoonful of meat stock.

In the demonstration on the opposite page, eggs are baked, uncovered, on a bed of chopped spinach with cream. The flavouring elements themselves provide protection against the enveloping dry heat of the oven: the eggs are placed in depressions in the bed of spinach, and partly submerged by the cream, which also provides a sauce for the cooked eggs.

Gentle Cooking in Ramekins

1 Preparing the ramekins. Lightly butter several ramekins. Warm some cream in a saucepan over a medium heat. When the cream is hot but not boiling, spoon a little into each ramekin. Break an egg into the cream in each dish (above).

A purée of peas, mushrooms or tomatoes would also make a good base for the eggs. Here, several eggs are baked together in one large dish; you could equally well bake the eggs on a vegetable base in individual serving dishes.

2 Adding butter. Place a small piece of butter on top of each yolk. If you like, you can season the eggs at this stage. Salt and pepper on the yolks will mar their smooth finish, however, so most cooks season the eggs just before serving. Place the ramekins on a wire rack in a large, shallow pan. Pour enough hot water into the pan to come two-thirds of the way up the sides of the ramekins. Put the dish in a moderate oven preheated to 180°C/350°F/gas 4. The eggs will take about 8-10 minutes to cook. They are done when the whites are barely firm and the yolks remain liquid. Lift the ramekins out of the water with a spatula. Serve immediately in the ramekins.

Eggs Baked on a Bed of Creamed Spinach

FOR 4

1 kg / 2¹/₄ lb spinach
25 g / 1 oz butter
150 ml / ¹/₄ pint double cream
pinch of freshly grated nutmeg
4 large eggs
salt and pepper

1 Preparing a spinach base. Stem the spinach leaves; wash them thoroughly in several changes of water to remove grit. Parboil the leaves for 2 minutes, then drain off the hot water. Run cold water over the leaves to cool them; squeeze out the excess moisture. Chop the leaves. Melt the butter in a pan, and add the spinach.

2 Adding cream. Toss the chopped spinach in the butter over a medium heat; reduce the heat, then pour all but about 4 tablespoons of the cream over the spinach. Stir the spinach and cream together. Season to taste with salt, pepper and a pinch of nutmeg.

3 Adding the eggs. Transfer the spinach to a buttered gratin dish. With the back of a spoon, form 4 shallow evenly spaced pockets in the spinach. Break an egg into each depression.

4 Topping with cream. When all the eggs are in place, spoon a tablespoon of the reserved double cream over each of the tops. Set the dish in a moderate oven, preheated to 180°C/350°F/gas 4.

5 Serving. After about 8 minutes, check whether the eggs have cooked; if the whites have not set, cook the eggs for a few minutes more. Serve the eggs on to a warm plate as soon as they are cooked, presenting each egg on its own base of spinach. Season to taste.

Pâté de Campagne

The simplest way to make a pâté or terrine is to combine raw, coarsely chopped meats and fat with eggs, breadcrumbs and a variety of lively seasonings. Wrapped in caul and a lattice of back fat, and baked in a shallow, ovenproof dish, the mixture will turn brown and crusty on the outside, tender and succulent within.

A pâté or terrine should contain enough lean meat to give it body, and sufficient fat to nourish the mixture and keep it moist. For a result that is neither too dry nor too fatty, use about twice as much lean meat as fat, including the back fat or caul that lines and covers the terrine.

Like many meat pâtés, the mixture demonstrated here is composed mainly of pork along with veal. The pig's liver contributes its smooth texture. The veal, included for its leanness and mild flavour, could be replaced by chicken or turkey, or it could be made with pork alone. Whatever meats it contains, the mixture is bound together with eggs and lightened with breadcrumbs.

Pâtés and terrines are usually served cold and, like most cold foods, need to be seasoned more highly. Enliven the mixture with aromatics – such as onion or garlic – herbs, spices and wine or spirits. The terrine on the right is also flavoured with a mixture of garlic and parsley known as a persillade. By varying the seasonings, you can change the character of the finished terrine.

Baked uncovered, the pâté will acquire an attractive brown lattice-work finish as the heat sears the criss-crossed fat. After it is cooked, it should be chilled overnight to make it solid enough to slice without crumbling. The flavours will improve if it is given three to four days to mature.

MAKES ABOUT 2.5 KG / 5 LB

350 g / 12 oz pork belly
350 g / 12 oz pork shoulder
350 g / 12 oz pork back fat
500 g / 1 lb lean veal
500 g / 1 lb pig's liver and cut it into cubes
2 onions, finely chopped
butter
4-5 garlic cloves
1 tablespoon coarse salt, plus more if necessary
3 tablespoons finely chopped parsley
250 g / 8 oz day-old bread
5 eggs
1 teaspoon freshly ground black pepper
1/2 teaspoon freshly grated nutmeg
1/2 teaspoon cayenne pepper
1 1/2 tablespoons mixed dried herbs, including marjoram, savory, oregano and thyme
3-4 tablespoons brandy
125 g / 4 oz caul fat

1 Preparing the meats. With a sharp knife, remove the rind from pork belly, shoulder and back fat. Cut the meats and fat into 2.5 cm (1 inch) strips, then into cubes. Pass the meat, back fat and liver through the coarse disc of a meat grinder.

5 Tasting for seasoning. Fry a small piece of the forcemeat mixture before tasting it for seasoning. Add more salt if necessary, bearing in mind that cold foods need more seasoning than those served hot.

6 Forming the pâté . Line a large shallow ovenproof dish – here, an earthenware gratin dish is used – with caul, allowing the caul to hang over the sides. Fill the dish with forcemeat; with your hands, mound and smooth the mixture into a dome.

2 Stewing onions. Melt the butter in a pan set over a low heat. Add the chopped onions. Stirring occasionally, cook the onions without letting them brown, for 10 to 15 minutes or until soft. In a mortar with a pestle, pound the garlic with the coarse salt to a smooth paste. Blend the chopped parsley into the paste with your fingertips.

3 Assembling the ingredients. Remove the crust from the bread; crumble the bread finely in a food processor. Place the crumbs in a large bowl with the meats, fat, onions, the persillade, eggs, pepper, nutmeg, cayenne pepper and dried herbs. Pour in the brandy.

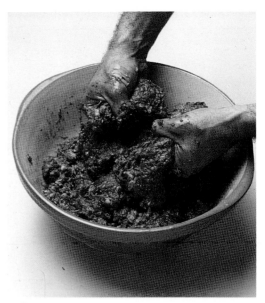

4 Mixing the forcemeat. With your hands mix the ingredients well, squeezing the forcemeat through your fingers several times to make sure that all its elements are thoroughly combined. If the mixture is too loose, scatter on more breadcrumbs; mix and squeeze again.

7 Covering with fat. Cut the back fat into strips about 1 cm (1/2 inch) thick. Arrange the strips of fat in a criss-cross pattern on top of the pâté. Lift the edges of the caul hanging over the sides and fold it over the lattice of back fat. If necessary, add more caul in order to cover the top of the pâté completely.

8 Baking the pâté. Bake the pâté for about 1 1/2 hours in an oven preheated to 180°C/350°F/ gas 4. Test it for doneness by inserting a thin skewer into the centre of the meat; if the juices run clear and the point of the skewer is fairly hot to the touch, the pâté is cooked. The top should be brown, with the criss-cross pattern of the fat still visible.

9 Serving the pâté. Let the pâté cool, then place it in the refrigerator to chill overnight. To improve the flavour, cover it with film and store it in the refrigerator for three to four days before serving it. Remove the film and cut the pâté into 1 cm (1/2 inch) slices for serving.

Candidates for Baking

Vegetables baked whole need minimal preparation – only enough to ensure that none of their flavour is lost while they cook. The demonstrations below explain how to deal with three commonly baked vegetables – potatoes, beetroot and onions – each of which requires slightly different treatment.

Potatoes are the vegetable most often baked, undoubtedly because they are so simple to prepare: just scrub them and place them, unpeeled, in the oven (below, left). The skin of a potato protects the vegetable's interior in a hot oven, the skin itself becoming crisp and delicious on baking. Sweet potatoes are baked in the same way as the common potato.

Aubergines, too, can be baked in their skins without added protection. First prick the skins all over with a skewer and cook them in a moderate oven – 170°C/325°F/gas 3 – for about 1 hour or until the flesh is purée tender when pierced. Serve accompanied by coarse sea salt, a pepper grinder and some good olive oil.

Onions should be placed in a shallow ovenproof dish for baking (opposite, below right). Although the onions require no protection other than their skins, a little water must be added to the dish before baking to prevent escaping juices from burning. If the roots have been cut off to prevent the onions from rolling to and fro, some of the juices will seep out; the water in the dish will allow the escaping juices to caramelize gently rather than burn.

Beetroots take three to four times as long to bake through as potatoes of comparable size. To keep them from drying out during their long spell in the oven, they must be individually wrapped in foil (opposite, below left).

The simple preparation of whole vegetables is often best complemented by an equally simple presentation: serve them slit open or, in the case of onions and beetroot, peeled, and graced only with a knob of butter, salt and pepper. For a more formal effect, however, the soft mealy flesh of baked potatoes and sweet potatoes may be scooped out, mixed with cream, butter and seasonings (below) and then spooned back into the emptied potato skins for reheating in the oven. As for aubergines, interesting flavours can be added before baking by inserting small pieces of bacon and garlic into slits cut in their skins.

Baking potatoes in their skins. Scrub the potatoes and arrange them on a baking tray or oven rack. Put them in a fairly hot oven preheated to 190°C/375°F/gas 5 for about 1 hour. Test them for doneness by piercing them with a skewer (above, left); if the skewer penetrates easily after piercing the skin, they are cooked through. Cut a cross on top of each potato; squeeze the potato at both ends (above, right) to widen this opening – protecting your hands with oven gloves if the potato is too hot – and drop a generous lump of butter inside before serving.

Stuffing baked potatoes. Slice off the top of each potato and scoop out the flesh. With a pestle, press the flesh through a sieve, season with salt and pepper and stir in butter and cream (above, left). Refill the skins with the mixture, make a shallow well in the filling, sprinkle grated cheese into it and add a knob of butter. Return the potatoes to a 200°C/400°F/gas 6 oven for 10 minutes, until their tops brown and they are heated through (above, right).

Garlic Purée from the Oven

Baked garlic, puréed and blended with olive oil, can be used as a flavouring with many meat or vegetable dishes, or added to a vinaigrette (page 00). A little more oil, poured on top of the mixture (far right), will protect it from the air and enable you to keep it, refrigerated, for up to three months.

To make $^1/_4$ litre (8 fl oz) of purée, you will need about 20-25 heads of garlic. Do not separate them into individual cloves or peel them; the skin will keep in the flavour. Bake in an oven set at 190°C/375°F/gas 5 for 1 hour. Pass through a sieve and combine the purée with oil to make a smooth paste.

Wrap the garlic in a foil parcel for baking (above, left). After baking, unwrap the heads and separate them into individual cloves. Squeeze out the contents of each clove and discard the skin (above, centre). Sieve the garlic, add olive oil – about 1 tablespoonful to every 10 heads of garlic – and salt to taste. Mix the purée well and it is ready for use. For storage, smooth the top of the mixture and cover it with a little olive oil (above, right).

Baking beetroot. Wash the beetroot; to avoid losing juices and colour, do not trim or peel it. Wrap the beetroot in foil and bake it in a moderate oven preheated to 170°C/325°F/gas 3 for 3 to 4 hours. Do not increase the heat to speed cooking, since high heat will dry out the beetroot even in its foil wrapping. Peel back the foil (above, left) and, with a skewer or knife point, test the beetroot for doneness, the sharp point should penetrate easily. Unwrap the beetroot and peel it (above, right) before serving.

Baking onions. Arrange the onions in a baking dish large enough to hold them snugly. Pour water into the dish to cover the bottom. Bake the onions in an oven preheated to 200°C/400°F/gas 6 until they are soft; about 1 to 1$^1/_2$ hours. Test for doneness by squeezing them between finger and thumb (above, left); they should give slightly. With a knife, peel the outer skin (above, right) before serving the onions with salt, pepper and butter.

Creamy Vegetable Gratins

Cream brings luxury to vegetable gratins and because such gratins depend for their success on the cream's own unaltered flavour, they are rarely complicated. Parboiled small onions, for example, smothered in cream and baked in a hot oven until covered with a brown crust, are as delicious as they are easy to prepare.

Any cream gratin may be topped with grated cheese or, as here, breadcrumbs. The breadcrumbs will provide a crisper contrast to the smooth cream underneath, and will brown evenly if they are first sautéed briefly in butter.

But the cream will also bake to a golden crust without the addition of cheese or crumbs – as in the gratin of thinly sliced potatoes demonstrated opposite. In the language of classical French cuisine, such a dish is called a gratin dauphinois; in traditional English and American cooking, it is known as scalloped potatoes. For this dish, choose waxy potatoes (page 40) that will retain their firm texture during cooking. To produce slices that will keep their shape, use a knife or mandoline to cut the potatoes lengthwise to a thickness of approximately 3 mm ($^1/_8$ inch). A cut garlic clove, rubbed around the inside of the gratin dish before it is filled, adds interest. Milk poured over the potatoes serves as their cooking liquid; double cream spread on top floats on the surface of the milk and browns in the oven to form the gratin's thin crust.

Shredded Root Vegetable Gratin

FOR 4

750 g / 1 $^1/_2$ lb turnips, swedes, parsnips or celeriac (or mixtures of them)
90 g / 3 oz butter
150 ml / $^1/_4$ pint double cream
30 g / 1 oz fresh breadcrumbs
generous pinch of mustard powder
generous pinch of paprika
salt and pepper

1 Tenderizing the turnips. Peel and halve the turnips, then grate them coarsely and sprinkle them with a little salt. Melt one-third of half the butter in a frying pan and cook the turnips over a low heat, stirring constantly to prevent sticking (above).

2 Pouring in cream. After 15 minutes the turnips will be tender and impregnated with the butter. Transfer the grated turnips to a buttered gratin dish and add enough cream to cover them.

3 Adding breadcrumbs. Sauté the breadcrumbs with the mustard and paprika in the remaining butter over a low heat until they are lightly coloured. Scatter the buttered crumbs over the cream, then bake the gratin in the oven preheated to 200°C/400°F/gas 6 for 30 minutes. When the surface is a deep golden-brown, remove the dish and serve the gratin while it is still bubbling hot.

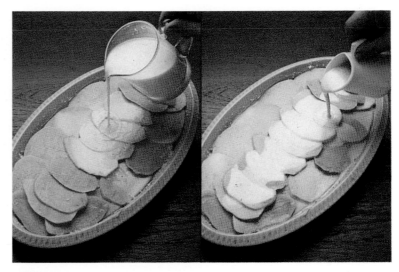

1 Layering the potato slices. Rub the inside of a gratin dish with a cut garlic clove. Let the juice dry, then smear the dish thickly with butter. Arrange potato slices in the dish in rows, overlapping both the slices and the rows slightly. Salt each layer of potato slices as you complete it. Do not fill the dish more than two-thirds full.

2 Adding milk and cream. Pour milk into the dish until the layers of potatoes are about half covered, then top the gratin mixture with a layer of cream until the slices are just covered. To help the crust to form, scatter thin shavings of the remaining butter over the cream.

Gratin Dauphinois

FOR 4-6

1 kg / 2¹/₂ lb waxy potatoes, thinly sliced
1 garlic clove
60 g / 2 oz butter
about 450 ml / ³/₄ pint milk
about 200 ml / 7 fl oz double cream
salt

3 Baking the gratin. Put the dish in the oven preheated to 200°C/400°F/gas 6. After 15 minutes, reduce the heat to 180°C/350°F/gas 4 and bake for a further 45 minutes, until the milk has been absorbed by the potatoes and the cream has formed a golden crust over the surface. The potatoes will be very tender. Serve them carefully, lifting them out with a fork and a spoon.

A Classic Cheese Soufflé

Basically a soufflé is no more than a thick white sauce enriched with egg yolks and lightened with firmly beaten egg whites. In the oven the moisture in the soufflé turns to steam and the soufflé puffs up.

Any cheese that is hard enough to grate makes an excellent flavouring for the soufflé. Before the grated cheeses are melted in the sauce, a small portion is used to line the dish. This lends extra texture and flavour to the soufflé's crust.

The ratio of sauce and cheese to eggs is critical. As a general rule 300 ml (¹/2 pint) of white sauce and 100 g (5 oz) of cheese call for 4 eggs, although many recipes include one more egg white than yolk, to give a well-risen soufflé. Varying the proportions significantly could well result in a mixture that is either too heavy to rise properly or too light to hold its shape.

The egg whites must be whisked to a voluminous foam before being mixed with the other ingredients. If care is taken to combine them gently with the base, well-whisked egg whites will lose little of their volume. However, the mixture should be put in the preheated oven immediately, lest the whites deflate.

Timing and temperature depend partly on the size of the soufflé: a large soufflé baked in a moderate oven takes 30 to 40 minutes, while small individual soufflés cooked at a higher heat require only half that time. For a very moist soufflé, reduce the time and increase the temperature; for a firmer, drier texture, increase the time and reduce the temperature.

FOR 6

85 g / 3 oz Parmesan cheese
85 g / 3 oz Gruyère cheese
30 g / I oz butter, plus more for greasing
30 g / I oz flour
300 ml / ¹/2 pint milk
5 eggs
generous pinch of grated nutmeg
salt and pepper

1 Preparing the cheese. Grate the Parmesan against the smallest holes of the grater. The Gruyère, a slightly less hard cheese, should be shredded more coarsely against larger holes.

2 Lining the dish. Generously butter a straight-sided ovenproof dish. Put in a few spoonfuls of grated cheese, then tip and roll the dish until its interior surfaces are well coated. Shake out and reserve any excess cheese.

6 Folding in the egg whites. Spoon the sauce gently into the bowl containing the remaining beaten egg whites. With your hand or a spatula, gently fold the whites into the sauce. Do not over-mix: a few streaks of unmixed egg whites are preferable to a heavy soufflé.

7 Shaping a cap. Pour the mixture into the prepared dish; the dish should be three-quarters full. If you want the soufflé's centre to rise in a high cap, run your thumb round the edge of the soufflé to make a deep groove. Bake the soufflé for 35 to 40 minutes in an oven preheated to 190°C/375°F/gas 5.

3 Making a white sauce. Melt the butter in a heavy pan. Stir in the flour and cook the roux for 2 to 3 minutes. Add the milk to the roux, whisking briskly to prevent lumps from forming. Cook the sauce uncovered, over a very low heat, for about 10 minutes, stirring it from time to time. Let it cool slightly.

4 Separating the eggs. Separate the eggs and transfer the whites to a large bowl, preferably of copper. Off the heat, drop all the yolks but one into the sauce, reserving the final yolk for another use. Whisk the yolks into the sauce (above). Stir the grated cheese into the sauce.

5 Lightening the sauce. Season the sauce with salt, pepper and grated nutmeg. With a wire whisk, beat the egg whites until they stand in soft peaks (above). To lighten the sauce and thus make it easier to incorporate into the bulk of the whites, gently mix about a quarter of the beaten egg whites into the sauce with the wire whisk.

8 Serving the soufflé. The soufflé is ready when it has risen well above the rim of the dish and its top is golden. Serve it without delay; make sure each helping includes some of the crust as well as some of the moist centre.

Shallow-frying Eggs

Like grilling, frying involves cooking food rapidly, this time in contact with a hot pan and usually in a shallow layer of fat in the pan. Dry-frying in cast-iron or non-stick pan can, however, achieve results very similar to that of grilling. Sautéing usually involves initial rapid shallow-frying, often of smaller pieces of food which are moved continuously to brown them evenly, followed by some gentle stewing, usually in a flavouring sauce.

When eggs are cooked in a thin layer of fat, heat is directed at them from one direction only – below. The cook's task is to ensure that the tops of the eggs cook at the same time as the bottoms, so that the thick rings of white surrounding the yolks set before the undersides burn. Basting the eggs by spooning fat over them will help to start the tops cooking. In addition, you can cover the frying pan with a lid to reflect heat downwards, as shown in the demonstration on the right.

Alternatively, you can turn an egg over mid-way through frying, so that both the top and the bottom are brought into contact with the hot surface of the pan (right, below).

Whichever frying method you choose, you should add the eggs to the pan as soon as the fat is warm, to prevent it from burning and spoiling the taste of the finished dish. The fresh flavour of melted butter marries well with eggs; so does that of oil or bacon dripping. Most cooks break the eggs directly into the fat, but some prefer to crack eggs on to a small dish and then slide into the pan so that if a yolk accidentally breaks, the egg can be reserved for another use.

Shirring eggs is an extension of the pan-frying technique: the eggs start cooking on the top of the stove, and are then finished in an oven (box, opposite page) or under a grill. Gratin dishes just large enough for one or two eggs are traditionally used for this method.

Reflecting Heat with a Pan Lid

1 Breaking the eggs. Over a low to medium heat, warm sufficient butter in a frying pan to cover the bottom of the pan generously. As soon as the butter melts, break into the pan as many eggs as it will hold easily – up to four eggs in a pan 30 cm (12 inches) in diameter.

2 Basting the eggs. Once all the eggs have been added, tilt the pan slightly and use a spoon to collect the fat that runs to the lower side. Baste the tops of the eggs with the hot fat two or three times to start them cooking. If the pan is completely filled with eggs, it may be difficult to collect the fat; in that case, melt some butter in a separate pan and use it for basting.

Turned Eggs with a Simple Sauce

1 Adding the egg to the pan. Melt butter over a low heat until it starts to foam. Break an egg into the hot butter (Step 1, above). Alternatively, break the egg on to a small dish and slide it into the pan (above). Allow the egg to cook until the underside sets – about 1 minute.

2 Turning the egg over. Slide a spatula under the egg so as to support the yolk and as much as possible of the white. Raise the spatula a little, then turn it over sideways so that the egg slips back into the pan, yolk side downwards.

3 Covering the pan. To set the thick layer of white surrounding each yolk, cover the pan with a tight-fitting lid to reflect heat on to the tops of the eggs. After about 1 minute, remove the lid. The eggs are ready as soon as the whites are set; the yolks should remain soft and glistening.

4 Serving the eggs. Take the pan off the heat. Gently shake the pan to free the eggs, then carefully tilt it to slide the eggs on to a warmed plate. Season to taste with salt and pepper. Serve at once.

1 Adding cream. Place a gratin dish over medium heat – with a fireproof mat if the dish is ceramic. Melt enough butter to coat the dish, then break in the eggs. Cook for about 1 minute, until the undersides set, take off the heat and pour enough cream over the eggs to coat the tops.

3 Tipping out the egg. Cook the egg for a few seconds more to allow the white around the yolk to set, then take the pan off the heat. Tilt the pan to slide the egg out on to a warmed plate (above).

4 Making a pan-juice sauce. Turn up the heat slightly. Melt a little more butter in the frying pan; when it foams, add a dash of vinegar. Stir the butter and vinegar mixture for a few seconds, then pour it over the egg. Serve at once.

2 Serving the eggs. Place the dish in an oven preheated to 180°C/350°F/gas 4 for 4 to 5 minutes, until the whites have set uniformly. Remove from the oven and serve the eggs in the dish, set on a plate to protect the table from its heat.

Omelette Fine Herbes

A perfect rolled omelette is an object lesson in culinary economy. Its making takes very little time and no special equipment other than a heavy, carefully seasoned omelette pan. The only ingredients required are eggs, butter, and any flavourings you have chosen to use.

The eggs should be beaten only lightly, to preserve their fresh yolk taste and tenderness. Beating is best done immediately before cooking. Butter, cubed for fast even melting, lends a silken texture to the omelette; allow 15 g ($^1/_2$ oz) for three eggs.

The mild taste of the eggs can be enhanced by any of a wide range of flavourings. Here fines herbes (box, right, below) bring a breath of fragrance; if fresh herbs are unavailable, dried marjoram or oregano are good aromatic substitutes. Other ingredients that can be added before the eggs are cooked include slices of asparagus, chopped anchovy fillets or steamed mussels. Whatever flavourings you use, cooking must be brisk, and the pan should be well heated before the eggs are added. The omelette should set and be ready to serve in less than a minute; cooked slowly, it would lose its moistness.

While integral flavourings such as herbs are added to the egg mixture before cooking, more substantial garnishes – diced salami, for example or a mixture of wild mushrooms, sautéed and moistened with a cream sauce – can be prepared in advance and added hot, just before the omelette is folded (Step 6, right). This is also the best time to incorporate cheese; if added at the start of cooking it will cause the omelette to stick as it melts.

FOR I

2-3 eggs
about 30 g / I oz cold butter
I teaspoon each finely chopped parsley,
**   chervil and chives**
$^1/_2$ teaspoon finely chopped tarragon
salt and pepper

1 Assembling the ingredients. Break the eggs into a shallow dish – the shallowness will facilitate rapid beating. Add salt, freshly ground black pepper and some of the cold butter cut into small cubes. Add the finely chopped fresh herbs (box, below).

2 Beating the eggs. Warm a seasoned omelette pan for a few seconds over a high heat. Add a piece of butter – about 15 g ($^1/_2$ oz) is enough to coat a 20 cm (8 inch) pan. While the butter melts, beat the seasoned eggs and butter lightly with a fork. Beat just enough to combine the yolks with the whites.

Fines Herbes

Equal quantities of parsley (above, right), fresh chervil (foreground) and chives (centre), plus a small quantity of powerful tarragon (background), make up the classic fines herbes mixture. Strip the tarragon leaves from the stalks and chop finely. Hold parsley and chervil tightly by the stems while you slice the leaves; discard stems. Bunch the chives and chop.

6 Rolling the omelette. With the fork, fold the near edge of the omelette into the omelette's centre. Tilt the pan away from you, then slide the prongs of the fork under the fold and roll the omelette over towards the far edge of the pan.

3 Adding the eggs. Tilt the pan in all directions to coat the base evenly with the melted butter. When the butter begins to foam and just before it starts to brown, pour in the beaten eggs.

4 Stirring the mixture. Pass the flat (not the prongs) of the fork 2 or 3 times through the eggs so as to expose as much of the mixture as possible to the heat of the pan.

5 Lifting the omelette's edge. When the base of the omelette has begun to set, use the fork to lift the edge of the omelette. Tilt the pan at the same time, so that any egg which is uncooked will run underneath the cooked egg and set. Repeat the lifting and tilting process around the pan's side to allow as much liquid egg as possible to run under.

7 Sealing the fold. With the prongs of the fork, pull the far edge of the omelette back from the side of the pan over the folded section. Seal the fold by gently pressing down on the top of the omelette with the flat of the fork for a second or two. Keep the tilted pan over the heat for 3 to 4 seconds so that the bottom of the folded omelette browns slightly. Remove the pan from the heat.

8 Serving. Tip the pan sharply against the edge of a warmed plate so the omelette rolls on to the plate browned side uppermost (inset). To give the omelette a sheen, you can draw a small piece of butter across the surface. Serve immediately, while the omelette is still hot and moist and soft inside.

Poulet Sauté à la Crème

In the three-stage sautéing process illustrated here, the poultry pieces are first browned in an open pan. Then the pan is covered and they are cooked through gently. Finally, when the pieces are done, they are removed, and the juices and the caramelized residue remaining in the pan used as the base of a sauce.

Ideally, the pan for sautéing should be just wide enough to hold the chicken pieces side by side. If they overlap, the moisture they exude will not evaporate readily and the pieces will start to stew instead of browning. On the other hand, too much space between the pieces will allow the oil or fat to overheat and burn.

During the gentle-cooking stage, a vegetable garnish may be added to the poultry to enhance the flavour of the finished dish. The vegetables should always be introduced after the poultry has browned, so that their moisture does not interfere with the sealing process.

When the meat and garnish are done, the excess fats are poured off and a liquid is used to dissolve the brown bits of coagulated juices adhering to the bottom of the pan. This process is called deglazing and it is the first step in making the sauce. In this demonstration, white wine is used to deglaze the pan, but any liquid – such as stock or water – will do.

FOR 6

6 chicken portions
1 tablespoon oil
30 g / 1 oz butter
1 cucumber, peeled, parboiled in salted
  water, drained, cut into chunks, then
  briefly stewed in a little butter
150 ml / ¼ pint white wine
150 ml / ¼ pint double cream
about 1 teaspoon lemon juice
salt and pepper

1 Browning the chicken. In a sauté pan, melt the butter with the oil to coat the bottom. Dry the chicken pieces – any moisture clinging to them will interfere with the browning process – and arrange them in the pan. Fry the seasoned pieces, turning them with tongs until they are evenly browned. This will take 15 to 20 minutes.

2 The gentle cooking stage. Reduce the heat and cover the pan. If cooking any breasts, they will be done after about 8 minutes. You can test by pressing with a finger; when the meat feels springy, it is done. Remove the breasts and transfer to a warmed dish, replace the lid and cook the other pieces for 10 minutes more.

Elaborating a Sauté with Vegetables and Herbs

By adding various garnishes to sautéed poultry pieces and finishing the sauce in different ways, a surprising number of dishes can be created. A small bundle of fresh herbs, for example, contributes an aromatic presence that eliminates the need for any additional garnish; simply add the herbs at the start of the gentle-cooking phase and remove them when cooking is completed. Prepare a sauce in the same pan by bringing wine to a boil and simmering it to half its original volume.

For a dish in the tradition of Provençe, garnish the poultry with tomatoes, peppers, black olives, garlic and parsley (above, left). Or garnish the chicken with sautéed mushrooms and sliced leeks stewed in butter (above, right). Finish the sauce with white wine and butter, as here, or with cream.

3 Adding the garnish. After any breast pieces have been removed, add a vegetable garnish if you want one. The exact moment depends on the ingredients chosen and the time they take to cook. Here, the chunks of cucumber that were first stewed in a little butter constitute the garnish.

4 Pouring off excess fat. The juices exuded by the chicken are a delicious complement to the flesh, but the frying fat is unpalatable. Put the remaining chicken pieces and the garnish in the warm dish containing the breasts. Pour off and discard the fat, but stop before the darker meat juices in the pan run out.

5 Deglazing. Add a generous dash of liquid – in this case, white wine – to the pan. Over high heat, stir and scrape with a wooden spoon until the coagulated meat juices sticking to the pan have been loosened and dissolved in the liquid. Boil the enriched liquid briskly for a few minutes to reduce and concentrate it.

6 Finishing the sauce. Sauces for sautéed poultry are usually completed by adding an element that enhances the flavour and consistency. Here, double cream is added and stirred constantly over a high heat until the sauce thickens to a consistency that will smoothly coat the poultry. Add the lemon juice and adjust the seasoning, if necessary.

7 Assembling the finished sauté. Reduce the heat to low, then return the chicken pieces and the garnish to the sauce in the sauté pan. Replace the lid and warm through for a few minutes.

Lyonnaise Potato Cake

Vegetables cooked gently in a small quantity of fat often profit from being covered, at least during a part of the process, to hold in the heat. The steam created within the enclosed vessel condenses on the underside of the lid, which should be lifted up without tipping and moved aside before being tipped and wiped clean, to prevent water dropping on the food, which may cause it to stick. Vegetables that require longer cooking times than those involved in rapid pan-frying are particularly suited to this method, demonstrated below.

A popular application of this technique is the potato *paillasson,* or 'straw cake', composed of vegetables cut into coarse shreds so that they are easily penetrated by heat. A straw cake is often made with potatoes alone, but other vegetables can be sandwiched between layers of potato; try shredded carrots or onions.

FOR 4

850g / 1¾ lb potatoes
about 100g / 3¼ oz butter
salt and pepper

1 Preparing the potatoes. Peel the potatoes, cut them into pieces and shred them (top). Rinse the shreds in cold water, then drain; repeat both steps. Place the shreds in a clean towel and roll them up as tightly as you can (above) to dry.

2 Forming the cake. Over a medium to low heat, melt half the butter in a heavy shallow frying pan, swirling to coat the sides. Put the potato shreds in the pan. Gently press them down with a fork to form a single firm cake with a smooth slightly domed top surface.

Slow Frying Under Cover

To pan-fry vegetables that require prolonged cooking, put them in a pan with enough hot butter or olive ail to coat them well. Cover the pan and set it over low heat until the vegetables soften – about 30 minutes for the new potatoes shown here. Shake the pan often and remove the lid occasionally to wipe away any moisture that condenses on its underside. Test the vegetables to make sure they are done as shown; then cook them uncovered, for another 10 minutes to evaporate any remaining moisture.

Potatoes especially benefit from this method: since they give off relatively little moisture on contact with the heat, they turn brown and slightly crisp in a covered frying pan in spite of contact with their own steam. Small new potatoes may be cooked whole and unpeeled; their skins will trap starch that would otherwise cause them to stick. If you use larger potatoes, cut them into pieces and wash them to remove surface starch: then dry them thoroughly.

You can also gently pan-fry any other vegetable which gives off little moisture. Coarsely chopped carrot and turnips, and thinly sliced artichoke hearts can all be cooked by this method.

Test that the vegetables – here new potatoes cooked with unpeeled garlic cloves – are tender with the tip of a sharp knife. The knife should pierce them easily.

3 Cooking the first side. Sprinkle the cake lightly with salt and pepper. To prevent the edges of the cake from sticking to the pan, distribute fingers of butter around the side. Cover the pan and cook over low to medium heat for about 20 minutes, removing the lid two or three times to wipe away any condensation that appears on its underside. When you smell the nutty aroma of browned butter and see that the edges of the potato cake are beginning to brown, it is ready to turn. To make sure the cake slides freely, shake the pan. If necessary, slip a spatula under the cake to loosen it.

4 Turning the cake. Dry the underside of the pan lid and hold it securely on the pan; turn pan and lid over. If you do not have a flat lid use a plate instead. Return the pan to the heat, melt a little more butter to coat and slide the cake – uncooked side down – from the lid back into the pan. Fry the cake, uncovered for about 15 minutes to brown the uncooked side. Slide it on to a warmed round platter and serve immediately, cut into wedges.

Deep-fried Marinated Chicken

Deep-frying subjects food to very high temperatures in hot fat. For this reason the food is often given a protective coating of egg and breadcrumbs or batter, which seals in its moisture. The contrast between this and the crisp and tasty cooked coating constitutes part of the joy of deep-fried food.

The oil for deep-frying must be of a kind that will not smoke or burn when heated to temperatures of 190°C/375°F or more. Its inherent flavour is another important factor: some fats and oils have a distinctive taste which is imparted to the food that is cooked in them, while others have almost no flavour at all.

Most vegetable oils stand up to deep-frying temperatures well. These oils are extracted from such diverse sources as corn and coconuts, sunflower seeds and soy beans. Groundnut oil is a good choice; its faint flavour will not mask that of the food being deep-fried, its smoking point is 230°C/450°F and it stores well.

Many commercial cooking oils are blends of several vegetable oils and most of them are processed to provide a clear, pale colouring and virtually no taste. Nearly all of them produce satisfactory, if undistinctive, results in deep-frying.

The oil used for deep-frying can be re-used several times. After cooking, let it cool, then strain it to remove any small particles of food that would burn if the fat were reheated, affecting its flavour. Such bits also turn the oil rancid.

When deep-frying, observe a few simple safety measures. To avoid spillage, use a high-sided pan specially designed for deep-frying; fill the pan no more than half full. Dry all utensils thoroughly before use; when water comes into contact with very hot fat, the water vaporises instantaneously and makes the fat splatter. If you regulate the heat properly, there is little chance of the oil or fat catching fire; but keep a tight-fitting lid close to the frying pan so that flames can be quickly smothered.

FOR 3-4

1 chicken, weighing about 1.5 kg / 3 lb, cut up into pieces
vegetable oil, for deep-frying
salt and pepper

FOR THE MARINADE:
1 small onion, sliced
1 bay leaf
1 young celery stalk, sliced
2 garlic cloves, crushed
1 tablespoon chopped parsley
1 teaspoon dried oregano
juice of ½ lemon
4 tablespoons white wine

FOR THE BATTER:
85 g / 3 oz flour
generous pinch of salt
2 tablespoons olive oil
2 eggs
150 ml / ¼ pint beer

The Secrets of a Light Puffy Batter

Batter for coating deep-fried poultry should be prepared at least an hour in advance. If used immediately, the batter will be too elastic to cling properly to the poultry pieces, and it will shrink and split when it comes into contact with the hot fat. An hour's rest enables the batter literally to relax.

A simple batter can be made with water, flour, oil and eggs alone; replace water with milk or wine, for a more flavourful batter. To make a fluffier coating, blend the flour with beer, and fold beaten egg whites into the batter just before frying. The carbon dioxide in the beer, together with the egg whites, gives the batter a light, airy texture. Pale ale was used here, but any other beer will serve equally well.

1 Mixing the batter. Put the flour, salt and oil into a mixing bowl. Separate the eggs, add the yolks to the bowl and reserve the whites. Slowly pour in the beer, beating the ingredients together with a wire whisk. Cover the bowl with a towel and set aside for 1 hour at room temperature.

2 Folding in the whites. Beat the egg whites until they form soft peaks. With a wooden spoon or spatula, gently fold the whites into the batter mixture.

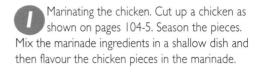 Marinating the chicken. Cut up a chicken as shown on pages 104-5. Season the pieces. Mix the marinade ingredients in a shallow dish and then flavour the chicken pieces in the marinade.

2 Heating the oil or fat. Fill a deep pan with oil or fat to a depth of 8 to 10 cm (3 to 4 inches), and place it over a high heat. Drop a dab of batter into the fat to test the temperature; if the batter sizzles on contact, the fat has reached the right temperature (about 180°C/350°F).

3 Coating the pieces with batter (left). Remove the chicken pieces from the marinade and pat them dry with a towel. Holding each piece by one corner, dip it into the batter, then slip it into the pan, using tongs. Handle the chicken carefully to avoid wiping off the batter. Do the same with each remaining piece, but do not crowd the pan; you may well need to deep-fry in at least two batches.

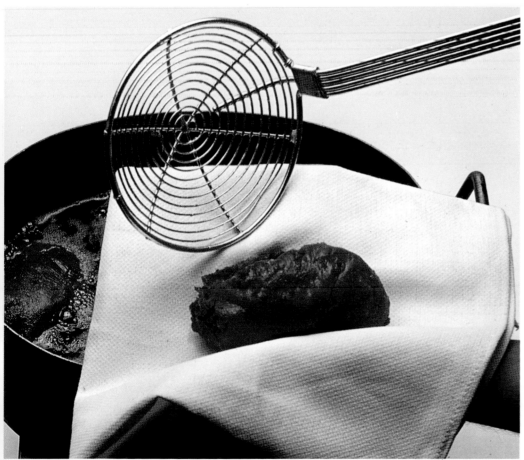

4 Cooking the pieces. Adjust the heat during the 15 to 20 minutes it takes for the chicken to cook through so the batter browns in the same time. The poultry pieces will float in the fat; turn them occasionally with a fork or a wire skimmer so they cook through evenly. When they are done, remove them with the skimmer. Place them on paper towel to drain off excess fat. You can keep the pieces warm in a low oven while you deep-fry subsequent batches.

Doing Justice to the Potato Chip

There are several ways to prepare potato chips. Before frying chips, some cooks wash and dry them, as shown here, to remove their surface starch and to keep them from spluttering in the hot fat; other cooks simply wipe the chips with a towel or omit this step altogether. Washed potato chips will be crisper, but some people prefer the softer quality of chips that have not been washed or wiped.

There are also two different approaches to frying. They can be fried a single time, as in this demonstration, in fat heated to 190°C/375°F; or they can be fried twice: first at 185°C/360°F, to cook them through without browning, then a second time, just before serving, in very hot fat – 195°C/390°F. This browns the chips very quickly and sometimes puffs them up. Either way, cook in small batches, so that the temperature of the fat does not fall too much as each new batch is added to the deep-frying pan.

1 Preparing the chips. Peel the potatoes – waxy-textured ones (page 40) are best for frying – and cut each potato lengthwise into slices about 1 cm (1/2 inch) thick. Cut each slice into 1 cm (1/2 inch) thick strips (above, left). Rinse the chips in plenty of cold water (above, centre), rubbing them gently with your fingers to remove surface starch. In order to avoid dangerous spluttering when the chips are put into hot fat, dry the chips thoroughly beforehand in a kitchen towel (above, right).

2 Heating the fat. Put enough fat or oil into a deep-frying pan to immerse a small batch of chips; do not fill the pan to more than half its depth. Place the pan over a moderate heat. You can test the fat's temperature by touching the end of a raw chip to it: if the chip sizzles, the fat is hot enough for frying.

3 Adding the chips. Lower an empty deep-frying basket into the hot fat to coat it, so that the chips will not stick to it. Lift out the basket, add a batch of chips and lower them into the fat.

4 Frying. Fry the chips for about 10 minutes, adjusting the heat to maintain a constant gentle sizzling in the pan. When the chips are an even golden colour, lift out the basket and hold it over the pan to allow the chips to drain. Empty the basket into a nest of paper towel, which will soak up excess fat. Fold it over the chips to keep them warm.

Six Ways with Deep-fried Potatoes

Shoestrings. Peel the potatoes and cut them into pieces that will fit into the feeder of a rotary shredder. Insert a drum with large holes for cutting coarse shreds. Piece by piece, pass the potatoes through the shredder to fashion the shoestrings (above, left). Rinse the shoestrings well to wash off surface starch; then dry them thoroughly and deep-fry them in very hot fat until they are crisp and golden. Shoestring potatoes may also be shaped with a disc-type shredder or an electric food processor.

Matchsticks. Peel the potatoes and cut them lengthwise into slices about 3mm (1/8 inch) thick. Stack a few pieces together and slice them lengthwise again into thin strips (above, left). Repeat until all the potatoes are cut up. Rinse the strips and dry them thoroughly. Deep-fry them in very hot fat until they are golden.

Crisps. The wafer-thin slices necessary for crisps are most easily fashioned with a mandoline. Use the mandoline's ordinary slicing blade adjusted to the thinnest cutting width. Press one side of a peeled potato against the mandoline with the palm of your hand. Slide the potato down the frame to cut the slices, keeping your fingers spread clear of the mandoline for safety (above, left). Soak the slices in water for a few minutes to remove surface starch; soaking also helps to give a characteristic wavy appearance. Dry them thoroughly and deep-fry them until they are crisp.

Waffles. Use the corrugated blade of a mandoline to make potato waffles. Slide a peeled potato down the mandoline; the blade will cut a ridged pattern. Then rotate the potato through 90 degrees and cut again, to produce a thin slice cut with a criss-cross pattern (above, left). You have to adjust the blade so that it neither cuts the waffles too thickly nor shreds the potato. Rinse and dry the waffles well before deep-frying them.

Pineapple and Frangipane Fritters

When pieces of fruit are dipped in batter and deep-fried, the hot oil quickly seals the batter into a crisp golden parcel that encapsulates the moistness and flavour of the fruit. Before dipping it in batter, you can coat a firmer-fleshed fruit – apple or pineapple, for instance – with a flavoured paste. Here, pineapple chunks are first covered with frangipane.

While a frangipane covering suits only some fruits, almost any type of fruit – fresh or dried – is suitable for deep-frying in a batter coat. Apples, pears and peaches need to be peeled, cored or stoned as appropriate, then cut into sections or slices so that the fruit will cook through during its brief immersion in oil. Bananas may be halved lengthwise or cut into pieces. The batter should be prepared well in advance so that it loses its elasticity and adheres to the fruit more readily. To lighten the mixture further, fold in beaten egg white just before the batter is used.

FOR 4

1 pineapple
flavourless vegetable oil, for deep-frying

FOR THE FRANGIPANE:
250 ml / 8 fl oz milk
1 vanilla pod
3 tablespoons sugar
45 g / 1½ oz flour
1 egg, plus 1 extra yolk
2 dried almond macaroons
30 g / 1 oz butter
1 tablespoon pistachio nuts, chopped

FOR THE SWEET BEER BATTER:
85 g / 3 oz flour
small pinch of salt
1½ teaspoons sugar
1 egg, separated
4 tablespoons warm beer
30 g / 1 oz melted butter

1 Combining frangipane ingredients. Pour the milk into a pan; add the vanilla pod and sugar and bring to the boil. Remove from the heat and leave to cool. Sift the flour into a separate pan. Add the whole egg and extra egg yolk and stir gently with a wooden spoon until the flour is absorbed. Remove the vanilla pod from the milk; slowly add the milk to the flour mixture, stirring continuously.

Batter Lightened with Beer

1 Adding beer. Sift flour into a bowl and add salt and sugar. Add the egg yolk. Gradually pour in beer and stir the mixture to a smooth consistency. Stir in melted butter and just a little water, until the consistency of double cream. For a different flavour, replace the beer with brandy.

2 Finishing the batter. Cover the batter with a plate and leave it to stand at room temperature for about 1 hour. Just before using the batter, beat the reserved egg white in a separate bowl until it forms stiff peaks. Fold the egg white into the batter.

5 Coating the pineapple. Butter a plate using a metal spatula and spread half the frangipane over the plate in an even layer. Arrange the pineapple chunks in rows on top of the frangipane; leave enough space between the chunks for them to be separated easily later. Press the pineapple pieces down firmly to make the frangipane adhere.

2 Cooking the mixture. Place the pan over a medium heat and, stirring all the time, cook the mixture until it is very thick; it should have a stiff paste consistency. Remove the pan from the heat.

3 Finishing the frangipane. Add the almond macaroons to the cooked mixture, finely crumbling them between your fingers and thumbs. Cut the butter into cubes and stir into the mixture. Add the chopped pistachio nuts and stir the frangipane thoroughly until all the ingredients are evenly distributed. Leave the mixture in the refrigerator until cool.

4 Cutting pineapple. Using a sharp knife, cut the top and bottom off a pineapple. Slice the pineapple into rounds about 1 cm ($^1/_2$ inch) thick. Cut away the outer skin from each round. Slice the rounds in half and then quarters, and cut away the hard core from each quarter.

6 Covering with frangipane. Spread the remaining frangipane evenly over the pineapple pieces. Cover the plate and refrigerate the coated pineapple for about 2 hours. Separate the pieces with a metal spatula.

7 Frying the fritters. In a deep pan, heat 5 to 7.5 cm (2 to 3 inches) of oil until it sizzles on contact with a drop of batter. Dip each pineapple piece in batter (box, opposite page), then place it in the oil (above). After a couple of minutes, turn the pieces over with a fork. When the fritters are evenly crisp and golden, transfer them to kitchen paper to drain. Sprinkle with sugar and serve.

Making Veal or Chicken Stock

Pure veal stock, produced by simmering bones and meat in water with aromatic vegetables, has a subtle flavour and smooth body that are indispensable to some dishes. The bony and cartilaginous cuts of veal that are best for making it are relatively inexpensive and so well endowed with natural gelatine that the cold stock sets as a clear jelly.

To make stock, choose cuts from the legs, neck and ribs with plenty of meat left on; include a knuckle bone for its gelatine. If you like, you can retrieve the meat to eat after about 1¹/₂ hours of cooking. For chicken stock replace the meats with a boiling fowl or 2 g (4 lb) of chicken carcasses, trimmings and giblets and cook for half the time.

Start the meat and bones in cold water, and allow plenty of time for the liquid to come to the boil – it may take up to an hour. A quantity of foamy scum will appear on the surface as albuminous proteins in the meat are drawn out.

MAKES 2-3 LITRES / 3-5 PINTS

- 1 veal knuckle bone, sawn into 5 cm / 2 in pieces
- 2 kg / 4 lb meat trimmings (neck, shank or rib tips)
- 4 carrots
- 2 large onion
- 2-3 cloves
- 1 head of garlic, whole and unpeeled
- 1 large bouquet garni (ideally consisting of celery, leek, bay, thyme and parsley)
- salt

1 Removing scum. After putting bones and meat into the pot, add cold water to cover by about 4 cm (1¹/₂ inches). Bring slowly to the boil. With a large spoon or ladle, carefully remove the thick grey scum that rises to the surface.

2 Retarding the boil. If the liquid reached a rolling boil, its turbulence would prevent scum from forming on the surface. When it starts to boil, add a dash of cold water to bring it to just below boiling point, and thus allow more scum to collect.

3 Completing the scumming. Remove the lighter scum that forms on the liquid's surface, adding more cold water when the liquid returns to the boil. Repeat once or twice until only a white froth appears on the surface.

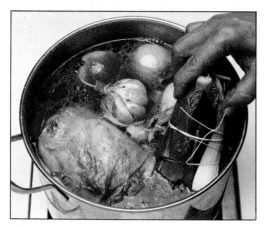

4 Adding aromatics. Aromatic vegetables are essential to a well-flavoured stock. Here carrots, onions – one stuck with 3 cloves – and a whole unpeeled head of garlic are used, with a bouquet garni.

5 Salting. Season the stock with salt. Since the liquid will reduce in quantity while it simmers, relatively little salt is necessary – about a tablespoon of course sea-salt will season 5 litres (8 pints) of water.

6 Bringing to the boil. After adding the vegetables, and thus lowering the temperature inside the pot, allow the liquid to return slowly to the boil. Skim off any new traces of scum that may appear on the surface. Reduce the heat so that the liquid barely simmers.

7 Adjusting the temperature. Place the lid on the pot, slightly ajar so that steam does not build up inside and raise the temperature to bring just to the boil. For the next 15 to 30 minutes, continue to check the stock and adjust the temperature so that the surface is rippled only by a continuous gentle murmur of bubbles. Cook at this bare simmer for about 4 hours (only 2 hours for chicken stock), skimming off any surface fat from time to time.

8 Straining. Spoon off any fat from the surface. Strain the stock through a colander set in a large bowl. When the meat and vegetables are drained, strain the stock again through a sieve lined with a double layer of dampened cheesecloth or muslin.

9 Degreasing. Refrigerate the stock for 8 to 12 hours, then the fat can be scraped off the firmly gelled stock (upper picture). Dab away the last particles of fat with a cloth or paper towel wrung out in hot water (lower picture).

10 Storing the stock. Spoon convenient quantities (about 6 tablespoons) of the cold gelled stock into small plastic bags (right) for freezing, or store the stock in an uncovered bowl in the refrigerator. To keep the refrigerated stock from spoiling, bring it to the boil every few days, cool it and return it to the refrigerator.

Court-bouillon and Fumet for Fish

Seafood can, of course, be poached or steamed in plain water. But the inherent taste of any fish or shellfish can also be enhanced easily by cooking it in a flavoured liquid. A court-bouillon usually combines water with wine or vinegar, but may be based on milk. A fumet, or fish stock, is made with water, wine, fish or fish trimmings, aromatic vegetables and herbs.

Thyme, bay, parsley, onion, carrot and garlic are usually present in a wine and vegetable court-bouillon (below, left). Leek, celery, fennel stalks or dill, are optional additions.

To draw out the flavours of the vegetables and herbs, simmer them in water for 30 to 40 minutes. Wine inhibits the release of the vegetables' flavours, so it should be added about halfway through the simmering time. If you include peppercorns, add them for the last few minutes, since they will impart a bitter taste to the liquid if cooked too long.

A vinegar court-bouillon (below, centre) substitutes wine vinegar for wine, but in a smaller proportion to the water. Its piquancy suits such freshwater fish as carp, trout and pike. Keep in mind that when a freshly caught fish is plunged into a simmering vinegar court-bouillon, the acid will turn its skin a delicate shade of blue. A fish which is treated in this way is said to be cooked au bleu.

A milk and lemon court-bouillon (below, right) helps keep fish steaks and fillets white. Turbot, brill, cod and smoked haddock are often poached in this mild liquid and emerge with their flavour heightened by the lemon's acidity.

A fumet is usually prepared with water and wine, but generally contains less water than a court-bouillon. Indeed, a fumet can simply be a court-bouillon that has already been used for poaching fish.

After the poaching, a fumet can be transformed into a sauce or reserved for a stew or braise. And if it is clarified and strengthened with gelatine, it becomes an aspic jelly that can be used to coat cold poached fish or other dishes.

To store a fumet for future use, simply place an intact plastic freezing bag in a small loaf tin or other suitably sized container, pour in the cooled fumet, tie up the bag, label it and freeze. It can be stored for up to three months.

A Trio of Court-Bouillons

A wine and vegetable court-bouillon. Slice an onion, a carrot and a leek, and dice a celery stalk. Add the vegetables, together with parsley, thyme, dill, a bay leaf and salt to about 1 litre (1³/4 pints) salted water. Simmer for about 15 minutes, then pour in 300 ml (¹/2 pint) of white wine. Simmer for a further 15 minutes, adding a few peppercorns for the last 10 minutes.

A vinegar court-bouillon. To the same water and vegetable mixture used for the wine court-bouillon, add white or red wine vinegar to taste; as a rough guide, allow 5 tablespoons wine vinegar to 600 ml (1 pint) water. Simmer the court-bouillon for about 30 minutes.

A milk and lemon court-bouillon. Peel the skin and bitter pith from a lemon. Slice the lemon finely and remove the seeds. Add as many lemon slices as you like to a mixture of one part milk to four parts salted water. The court-bouillon requires no preliminary cooking before the fish is placed in it.

Fumet: an Essence Made with Trimmings

1 Assembling the ingredients. Prepare a selection of vegetables and herbs as for a court-bouillon (opposite page). Rinse some fish trimmings – here, the heads and the bones of sole and whiting – and tear out and discard the gills. Break into convenient sizes. Place all the ingredients in a pan, cover with cold water, and salt lightly.

2 Skimming the liquid. Bring the liquid to the boil. With a spoon, remove the scum that forms on its surface as its reaches a simmer (above). Simmer for 15 minutes, then add white wine in the proportion of up to one part of white wine to one part of water, according to taste. Simmer for a further 15 minutes.

3 Straining the fumet. Strain the fumet through a colander set over a deep bowl. The strained liquid is now ready for use as a poaching medium.

4 Removing small particles. If you want to make aspic from the fumet, strain the liquid a second time, through a damp muslin cloth draped inside a fine sieve (left). Leave the strained fumet in a refrigerator for several hours to allow the fine solids it contains to form a sediment (above). Decant the liquid for making aspic.

Basic White Sauce

One of the most useful thickening agents in the whole of sauce-making is a roux – butter and flour blended to a smooth paste over gentle heat. The white sauce shown here is perhaps the most fundamental roux-based sauce, consisting simply of the paste itself, milk and a little cream.

The blandness of a plain white sauce makes it an ideal base. Here, for example, it provides the foundation for a more elaborate cheese sauce for vegetables.

To make the roux, the butter is first melted so that the flour will combine with it smoothly and evenly. The resulting paste is cooked for only a minute or two – until it begins to bubble – before milk is whisked in. Longer cooking at this stage would not only lessen the flour's thickening power but discolour the roux and hence the finished sauce. After the milk is added, the mixture should be whisked until it comes to the boil to prevent flour lumps from forming, and then simmered gently for at least 20 minutes. This long cooking improves both the texture and the flavour of the sauce: the liquid reduces and thickens and any taste of raw flour is eliminated. After sieving, the sauce is seasoned and thinned with cream.

Special flavourings and colourings for a white sauce are usually added at this stage. You can stir in grated cheese, finely chopped herbs or capers, or a spoonful of prepared mustard, or you can whisk in a few pieces of a flavoured butter. Alternatively, the milk used for the sauce can be first infused with aromatics such as carrot, onion and a bouquet garni.

MAKES ABOUT 300 ML / ½ PINT

30 g / 1 oz butter
30 g / 1 oz flour
600 ml / 1 pint milk
about 300 ml / ½ pint double cream
little freshly grated nutmeg (optional)
salt and white pepper

1 Adding milk. Over low heat melt the butter in a heavy pan and add the flour. With a whisk, stir the flour rapidly into the butter. Cook the resulting paste for a minute or so, then slowly pour in the cold milk, whisking all the time (above).

2 Cooking the sauce. Increase the heat and, to prevent the formation of lumps whisk the sauce until it boils. Season with a little salt. Reduce the heat to very low and simmer the sauce gently for at least 20 minutes. To keep the sauce from sticking to the pan, stir it from time to time with a wooden spoon or a whisk, scraping the pan's bottom and sides.

Vegetable Gratin Mornay

1 Adding grated cheese. Finely grate hard cheese – in this case, 30 g / 1 oz each of Gruyère and Parmesan. Make the basic white sauce (Steps 1 to 4, above), using extra cream (about 200 ml / 7 fl oz in total) to give it a thin consistency. Off the heat, stir in the cheese until it is melted.

2 Pouring on the sauce. Arrange prepared vegetables – here, boiled cardoons – in a gratin dish. Ladle the sauce mornay evenly over the vegetables, then sprinkle more grated cheese on top.

3 Sieving the sauce. To remove any lumps that may have formed during cooking, place a sieve over another pan, and strain the sauce through. Then return the strained sauce to the heat.

4 Finishing with cream. To enrich the sauce and thin it to the right consistency, whisk in double cream. Add white pepper to taste, and, if you like, a little freshly grated nutmeg. Serve at once over vegetables, or finish the sauce with additional flavouring.

3 Serving the gratin. Put the gratin dish in an oven preheated to 190°C/375°F/gas 5. After 15 to 20 minutes, when the sauce is slightly reduced and thickened and the surface of the gratin is pale golden, remove from the oven. Serve the gratin straight from the dish.

A spoonful or two of prepared mustard stirred into Basic White Sauce produces an excellent dressing for grilled or fried steak.

Basic Brown Sauce

The richly flavoured variation on basic stock that is known as brown sauce or demi-glace provides a foundation for many other sauces to serve with meat and game.

Browning the meats and vegetables for the sauce in oil intensifies their flavour and deepens the colour of the finished product. Flour is then added to the pan, mingling with the fat to form a roux. Further cooking in a hot oven causes the flour to darken: the resulting brown roux also colours the sauce as well as thickening it. During this preliminary cooking of the ingredients, juices are drawn out from the meats and caramelize in the bottom of the pan and these are then dissolved in wine.

Once these steps are complete, the brown sauce can be made with plain water. But to achieve a much greater depth of flavour, veal stock (page 242) can be used, as here. A game brown sauce can be prepared in the same way, using game carcasses with game or veal stock.

Strips of ham, stewed mushrooms or tiny onions, or tomato purée are just a few of the many garnishes and flavourings that combine well with a brown sauce.

MAKES ABOUT 600 ML / I PINT

I sheet of pork rind, about 20 x 15 cm (8 x 6 in)
500 g / I lb shin of beef
I kg / 2 lb lean veal
I veal knuckle, broken up
500 g / I lb chicken wing tips
2 carrot, coarsely chopped
2 onions, coarsely chopped
2 leeks, coarsely chopped
I celery stalk, coarsely chopped
4-5 garlic cloves, crushed
2 sprigs of thyme
2 bay leaves
about 4 tablespoons olive oil
4 tablespoons flour
about 750 ml / I ¼ pints dry white wine
about 2 litres / 3 ½ pints veal stock (page 242)

1 Coating with oil. Parboil the pork rind for 2 to 3 minutes, rinse it and chop it coarsely. Cut the shin of beef and veal into chunks; put them in a roasting pan with pieces of veal knuckle, chicken wings and the rind. Add the carrot, onion, leek and celery, crushed garlic, thyme and bay leaves. Sprinkle with oil and toss with your hands.

2 Adding flour. Put the pan in an oven preheated to 230°C/450°F/gas 8. After about 15 minutes, remove the pan and turn the ingredients with a spatula so that they will brown evenly. Return the pan to the oven for a further 15 minutes, or until all the ingredients are well browned. Sprinkle on the flour and stir it well into the mixture with the spatula.

5 Removing the meat and bones. Take the pan off the heat. Set a sieve over a large bowl and put a few ladlefuls of the cooked meat into the sieve (above, left). Pick out any bones and discard them. To extract the meat juices, press the meat with a wooden pestle (above, right). Discard the pressed meat and extract the juices from the rest of the meat in the same way. Strain the cooking liquid from the pan into the bowl; remove the sieve and let the liquid cool slightly, then skim off any fat on the surface of the liquid.

3 Deglazing. Return the pan to the oven for about 10 minutes, until the flour has browned. Then set the pan on a medium heat. Add enough wine to moisten all the ingredients and dissolve the meat juices that have caramelized

(above, left). Using the spatula, scrape free the deposits on the bottom of the pan (above, right). Increase the heat, bring the liquid to the boil and cook rapidly for about 10 minutes, or until almost all the liquid has evaporated.

4 Adding stock. Transfer the contents of the roasting pan to a large saucepan. Add enough stock to cover all the ingredients generously. Bring the liquid to the boil; reduce the heat and set a lid slightly ajar on the pan. Simmer very gently for at least 3 hours, preferably for 5 to 6 hours.

6 Straining the sauce. Strain the liquid, a ladleful at a time, through a chinois – a conical sieve with a very fine mesh – held over a pan. Move a small ladle up and down, very gently, in the liquid to help it pass through the mesh, but take care not to press any solids through the mesh. Discard the solids.

7 Cleansing the sauce. Place the pan over a medium heat. Bring to the boil, set the pan half off the heat and leave the sauce to reduce. Repeatedly pull to one side and discard the skin of impurities that collects on the cooler side of the

pan. When the sauce has reduced to the desired consistency, taste and add salt if necessary, then remove from the heat. Use at once or store as veal stock.

Some Classic Sauces

Good food often needs no more than its own juices or a simple glistening coat of butter or good olive oil or a squeeze of lemon juice to dress it for the table. However, to add variety to your menus you will also want to experiment with some of the basic – and surprisingly easy – sauces on the following pages.

From olive oil and lemon juice is a but a short step to vinaigrette. Best known as a salad dressing, its blend of fruitiness and acidity is also welcomed by hot vegetables and some white fish dishes. Vinaigrette is an emulsion: rapid stirring disperses the oil evenly throughout the vinegar, but it separates in minutes – so the sauce must always be stirred again just before serving.

Hollandaise sauce is also an emulsion – of butter in egg yolk – but it is stable and will not separate unless it is overheated. It can serve as a base for a whole family of sauces with other flavourings.

The closely related sabayon is a perfect partner for all hot poached white fish dishes. Egg yolks are whisked into an equal volume of reduced fumet in a pan set in a water bath and the mixture becomes frothy and slightly thickened. Butter is incorporated in batches and the sauce whisked to a light custard.

Beurre blanc, a shallot-flavoured combination of butter, wine and vinegar, is a sauce that many cooks think requires special skill. The trick is simply to keep the heat very low and whisk continuously.

Sauce bâtarde is also thickened with egg yolks and served warm but its preparation is less finicky and very quick as it is based on a simple roux. Both sauce bâtarde and hollandaise can be transformed into the airy sauce mousseline by the addition of lightly whipped cream.

Aïoli is simply a mayonnaise that incorporates pounded garlic. For a successful mayonnaise, the oil and egg yolks must be at room temperature. Pesto and salsa verde are uncooked sauces combining aromatic herbs with pungent flavourings like garlic and anchovies.

Sabayon: for Fish Terrines and Poached White Fish

1 For about 300 ml (¹/2 pint): boil that volume of fumet (page 245) until reduced to a few tablespoons. Put pan in a water bath.

2 Whisk in 2 or 3 egg yolks. When it starts to thicken, add 175 g (6 oz) diced butter, a handful at a time, whisking between each addition.

3 Continue adding up to 75 g (3 oz) more butter dice, whisking constantly, until the sauce coats the sides of the pan.

4 Take the pan off the heat. Continue whisking for about 30 seconds as it cools. Pour the sauce into a warmed sauce-boat to serve.

Beurre Blanc: for Hot Poached Fish

1 For 300 ml (¹/2 pint): boil 100 ml (3¹/2 fl oz) each dry white wine and white wine vinegar with 3 very finely chopped shallots.

2 Take off heat. Season, then put on a fireproof mat over a very low heat. Whisk in 250-400 g (8-14 oz) diced butter until creamy.

Vinaigrette: a Dressing for Salads or Hot Vegetables

1 Mixing seasonings and vinegar. Put salt and pepper in a bowl and pour in vinegar – here, red wine vinegar. Stir until salt has dissolved.

2 Pouring in olive oil. Add about four or five times as much oil as vinegar; exact proportions will depend on your taste.

3 Blending the vinaigrette. Stir just long enough to mix the oil and vinegar; excess beating would disperse volatile flavouring elements.

Sauce Bâtarde: a Butter Sauce for Vegetables, Veal and Boiled Fish

1 Beating egg yolks with water. For about 600 ml (1 pint): drop 2 egg yolks into a bowl, add a tablespoonful of cold water and beat the mixture until it is smooth. Set it aside.

2 Making the roux. Melt 50 g (2 oz) butter in a heavy pan and add the same volume of flour (about 3 tablespoons). Stir the mixture over a low heat until it begins to bubble.

3 Pour in water. Remove the pan from the heat and add 600 ml (1 pint) lightly salted hot water, whisking constantly. Continue whisking over heat until the mixture boils.

4 Adding the egg. Remove the sauce from the heat to cool for a moment, then whisk in the beaten egg mixture. Continue to whisk over a low heat.

5 Adding lemon juice and butter. When the sauce thickens (without boiling), take it off the heat and add lemon juice to taste. Start whisking in 170 g (6 oz) butter cut into chunks.

6 Finishing the sauce. Off the heat, gradually whisk in the rest of the butter. Adjust the seasoning and serve the sauce immediately.

Hollandaise: A Butter and Egg Emulsion for Poached Fish and Vegetables

1 Preparing a bain-marie. Half fill a large pan with water and place a trivet inside it. Heat until it simmers, then reduce to just a bare simmer.

2 For about 300 ml (1/2 pint): place 3 egg yolks in a pan. Add a tablespoonful of cold water. Set pan on trivet and beat yolks smooth.

3 Whisk in 250 g (8 oz) butter cut into chunks, in 3 or 4 batches. Allow the egg yolks to absorb each before adding more.

4 Beating to thicken the sauce. When all the butter has been added, continue whisking until the sauce becomes thick and creamy. Keep the heat very low.

5 Adding lemon juice. Season with white pepper, cayenne pepper and salt. Then add lemon juice to taste; squeeze the lemon through a strainer.

6 Adjusting consistency. For a thicker sauce, whisk it over low heat until it reaches the desired consistency. To thin the sauce, whisk in a little warm water.

Sauce Mousseline: Lightened with Whipped Cream for Asparagus and Sole

1 Whip double cream to soft peaks. Take a basic hollandaise or bâtarde off the heat and spoon over it 1 part whipped cream to 3 of sauce.

2 Still off the heat, fold the cream quickly but gently into the sauce with a wooden spatula until the mixture is completely smooth.

3 The finished sauce mousseline is lighter in texture than the basic hollandaise or sauce bâtarde. Serve it immediately.

Aïoli

1 Mixing egg yolks and garlic. For about 600 ml (1 pint): in a mortar, pound to a purée 3-4 peeled garlic cloves and a little salt. Stir in 2 egg yolks to combine.

2 Incorporating oil. Add about 500 ml (16 fl oz) olive oil, to begin with drop by drop at the side, stirring briskly all the while. When sauce starts to thicken, add oil in thin steady stream.

3 Finishing. When sauce is quite stiff, add the juice of ½ lemon and spoonful of warm water. Use with fish soups and stews, salt cod, snails, grilled prawns, roast chicken and cold roast lamb.

Pesto

Pesto – a word that simply means 'pounded' – is an uncooked mixture of basil, garlic, pine nuts and salt, pounded with olive oil to make a smooth paste. Grated Parmesan or Pecorino cheese gives it body and extra flavour. A little of the pasta's cooking liquid moistens the sauce, making it easier to mix with pasta.

1 For 250 ml (8 fl oz): In a mortar, grind 3 garlic cloves, 2 tablespoons pine nuts and a little coarse salt to a pulp. Pound in 60 g (2 oz) basil leaves and. Add 100 g (3½ oz) grated cheese and a trickle of olive oil.

2 Completing the sauce. Add more olive oil in a slow trickle; stir the sauce with the pestle, until the sauce is smooth and creamy. Before using the pesto sauce, add a little of the pasta's cooking liquid.

Salsa Verde

1 For about 350 ml (12 fl oz): Soak, fillet, rinse and dry 2 salted anchovies. In a mortar, pound the anchovies with 2-3 peeled garlic cloves and a little coarse salt until the mixture forms a smooth paste.

2 Stir in juice of 1 lemon and 150 ml (¼ pint) olive oil. Add 125 g (4 oz) mixed finely chopped herbs – parsley, chives, tarragon, basil, chervil – 1 tablespoon chopped capers and 100 g (3½ oz) chopped drained parboiled spinach.

3 Serving the sauce. Serve the sauce with a dish of mixed poached meats – here, boned shin of beef, pickled ox tongue, chicken and pork sausage.

A Trio of Dessert Sauces

Sauces based on sugar syrups and on melted chocolate are mainstays for enhancing desserts. At its simplest, a syrup sauce is nothing more than sugar and water boiled together. The proportions of water and sugar, and the temperature to which the syrup is boiled, determine the sauce's consistency. The sauce on the right contains butter and cream, and is known as butterscotch; because the addition of extra flavourings can cause a syrup to turn grainy, the mixture includes some liquid glucose, which inhibits crystallization.

If a syrup is cooked until all the water evaporates, the molten sugar that remains turns rapidly into caramel – a useful foundation that can be diluted with water to make a pouring sauce (below).

To give chocolate a pouring consistency, it is melted with a little water or cream over low heat – overheating would scorch it, impairing its flavour and texture.

Butterscotch Sauce: a Deep Golden Coating

1 Dissolving sugar. To warm a sugar thermometer, put it in a jug of very hot water. For about 250 ml (8 fl oz): Put 230 g (7 oz) soft brown sugar, 150 ml (¼ pint) water and 75 g (2½ oz) butter in a heavy pan. Add 2 tablespoons liquid glucose. Set the pan over a medium heat and stir until the sugar has dissolved. Do not let the mixture boil until the sugar has completely dissolved.

2 Boiling the syrup. When all the sugar has dissolved, stop stirring. Put the warmed sugar thermometer in the pan, bring the syrup to the boil and continue to boil until it reaches 116°C (240°F) – the soft-ball stage. Take the pan off the heat and dip it in cold water to arrest cooking.

Caramel: an Amber Pool of Molten Sugar

1 Diluting caramel. For about 500 ml (16 fl oz): Put 150 ml (¼ pint) of water in a heavy pan and add 500 g (1 lb) of sugar. Stir gently over a medium heat until the sugar has dissolved. Bring the syrup to the boil and boil it, without stirring, until it turns reddish-amber. Dip the pan in cold water. Let the caramel cool a little; pour in cold water.

2 Dissolving the caramel. Return the pan to the heat and stir the water and caramel together until the caramel is smoothly dissolved. Once diluted, the caramel will not harden even when quite cold.

3 Serving caramel sauce. Refrigerated in a stoppered bottle, the sauce will keep for weeks. Serve caramel sauce hot or cold, with a hot or cold dessert. Here, it is served hot with bread pudding.

3 Testing the syrup. Place a teaspoonful of syrup in a bowl of iced water. Mould the cooled syrup into a ball in the water, then lift it out. Squeeze the ball gently between your finger and thumb. If it holds its shape under the water but flattens when taken out, the syrup has reached the correct stage.

4 Stirring in cream. If the syrup is too liquid, return it to the heat and test it again when the temperature has risen by a few degrees. Once the syrup has reached the soft-ball stage, let it cool slightly. Pour in up to 100 ml (3 1/2 fl oz) double cream, stirring well until well blended and the sauce has a good pouring consistency.

5 Serving the sauce. Serve the sauce hot or cold; in this case, it is served hot with ice cream. The butterscotch sauce can be kept, covered, in the refrigerator for up to two weeks.

Chocolate Sauce: a Dark Delight

1 Melting chocolate. For about 300 ml (1/2 pint): Break 250 g (8 oz) plain dark eating chocolate into pieces and put them in a bowl with a little cold water. Place the bowl in a pan of hot water over a medium heat. Stir the chocolate until all the pieces have melted smoothly.

2 Incorporating butter. Cut 60 g (2 oz) cold butter into cubes. Remove the pan from the heat and stir a few cubes into the chocolate. When the butter is blended in, add more. Continue until all the butter is stirred in and the mixture is smooth.

3 Serving the chocolate sauce. Serve the chocolate sauce immediately, while it is still hot: it sets as it cools. Here, the sauce is poured over a cold dessert – choux pastries filled with ice-cream.

Creams and Custards

Custards and creams are all based on a smooth amalgam of egg yolks, sugar, and milk, thickened over gentle heat.

Pouring custard, or *crème anglaise* is a traditional accompaniment for fruit pies and puddings. It is made by adding milk that has been scalded – heated until small bubbles form on the surface – to blended egg yolks and sugar, then heating the egg and milk mixture slowly until it has the consistency you want. Scalding the milk first reduces the custard's cooking time; since a mixture containing egg yolks must be cooked very gently to prevent the yolks curdling, a custard begun with cold milk would need to be heated for much longer before it thickened.

By increasing the proportions of egg yolks and sugar to milk, and freezing the result, you can make ice-cream.

Bavarian cream (right, below), a custard firmed with gelatine, enriched with whipped cream and set in a mould, may be served with fruit sauces and fresh or poached fruit. Since gelatine sets rapidly once it starts to cool, a smooth cream depends on careful timing.

First, a custard is made and kept warm while the cream is whipped. Next, gelatine is dissolved and stirred into the warm custard. Once the gelatine is incorporated, the custard is stirred over ice and water until it starts to gel. The cream is added when the custard reaches a similar consistency; finally, the mixture is poured into a mould and chilled until set.

Like Bavarian cream, pastry cream (opposite page, below) is essentially a thickened custard, but in this demonstration, the thickening agent is flour. You can enrich pastry cream by folding in stiffly beaten egg whites or whipped cream after cooking. Used plain, or flavoured with chopped fruit, candied peel, nuts or a liqueur, this is a luxurious filling for layered desserts and pastries.

Custard: A Sauce from Egg Yolks and Milk

1 Whisking yolks and sugar. For about 600 ml (1 pint): Separate 6 eggs and reserve the whites for another use. In a mixing bowl, whisk the yolks with 125 g (4 oz) sugar. After about 10 minutes, the mixture will be creamy and almost white. Continue until a little of the mixture, dribbled from the whisk, forms a trail across the surface.

2 Adding milk. Over medium heat, scald 500 ml (16 fl oz) milk in a pan, with a vanilla pod if you like. Remove the pod and slowly pour the hot milk into the yolk and sugar mixture, whisking constantly but gently.

Bavarian Cream: Gelatine and Whipped Cream

1 To serve 4-6: Make a custard (Steps 1 to 4, above), strain it into another pan, and place in a hot water bath. Whip 450 ml (3/4 pint) double cream to soft peaks. Sprinkle 15 g (1/2 oz) gelatine powder on to a little hot water; when the gelatine has absorbed the liquid, remove the pan from water bath and stir the gelatine into it.

2 Stir until the gelatine dissolves, then pour the mixture into a bowl set over a bowl of ice and water. Stir frequently. When the mixture has the consistency of lightly whipped cream, remove it from the bowl of ice and water and add the cream. Blend well, pour into an oiled mould and chill until set.

3 Getting the right consistency. Transfer the mixture to a heavy pan and set it over a low heat. Stir the custard continuously with a figure-of-eight motion, to distribute the heat evenly throughout the mixture, and bring the custard to just below simmering point. Do not allow the custard to reach a boil.

4 Cooling the custard. When the custard coats the spoon evenly, stop stirring and remove the pan from the heat. Place the pan immediately in a bowl of ice (above), to prevent the custard from thickening any further; continue to stir the custard for a further 5 minutes or so.

5 Straining the custard. To remove any lumps that may have formed, strain the custard through a sieve into a bowl. Serve immediately; or keep the custard warm by placing the bowl in a hot water bath. If you wish to serve the custard cold, stir it over ice until it is sufficiently chilled, or stir it until cool, cover it with plastic film and refrigerate.

Classic Pastry Cream

1 Mixing ingredients. For about 750 ml (1¼ pints): In a large bowl, use a spoon to mix together 125 g (4 oz) sugar and 5 egg yolks, beating until the mixture is thick and cream-coloured. Gradually sift in 45g / 1½ oz flour to which a tiny pinch of salt has been added, stirring to blend it well.

2 Adding milk. Scald 500 ml (16 fl oz) milk with a vanilla pod in it. Remove the pod and, stirring constantly, pour the milk into the flour mixture in a thin stream. Transfer mixture to a heavy saucepan. Over medium heat, bring it to a

boil, stirring vigorously (left). Turn down the heat and stir for 2 minutes until the mixture is thick (right). Strain the pastry cream and allow it to cool, stirring occasionally to prevent a skin from forming on the surface.

Chilled Consommé

Attractively garnished, a basic meat or chicken broth is an excellent soup in its own right. The soup can be endowed with a greater subtlety and complexity of flavour, however, by enriching the broth a second time with fresh meat and vegetables. The result is what the French call a consommé, or consummate broth.

If the consommé is to be served cold and jellied, one of the enriching ingredients must be high in natural gelatine. In the demonstration here, a consommé à la Madrilène based on chicken broth receives its secondary infusion from lean beef, chicken parts, aromatic vegetables and tomatoes, which add a rosy colour as well as flavour. The chicken parts, particularly the chopped wings and feet (blistered over a flame and skinned), provide enough gelatine to set the broth – when chilled – to a light jelly that turns to liquid in the warmth of the mouth.

The mark of a successful consommé, whether jellied or not, is perfect clarity. Prepare a chicken stock by the slow-cooking method demonstrated on page 00, making sure that you skim and strain it meticulously. Chill it, then remove every speck of fat that solidifies on the surface.

Combine the cold broth with the enriching ingredients and simmer them gently for about 1 hour. During the cooking, very small particles of food, particularly from the tomato pulp in this case, are released into the soup. Some of these are too fine to be strained out, but they can be trapped by a protein molecule

1 Enriching the broth. Put the beef, chicken and vegetables into a heavy pan. Add the egg whites (left) and stir them well into the solids. Ladle in the cold chicken broth (right) and stir to combine it with the other ingredients. Heat the cold broth very slowly and gently so that the albumin does not solidify too soon.

called albumin, some of which is contributed by the beef. Extra albumin is supplied by egg whites.

While the soup is heating, the albumin will coagulate and gather up the particles. But the cooking must by very gentle or the albumin will solidify before it has done its job. The cooked albumin, along with the trapped particles, is filtered out when the consommé is strained.

To display the clarity and jewel-like colour of a hot consommé, serve it from a warmed white tureen. A jellied consommé merits a more elaborate presentation: put it in a clear glass bowl nestled in a larger vessel and surrounded with crushed ice.

FOR 8-10

750 g / 1½ lb lean chuck beef, trimmed of all fat and finely chopped

1 kg /2lb chicken wings, skinned feet, necks, coarsely chopped

2 carrots, trimmed and finely chopped

2 leeks, trimmed and finely chopped

500 g / 1 lb tomatoes, coarsely chopped.

whites of 2 eggs

3 litres (5½ pints) cold chicken broth (page 242)

1 red sweet pepper, grilled and skinned (page 210), then diced, to garnish

2 Simmering the broth. Stir occasionally as the liquid slowly comes to the boil. Skimming is not necessary, since the impurities will be removed later. Partially cover, adjust the heat and let the soup barely simmer for an hour to extract all the flavour from the solid ingredients.

3 Straining out the solids. Line a fine sieve with several layers of muslin wrung out in cold water. Pour the cooked broth into the lined sieve and let it drain through into a bowl. To keep the broth absolutely clear, do not press the solids to extract extra drops of liquid. Adjust the seasoning if necessary.

4 Serving the consommé. Chill the consommé until it sets to a light jelly. To serve, put the bowl of consommé inside a larger bowl containing crushed ice. Ladle the soup into chilled consommé cups (left). Garnish (below) with diced red sweet pepper that has been grilled and skinned.

Two Classic Onion Soups

Onions, which carry an important supporting role in many dishes, can be used in quantity to make soups that are fragrant and warming. Properly cooked, an onion soup has none of the harshness many associate with the raw vegetable.

The sturdy soup shown on the opposite page, above, may well be the ancestor of all onion soups. Its basic ingredients are slices of coarse dry bread, sliced onions cooked to a golden-brown and shredded cheese. The bread slices are coated with cooked onions and cheese, layered in a broad casserole and moistened with water. The casserole is first simmered on top of the stove, then baked in the oven until a richly coloured crust forms on the surface.

The same ingredients used in different proportions appear in the onion soup so often featured on the menus of French bistros – in France and around the world. For this soup (opposite, below), the cooked and browned onions are simmered briefly in the soup liquid – beef broth, as here, or plain water. Then the broth is divided among individual casseroles and each portion is crowned with a single bread slice and a handful of cheese. Before serving, the cheese is passed under a grill until it has melted and is bubbling. Strictly speaking, the bread and cheese are merely a garnish, but they are such an invariable accompaniment that the dish would be unrecognisable without them.

The onions used in either soup should be tender and sweet; large white summer onions, violet Bermudas or large Spanish onions are suitable. They are cooked for about 1 hour, in two stages – a long, slow simmer followed by a thorough browning over a slightly higher heat (box, below) – and any traces of rawness are eliminated. Cooked this way, raw sliced onions will reduce to about one-third of their original volume by the time they are ready to be added to the liquid.

Freshly grated Gruyère and the sharper Parmesan – used singly or together – are the traditional cheeses for onion soup. If you substitute a Cheddar, Romano or other sharp cheese, pick one that is mature and relatively dry so that it shreds or grates easily. Any rough-textured bread is appropriate for the layered onion soup. Dried-out slices of baguette – the long, narrow French loaf – are the traditional choice for onion soup bistro-style.

The Gentle Process of Caramelizing Onions

Colouring without burning. For enough onions to make soup for 4-6: In a sauté pan, melt 50 g (2 oz) butter over a very low heat. Fill the pan with 250 g (8 oz) thinly sliced onions. Add a pinch of salt, then cover (above, left) and cook, stirring occasionally, until the onions are very soft but not coloured – about 40 minutes. Uncover the pan, raise the heat slightly and stir regularly (above, centre), until the onions turn a rich caramel (above, right) – about 30 minutes; if they are browning too quickly, reduce the heat.

An Onion Soup Gratinéed

1 Spread 16 thin dry bread slices with caramelized onions. (For even more flavour add 2 or 3 finely chopped garlic cloves to the onions as they cook.) Put a layer in a casserole and sprinkle with 40 g (1 1/2 oz) grated cheese. Repeat until two-thirds full. Insert a funnel down the side and pour in boiling water (inset) until the bread floats a little.

2 Cooking the soup. Simmer the soup, uncovered, for 30 minutes. Meanwhile, preheat the oven to 170°C/325°F/gas 3. Top up the soup, if necessary, with boiling water, then sprinkle on more cheese and a few thin shavings of butter. Bake, uncovered, for about 1 hour and serve in shallow soup plates.

Onion Soup Bistro-Style

1 Preparing the onion broth. Pour 1.5 litres (3 pints) boiling liquid – here, beef broth – into a pan containing the caramelized onions. Bring the mixture to the boil, then lower the heat to maintain a simmer.

2 Ladling into bowls. Simmer the broth for 10 minutes to allow the onions' flavour to permeate the liquid. Skim off any butter that rises to the surface. Ladle the broth and the onions into individual, heatproof bowls.

3 Finishing the soup. Top each bowl with a slice of dry French bread, season with pepper and cover with shredded cheese. Put the bowls under a hot grill until the cheese begins to bubble, then serve immediately.

A Borscht on a Grand Scale

Soups made with beetroot are standbys in the kitchens of Russia, Poland and the Ukraine. These soups, known in the West by their Russian name borscht vary from simple purées of beetroot with soured cream to the lavish Ukrainian speciality demonstrated here. This bountiful offering, which includes several different kinds of meat and shredded cabbage, is served with a medley of traditional garnishes.

The first step in making borscht as the Ukrainians do, takes place several days in advance of actual cooking, when a fermentation of beetroot is begun (box, below, right). The liquor produced by this fermentation is necessary to give the soup its characteristic sour tang and deep ruby colour. Passably tangy borscht can also be made by using beetroots macerated in vinegar in place of fresh beetroots, and adding a little of the vinegar to the broth.

The cooking gets under way at least four hours before the soup is to be served. A selection of fresh and salted meats is set simmering to make a broth, and beetroots – left whole and unpeeled to preserve all their juices – are put in the oven to bake. After baking, the beetroots are cut up and simmered, along with shredded cabbage, in broth that has been mixed with beetroot ferment. The meats themselves are served separately.

The lengthy cooking process leaves adequate time to prepare a selection of the traditional borscht accompaniments. Pirozhki, little crescent-shaped pasties made with a sour-cream dough, are served alongside the soup. Roasted buckwheat, or kasha, is baked with water and butter and spooned into the individual soup plates before the broth.

Since a lot of time and effort go into making the soup, it is sensible to make a large quantity. Any leftover borscht will keep well in the refrigerator for up to a week, and can be served again; either reheated or chilled.

FOR 8-10

1.5 kg / 3 lb mixture of beef shin and chuck, smoked bacon hock and salted bacon in a slab
2 whole onions, peeled
2 bay leaves
6 beetroots
1 white cabbage
salt and pepper
soured cream and chopped dill or parsley, to garnish
pirozhki and kasha to serve (optional)

1 Cooking the meats. Put meats, onions and bay leaves in a large pan with some salt. Cover with cold water and bring to the boil, removing the scum. Simmer, partially covered, until meats are tender – about 3 hours. Transfer meats to a casserole, cover, and keep warm. Reserve broth.

Making a Beet Liquor

Peel 5 or 6 raw beetroots and grate into a pot. Add 2 litres (4 pints) of warm water and, to encourage fermentation, stale rye bread and a teaspoon of sugar. Cover and leave in a cool room for 3 to 4 days, then strain: the ferment is ready but will keep in a corked bottle in the refrigerator for several weeks.

4 Assembling the borscht. Bring the liquid to a simmer over a medium heat and cook the cabbage until it is just tender – about 10 minutes. Add the cooked beetroot strips (above), and reduce the heat to the barest simmer to warm the ingredients through. Season with pepper and salt, if necessary.

2 Baking the beetroots. While the meats simmer, lightly scrub and then rinse the beetroots, do not peel or pierce them. Put the beetroots in a baking dish, cover it with foil and place it in a cool oven, preheated to 150°C/300°F/gas2. Bake for 3 to 3¹/₂ hours, depending on the beetroots' size. When they cool, peel them with a small sharp knife and cut into thick strips

3 Preparing the cabbage. Pull off the leaves of a white cabbage. Cut out the tough ribs, then roll up and slice the leaves into narrow strips and put them in a large cooking pan. Cover the cabbage with the strained meat broth (above, left) and then about ¹/₂ litre (18 fl oz) of the strained beetroot ferment (above, right).

5 Serving. Take the meats from the casserole. Cut them into slices, removing any bones, and arrange the meats on a large warmed platter. Serve the borscht from a warmed tureen, accompanied by the meats and other side dishes – here, pirozhki and kasha. Place a spoonful of kasha in each soup plate and ladle the borscht over it (right). Garnish the soup with a dollop of soured cream and a sprinkling of chopped dill or parsley.

Crayfish Bisque

A purée based on shellfish – which may be anything from oysters to lobster – is generally known by its French name, *bisque*. Like most purées, a bisque requires a thickener – a few tablespoons of cooked rice or a handful of breadcrumbs – to give it just the right velvety body.

If the basis of the soup is a crustacean – whether crab, prawns, crayfish or a small lobster – the consistency can be further enhanced by the shells and their contents. By breaking up the emptied shells and other discarded parts of the body and simmering them in the soup, every tiny crevice containing meat and juices will offer up its substance; additionally, the shell particles will give the soup an extra depth of flavour and colour.

After brief simmering with the soup, most of the inedible shell is removed by passing the mixture through a food mill, which both extracts more juices from the crayfish and traps most of the shell debris. After thickening, strain the soup through a fine sieve, to amalgamate the ingredients and filter out any remaining shell fragments, leaving the bisque with a luxurious satin texture.

FOR 8

about 30 live crayfish, washed
30 g / 1 oz butter
1 large onion, finely chopped
1 large carrot, finely chopped
1 celery stalk, finely chopped
1 bay leaf
generous pinch of mixed dried herbs
600 ml / 1 pint dry white wine
2-3 tablespoons brandy
about 1 litre / 1¾ pints fish fumet (p. 244)
salt and a little cayenne pepper
125 g / 4 oz semi-dry white breadcrumbs
150 ml / ¼ pint double cream

1 Cooking the crayfish. Melt the butter in a frying pan over a low heat. Add the chopped vegetables, bay and mixed herbs and cook, stirring frequently (top), for about 15 minutes until the vegetables are soft but not coloured. Add the wine and brandy, turn up the heat and bring to the boil. Drop in the crayfish and stir (above) until they turn red. Cover the pan, reduce the heat and simmer for 7 to 10 minutes.

2 Shelling the tails. When the crayfish are cool enough to handle, twist each tail free from the carapace (above), and put the carapace into a large mortar. Using your thumbs, split open the underside of the tail to remove the meat (left); put the shell into the mortar, and reserve the meat. Put the vegetables and liquid into a saucepan.

3 Pounding the crayfish. With a pestle, pound the carapaces and tail shells into coarse fragments in the mortar. Then add them to the vegetables and cooking liquid. Add the fish fumet and a little cayenne pepper.

4 Extracting more flavour. Simmer uncovered, for 2 to 3 minutes. Add a little more broth if the mixture seems too thick, then pass it through a food mill set over a large bowl. Discard the shell fragments that remain in the mill.

5 Thickening the bisque. Return the milled pulp and its liquid to the saucepan, and set the pan over a moderate heat. Add white breadcrumbs and cook, stirring to distribute them evenly, until the bisque comes to a simmer.

6 Sieving the bisque. To smooth the soup and remove inedible pieces of shell, pour the mixture into a fine-meshed, heavy-duty sieve set over a large bowl. Press the mixture through the sieve with a broad heavy pestle. Discard fragments that remain in the sieve. Adjust the seasoning with more salt and cayenne if necessary.

7 Serving. Return the soup to the pan, set it over a moderate heat, and stir in the cream as you bring the bisque back to a simmer. Combine the reserved crayfish tail meat with the soup, and serve from a warmed tureen (left).

Basic Bread-making

Bread is most often made from a simple mixture of flour, yeast, a moistening agent and usually a seasoning. The most readily available and commonly used ingredients are plain white wheat flour, commercial yeast, water and salt, as here. You may vary this mixture by adding other flours, like wholemeal and rye, and a sourdough leaven, but the basics remain unchanged.

The ingredients are mixed together into a shaggy-textured dough, which is kneaded (Step 4) to form a network of gluten – the substance that gives dough its elasticity. When the dough is supple and smooth, it is covered and set aside to 'prove': the yeast produces bubbles of carbon dioxide which gently stretch the gluten, raising the dough.

If baked after this first rising, the bread would have a loose, cottony texture and be full of large holes. To redistribute the yeast cells and to expel large gas bubbles, for a finer and more even crumb, the dough is next kneaded into a round (Step 7). After a short rest to relax the gluten, the dough can be handled further without tearing and moulded into its final shape.

To give lightness to the finished bread, the shaped loaf must then be left to rise briefly once more before it is baked. At any time during this final rising, the surface may be slashed or scored (Step 9, overleaf. The slashes increase the area of the crust; the earlier the slashes are made, the more they will open as the loaf rises.

When the loaf is placed in a preheated oven, it expands even more during the first 20 minutes or so, until the yeast dies and the crust forms. To delay the crust's formation and thereby promote expansion, make the oven humid during this critical period (steps 8 and 9, overleaf).

FOR 2 MEDIUM LOAVES

about 1.5 kg / 3 lb strong plain flour
1 tablespoon fine salt
**30 g / 1 oz fresh yeast or 1 tablespoon
   dried yeast**
900 ml / 1½ pints tepid water

1 Combining the ingredients. Place the flour in a mixing bowl and put the bowl in an oven at its lowest setting for 3 to 5 minutes; warming the flour will help the dough to rise. Add salt to the flour. Mix the yeast in a little of the tepid water and pour it with the remaining water into the centre.

2 Mixing the dough. Holding the bowl steady with one hand, with the other mix the flour and liquid together, scooping and turning them until they are thoroughly combined, forming a shaggy mass.

5 Leaving the dough to rise. Replace the dough in the bowl. To keep the dough moist, cover the bowl with plastic film. Set aside in a warm place until the dough has doubled in bulk – from 1½ to 2½ hours. To test that the dough has risen enough, press a finger into it: if the indentation remains, filling in only very slowly, the dough is ready.

6 Dividing the dough. Turn the risen dough out on to the work surface. If, as here, you have made enough for two loaves, use a knife to divide the dough in half. Cover one portion of dough with a damp cloth or plastic film to keep it from drying, and set it aside while you work with the other.

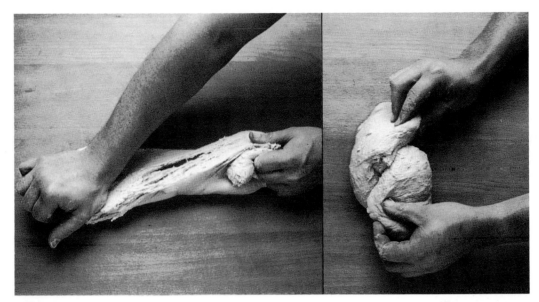

3 Tipping out the dough. If the dough feels very dry and stiff, mix in a little more water; if it is too loose and wet, work in some more flour. Empty the dough from the bowl on to the work surface. Wash out and dry the mixing bowl.

4 Kneading the dough. Holding the dough with one hand, with the heel of the other hand, push the dough away from you until it begins to tear (above, left). At first, the dough will be sticky and will tear very easily. Fold the dough back and at the same time give the mass of dough a slight turn (above, right). Continue to push, fold and turn the dough with a regular, rhythmic motion for 10 to 15 minutes. To develop the gluten further, occasionally lift up the dough and throw it down on to the work surface. The dough is ready when it is no longer sticky, is easy to stretch and feels smooth.

7 Kneading the dough into a round. Exerting a light, even pressure with the heel of your hand, push away a corner of dough, at the same time, give the corner a slight anti-clockwise twist (far left) to turn the whole mass of dough slightly. Fold the pushed-out piece of dough back into the middle (centre, left) and begin the process again with the adjacent section (centre, right). Repeat the process with a regular, rhythmic motion until the loaf is rounded (far right). Turn over the dough so that its pleats are on the bottom. Cover the round and repeat the process with the other piece of dough.

8 Leaving the dough to rise a final time. Cover and rest the loaves for 10 to 15 minutes. Repeat the rhythmic kneading motion (Step 7) to mould the loaves into neat rounds. Place them on boards sprinkled with flour; cover with a cloth and leave to rise for about 50 minutes. Preheat the oven to 230°C/450°F/gas 8; to produce a steamy atmosphere, place a wide dish at the bottom of the oven and fill it with hot water. Place a baking sheet in the oven.

9 Slashing the loaves. Test with your finger to see if the loaves are fully risen. With a razor blade, make a long shallow slash across the top of one loaf; at right angles to the first, make two additional slashes from the edge to the centre. For variety, give the other loaf extra crust by slashing it more deeply (above, right). With a sharp, pushing movement, slide each loaf from its board on to the baking sheet. Spray fresh water into the oven from a plant sprayer.

10 Baking the loaves. After 20 minutes remove the dish of water. After a further 15 minutes, if the loaves are browning too quickly, lower the heat to 200°C/400°F/gas 6. When the loaves have baked for about 45 minutes, test for doneness: rap the bottom of each loaf with your knuckle. The loaf should sound hollow; if not, bake 10 minutes more and test again. Put the loaves on a wire rack to cool.

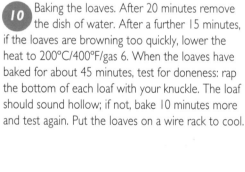

Making Croissants

A lightly enriched yeast dough interleaved with thin layers of butter produces a leavened puff dough – the raw material for a variety of delectable breads and pastries. The dough is raised not only by yeast but also by the butter's moisture, which turns to steam during baking and separates the layers into light flakes. Croissants, favourites of the French breakfast table, are demonstrated here.

The basic preparation of a leavened puff dough is shown in Steps 1 to 5. The rolled dough is spread with softened butter, folded to enclose the butter, rolled out to compress the layers together, and folded once again. So that the leavened pastry will have enough layers to puff up handsomely, this folding and rolling-out sequence must be repeated at least once – more often if you wish.

Because the dough undergoes so much handling during its preparation, the initial kneading should be lighter than for an ordinary bread dough. Otherwise, the dough would become too elastic to work easily. In any case, to allow the dough to relax after each sequence of rolling and folding, it must be left to rest for an hour.

During the resting periods, the dough should be kept in the refrigerator, so that the butter remains firm enough to separate the layers of dough. Even with this precaution, the butter can easily become too soft, and the dough is best handled on a very cool work surface such as marble.

MAKES ABOUT 12

500 g / 1 lb strong plain white flour
1 teaspoon salt
1 teaspoon sugar (optional)
250 g / 8 oz butter, softened
15 g / ¹/₂ oz fresh yeast or 1 teaspoon dried yeast
300 ml / ¹/₂ pint tepid milk
1 egg yolk

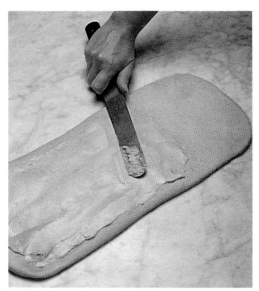

1 Prepare dough by putting flour, salt and sugar, if you like, in a large bowl and adding 60 g (2 oz) of the butter, in small pieces. Mix yeast into milk and add to mixture, Mix and knead as for basic bread dough (pages 266-7). Let dough rise twice. Roll out into rectangle about 8 mm (³/8 inch) thick. Spread remaining butter on dough over two-thirds its length (above), leaving a 2 cm (³/4 inch) margin at edges.

2 Folding the dough. Fold the unbuttered third over half of the buttered dough, and bring over the remaining buttered section to cover these two layers. There are now two thicknesses of butter sandwiched between three layers of dough.

3 Sealing the edges. With a rolling pin, lightly squeeze together the three open sides of the rectangle. The gentle pressure will seal in the softened butter and prevent it from escaping when the dough is rolled out again.

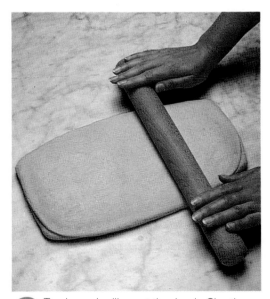

4 Turning and rolling out the dough. Give the dough a quarter turn. Roll out lightly: too much pressure would force out the softened butter. Continue to roll the dough until it is a rectangle twice as long as it is wide . Fold into thirds again (Step 2). Six thicknesses of butter are now sandwiched between seven layers of dough. Wrap in plastic film and chill it for an hour.

5 Folding the dough. Remove the dough from the refrigerator. Place the rectangle on the work surface with one of its short sides facing you. Roll out the dough lengthwise, fold it again (above, left), and give it a quarter turn. Roll it out into a rectangle and fold the dough into thirds once more (above, right). After the fourth folding, 54 thicknesses of butter are sandwiched between 55 layers of dough. Wrap the dough in plastic film and chill for another hour.

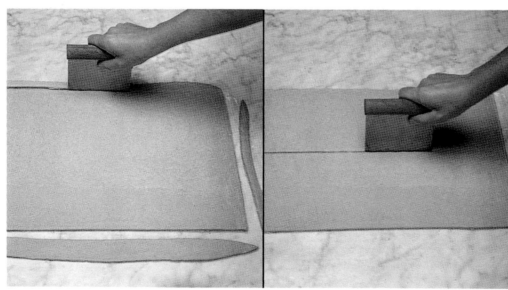

6 Trimming the dough. Roll out the layered dough to a thickness of about 3 mm ($^{1}/_{8}$ inch). Neatly trim the sides of the dough into a rectangle with a dough scraper (above, left), guiding the blade with a ruler if necessary. Cut the dough lengthwise into strips about 15 cm (6 inches) wide (above, right).

7 Cutting out triangles. With the dough scraper, mark points about 15 cm (6 inches) along one side of each strip, starting 15 cm from the end. On the opposite side of the strip, mark points 15 cm apart, but start 7.5 cm (3 inches) from the end. Make diagonal cuts between the marks to produce triangles.

8 Shaping the croissants. Gently separate one triangle from the rest. Elongate the triangle slightly by giving it a light roll lengthwise with a rolling pin. Gently stretch the two corners of the triangle's base so that they are well defined (above, left). Starting at the base, roll up the triangle tightly (above, centre). Tuck the tip of the triangle just under the roll: it will emerge during baking. Shape the dough into a crescent by curling the ends of the roll so that they point inwards.

9 Glazing the croissants. Butter a baking sheet. Place the crescents on the sheet, leaving at least 2.5 cm (1 inch) between them to allow room for expansion. Cover the rolls with a cloth and leave them to rise for about 1 hour – or overnight in the refrigerator. Mix egg yolk with a little water and brush it over the croissants.

10 Baking and serving. Place the baking sheet of croissants in the centre of a preheated 240°C/475°F/gas 9 oven; after 2 minutes reduce the heat to 190°C/375°F/gas 5 and bake for 15 to 20 minutes, until the croissants are golden-brown. Allow them to cool on a rack for 10 to 15 minutes. Serve the croissants warm, in a napkin-lined basket. Pull them apart to eat them.

Making Long Loaves

By repeatedly rolling a shaped cylinder of dough, you can extend it into a thin, elongated shape (see right) reminiscent of the classic French loaf. The loaf can be as long as you wish: the only limiting factor is the size of your baking sheet and oven.

Like all of the basic dough shapes, the long loaf is open to all kinds of variations. For example, if you roll the cylinder out very thinly, then coil it neatly, you can make a spiral, turban-shaped loaf (box, below). To ensure that the spiral has a compact, circular outline, taper one end of the cylinder as you roll out the dough so that the tip will merge smoothly into the side of the loaf.

A more elaborate version of the basic long loaf is shown opposite. The surface of the elongated cylinder of dough is deeply cut with scissors and shaped into a knobbly pattern that is easily torn apart by hand. The baked loaf's form inspires its common French name, *épi*, which means 'ear of wheat'.

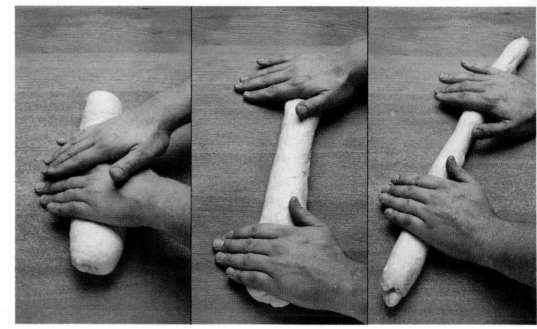

1 Lengthening the dough. Make a basic dough (page 266), and knead it into a round. Cover dough and leave to rest for 10 to 15 minutes. Then shape into a cylinder by rolling it out to a round and then rolling this up and folding in the resulting edges.

Rest again. Roll cylinder back and forth under your palms with a steady pressure; to ensure that it lengthens evenly, place your hands at the centre, move them outwards as you roll, and repeat. If dough resists, rest it for 5 to 10 minutes, then continue.

Coiling a Turban

Roll out a cylinder of dough (Step 1, above) about 75 cm (2^1/$_2$ feet) long. Coil the dough into a spiral, tapering the free end by rolling it with your palm (left). Put on a baking sheet, cover and leave to rise for about 45 minutes. Bake in an oven preheated to 230°C/450°F/gas 8 for 40 minutes then allow to cool on a rack.

2 Slashing the dough. Put the shaped loaf on a baking sheet that has been sprinkled with semolina. With a razor blade held almost horizontally, score the surface of the loaf: in this case, four long shallow, overlapping cuts are made almost parallel to the loaf's length.

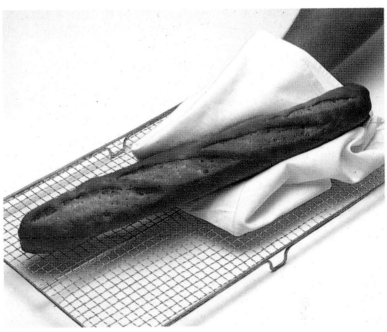

3 Baking the loaf. Cover the loaf and leave it to rise in a warm place for about 45 minutes. Bake the loaf in an oven preheated to 230°C/450°F/gas 8 for about 30 minutes, until well browned. Transfer the loaf to a wire rack and leave it to cool for an hour. Slice the bread for serving or break it apart by hand.

Scissor Cuts for a Knobbly Crust

Roll out a thin cylinder of dough and put it on a baking sheet dusted with semolina. With a pair of scissors held almost horizontally, make cuts about three-quarters of the way through the dough's diameter and about 5 cm (2 inches) apart. As you cut, pull the sections to alternate sides (left). Leave the loaf to rise, then bake it in an oven preheated to 230°C/450°F/gas 8.

Pizza: Moist Toppings for Breads

The simplest way to flavour a plain dough is to spread it out thinly – with a rolling pin or by hand – and cover it with a moist topping that will be partly absorbed by the bread as it bakes. Cooked quickly in a hot oven, the bread will develop a crisp bottom crust; its upper surface, shielded by the topping, will stay soft.

So that individual flavours will stand out, make the topping from just a few complementary ingredients. Any elements that take longer to cook than the 30 minutes or so required by the dough – meats and root vegetables, for example – should be pre-cooked. Otherwise, the choice of topping is limited only by your preferences and by what is available.

The traditionally flavoured French breads demonstrated here exploit local produce from their respective regions. On the right, a Provençal pissaladière is covered with onions that have been stewed in olive oil and is garnished with salt anchovies (a substitute for *pissala*, a salted purée of fish that originally flavoured the bread) and black olives. On the opposite page, below, a time-honoured Lorraine variety of quiche, which differs markedly from the familiar filled pastry of today, is topped with bacon and bathed with cream.

Another good topping for this sort of bread is a thick sauce made from skinned and seeded fresh tomatoes or sieved tinned tomatoes. Simmer them with garlic, onions or sweet peppers, and dried oregano or fresh basil. Mashed soft or semi-soft cheeses – cream cheese, goat cheese or Roquefort also make excellent toppings, alone or accompanied by a little cream. Or, for a sweet variation, cover the dough with fresh fruit – apricots, plums or cherries are especially suitable. Stone, and halve or slice the fruits; before baking, sprinkle them with sugar and, if you like, dust them with cinnamon.

Pissaladière: a Neat Display of Onions, Anchovies and Olive

1 Rolling out dough. Mix a bread dough (page 266), adding 2 tablespoons of olive oil with the liquid. Then knead and let rise. Stew 1 kg (2 lb) thinly sliced onions in 3 tablespoons of olive oil until soft. Soak 12 anchovies in water. Knead dough into a round; rest for 10 minutes. Break off a handful. Form the remaining dough into a rectangle 5 mm (¹/4 inch) thick.

2 Flavouring the surface. Place the rolled-out dough on to a lightly oiled baking sheet. Leaving a narrow margin round the edge of the dough, spread out the onions evenly over its surface. Fillet the anchovies, rinse them with water and dry them on paper towels. Arrange the anchovies on top of the onions in a regular criss-cross pattern (above).

6 Baking and serving. Leave the flattened and flavoured dough at warm room temperature to rise slightly for about 10 minutes. Bake it in an oven preheated to 220°C/425°F/gas 7 for about 30 minutes, until the exposed dough is evenly browned. Serve hot, cut into squares, straight from the sheet.

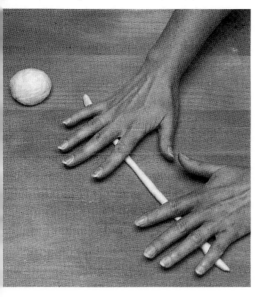

3 Rolling dough strips. Pull walnut-sized pieces from the reserved dough. With your fingers, roll each piece back and forth on a board to make a long, even strip the thickness of a pencil.

4 Attaching the dough strips. To make a decorative lattice-work effect, place the strips of dough on top of the flavourings to divide the surface into a series of neat squares – each one containing a pair of anchovy fillets. To secure each strip of dough, brush the underside of both ends with water, then press the ends into the rim of the dough base.

5 Brushing with olive oil. Complete the pattern by distributing some stoned black olives over the surface. To add more flavour and to help keep the surface moist, sprinkle more olive oil over the flavourings. Brush the oil evenly over the exposed dough.

Old-fashioned Quiche Lorraine: A Bacon and Cream Embellishment

1 Preparing the dough base. Mix and knead a basic bread dough and let it rise. Transfer the dough to a lightly floured surface. Use the heels of your hands, or a rolling pin, to spread out the dough to a thickness of about 5 mm (^{1}/4 inch). Transfer it to an oiled baking sheet. To form a rim to contain the fairly liquid topping, pinch up the edge of the dough.

2 Adding flavourings. Cut 125 g (4 oz) rindless streaky bacon into pieces about 1 cm (^{1}/2 inch) square and 2.5 cm (1 inch) long. Fry the pieces in a little oil over a low heat for 5 to 7 minutes, until lightly browned. Drain the bacon, then gently press the pieces into the dough at regular intervals. Spoon a thin coating of about 200 ml/ 7 fl oz double cream over the dough and bacon.

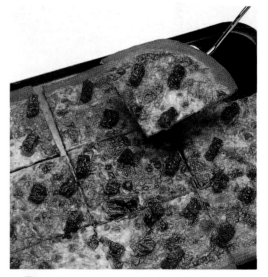

3 Baking and serving. Put the bread in an oven preheated to 220°C/425°F/gas 7. After about 15 minutes, when the cream has been absorbed, take out the bread and spoon over it another coating of cream. Return the bread to the oven and bake for 15 minutes more, until it is golden. Cut the bread into squares while still hot, and serve immediately.

Making Shortcrust Pastry

Crisp, light and easy to prepare, shortcrust is the most frequently used of all pie and tart pastries. Its firm texture complements most fillings, such as custard, apple or rhubarb, while a base of baked shortcrust can provide the foundation for elaborate assemblies.

Shortcrust dough is made from flour, butter, water and a little salt – usually, half the amount of butter to flour. The dough takes very little time to make. Indeed, to achieve perfect, tender shortcrust pastry, speed is essential; overworking would only strengthen the gluten in the dough and make the butter oily – resulting in a mixture that will become hard and tough on baking.

To help keep the dough cool, chill the water and butter and use your fingertips to rub the butter lightly together with the flour. Lift the mixture well out of the bowl and let it fall back through your fingers (Step 2), shaking the bowl

occasionally to bring the larger crumbs to the surface. Some cooks minimize handling even further by using an electric food processor which can combine the ingredients in seconds. Another method of making shortcrust dough is to cut the butter into the flour with two knives (box, opposite page, below) – a technique that produces a less uniform mixture that bakes to a flakier pastry.

Whichever method of incorporating the butter you use, finish the dough by adding just enough water to make the dough cohere (Step 4, below). Too much water will produce a sticky dough that is difficult to roll out, too little water leaves it unmanageably dry. In either case, the resulting pastry will be hard. Start with less water than you think you need and supplement it – if necessary – by adding more water a drop or two at a time.

Chilling any dough before use relaxes the gluten, making the dough less elastic

and thus softer and easier to roll out. To prevent air from drying out the resting dough and forming hard, crusty streaks on its surface, wrap the dough in film, greaseproof paper or foil before placing it in a refrigerator or other cool place. If it is not required immediately, the dough can be stored in this way for up to three days.

MAKES 750 G / 1 ½ LB

250 g / 8 oz cold butter, cut into pieces
500 g / 1 lb flour
pinch of salt
5-8 tablespoons iced water

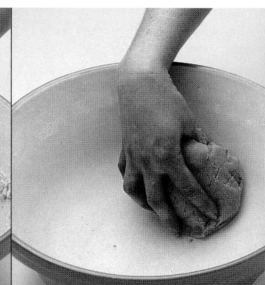

3 Finishing the dough. Quickly stir in the water with a knife to distribute the water evenly without overworking the dough (above, left). Gather the mixture together with one hand, if it feels too crumbly, add a little more water until the dough begins to cohere (above, centre). Press the dough into a ball (above, right). To make the dough easier to roll out, wrap it in film, greaseproof paper or foil and chill for 15 minutes before using.

1 Rubbing the butter into the flour. Add the salt to the flour and sift them into a large mixing bowl. Add all of the butter cubes to the flour. Using the tips of your fingers and thumbs, pick up a small amount of butter and flour, lightly rub

them together and let the mixture fall back into the bowl (above, left). Continue for about 2 to 3 minutes, until all of the butter is incorporated and the mixture resembles very coarse breadcrumbs (above, right).

2 Adding water. Use a spoon to make a shallow well in the mixture; spoon in a little iced water. Because some flours absorb more water than others, the quantity of water you need may vary; always start with a minimum amount in order to avoid soggy results.

An Alternative Approach: Working with Knives

1 Cutting in the butter. Chill water and butter. Cut the butter into cubes and put them into a mixing bowl with sifted flour and salt. With two knives, cut the butter into the flour using a rapid criss-cross movement until the lumps of butter are about the size of peas.

2 Adding the water. Sprinkle a little cold water over the mixture and blend it in lightly with a knife. Then, use your hands to lightly gather the dough together. Add a little more water if necessary; the mixture should cling together without being damp.

3 Finishing the dough. Lightly press the dough together and form it into a ball. Wrap the dough in film, greaseproof paper or foil to prevent drying out, and chill the dough for about 15 minutes before use.

Double-crust Apple Pie

The trick in making a double-crust pie is to keep the base from getting soggy, a disaster you can prevent with simple precautions. In the first place, you should choose a filling that will not render much liquid as it cooks – the firm apples used in this demonstration, for example, or a thick cream filling or a mincemeat.

For extra insurance, you can brush the bottom layer of pastry dough lightly with whisked egg white before adding the filling. In the oven, the egg white will cook to a thin glaze that will prevent the filling's moisture from seeping into the dough. A little flour added to a fruit filling will absorb some of the juices that are exuded during cooking. A few slits cut into the upper pastry crust will allow much of the remaining moisture to escape.

To make the pie base and top, you can use any shortcrust or puff dough (recipes, pages 276-7 and 282-3). A plain, simple-to-make shortcrust dough is well-suited to the traditional apple pie illustrated here.

Although the pie can be baked and served without adornment, you can, if you like, glaze it before baking by brushing the top with a lightly whisked egg white and sprinkling on some caster sugar. For an attractive matt finish, sift a little icing sugar over the baked pie.

FOR 6-8

1 kg / 2¹/₂ lb tart apples
2 tablespoons flour, plus more for dusting
pinch of salt
300 g / 10 oz sugar
¹/₂ teaspoon freshly grated nutmeg
³/₄ teaspoon ground cinnamon
500 g / 1 lb shortcrust pastry dough
**   (page 276)**
30 g / 1 oz butter
¹/₂ lemon (optional)
whipped double cream, to serve
**   (optional)**

1 Mixing the apple filling. Place the flour, salt, sugar and spices in a mixing bowl. Peel, core and slice the apples, and add them to the bowl. With your hands, toss the apples until they are evenly coated with the dry ingredients.

2 Preparing the dough. Divide the dough into halves, one for the top of the pie and one for the base. Wrap one half of the dough in film or foil to prevent it from drying out.

5 Fitting the pastry base. Use your fingers to mould the dough firmly to the shape of the tin. Try not to stretch or tear it; if necessary, patch any damaged area with a bit of extra dough.

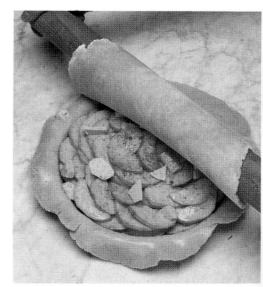

6 Filling and covering the pie. Fill the base with the apples and dot them with butter. If the apples are sweet, sprinkle them with lemon juice and grated lemon rind. Using a pastry brush, moisten the dough round the edge of the tin with water. Roll the remaining dough to a thickness of about 5 mm (¹/₄ inch) and place it over the filling.

3 Rolling into a circle. Sprinkle a little flour on to the work surface to prevent the dough from sticking. To make the base, roll the dough forwards only, using firm, light strokes; then, for an even surface, give the dough a quarter turn and roll it again. Roll and turn the dough until it forms a round about 5 mm (^{1}/4 inch) thick.

4 Lining the tin. To ensure that the round of dough is big enough to cover the base and overlap the sides of the tin, hold the tin over the dough as a guide; the pastry should be slightly wider than the tin all round (inset). To lift the dough, roll it loosely round the rolling pin and then unroll it over the pie tin.

7 Finishing the edges. Use a knife to trim away the excess dough, angling the blade up and outwards so as to leave a slightly overhanging margin of dough. Using your thumb and index finger, pinch the dough firmly to seal the base and top. With the knife, pierce the top in several places to allow steam to escape as the pie bakes.

8 Serving the pie. Bake the pie in an oven preheated to 220°C/425°F/gas 7 for 10 to 15 minutes, then at 180°C/350°F/gas 4 for 40 to 45 minutes, or until the pastry is firm and golden-brown.

Hot pastry crumbles easily: let the pie cool for a few minutes before cutting it. Serve the pie warm or cold, with whipped double cream.

Pear Upside-down Tart

A tart can be made upside down by baking a lid of pastry dough over a filling of cooked fruit and reversing the finished assembly on to a serving plate. For the classic *Tarte Tatin* apples are first caramelized. Pears, apricots and peaches can be cooked in the same way in a sugar syrup (see page 254).

Choose a good deep-coloured wine which is young and full-bodied. Cooking concentrates the flavour and the quality of the wine will be reflected in the finished tart.

To prevent the juices from the filling seeping into the pastry and making it soggy, unmould the tart only at the last possible moment before serving. Serve warm or cold, accompanied by thick fresh cream if you wish.

SERVES 8-12

7 firm, slightly under-ripe pears
100g / 3¹/₂ oz sugar
¹/₂ tsp ground cinnamon
about 600ml / 1pt red wine
250g / 8oz shortcrust pastry (see page 276)

1 Preparing the pears. Assemble the ingredients. Using a small sharp knife, halve, peel and core the pears. Arrange the halves, cored side up, in a heavy-based pan so that the wide ends of the pears fit snugly against the edge of the pan.

2 Covering the pear with wine. Fill the centre of the pan with more pear halves. Arrange them with the narrow ends pointing outwards so that the fruit will form an attractive symmetrical design when the tart is unmoulded. Sprinkle the cinnamon and sugar over the pears, then pour enough red wine into the pan just to cover the fruit.

6 Preparing the pastry lid. Roll the pastry into a circle just slightly larger than the pan and about 5mm/¹/₄ in thick. Pierce the dough circle all over with a fork to create steam vents. Make a pastry border by folding over the edge, pressing the edge flat and crimping it with a fork.

7 Covering the pears. Carefully lift the dough and place it over the pears with the folded edge down. Bake in an oven preheated to 190°C/375°F/gas5 for about 40 minutes, until the pastry is golden-brown and crisp.

3 Poaching the pears. Place the pan of pears and wine over a high heat. Bring the wine to a boil, then cover the pan, reduce the heat and simmer the pears for about 1 hour or until tender. Test the fruit by gently inserting the tip of a knife into one of the pears.

4 Making the syrup. Holding the lid of the poaching pan firmly against the pears to keep them in place, pour off the liquid into a small saucepan. Set the pears aside. Put the pan of cooking liquor over high heat and boil, stirring occasionally with a wooden spoon. Reduce the heat, if necessary, to prevent the liquid from boiling over.

5 Reducing the syrup. Continue to cook the syrup until it is thick and has reduced in volume by between two-thirds and three-quarters – about 10 minutes. Pour the syrup evenly over the pears.

8 Serving the tart. Remove the tart from the oven and leave it to cool slightly. To unmould the tart, invert a serving dish over the pan and turn the dish and pan over together. If the pan's handle prevents you from unmoulding the tart into the centre of the dish, slide it into place with your hand. Serve at once.

Making Puff Pastry

Puff dough rises to the lightest and highest of all pastries, it can be baked with a light filling of jam or pastry cream, or pre-baked and filled with fresh fruit or almost any type of flavoured cream.

The ingredients for puff – flour, butter and water – are the same as for shortcrust (page 276). Only proportions differ.

The technique for making puff dough is essentially the same as for flaky (page 00); the dough and butter are repeatedly rolled and folded to create multiple layers. However, the method of incorporating the butter is very different. For puff, a small amount of the butter – about one eighth of the total amount – is used to make the basic mixture; the remainder is pounded into a sheet and the rolled out dough is folded over it (Step 5). To give the pastry its characteristic height and leafy layers, the parcel of dough and butter is rolled and folded six times, instead of the usual four times for flaky.

Between each rolling sequence the dough is chilled in order to firm the butter and relax the gluten in the dough.

You can use a food processor to make the basic mixture, as you can for shortcrust and flaky dough. The food processor will save very little time, however, since the rolling out must be done by hand. Because puff dough takes so much time to make – about 3 hours in all – it is well worth making a large quantity and storing it. Wrapped in plastic or foil to prevent it from drying out, puff dough will keep in a refrigerator for up to 4 days or for several months in a freezer.

MAKES 1 KG / 2 LB

500 g / 1 lb flour, plus more for dusting
2 teaspoons salt
500 g / 1 lb cold butter
about 200 ml / 7 fl oz cold water

1 Preparing dough. Sift flour and salt into a bowl, add one-quarter of the butter, cut into small pieces, and rub together with your fingertips. Gradually add enough cold water to bind, working the dough lightly. Sprinkle a little flour into a plastic bag to prevent the dough from sticking, put the dough mixture inside and chill for about 30 minutes.

4 Placing the butter. Peel the top sheet of greaseproof paper from the butter. Invert the butter over the rolled-out dough, placing it diagonally on the dough. Then peel the second sheet of paper from the butter.

5 Enclosing the butter. Draw up the four corners of the dough and fold each one over the butter to make an envelope, leaving about 1 cm (1/2 inch) all round the butter. Press the edges and seams of the envelope gently together with your fingers or the rolling pin.

6 Rolling the folded dough. Pressing evenly but lightly, so as not to squeeze out the butter, roll the dough into a rectangle three times as long as it is wide. Pat the edges of the dough with the sides of your hands to keep the edges neat. Brush off any surplus flour.

2 Flattening the butter. Take the dough out of the refrigerator. Put a sheet of greaseproof paper on a work surface, place some cold butter on top and cover it with another sheet of greaseproof paper. The paper will prevent the butter from sticking to both the rolling pin and the work surface. With a rolling pin, beat the butter into a square about 2 cm ($^3/4$ inch) thick.

3 Rolling the dough. Remove the dough from the bag and place it on a lightly floured work surface. Roll the dough into a square about 1 cm ($^1/2$ inch) thick, and large enough for its corners to fold over and envelop the butter. Use light, quick strokes to roll the dough, turning it so that it is rolled evenly.

7 Folding the dough. Fold the top third of the dough over the centre, then fold the bottom third over, to make three layers of dough. Seal the air inside the layers by pressing the edges of the dough down lightly with the rolling pin.

8 Completing the sequence. Repeat Steps 6 and 7 – always rolling with the folded edges at the sides (above). Mark the dough with two fingers (right) to show you have rolled it twice. Wrap and chill the dough for about 30 minutes. Repeat Steps 6, 7 and 8 twice, imprinting the dough each time.

Fruit Cases Fashioned from Puff

Pre-baked puff dough can yield pastry cases of all shapes and sizes, ready for filling with fruits, cream or pastry cream. Fully risen puff, however, would be too fragile for this purpose. To restrict its expansion – as well as helping the dough to rise evenly – some or all of the shaped dough must be pricked before baking.

In the demonstration on the right, pricked and baked puff pastry is built up into a roomy basket. One piece of pastry forms the base of the basket, while the sides are constructed from stacked pastry rings. Layers of meringue hold the pastry pieces together; a final spell in the oven sets the meringue and browns it lightly. The more rings you bake, the deeper the basket will be: here, three rings produce a capacious container for lightly sugared strawberries.

In the demonstration below, strips of puff pastry dough form a rim around a puff base to create a pastry tray; further strips of dough subdivide the tray into several compartments, each of which can be filled, after baking, with a different fruit or cream. The strips, brushed with egg to make them adhere, are placed on the base before cooking. Only the base of the pastry is pricked, to prevent it from rising too much and buckling; the strips of dough must rise to their full height in order to provide effective – and attractive – partitions.

You can make such a free-form pastry case as small or as large as you like, so long as it will fit inside your oven. The number of partitions is equally variable. In this demonstration, the basic tray is subdivided into eight, and once it has cooled, the compartments are filled with poached cherries and apricots, and with chilled pastry cream (page 257).

A Layered Basket for Sugared Berries

1 Cutting the puff dough. Make puff dough (page 282) and roll it to a thickness of 3 mm (1/8 inch). Use an inverted plate as a guide to cut four pieces of dough; transfer them to ungreased baking sheets. Using a similarly shaped but smaller plate, cut out the centres from three of the pieces.

Choose a plate that will leave a pastry rim about 2 cm (3/4 inch) wide. With a fork, prick the dough all the way through at even intervals and refrigerate it for 20 to 30 minutes. Bake the dough in an oven preheated to 220°C/425°F/gas 7 for 20 to 25 minutes.

A Patchwork of Fruit and Pastry Cream

1 Making the case. Roll out puff dough to a thickness of 5 mm (1/4 inch); cut out a large rectangular base, put it on an ungreased baking sheet and prick it with a fork. Cut remaining dough into long strips 2.5 cm (1 inch) wide. Brush outside edge of base with beaten egg and position the strips to make a rim and geometric partitions.

2 Preparing the fruits. Glaze the rims of the pastry with egg and bake it for about 30 minutes, until risen and golden-brown. Cool it on a rack. Stem 450 g / 1 lb cherries and stone them with a cherry stoner. Halve, stone and poach 12-16 apricots in sugar syrup (page 254) for 8 to 10 minutes. Peel them, then drain on paper towels.

2 Constructing the case. Prepare a meringue mixture (page 290). When the pastry is cool, set the base on an ovenproof plate. With a metal spatula, spread the outer edge with a ring of meringue about as wide as the baked rims. Place a rim on top. Spread the rim with meringue, top it with another, and repeat to complete the container.

3 Piping a decorative trim. Fit a piping bag with a large star nozzle and fill the bag with the remaining meringue. Pipe the meringue along the top rim of the pastry case. Sprinkle the meringue with caster sugar. Bake the case in an oven preheated to 200°C/400°F/gas 6 for about 10 minutes – until the peaks of the meringue turn lightly golden-brown.

4 Filling the basket. Pick the hulls from strawberries and put the fruit in a bowl. To heighten their flavour, sprinkle the berries with icing sugar, turn them gently with your hands and leave them for 10 to 15 minutes. Pile the strawberries in the case (above), leaving the excess juice which would make the pastry soggy.

3 Spooning in the cream. Cook the cherries in a separate pan of sugar syrup for about 5 to 7 minutes, then lift them out with a slotted spoon and leave to drain and cool on paper towels. Prepare glazes from the two syrups by boiling them down, adding 2-3 spoonfuls of good-quality jam if you like, and straining them. Allow them to cool before using. Spoon chilled pastry cream (page 257) into alternate sections of the case (above) smoothing it with the back of a spoon.

4 Arranging the fruit. Pack the apricot halves and the cherries into the remaining sections of the pastry case, using separate sections for each fruit. With a pastry brush, coat each of the fruit sections with its respective glaze. To appreciate best the contrasts between crisp pastry, chilled cream and freshly cooked fruits, serve the tart as soon as possible, cut into rectangular portions of roughly equal size.

Making Choux Pastry

Whereas most other pastry doughs require cold butter and water, choux is made by bringing butter and water to the boil together and then stirring in the flour, off the heat. When the flour comes in contact with the hot liquid the mixture thickens. Finally, eggs are beaten into the hot paste to produce a soft light dough. Choux is too sticky to be rolled out like other doughs; it must be piped or spooned on to a tray for baking.

In the oven, the moisture in the dough becomes steam and causes it to swell up to about three times its unbaked size, leaving a hollow interior. The feather-light result is delicious served simply dusted with icing sugar, or balls or strips can be used to make the pastries overleaf.

MAKES 15 CHOUX PUFFS OR 10 ÉCLAIRS

60 g / 2 oz unsalted butter
75 g / 2¹⁄₂ oz flour
large pinch of salt
2-3 eggs

1 Preparing the ingredients. Put 125 ml (4 fl oz) water into a heavy saucepan and place it over a low heat. Add the butter. Sift the flour and salt on to a piece of greaseproof paper.

2 Boiling the water. Once the butter has melted, increase the heat to bring the water to the boil. Turn off the heat immediately: prolonged boiling would evaporate enough water to alter the proportions of the ingredients.

5 Adding eggs. Cool the dough briefly to prevent the eggs from setting as they are added. Break an egg into a bowl and add it to the pan (above, left). Beat the dough to incorporate the egg thoroughly. Beat in the remaining eggs one by one.

3 Adding the flour. Pick up the piece of greaseproof paper and slide the flour and salt into the hot liquid. Add all the flour mixture at once: added in stages, it would form lumps.

4 Stirring in the flour. Stir the mixture as soon as the flour is added (above, left), and continue until the ingredients are thoroughly combined. Turn on the heat – a moderate heat will eliminate any extra moisture in the dough. Continue stirring the mixture vigorously, until the dough forms a solid mass that comes away from the sides of the pan (above, right). This should take about one minute. Remove the pan from the heat.

6 Filling a piping bag. Continue beating until the ingredients are thoroughly blended (left). Use a piping bag to shape the choux for cooking. To fill the bag easily, fold the top third back over your wrist. Spoon the mixture into the folded bag (above) until it is about two-thirds full. Unfold the bag and twist the top to secure its contents.

Cream-filled Chocolate Éclairs

Airy shells of choux are made by piping the dough (previous pages) into mounds or, as here, strips, and baking them until the pastry is puffed and brown. In the oven, cavities form inside the shells as the moisture in the dough turns to steam and expands. These hollows can be filled with sweetened, lightly whipped cream or pastry cream (page 257) or with ice-cream – flavoured, if you like, with vanilla, praline, chocolate or coffee.

Choux pastry that has browned on the outside but remains moist inside will collapse and toughen as it cools. To release any residual moisture, remove the choux from the oven during the last few minutes of baking and pierce the shells with the tip of a knife (Step 2). Return the choux to the oven to complete the baking and to dry out the inside of the pastries. When they are done, the shells will feel light and remain firm.

In the main demonstration here, thick fingers of choux, known as éclairs, are piped on to a baking tray. If you like, you can give the pastries a glossy finish by brushing the tops and sides lightly with a mixture of egg yolk and milk before baking them. Make sure that the glaze does not touch the baking tray or it will seal down the dough and prevent it from rising. After the éclairs are cooked, they are split in two and filled (Step 3) – pastry cream is used in this instance. The éclairs can then be covered with caramel, glacé icing or, as here, chocolate fondant.

To make chocolate fondant dissolve 500 g (1 lb) sugar in 150 ml ($^1/4$ pint) water over a low heat. Add $1^1/2$ teaspoons of glucose or a pinch of cream of tartar and 3 tablespoons of grated dark chocolate and bring to the boil quickly. Boil to a temperature of 115°C (238°F) and then pour out on an oiled slab. When a little cooler, work it with a palette knife until cool and then knead with the hands.

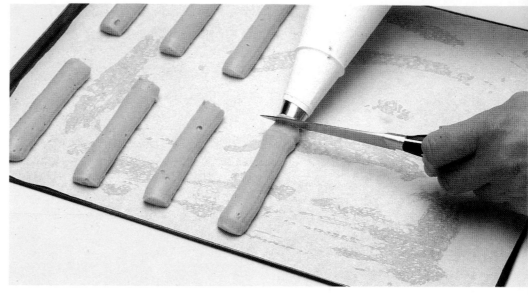

1 Piping the dough. To prevent the choux dough from sticking, cover a buttered baking sheet with greaseproof paper. Fit a 1 cm ($^1/2$ inch) plain nozzle to a piping bag, fill the bag two-thirds full with dough and pipe the dough into strips about 7 to 10 cm (3 to 4 inches) long, cut off each length with a knife. Leave about 4 cm ($1^1/2$ inches) between the strips to allow for expansion.

2 Baking the shells. Place the éclairs in an oven preheated to 200°C/400°F/gas 6. After about 15 minutes, reduce the heat to 190°C/375°F/gas 5 to prevent burning; bake them for 10 more minutes or until they are firm and golden. Remove the éclairs from the oven and pierce the ends of each shell with a knife; bake for a few more minutes.

3 Filling the bases. While the pastry is baking, prepare the pastry cream filling (page 257) and the chocolate fondant icing (left). To use the fondant, soften it in a bowl set over hot water. When the éclairs are cool, slice each one lengthwise and spoon the cream on to the bottom half. Replace the tops and put the éclairs on a wire rack for icing.

Spanish Churos: Deep-fried Strips of Choux

Deliciously crunchy churos, the Spanish breakfast pastries can be made by deep-frying dough in a relatively flavourless oil such as the groundnut oil used here. You could flavour the choux dough with a few drops of vanilla essence, or 2 teaspoons of rum or lemon juice. In this demonstration, the dough is piped directly into the hot oil; but you could simply drop in spoonfuls.

To cook the dough quickly, but without burning, the temperature of the oil should be 180° to 190°C (350° to 375°F). Measure the temperature with a deep-frying thermometer, or test the heat by dropping a small piece of dough into the oil. If the dough sizzles on contact, the oil is hot enough. To keep the oil at the right temperature, fry only a few pastries at a time.

1 Deep frying choux. Pour 7.5 cm (3 inches) of oil into a heavy-bottomed pan and heat it to 180° to 190°C (350° to 375°F). Fit a plain or star nozzle to a piping bag; fill it with dough. Pipe 20 to 30 cm (8 to 12 inch) lengths into the oil cutting off the dough near the nozzle.

2 Serving the pastry. Fry the pastries for 5 to 7 minutes, or until they are golden. Remove them with a slotted spoon and drain on paper towels. Continue until the dough is used up. Sprinkle icing or, as here, caster sugar over the pastries and serve them warm or cold.

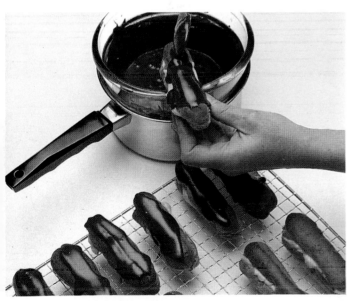

4 Icing the éclairs. Spoon the fondant over the top of each éclair. Use a spoon or knife to scrape up any drips of icing and add them to the fondant in the bowl so that nothing is wasted. Arrange the éclairs on a dish and serve.

Making Meringue

When egg whites are beaten, they trap air and mount into a stiff, foamy mass. The addition of sugar stiffens the egg whites further, enough for them to retain their shape when piped or spooned on to baking sheets. This light, airy mixture, known as meringue, is usually baked very slowly until it is dry and crisp.

The texture of the meringue, which largely determines its uses, depends on the way the egg whites and sugar are combined. Each of the three types of meringue shown here – French, Swiss and Italian – has its own particular advantages.

French meringue is the simplest to prepare. It is made by whisking the whites and then gradually beating in the sugar (right, above). The result is best suited for spooning or piping simple shapes that, after baking, make delicate meringues for filling and decorating (overleaf).

For Italian meringue, the sugar is added to the whites in the form of a boiling syrup (right, below). This method partly cooks the ingredients, producing a stable meringue that can be used, without any further baking, to lighten mousses, etc.

The third type of meringue – Swiss – is made by beating egg whites and sugar over boiling water (box, opposite page). This produces a dense mixture that holds its shape well and bakes to a particularly firm meringue. It is suitable for piping into complex shapes, and is the best choice for ornate decorations.

Whichever mixture you are making, the whites must be free from any trace of egg yolk, which would prevent the whites from mounting fully. The mixing bowl should be made of a material that does not retain grease, such as glass, porcelain or stainless steel. Best of all is copper, which due to a catalytic reaction with egg whites produces a very stable foam.

French meringue should be shaped and baked immediately after you have prepared it, as it easily absorbs moisture and starts to separate. Italian and Swiss mixtures will keep for a few hours.

1 Separating eggs. For enough to make about 20 meringues, use 4 eggs. Over a small bowl, crack each egg sharply and prise apart the two halves of the shell. Pass the yolk from one half to the other, letting the white fall into the bowl. Put the yolk in a second bowl and transfer the white to a large mixing bowl. Reserve the yolks for enriching a sauce.

2 Beating the whites. Using a balloon whisk, beat the egg whites slowly and regularly with a figure-of-eight motion. When the egg whites have formed a froth, whisk more rapidly with a circular motion, lifting the whites to incorporate the maximum amount of air.

Italian Meringue: Made with Boiling Syrup

1 Prepare a sugar syrup using 250 g (8 oz) sugar and 100 ml (3 1/2 fl oz) water, and cook it to the hard-ball stage (pages 254-5, 123°C/ 250°F). Separate 4 eggs and whisk the whites until stiff (above, Steps 1 and 2). Whisking all the time, pour the boiling syrup into the whites in a thin steady stream; this operation is easier with help.

2 Finishing the meringue. When all the syrup has been beaten into the whites, continue to whisk the meringue mixture vigorously while it cools. Once cool, the meringue will be very thick and glossy and ready for use.

3 Adding sugar. Continue whisking the whites until a stiff peak is formed on the whisk when you lift it from the bowl. Sprinkle a little caster sugar over the whites. Beat the sugar into the whites until the mixture is stiff and shiny.

4 Finishing the meringue. Sprinkle the rest of a measured 250 g (8 oz) of caster sugar over the beaten egg whites, a little at a time, beating well after each addition until the mixture has regained its stiff texture and shiny appearance. When all the sugar has been incorporated, the meringue will be very stiff and glossy.

Swiss Meringue: Cooked to Stability Over Heat

1 Beating egg whites and sugar. Bring a pan of water to a gentle simmer over low heat. Separate the 4 egg whites and put them into a large mixing bowl; add 250 g (8 oz) sugar. Set the bowl over the pan, making sure the bottom of the bowl does not touch the water. Whisk the mixture gently until the sugar has melted.

2 Whisking the meringue. Whisk the egg white and sugar mixture with more speed, until it becomes white and foamy (above, left). Then continue to whisk, lifting up the whites to incorporate air. Beat until the meringue is thick and shiny and will stand in stiff peaks when the whisk is lifted from the bowl (above, right).

Crisp Spheres Masked in Chocolate Flakes

1 Piping mounds. Line a baking sheet and draw circular guidelines using a round metal cutter. Prepare French meringue (page 290) and spoon it into a piping bag fitted with a large plain nozzle. Pipe out mounds, finishing each with a twist. Flatten any sharp peaks with a knife.

2 Sandwiching the meringues. Bake the meringues and let cool. Prepare buttercream; add 90 g (3 oz) melted chocolate. Spread the base of one meringue with the cream. Join a second meringue to the base of the first and then place the sandwiched meringues on a tray.

3 Coating with buttercream. Chill meringues for 15 minutes to firm the buttercream and bond the meringues. Grate chocolate coarsely. Have ready paper cases. Spear one sandwiched meringue on the tip of a small sharp knife; spread buttercream over its surface.

Graceful Whirls of Strawberries and Cream

1 Piping coils. Prepare a baking sheet (Step 1, above). Spoon French meringue (page 290) into a piping bag fitted with a large plain nozzle. Pipe the meringue in a spiral from the outside in, making the mound slightly higher in the middle and finishing with a peak.

2 Coating with fondant. Bake the meringues, let cool and transfer to a wire rack set over a tray. Melt fondant flavoured with a few drops of vanilla essence rather than chocolate to a coating consistency and keep liquid over a pan of hot water. Spoon fondant over the meringues.

3 Mixing a filling. Leave the coatings to set: the fondant will harden to a glossy finish. Meanwhile, prepare a fruit purée (page 163) – here, strawberry is used. Pour 600 ml (1 pint) double cream into a bowl and add the purée to the cream. Whisk the two together until thick.

4 Covering with grated chocolate. When the meringue is coated with buttercream, hold it over a bowl of chocolate flakes and sprinkle them over the surface; the chocolate will adhere to the buttercream. Put meringue in a paper case resting on the base where it was speared by the knife.

5 Serving the meringues. Coat the remaining meringues first with the buttercream and then with the chocolate flakes until all have been covered. Serve the meringue assemblies the same day, keeping them in a cool place before serving.

4 Piping the filling. Loosen meringues from the rack and trim off any fondant drips with a small, sharp knife. Spoon strawberry cream into large piping bag fitted with a medium-sized star nozzle. Pipe spiral on the base of one meringue and press a second, flat side down, on to the first.

5 Serving the meringues. Continue to sandwich pairs of fondant-coated meringues together, putting each one into a paper case as you finish. Serve the meringues arranged on a cake stand and present one serving on an individual plate garnished, if you like, with a single fresh strawberry.

Whisked Sponge Cakes

In this classic method of making light, delicate sponge cakes whole eggs and sugar are initially whisked together over a gentle heat then sieved flour and melted butter are folded in. Another method whisks the yolks separately with the sugar – not over heat – then the whites are whisked to firm peaks and folded into the yolk and sugar mixture with the flour. Although cakes made by either method can be cut and decorated in exactly the same way, whisking whole eggs produces a cake with a soft, springy texture; sponges made with separated eggs are slightly firmer. Butter can be used or not, as you prefer – its addition results in a richer cake that stays moist for 2 or 3 days.

Whichever method you use, the secret is to whisk as much air as possible into the eggs and sugar and to bake the cake immediately to prevent the mixture from deflating. In the oven, the air expands and causes the cake to rise.

Warming the eggs and sugar is a time-saving technique: heat coagulates the protein in the eggs, enabling them to trap and hold large quantities of air and thus increase quickly in volume. The sugar dissolves into the warm eggs to form a homogenous mixture (Step 1).

To heat the eggs and sugar gently, put them in a bowl that will fit snugly over a saucepan of hot water. Be sure that the base of the bowl does not touch the water and that the water does not boil, otherwise, the eggs would cook. As you whisk, the air beaten into the eggs turns the mixture a pale cream colour and causes it to treble in volume (Step 2).

FOR ONE 20 CM / 8 INCH CAKE

6 eggs
175 g / 6 oz sugar
150 g / 5 oz flour
90 g / 3 oz butter, plus more for greasing

1 Whisking eggs and sugar. Whisk the eggs and sugar together lightly in a large bowl. Put a little hot water into a saucepan, set it over a low heat and place the bowl on top. Heat the mixture until lukewarm, whisking constantly for 5 to 10 minutes. Remove the saucepan and bowl from the heat and continue to whisk until the mixture has tripled in bulk and falls from the whisk in a thick ribbon (above, right) – about 20 minutes by hand or 10 by electric mixer

3 Filling the tin. Pour the batter into a cake tin lined with buttered and floured greaseproof paper – here, a 7.5 cm (3 inch) deep spring-form tin is used to help unmould the cake easily. Bake the cake in an oven preheated to 180°C/350°F/gas 4 for about 35 to 40 minutes (20 to 25 minutes for a shallow tin) until it feels springy and begins to shrink from the sides of the tin.

4 Unmoulding the cake. Using a cloth to protect your hands, remove the cake tin from the oven, and place it on a wire rack to cool for 5 minutes. Run a knife around the inner edge of the tin to loosen the cake. Pull back the clip of the spring-form to release the ring from the base and lift away the ring.

2 Adding flour. Put the butter in a saucepan and melt it over a low heat: allow to cool. Sieve the flour into the egg and sugar mixture in two or three stages, adding it alternately with the cooled butter. Use a metal spoon or a whisk to fold in the ingredients gently after each addition, starting from the centre of the mixture, draw the spoon along the bottom of the bowl and bring it up around the sides (above, centre). Continue until the ingredients are blended.

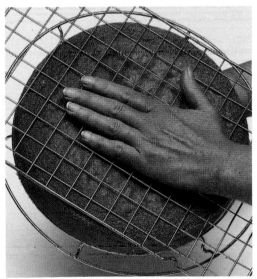

5 Cooling the cake. Place a wire rack over the top of the cake. Place one hand under the bottom rack and lift up the cake, reversing it on to the top rack. Lift off the base of the spring-form tin and peel away the greaseproof lining paper. Leave the cake to cool.

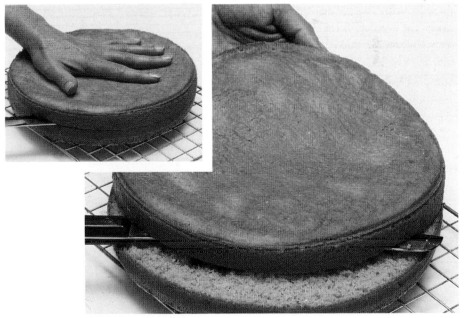

6 Slicing the cake. To serve the cake plainly, simply cut it into wedges. For a layered cake, either assemble two cakes or slice one cake into 2-4 layers, depending on its depth. Use a long serrated knife to score a guideline round the sides (inset) then slice through the cake following the guideline. Jam or whipped cream and brightly coloured fruit offer sumptuous ways to fill and decorate such cakes. The cream may be sweetened or not, flavoured with brandy or liqueur as you like.

Rich Fruit Cake

Because rich fruit cakes have a high fat content, they are prepared by the creaming method. They always contain eggs and are usually made with equal amounts of flour, butter and brown sugar.

The density of a rich fruit cake batter means that the cake requires a long baking time. To prevent the surface from burning, the oven temperature must be kept low. Put the cake into a fairly warm oven to begin with, to heat the batter through and start the cooking. After about 20 minutes, reduce the heat slightly. After a further 40 minutes, reduce it again.

Because of the fruit and brandy it contains, as well as its high proportion of butter, the finished cake will be a moist one that matures and improves with keeping. It may be kept, un-iced, for up to a year. Indeed the un-iced cake should be stored for a minimum of 2 weeks to let its flavour develop properly.

The matured cake can be served simply sprinkled with icing sugar or decorated more elaborately with icing. For a smooth finish and a rich flavour, you can cover the cake with marzipan before you ice it.

FOR ONE 2 CM / 9 INCH CAKE

500 g / 1 lb each sultanas, seedless raisins and currants

5-6 tablespoons brandy, plus more for spiking

300 g / 10 oz butter, plus more for greasing the tin

300 g / 10 oz soft brown sugar

grated zest of 1 orange and 1 lemon

1 tablespoon black treacle

6 eggs, lightly beaten, plus white of 1 more egg for the marzipan

300 g / 10 oz flour

pinch of salt

$^1/_2$ teaspoon freshly grated nutmeg

$^1/_2$ teaspoon mixed spices

200 g / 7 oz glacé cherries, halved

150 g / 5 oz blanched almonds, chopped

200 g / 7 oz candied mixed peel, chopped

1 kg / 2 lb marzipan

1 Combining the ingredients. Put the dried fruit in a bowl and pour over the brandy. In a large bowl, cream the butter and sugar with a wooden spoon until light and fluffy. Add the orange and lemon zest. Stir in the treacle. Beat in the eggs one at a time, then fold in the sifted flour, salt and spices. Pour in the brandy-soaked fruit, the cherries, nuts and chopped peel, and mix thoroughly.

2 Filling the tin. Grease and line a deep cake tin with a double thickness of greaseproof paper. Mix the batter with your hand to make sure that the fruit is evenly distributed, then put the batter into the tin and smooth it flat. Tie a band of brown paper or newspaper around the tin, about 2.5 cm (1 inch) higher than the sides of the tin, to shield the sides and top of the cake from the heat of the oven.

6 Preparing to decorate. Unwrap the cake, turn it over for a smooth icing surface and measure its circumference with string. Roll out two long strips of marzipan about 5 mm ($^1/_4$ inch) thick. Using the string as a guide, trim the strips so that each is almost as long as half the cake's circumference to prevent a bulge when they meet.

7 Brushing with egg whites. Trim both strips to the height of the cake. To help bond the marzipan to the cake, brush each strip with lightly beaten egg white. Press their coated surface against the cake; the strips should just meet on one side, leaving a 2.5 cm (1 inch) gap between them on the other side.

3 Cooking the cake. Bake it in an oven preheated to 170°C/325°F/gas 3 for 20 minutes, then reduce the heat to 150°C/300°F/gas 2. After 40 minutes, reduce the heat again to 140°C/275°F/gas1 and continue baking the cake – here for about 4 hours. When done, a skewer inserted into the cake will come out clean.

4 Storing the cake. Allow the cake to cool in its tin – about 2 hours – then remove it from the tin. To store the cake, place it on a large piece of plastic film. Cover the cake tightly with the film, then wrap it in foil and place it in an airtight container.

5 Adding brandy. If you are storing the fruit cake for a long period of time, refresh its flavours and keep the cake moist by adding brandy: unwrap the cake and use a small skewer to pierce the cake deeply several times. Dribble brandy over the cake and let it fill the pierced holes. Repeat at least every 3 to 4 months.

8 Ensuring a snug fit. To close the gap between the marzipan strips smoothly, steady the cake with one hand and roll a bottle or a drinking glass round the sides of the cake. Use a firm, even pressure so that the marzipan flattens out and stretches to close the gap.

9 Cutting a marzipan top. Roll out a circle of marzipan that is slightly larger than the diameter of the cake and about 5 mm ($^1/_4$ inch) thick. Use the baking tin as a template to cut the marzipan circle to the exact size.

10 Sealing the marzipan. Brush a little beaten egg white on the top of the cake to help the marzipan adhere. Lift the marzipan on to the cake. Run a rolling pin across to smooth the marzipan and press it into place. With a spatula, seal the top and sides. Wrap loosely in foil and store for 1 week before icing.

Serving Food

When you have put so much energy, enthusiasm and new-found skill into buying the right ingredients, preparing them to advantage and cooking them sympathetically, it is well worth spending the extra time giving some consideration as to how to serve it most appealingly at the table. There is no doubt that visual appeal stimulates the taste buds.

Some people feel daunted by this concept, believing that they have to attempt the picture-on-plate 'masterchef' approach, which so often — in all but the most expert hands —- looks overworked and detracts from the food. The truth is simple good food needs no artifice. All that is required is a little care: things like trimming off dangling pieces of skin and projecting bone from portions of meat and poultry, piling the food to give centre height rather than presenting a flat heap, wiping grease and/or sauce from the edge of the plate, and finishing with a little sprinkle of *appropriate* chopped herbs or a dusting of paprika to give a colourful garnish. Try to limit garnishes to herbs and spices used in the dish, or functional serving aids like lemon wedges where a squeeze of lemon juice will enhance the flavour. *Never* garnish with anything that is not edible.

If you are going to carve at the table, it helps to have nice large carving board or serving platter to give yourself room to work on and to set it on a folded napkin or tea cloth to keep it from sliding about. Also, it may be tempting to surround your joint or bird with vegetables but they will just get in the way when you have to go into action. A few handfuls of watercress, say, will set off the roast beautifully and can then be swiftly set to one side.

Make sure your carving knife is well-sharpened ahead of time rather than going in for theatrical stropping while the gravy congeals. Some preliminary work in the kitchen can also help simplify the process later in front of an audience, for example removing strings or excising the wishbone from poultry. Don't worry if you can't follow carving instructions to the letter, as long as you cut boldly and don't reduce the meat to sorry shreds no one will notice lack of expertise. It is always a good idea to cut against the grain to avoid possible 'shredding'.

Finally a word on tableware. Most food looks its best on plain white plates, particularly if it is highly coloured and elaborate in its own right. Some monochromatic dishes, like stews or casseroles, or things in white or creamy sauces, can benefit from having a coloured or patterned plate as a background. Try to match the plate size to the food, as cramped plates look clumsy and very large plates can make average-sized portions look lost. Perhaps the most important advice on plates is to make sure that they are nice and hot (or chilled, as appropriate) when they reach the table or the food reaches them.

Carving Leg and Saddle of Lamb

1 Carving the rounded side of the leg. If you have a manche à gigot, screw it on to the shank bone of the leg. Snip off the string and discard it. Using the manche à gigot as a handle, lift the shank end slightly to tilt the joint. If you do not have a manche à gigot, you can hold the shank end of the leg, wrapped in a napkin, in your hand. With a sharp knife, start carving from the rounded side of the leg (above, left). Slice the meat thinly – always cutting away from yourself – almost parallel to the bone (above, right).

2 Carving the long muscle. When you have carved a slice of meat for each diner turn the leg round and carve as many slices again from the elongated muscle on the opposite side of the bone.

3 Carving from the shank. Insert the knife close to the point where the shank is gripped. Carve the meat from the shank bone. Because it is so much smaller than the thick parts of the leg, the shank end is always well done. However, thanks to its gelatinous structure, this muscle acquires a melting succulence as it cooks.

4 Serving the meat. Transfer the sauce to a heated sauce-boat; spoon the juices exuded during carving into the sauce. Serve each diner meat from each of the three sections that you have carved. Offer the sauce and any other accompaniments – with the meat. Return any remaining meat to a low oven to keep warm.

An Alternative Method of Carving

Unless you make a specific request to the contrary, many butchers cut through the shank bone of a leg of lamb near the top end, in order that it can be bent back to fit into a small roasting pan.

Unfortunately, once the shank bone is cut, there is no 'handle' to grasp as you carve. As a result, the joint tends to slip when being carved. To prevent the leg from slipping, carve the meat on a wooden board and steady the joint with a carving fork.

 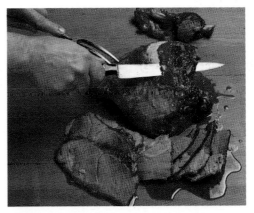

1 Cutting the shank bone from a leg. Place the meat on a wooden board. Steady the partially severed shank with the back of a carving fork. With a sharp knife, cut right through the flesh at the point where the bone was sawn.

2 Carving the rounded side. Set the cut-off shank to one side. Steady the meat with the back of the fork and slice through the rounded section of the leg. Carve a slice of meat for each diner.

3 Carving the long muscle. Turn the joint carved side downwards. Steadying the meat with the fork's prongs, carve the long, lean muscle. Take a slice for each diner, then carve as many slices again from the shank.

Elegant Slices from a Saddle of Lamb

1 Carving the saddle. Steady the saddle with a carving fork. Cut downwards, following the contour of the backbone, to separate the eye of the loin from the bone. Slice horizontally from the side to the centre of the saddle, to cut a slice 6 to 8 mm (¹/4 to ¹/3 inch) thick. Cut two more slices from this side. Turn the saddle round and carve the other side in the same way. Turn the joint over and slice off the rolled aprons. Cut each apron across into three.

2 Carving the fillet. If you have roasted the kidneys with the saddle, take them out. Slice each kidney across into three. Following the contour of the backbone with the knife blade, lift out the fillet in a single piece. Cut out the fillet from the other side of the bone and slice each fillet across into three. Serve each diner a piece of the eye of loin, a piece of fillet, a piece of apron and a piece of kidney if included.

Carving Leg of Pork

Roasting makes pork rind so brittle that it can simply be split down the middle, lifted away from the meat, and served in thin crisp strips.

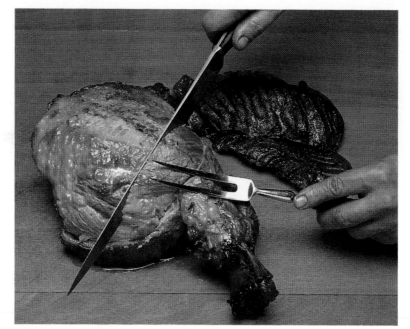

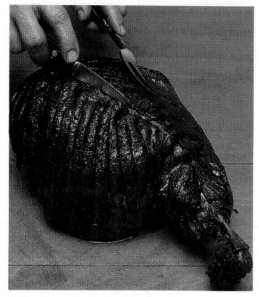

1 Removing the crackling. Holding the leg steady with the back of a carving fork slice down the central line scored along the length of the rind. With the knife and fork, lift away each half of the crackling and reserve it to serve with the meat.

2 Cutting a notch in the meat. With a knife-blade held at an angle cut into the leg at a point about 10 cm (4 inches) from the tip of the leg bone, where the leg begins to widen. Holding the leg steady with the back of the fork, make a second, vertical cut down to the bone to free a wedge of meat. Lift the wedge away, leaving a notch cut out of the roast.

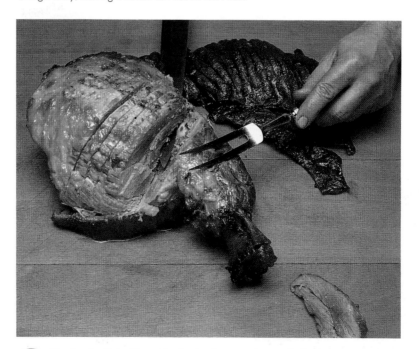

3 Carving in slices. Carve the leg in slices, cutting vertically down to the bone. To free the slices, make a horizontal cut along the bone from the notch previously cut in the leg. Serve the meat with the crackling and gravy.

Carving a Ham

Carving and serving. Cut two 1 cm ($^1/2$ inch) slices from the underside of the leg to make a flat base for the ham to rest on. Then slice the ham vertically, cutting down to the bone. Cut along the bone to free the slices (inset). Place the bone, with the remaining meat, on a serving plate; arrange the slices around it.

Alternatively, having made the ham stable, as before you can simply cut parallel to the bone, but this produces less uniform slices.

Carving Turkey and other Poultry

Carving a turkey is easy, provided you use the right tools. Pick a pointed knife with a very keen edge and a long flexible blade that can cut straight through a joint yet bend enough to follow the contours of the bird. And choose a large two-tined fork for holding the bird while you cut.

Carve the leg, wing and breast from one side of the turkey before you cut into the other side. Work with the back of the fork on the first side so that whenever possible the tines do not pierce the skin and flesh. Then stick the fork firmly into the carcass to hold it steady while you slice the other side. Carve only as much as you will serve at once so that the rest stays hot and moist.

Chickens and guinea-fowl are handled much like turkeys, but smaller birds are merely halved (see box below).

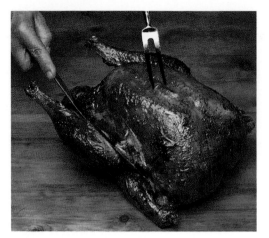

1 Removing the first leg. Lay the turkey breast-up on a carving board or a large platter. Steady the bird with the carving fork. Cut the skin between the thigh and breast. Bend the thigh outwards to locate the hip joint and slice down through the joint to remove the whole leg.

2 Separating thigh from drumstick. Hold the knife so that it bisects the angle between the thigh and drumstick bones and cut down firmly through the joint to sever the leg into two portions.

How to carve small birds

Roast chicken can be carved with the same long, flexible knife used for turkey – and by the same method except for its legs. If the chicken is large, separate the drumstick from the thigh and serve each half separately (but do not slice the meat off the bones). With small chickens, serve thigh and drumstick in one piece.

Carving poussins and other small birds requires a long but rigid knife. Half a bird is just the right amount for one serving. All you need do is split the bird in two.

A heavy rigid blade halves a small bird neatly.

A slender flexible blade curves as it cuts across a chicken breast.

3 Slicing the drumstick. Cut a thick slice off meat and skin from one side of the drumsticks, parallel and close to the bone. Rolling the leg over, cut three more slices in the same way, one from each side of the bone.

4 Slicing the thigh. Keeping the knife blade parallel to the bone and steadying it with the back of the fork, cut down through the thigh to slice it into four or more pieces, according to its size.

5 Removing the first wing. Slice down through the corner of the breast towards the wing. Move the wing to find the joint; cut through the joint as above. Remove the wing with the piece of breast attached. This will provide a single serving.

6 Carving the breast. Hold the back of the carving fork against the breast-bone on the side you will be carving and slice down diagonally through the meat. Lift each slice off between the fork and the knife. If you removed the wishbone before roasting the bird (see page 106), you can cut the breast cleanly into large slices as shown.

Serving a Whole Poached Fish

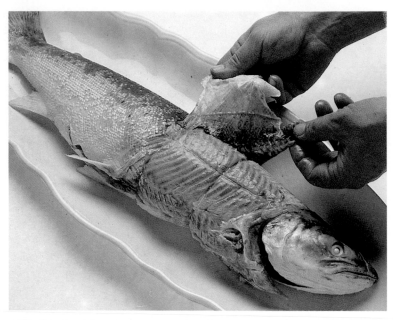

1 Skinning. It is easier to remove the skin while the fish is still hot and wet. Cut any trussing string and pull it free. With a small knife, cut out the fins. Slit the skin from head to tail along the back and the belly, then pull the skin away from the exposed upper side of the fish with your fingers.

2 Dividing the top fillets. With a flexible long-bladed knife, cut down one side of the fish along the line of the backbone. Then, turning the blade of the knife so that it is almost flat, reinsert it in the incision. Work down the length of the fish, easing the flesh of the top fillet away from the bones.

3 Serving the fish. When half the fillet has been freed, divide it into serving portions. Lift the servings on to plates. Detach and serve the second half of the upper fillet in the same way.

4 Final division of the fish. When the entire upper fillet has been removed, pull the tail forward to free the attached backbone and head from the lower fillet. Divide the lower fillet also into two segments, and lift these away from the underskin with a fish slice.

Serving Flat Fish Off the Bone

Flat fish retain much more flavour if cooked on the bone and also look more impressive presented this way. A little practice makes it easy to fillet the cooked fish on the serving plate.

Holding the fish steady with the back of a fork, cut away the fins on each side (above, left). Do not discard the fins; the crisp flesh, which is easily scraped from between the bones, is delicious. Cut along the length of the backbone (above, centre) to separate the two upper fillets, and lift them away from the bone. Peel the backbone from the lower fillets (above, right) and discard it.

Dressing a Whole Crab

By taking apart, or 'dressing', a whole cooked crab you can extract every shred of its delicate white meat and make full use of the tomalley, the crab's brown, creamy liver. Considered a delicacy, the tomalley can be combined with flavourings and with olive oil, cream or mayonnaise to make a sauce for the meat (Step 8). Depending on its size, a crab will provide two to four portions. And the shell, once emptied, becomes a logical serving dish.

Crabs are usually purchased already cooked. If you can, choose a male crab, which has more meat for its weight; you can identify it by its apron, the tail-like piece of cartilage on the shell's underside, which is markedly narrower on the male.

If you buy crabs live or catch them yourself, drop them into boiling salted water flavoured, if you like, with a bay leaf or two and a little vinegar or white wine. Simmer, uncovered, for 15 minutes, depending on size; then lift from the pan and leave to cool.

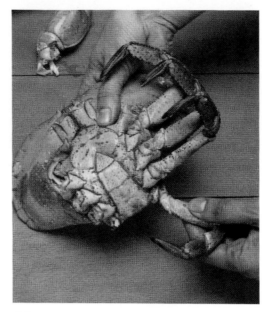

1 Removing the claws and legs. Hold the crab underside up. To break off the two large claws, grip each in turn and twist it against the direction its pincers face. Break off the eight legs in the same way, grasping each of them at the joint nearest the body. Reserve all the limbs.

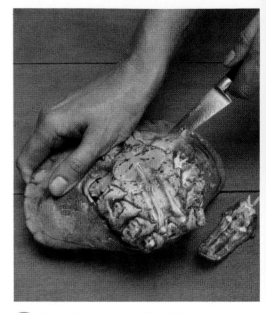

2 Loosening the underside. With your fingers, pull off the crab's hinged tail flap, the apron (above, foreground). Insert the tip of a small rigid knife at several points along the rim between the hard main shell and the softer underside to which the legs were attached. Holding the shell, prise the underside loose.

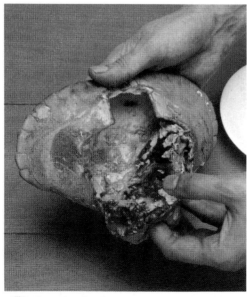

6 Emptying the shell. With your fingers pull out the brownish-red inner lining of the shell, which contains the bulk of the tomalley. In most cases the lining will come out in one piece, but if not, remove it in sections. With a teaspoon, scrape out any tomalley that remains in the shell.

7 Removing the tomalley. Scoop out and reserve the tomalley from the shell lining and reserve; discard the lining. Scrub the shell clean in warm water, then dry it. (If you like, you can enlarge the opening by snapping off the rim of the underside with pliers.) Rub the exterior of the shell with a few drops of oil to give it a glossy sheen.

8 Making the sauce. With a mortar and pestle, mash the yolks of 2 hard-boiled eggs. Stir in 1 or 2 teaspoons of mustard and the tomalley to make a smooth paste, then add just enough olive oil and freshly squeezed lemon juice to bring the sauce to the consistency of thick cream. Season the sauce with salt and pepper. Stir in the white crab meat.

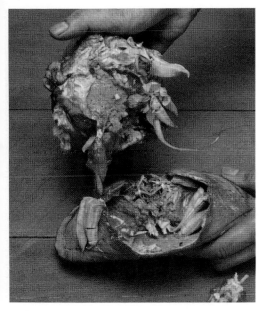

3 Opening the crab. Grip the shell firmly with one hand; with the other, pull away the underside, which contains the bulk of the white meat in its thin-shelled chambers. Most of the crab's finger-shaped, inedible gills will probably come out attached to the underside.

4 Halving the underside. From the main shell, pull out the transparent stomach sack and any remaining gills. From the underside, pick off the gills and pull out the feather-like back fins (above left, foreground); with a sharp, sturdy knife, cut the underside in half in order to expose the meat. Discard the gills, stomach, back fins and apron.

5 Removing the meat. With a teaspoon, scrape away any of the brown, pasty tomalley adhering to the halves of the underside, reserve the tomalley. To loosen the meat, crack open the shell of each half with your hands or, if the shell resists, cover the halves with a towel and tap them with a mallet. Pick out the meat and reserve it.

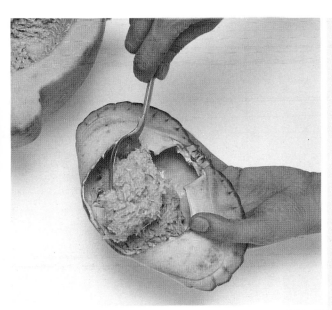

9 Stuffing the shell. Spoon the salad into the shell. With a heavy wooden mallet, crack the shell of the claws and legs to expose the meat inside. Present the stuffed shell on a plate, surrounded by the claws and legs and garnished with sprigs of fresh parsley.

Dressing Lobster

Boiled lobster – its meat carefully removed, sliced and served with a dressing in the shell – makes an opulent seafood salad. A pair of medium lobsters, as shown here, will amply serve four to six people as a main course, or eight to 12 as a starter.

Buy your lobsters live, and drop them into a large pan of boiling water or a white wine court-bouillon (page 244): the heat will kill them instantly. Reduce the heat and simmer each lobster 12 minutes for the first 500 g (1 lb) of its weight, 10 minutes for the next 500 g and 5 minutes for each additional 500 g. Lift the lobsters from the pan and set aside until cool enough to handle; or, for extra flavour, let them cool in their court-bouillon and, in this case, reduce the cooking time slightly.

A mayonnaise-based dressing is the classic accompaniment to a lobster's sweet firm flesh. Here, the mayonnaise is combined with mustard, chopped capers and gherkins, to make a tartare sauce.

1 Removing the roe. A female lobster, as shown above, may have reddish-brown, delicately flavoured roe clustered beneath the tail end of its shell. Grasp the cooked lobster firmly and pick off the eggs; reserve them for garnish.

2 Breaking off the claws. Put each lobster on its back and snap off its eight legs one by one; reserve the legs. Some of the lobster's feather-like gills, or lungs, may come out attached to the leg joints: pull off the gills and discard them. Snap off the two claws by holding each one close to its joint with the body and twisting it backwards.

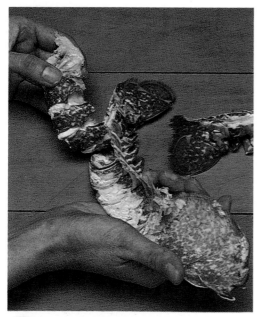

6 Lifting out the tail meat. With your fingertips, prise up the tail meat at one end of each shell half, then pull out the meat in one piece. Cut the meat along its natural markings into thick slices.

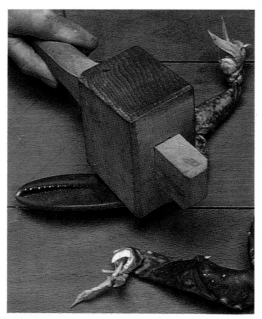

7 Cracking the claws. To break open the shell of each claw, tap it sharply with a mallet. Separate the upper part of the claw from the pincers by snapping the joint between them. Bend back the smaller pincer to expose a feather-shaped bone running through both pincers. With your fingers, pull out as much bone as possible and discard.

8 Extracting the claw meat. Using a skewer or a trussing needle, prise the meat out of both cracked pincer shells – keeping each piece of meat intact if possible. Using a pair of scissors, cut the shell away from the meat of the upper claw.

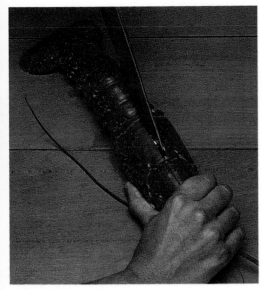

3 Splitting the tail. Turn the lobster over and steady it with one hand. Push the tip of a large sharp knife into the cross-shaped indentation that marks the point where the head and tail sections join; the shell is softest here. Cut down along the length of the lobster's tail.

4 Splitting the head. Turn the lobster around and steady its tail. Cut the head section in two along its length to split the lobster completely. From each half of the head section, pull out and discard the lobster's transparent gravel sac, located just behind and beneath the eyes.

5 Removing the chest section. Scoop out and reserve the greyish-green liver from each half of the head section. Lift out the bony chest structure from each shell half in a single piece; with a knife, dig out and reserve the meat from its crevices and scrape off any liver. Snap off and discard antennae.

9 Preparing a tartare sauce. Make a mayonnaise (see Aïoli, page 253) with 3 egg yolks and 500 ml (18 fl oz) olive oil. Season well and flavour with 1 or 2 tablespoons lemon juice, 1 or 2 teaspoons Dijon mustard, 2 tablespoons each finely chopped capers and gherkins and a good handful of chopped parsley. Stir in the reserved liver from the lobster.

10 Presenting the salad. Crack open the legs and remove their meat with a trussing needle. Put all the scraps of meat in the emptied shell halves, cover with tartare sauce, then slices of tail meat and reserved roe. Cover a dish with shredded lettuce and place stuffed shells and claw meat on top.

Assorted Garnishes

Cutting a Chiffonnade of Leaves

1 Preparing spinach or sorrel. Discard any leaves that are not fresh and green. Fold each leaf in half, with the ridged rib outermost. Pull the rib away down the length of the leaf.

2 Rolling and slicing. Stack several leaves on top of each other and roll up lengthwise. With fingertips turned slightly under for safety, steady the roll with one hand and slice it into strips.

Julienne and Brunoise

1 Slicing. Cut vegetables – here, carrot and turnip – into thin slices. To make julienne, stack several slices and cut them into strips. For brunoise, cut the strips into dice.

2 Cooking. Drop the cut-up vegetables into boiling salted water or broth and parboil them for about a minute. The vegetables should remain slightly firm.

Skinning Sweet Peppers

1 Peeling. Grill the peppers at a fairly high heat, turning so that the skins blister evenly. Leave to cool, covered with a damp cloth. Strip off the and pull out stems.

2 Seeding and slicing. Pull open the peppers at their stem ends. With a teaspoon, remove the seeds. Slice the flesh lengthwise into strips. Cut across the strips to make dice.

Croûtons

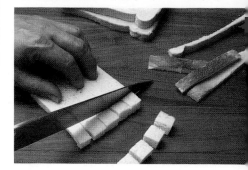

1 Slicing the bread. Cut slices from a stale, firm-crumbed loaf; remove the crusts. Cut each slice into fingers and cut across the fingers to make cubes.

2 Heating the bread cubes. In a sauté pan, melt plenty of butter over a very low heat. Add the cubes in a single layer, so that they soak up the butter evenly.

3 Tossing the croûtons. Fry the cubes gently so that they become crisp all the way through. To ensure even browning, toss them frequently.

Baked Bread Flavoured with Garlic and Olive Oil

1 Drying the bread. Cut thin slices from a narrow French loaf. Put the slices on a baking tray in a slow oven and dry them out without browning them.

2 Rubbing with garlic. Peel a large clove of garlic and cut off the root end. Rub one side of each toast slice with the cut surface of the garlic clove.

3 Sprinkling on olive oil. Dribble olive oil over the toast. You can regulate the flow by pouring the oil from a bottle with a cork in which a groove has been cut.

Colouring and Cutting Out Savoury Custards

1 Mixing custard. In a bowl, whisk egg yolks and whole eggs – 3 yolks to each whole egg. Whisk warm – not hot – stock or water into some of the whisked egg and sieve mixture.

2 Adding purées. Dilute separately puréed vegetables – here, tomatoes and peas – with a little stock or water. Make flavoured custards by whisking some whisked egg into each purée.

3 Baking. Pour the custards into well-buttered moulds and set them on a wire rack in a pan of hot water. Cook, covered, at 180°C/350°F/gas 4 for 15 to 20 minutes until firm..

4 Unmoulding. Firm up the custards in a dish filled with ice. To loosen the custard, run a small knife round the inside of each mould. Invert it over a plate and tap it sharply to turn out the custard.

5 Cutting to shape. Cut each custard into slices. Slices from small moulds may be used whole as individual garnishes; larger square or rectangular slices should be cut into small strips or dice.

6 Cutting decorative shapes. Occasionally you may like to garnish a dish such as soup with custards of more fanciful shapes. Use small biscuit cutters to stamp the custard garnishes from larger slices.

Piping Decorations

In the realm of fine cake decoration, the piping bag stands supreme. The device itself could scarcely be simpler: a conical bag filled with icing, with a hole or a shaped metal nozzle in its tip. But with this rudimentary equipment and a little practice, you can produce the exquisite array of adornments shown here.

Commercially produced piping bags are easy to obtain; it is even easier, though, to make your own from paper (right). If you are piping icing of different colours, make as many bags as you need and throw them away after use.

The pattern of the piping will depend on the size and shape of the hole in the bag. For lines and dots, snip off the tip of the bag; the less paper you cut away, the finer your piping will be. For fluted piping and for petals and leaves, make V-shaped cuts in the bag; for more intricate patterns still, insert a shaped nozzle.

Simple lines and borders are applied directly to the cake; more intricate decorations, such as flowers, are best made separately and fixed in place once they have dried completely. Use royal icing, which sets rock-hard, for these delicate structures. Because intricate shapes are difficult to form on a stationary surface, professional decorators pipe flowers on to a small platform called a flower nail, which can be turned to the most convenient position. You can buy flower nails in specialist shops but a good substitute can be made easily from a cork and a skewer (right, centre).

Delicate decorations known as lacework (right) are best made with the aid of a carefully drawn design. Icing – here, chocolate – is piped on to silicon paper placed over the drawing, which serves as a template.

Both flowers and lacework should be allowed to dry completely before they are disturbed. If you are making them in advance, store them without removing them from their paper; they will be less likely to suffer damage.

Making a Paper Piping Bag

1 Cutting triangles. Cut out a rectangle of greaseproof paper about 25 by 20 cm (10 by 8 inches). Fold the rectangle in half diagonally, then cut along the crease; reserve one triangle.

2 Folding. With the right angle of the triangle at the bottom left-hand side and the shortest edge near you, take the top corner in your right hand and the bottom right-hand corner in your left.

Piping a Narcissus on a Flower Nail

1 Making a flower nail. Stick a small skewer into the base of a cork. Cut a sheet of wax paper into little squares. Fix a square of paper to the top of the cork with a dab of icing.

2 Cutting a petal nozzle. Fill a paper piping bag two-thirds full with royal icing (see over). Fold over the top of the bag to secure it. Flatten the tip; cut diagonally from each side to make a V-shape.

Tracing Chocolate Filigree

1 Drawing a design. Draw a design on a strip of card or paper. Place silicon paper over the card. Melt chocolate fondant (page 288). Fill a piping bag with the icing.

2 Piping decorations. Cut a tiny hole in tip of bag. Hold bag above paper and, squeezing gently, follow lines of the drawing. Slide the paper along; pipe another decoration.

Making a cone. Bring your right hand under your left hand (above, left). Wrap the paper [roun]d your left hand to form a cone (above, centre). Pull the paper in your right hand towards you to make a very sharp point to the cone (above, right).

4 Securing the cone. Tuck corner held in your right hand inside the cone. To prevent the cone unwinding, make two small tears in the folded edge and press down the paper between them.

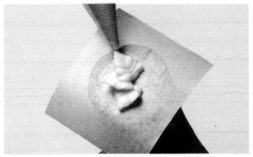

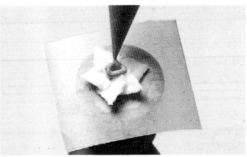

Piping first petal. Hold flower nail upright. Begin at the centre of the paper, holding the [nail a]t a 45-degree angle to cork. Squeeze bag gently, [movi]ng it back and forth slightly to ripple icing.

4 Piping more petals. When the petal is about 5 mm (1/4 inch) long, pull the bag away to create a point. Continue piping petals round the flower nail, overlapping the petals slightly.

5 Completing the narcissus. Fill a piping bag with royal icing of a contrasting colour. Cut across the tip to make a tiny hole. Hold the bag perpendicular to the flower; pipe a coil in its centre.

Forming a Rose with a Petal Nozzle

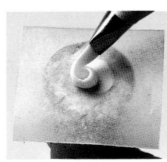

1 Fitting a metal nozzle. Make a paper piping bag; cut straight across the bag 1 cm (1/2 [inc]h) from the tip. Drop a metal petal nozzle into [p]osition. Make a flower nail (step 1 above).

2 Piping a rose. Fill the bag with royal icing. With the wide end of the nozzle tip nearest the flower nail, pipe a central scroll, rotating the nail anti-clockwise as you work (above, left).

Lower the nozzle to the scroll's base (above, centre). Starting and finishing at the base each time, pipe overlapping petals round the scroll (above, right).

Piping Using the Star Nozzle

The star is the most versatile of all commercially available nozzles. It produces a fluted cylinder of icing which, by manipulating the piping bag and varying the pressure you apply, you can turn into such diverse shapes as ropes, rosettes, shells and scallops. And the star nozzle will work equally well with royal icing, buttercream, whipped cream or meringue, provided the mixture to be piped is fairly stiff and free of lumps.

The simplest straight lines of fluted piping (right, above) can be criss-crossed to give a lattice effect. Rosettes make attractive single motifs (right, centre) or they can be piped in rows on a petit four. By moving the piping bag from side to side in a zigzag motion you can create a wide rope border (right, below). By bringing the nozzle round in a series of arcs you can produce a flowing shell design (opposite page, above) that makes an interesting shape for meringues as well as for small-scale ornaments. A raised flourish is achieved by varying the pressure you apply as you make the stroke (opposite, centre); by altering the direction and the pressure you can pipe a pretty curvilinear scallop (opposite page, below).

Royal Icing

MAKES 300 ML / ½ PINT

500 g / 1 lb icing sugar
whites of 2 eggs
juice of ½ lemon, strained

Sieve the sugar 2 or 3 times. In a bowl, beat the egg whites lightly. Then add three-quarters of the icing sugar, a tablespoon at a time, and lemon juice. Beat for about 15 minutes if working by hand or 7 if using an electric mixer.

When the mixture is smooth, clear and light, add the remaining sugar and beat again for a minute or two. If the icing is not stiff enough add a little more sugar.

Cover with a damp cloth until ready to use to prevent the icing developing a skin.

Releasing a Rope of Icing

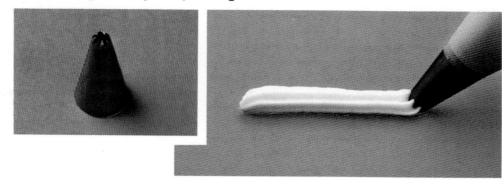

Hold paper piping bag with star nozzle at a 45-degree angle and 5 mm (¹/4 inch) above surface. Pipe towards yourself, raising bag slightly as the icing falls on surface. To finish, lower nozzle and pull away sharply.

A Single Action for a Neat Rosette

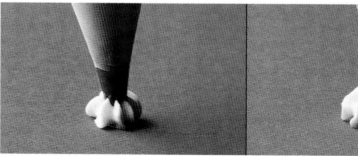

Squeezing gently. Hold the piping bag so that it is perpendicular to the work surface and just above it. Squeeze the piping bag gently to make

a rosette (above, left). When it is the size that you want, stop squeezing and lift the bag away (above, right).

A Tightly Woven Cable

Changing direction. Hold the bag at a 45-degree angle about 5 mm (¹/4 inch) above the surface. Pipe a short line to the left; reverse direction

and pipe a second short line to the right, close to the first. Continue piping from left to right to form a thick zigzag of icing.

A Continuous Spiral

Building up overlapping lines. Hold the bag at a 45-degree angle. Pipe a short line towards yourself, then move the bag a little to your left. Lift the bag up and over the previous line (above, left). Continue piping in arcs that increase in size towards the middle, then decrease towards the end (above, centre and right).

An Undulating Band of Shells

Varying pressure. Hold the bag at a 45-degree angle to the work surface. Squeeze a small mound, then move the bag up (above, left). Reduce pressure and bring the bag down to the surface and towards yourself (above, centre). Pull away sharply. Pipe another shell over the end of the previous one (above, right).

A Border of Interlocking Shells

Forming curves. Hold the bag almost perpendicular and pipe a small mound. Reduce pressure, move the bag to the right (above, left) in a half circle round the mound. Draw the nozzle downwards to form a tail (above, centre). Begin the next scallop by piping another mound over the tail of the previous one (above, right).

Decorating a Cake

1 Icing the top. Prepare royal icing (page 316). Spoon icing on to the top of the marzipan covered cake. Use a metal spatula to spread the icing about 2 mm (¹/₁₀ inch) thick. To smooth the icing, hold the spatula – or, as here, an icing ruler – flat against the top and draw it firmly towards you.

2 Icing the sides. Cover the sides of the cake with icing about 2 mm (¹/₁₀ inch) thick. Rotate the cake as you work; a jagged edge will form round the rim. Leave the cake uncovered for a day to allow the icing to harden, then scrape the rough edge with a knife. Repeat Steps 1 and 2 two or three times.

3 Making a stencil. Cut a strip of greaseproof paper to fit round the cake. To make a pattern with repeated loops use a ruler to mark off equal lengths and fold the paper over at each mark. Draw a semi-circle between two corners of the paper, from the fold to the opposite edge; cut it out.

4 Tracing the loops. Open the paper and place its straight edge along the base of the cake. Fasten each peak to the cake with a pin. To outline the pattern, use a pin to prick a series of small marks in the icing just above the looped edge of paper. Unpin the paper.

5 Completing the decoration. If necessary, thicken the royal icing by beating more icing sugar into it. Fit a small icing bag with a star nozzle, and fill it two-thirds full with the icing. Pipe garlands of shells following the pattern markings on the cake's sides, then pipe rows of pendant stars from the peaks of the garlands. Finally pipe borders of shells along the bottom and top edge of the cake.

Index

acidulated water 139
aduki beans 49, 143
aïoli 253
allspice 77
almonds 61
anchovies 26
angler-fish 30
apples 50, 159
    double-crust pie 278-9
apricots 52
artichokes 43, 141, 175
asparagus 42, 142, 175
aubergines 40, 222

bacon: quiche Lorraine 275
    stuffings 165
baking: eggs 218-19
    vegetables 222-3
bananas 58, 59
barbel 25
barding 80-1, 119
barley 63, 176
basil: pesto 253
bass 30
batter: beer 240
    for deep-frying 236
Bavarian cream 256
bay leaf 74
beans 48, 175
    see also individual types of bean
beef: barding 80
    beef Carpaccio 89
    beef olives 199
    boeuf à la mode 200-1
    borscht 262-3
    brown sauce 248-9
    chilled consommé 258-9
    cuts 10-11
    dressing and flavouring steak 85
    grilling steaks 206-7
    hamburgers 87
    larding 82-3
    marrow bones 13, 125
    mincing 86
    oxtail 125
    raw preparations 88-9
    roast rib 214-15
    roasting 212-13
    steak and kidney pudding 180-1
    steak tartare 88
beer batter 240
beetroot 38
    baking 222, 223
    boiling 175
    borscht 262-3
berries 54-5, 158
beurre blanc 250
bisque, crayfish 264-5
black beans 49, 143
black-eyed peas 48, 49, 143
blackberries 54
blackcurrants 55
blue cheese 68-9
blueberries 55
bluefish 30, 31
boeuf à la mode 200-1
bogue 30, 31
boiling: eggs 172-3
    pasta 177
    rice and grains 176
    vegetables 174-5
bones, marrow 13, 125
boning: chicken suprêmes 112
    feet 125
    fish 130-1
    lamb 90-3
    pork 100-1

poultry 106-7
bonito 28
borlotti beans 49, 143
borscht 262-3
bouquet garni 74-6
braising: boeuf à la mode 200-1
    osso buco 198
    vegetables 202-3
Brazil nuts 61
bread 266-8
    croûtons 312
    garlic 313
    long loaves 272-3
    pizzas 274-5
    stuffings 166
bream 25
brill 27
broad beans 44, 139
    dried 48, 49, 143
broccoli 37, 138, 175
brochettes, fish 209
brown sauce 248-9
brunoise garnishes 312
Brussels sprouts 36, 37, 175
buckwheat 63, 176
burbot 25
burghul 62
butter beans 49, 143
buttering under poultry skin 167
butterscotch sauce 254-5

cabbage 36-7, 138, 175
cakes: decorating 318
    rich fruit 296-7
    whisked sponges 294-5
calabrese 37
calf's foot 13, 125
cannellini beans 49, 143
Cape gooseberries 55
capercaillie 21
capon, roasting 216
caramel sauce 254
caramelizing onions 260
cardamom 77
cardoons 42, 43, 175
carp 25
carrots 38, 139, 175
    sugar-coating 204-5
carving: ham 303
    lamb 300-1
    pork 302
    poultry 304-5
cashew nuts 61
caul 119, 124
cauliflower 36, 37, 175
cayenne pepper 77
celeriac 38, 139, 175
celery 42
    boiling 175
    braised in stock 202-3
    stringing 142
ceps 45
chanterelles 45
chard 34, 42-3
chayote 41, 175
cheese 70-3
    soufflé 226-7
    vegetable gratin Mornay 246-7
cheese, soft 68-9
cherimoya 59
cherries 52, 159
chervil 76
chestnuts 61, 161
chick peas 48, 49, 143
chicken 18
    boning 106, 112
    carving 304

chilled consommé 258-9
coq au vin 191-3
deep-fried marinated 236-7
jointing 104-5
poule au pot 186-7
poulet sauté à la crème 232-3
spatchcocking 110-11
stock 242-3
stuffing breasts 113
stuffing under the skin 111
trussing 108-9
chicory 34, 46, 138
chiffonade of leaves 312
chilli peppers: rouille 195
Chinese cabbage 36-7
chips, potato 238
chives 76
chocolate: cream-filled éclairs 288-9
    filigree 314
    meringues 292-3
    sauce 255
chops, lamb 98-9
choux pastry 286-7
churos 289
cinnamon 77
citrus fruits 56-7
citrus rind, julienne strips 160
clams 33
clementines 56
cloves 77
cockles 33
coconut 61
cod 26, 27
coley 26
compotes, fruit 188-9
conger eel 30
consommé, chilled 258-9
coq au vin 191
coriander leaves 76
coriander seeds 77
corn 45, 63
cornmeal 63
courgettes 41, 175
court-bouillon 244
couscous 62, 144
crab 32
    dressing 308-9
crab apples 51
crackling, pork 103
cranberries 54-5
crayfish 32
    bisque 264-5
cream-filled chocolate éclairs 288-9
creams and custards 256-7
crisps, potato 239
croissants 269-71
croûtons 312
crustaceans 32-3
cucumber 40-1, 175
cumin 77
custards 256-7
    savoury 313
cuttlefish 32, 133

dab 26
damsons 53
dandelion 46
dates 52, 53
decorating cakes 318
decorations, piping 314-17
deep-frying: marinated chicken 236-7
    potatoes 238-9
deer 22-3
dentex 30, 31
dessert sauces 254-5
dicing vegetables 137
dill 76

discoloration, preventing 139
dogfish 28
dolphin fish 30, 31
dried fruit: winter fruit pudding 182-3
duck 18
    boning 106-7
    roasting 216
    see also wild duck
Dutch brown beans 49, 143

éclairs, cream-filled chocolate 288-9
eels 25
eggs 66-7
    baked 218-19
    boiling 172-3
    omelette fine herbes 230-1
    poaching 184
    shallow-frying 228-9
    shirred eggs 229
endive 34, 46, 175

fat: barding 80-1, 119
    larding 82-3, 119
feet: boning 125
    skinning poultry 125
fennel, Florence 42, 142, 175
fennel (herb) 76
field beans 48, 49, 143
figs 59
    in a wine syrup 188
    winter fruit pudding 182-3
filleting fish 128-9
fish 24-31
    boning round fish 130-1
    cleaning and trimming 126-7
    court-bouillon 244
    filleting 128-9
    fumet 244-5
    grilling 208-9
    lamb 98-9
    Mediterranean fish stew 194-5
    poaching 185
    serving 306-7
flageolet beans 49, 143
flounder 27
flower nails 314
flowers, piping 314-15
food processors 137
forcemeat, pork 165
frangipane: pineapple and frangipane 240-1
French beans 44
frigate mackerel 29
fritters, pineapple and frangipane 240-1
fruit 50-60
    poaching 188-9
    preparation 158-62
    puff pastry cases 284-5
    purées 163
fruit cake 296-7
frying: eggs 228-9
    vegetables 234
    see also deep-frying; sautéing
fumet 244-5

game, larding and barding 119
game birds 20-1
    plucking and drawing 114-15
    roasting 217
    trussing 116-17
garfish 30, 31
garlic 39
    aïoli 253
    baked bread with 313
    boiling 175
    peeling 142
    purée 223

garnishes 312-13
gelatine, calf's foot 13
giblets 167
gizzards 124
glazing vegetables 204-5
globe artichokes 43, 141, 175
goose 18, 216
gooseberries 55
grains 62-3, 176, 178
grapefruit 57, 159
grapes 55, 161
gratins: vegetable 224-5
    vegetable gratin Mornay 246-7
gravlax 168-9
grayling 25
greengages 53
grey mullet 30
grilling: fish 208-9
    steaks 206-7
    vegetables 210-11
grouper 30, 31
grouse 21
guavas 58, 59
gudgeon 25
guinea fowl 18, 216
gurnard 30
gutting fish 126-7

haddock 26, 27
hake 26, 27
halibut 26
ham: carving 303
    ham and cheese stuffing 165
hamburgers 87
hare 22-3
    jointing 118
haricot beans 49, 143
    lamb and haricot stew 190
hazelnuts 61
hearts 122
herbs 74-6
    chopping 136
    marinades 164
    omelette fine herbes 230-1
herrings 26
hollandaise 252
horseradish sauce 214

icing, royal 316
Italian meringue 290

Jerusalem artichokes 175
John Dory 30, 31
jointing: hare and rabbit 118
    poultry 104-5
julienne garnishes 160, 312
juniper berries 77

kale 36, 175
kidney beans 49, 143
kidneys 123
kiwi fruit 58, 162
kohlrabi 36, 37, 175
kumquats 56-7

lamb: boning joints 90-3
    carving 300-1
    chops 98-9
    crown roast 94
    cutlets 99
    cuts 14-15
    guard of honour 94-5
    lamb and haricot stew 190
    rack of lamb 94-5
    stuffing joints 96-7
lamb's lettuce 46
larding 82-3, 119

leaf vegetables 34-5
leeks 39, 175
lemon 57
lentils 48-9, 143
lettuce 34, 46
lime 57
ling 26, 27
liver 122
lobster 32, 132
  dressing 310-11
loganberries 54
loquats 50-1
lovage 76
lumpfish 31
lychees 60
Lyonnaise potato cake 234-5

mace 77
mackerel 28
maize 63
mallard see wild duck
mandolines 137
mange-tout 44-5
mangoes 52, 53
marinades 164
marjoram 74
marrow, vegetable 41
marrow bones 13, 125
marzipan, fruit cakes 297
Mediterranean fish stew 194-5
medlars 50
megrim 27
melon 60, 159
meringue 290-3
millet 63, 176
mincing beef 86
mint 76
molluscs, preparation 134
moules à la marinière 179
mulberries 54
mullet 30
mung beans 49, 143
mushrooms 45
  grilling 211
mussels 33, 134
  moules à la marinière 179

nectarines 52
noodles 150
nutmeg 77
nuts 61

oats 63, 176
octopus 32, 133
offal 122-5
okra 40, 41, 140
ombrine 30, 31
omelette fine herbes 230-1
onions 39
  baking 222, 223
  boiling 175
  caramelizing 260
  glazed 204-5
  pissaladière 274-5
  soups 260-1
oranges 56
oregano 74
osso buco 198
oxtail 125
oysters 33, 134-5

pandora 30, 31
papaya 58
paprika 77
parsley 76
parsnips 38, 175
partridge 20
passion fruit 60, 159
pasta 64-5

boiling 177
colouring and flavouring 152-3
making fresh 146-7
pasta machines 148-50
savoury fillings 154-7
shaping 150-1
pastry: choux 286-7
  puff 282-3
  shortcrust 276-7
pastry cream 257
pâté de Campagne 220-1
peaches 52
peanuts 61
pears 51
  upside-down tart 280-1
peas 44, 45, 175
  dried 48, 49, 143
pecan nuts 61
peeling vegetables 139
peppercorns 77
peppers 40, 140, 175, 312
perch 25
persillade 164
persimmons 58-9
pesto 253
pheasant 20
pie, double-crust apple 278-9
pigeon 18, 216
pigeon peas 49, 143
pike 25
pike-perch 25
pilchards 26
pine nuts 61
pineapple 60
  pineapple and frangipane fritters
    240-1
  preparation 160-1, 162
  pulping 163
pinto beans 49, 143
piping bags 314-15
piping decorations 314-17
pissaladière 274-5
pistachio nuts 61
pizzas 274-5
plaice 26
plucking game birds 114-15
plums 52-3
poaching: eggs 184
  fish 185
  fruit 188-9
  poule au pot 186-7
pods, trimming 139
polenta 145
pollack 26
pomegranates 60
porbeagle shark 28, 29
pork: boning joints 100-1
  carving 302
  crackling 103
  cuts 16-17
  forcemeat 165
  pâté de Campagne 220-1
  stuffing joints 102-3
potatoes 38
  baking 222
  boiling 175
  chips 238
  deep-frying 238-9
  gratin Dauphinois 225
  grilling 211
  Lyonnaise potato cake 234-5
  steaming 178
poule au pot 186-7
poulet sauté à la crème 232-3
poultry 18-19
  boning 106-7
  buttering under skin 167
  carving 304-5
  gizzards 124

jointing 104-5
livers 122
roasting 216
skinning feet 125
spatchcocking 110-11
stuffing under the skin 111
stuffings 166-7
trussing 108-9
poussins, roasting 216
powan 25
prawns 32
prickly pears 59, 162
puff pastry 282-3
  fruit cases 284-5
pulses 48-9, 143
pumpkin 41, 175
purées: fruit 163
  garlic 223
purslane 46

quail 20
quiche Lorraine 275
quinces 51

rabbit 22
  jointing 118
radicchio 46
raspberries 54
ratatouille 196-7
ravioli 155
rays 29
red cabbage 36
red kidney beans 49, 143
red mullet 30
redcurrants 55
redfish 30
rhubarb 60, 162, 163
rice 62, 63, 176, 178
roasting: beef 212-13
  game birds 217
  poultry 216
  veal 81
rocket 46
root vegetables 38, 178
  shredded root vegetable gratin 224
rosemary 74
roses, piping 315
rotary shredders 137
rouille 195
royal icing 316
runner beans 44
rye 63, 176

sabayon sauce 250
saffron 77
sage 76
salad leaves 46-7
salmon 25
  gravlax 168-9
salsa verde 253
salsify 38, 175
sar commun 30, 31
sardines 26
satsumas 56
sauces: aïoli 253
  bâtarde 251
  beurre blanc 250
  brown 248-9
  butterscotch 254-5
  caramel 254
  chocolate 255
  custard 256-7
  hollandaise 252
  horseradish 214
  mousseline 252
  pesto 253
  rouille 195
  sabayon 250
  salsa verde 253

vinaigrette 251
  white 246-7
sautéing: poulet sauté à la
  crème 232-3
savory 76
scad 30, 31
scales, cleaning fish 126
scallops 33, 135
scorzonera 38, 175
sea bass 30
sea bream 30, 31
sea lamprey 29
seakale 43, 175
semolina 62
shad 26
shallots, peeling 142
shallow-frying eggs 228-9
sharks 28-9
Sharon fruit 58
shellfish 24, 33, 179
shirred eggs 229
shortcrust pastry 276-7
shrimp 32
skate 29
skinning fish 126-7, 128-9
slicing vegetables 136-7
smelt 26
smooth hound 28
snipe 21, 115
sole 26, 27
sorrel 34, 46, 175
soufflé, cheese 226-7
soups: borscht 262-3
  chilled consommé 258-9
  crayfish bisque 264-5
  onion 260-1
soya beans 48, 49, 143
spatchcocking poultry 110-11
spices 77
spinach 34, 46, 138, 175
  eggs baked on a bed of creamed
    spinach 219
sponge, whisked 294-5
sprats 26
spring greens 36
spring onions 39
spring vegetable stew 196-7
spur dog 28
squashes 41, 175
squid 32, 133
star nozzles 316-17
steak 11
  dressing and flavouring 85
  grilling 206-7
  steak tartare 88
steak and kidney pudding 180-1
steaming: rice 178
  root vegetables 178
  shellfish 179
  steak and kidney pudding 180-1
  winter fruit pudding 182-3
stews: coq au vin 191-3
  lamb and haricot 190
  Mediterranean fish 194-5
  vegetable 196-7
stock, veal or chicken 242-3
stoning fruit 159
strawberries 54, 158
  meringues 292-3
string beans 44
stuffing: chicken breasts 113
  lamb 96-7
  pork 102-3
  spatchcocked poultry 111
stuffings 164-7
sturgeon 25
swedes 38, 175
sweet potatoes 38, 175
sweetcorn 45, 140, 175

Swiss chard 42-3, 175
Swiss meringue 291
swordfish 28, 29

tangerines 56
tarragon 76
tart, pear upside-down 280-1
teal 20
thyme 74
tomatoes 40, 140
tortellini 156-7
tripe 122, 124
trout 25
truffles 45
trussing: game birds 116-17
  poultry 108-9
tuna 28
turbot 26, 27
turkey 18
  carving 304-5
  roasting 216
turnips 38, 175
turtle beans 49

veal: barding 80-1
  brown sauce 248-9
  cuts 12-13
  grilling steaks 206
  larding 82-3
  osso buco 198
  roasting 81, 212
  stock 242-3
  stuffing breast 84
vegetable fruits 40-1
vegetables 34-47
  baking 222-3
  boiling 174-5
  braising 202-3
  glazing 204-5
  gratins 224-5
  grilling 210-11
  pan-frying 234
  preparation 136-42
  stews 196-7
  stuffings 165, 167
  vegetable gratin Mornay
    246-7
venison 22-3, 120-1
vinaigrette 251
vine leaves 34, 175
  grilling fish in 209

waffles, potato 239
walnuts 61
watercress 46
watermelon 60
weever 31
Welsh onions 39
wheat 62, 176
whelks 33, 134
whisked sponges 294-5
white currants 55
white sauce 246-7
whiting 26, 27
widgeon 20
wild duck 20
  removing oil glands 115
wild rice 63, 176
wine: coq au vin 191-3
  figs in a wine syrup 188
  marinades 164
winkles 33, 134
witch 27
wolf-fish 30
wood-pigeon 21
woodcock 21, 115
wrasse 30

Yorkshire pudding 214-15